THE FORGOTTEN HOLOCAUST

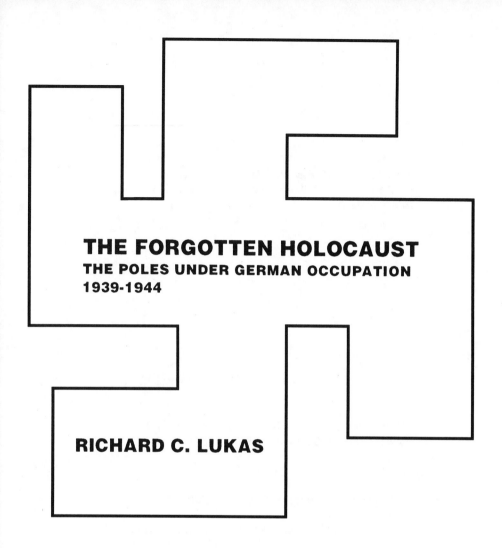

THE FORGOTTEN HOLOCAUST
THE POLES UNDER GERMAN OCCUPATION
1939-1944

RICHARD C. LUKAS

HIPPOCRENE BOOKS

New York

Publication of this new Revised Edition was facilitated by a grant from the Joseph B. Slotkowski Publication Fund of the Kosciuszko Foundation.

Originally published in the U.S.A. in 1986 by the University Press of Kentucky.

Original Hippocrene Books paperback edition published in 1990. Second Revised Edition published in 1997.

Library of Congress Cataloging-in-Publication Data
Lukas, Richard C., 1937-
　　　　The forgotten Holocaust : the Poles under German occupation.
　　1939-1944 / Richard C. Lukas. -- 2nd rev. ed.
　　　　　　　p.　　cm.
　　　　Includes bibliographical references and index.
　　　　ISBN 0-7818-0528-7
　　　　1. World War, 1939-1945--Poland. 2. Poland--History--Occupation,
　　1939-1945. 3. World War, 1939-1945--Atrocities. 4. World War,
　　1939-1945--Prisoners and prisons, German. 5. Holocaust, Jewish
　　1939-1945)--Poland. I. Title.
　　D802.P6L85　1996
　　940.53'438--dc21　　　　　　　　　　　　　　　96-50368
　　　　　　　　　　　　　　　　　　　　　　　　　　CIP

Printed in the United States of America.

**TO THE MEMORY
OF ALL THE VICTIMS
OF THE HOLOCAUST**

DID THE CHILDREN CRY?
Hitler's War Against Jewish and Polish Children, 1939-1945
by Richard C. Lukas

Winner of the 1996 Janusz Korczak Literary Competition for Books about Children

Based on eyewitness accounts, interviews and prodigious research by the author, this is a unique and most compelling account of German inhumanity to children in occupied Poland. An unprecedented aspect of Nazi genocide in World War II was the brutal and deliberate decision not to spare the children. Jewish children, first driven into ghettos, were marked for total destruction once "The Final Solution" was put into action. Gentile children were starved, killed or Germanized in order to reduce the Polish nation to a small complement of semi-literate slaves tending the Herrenvolk in their thousand-year Reich.

"Lukas systematically catalogues the varied aspects of Nazi occupation policies in Poland... for all levels." —*Choice*

"[Lukas] intersperses the endless numbers, dates, locations and losses with personal accounts of tragedy and triumph.... A well-researched book."   —*Catalyst*
320 pages   6x9   photos, index   0-7818-0242-3 $24.95hc   (145)

CONTENTS

Foreword

The history of wartime Poland is not a simple subject. Yet it is frequently oversimplified and misunderstood. There are people who do not even know that Poland fought against the Germans on the Allied side from start to finish. If British and Americans think of it at all, they think of a country which Hitler turned into the central laboratory of Nazi Germany's *Lebensraum* and which was the site of what the Nazis named euphemistically "The Final Solution of the Jewish Question."

Of course, it is absolutely true that German-occupied Poland was subjected to the most rigorous policies of racial planning, and that the genocide of the six million Jews was largely perpetrated there in circumstances rightly described as uniquely evil. The point is: these undoubted facts represent less than half the story. Between 1939 and 1945–that is during the war years but for reasons mainly unconnected with the conduct of the war–occupied Poland became the scene of numerous other campaigns of exterminatory violence. What is more, Poland was not just a land inhabited by Catholic Poles and Polish Jews. It contained a much richer array of ethnic and religious groupings, each of whom have reason to view their own particular sufferings as meriting the label of a "holocaust."

Not just Poles and Jews, but Poland's Germans, Ukrainians, Lithuanians, Byelorussians, Tartars and Gypsies, Catholic, Orthodox, Uniate, Protestant, Judaic and Moslem were all to pass through the mills of Hitler's and Stalin's human engineering. The result was a variety of atrocities, great and small, that knows no parallel. In 1939-1941, when the masters of the German zone were concentrating on the forcible Germanization of Polish provinces directly annexed to the Reich, the Soviet NKVD was conducting ethnic, social and political purges in the eastern zone of occupation that destroyed far more innocent lives than the SS could by that stage account for. In 1941-1944, when German power engulfed not ony the whole of Poland but also the Baltic states, Byelorussia and Ukraine, the Nazis' racial laboratory consumed all manner of human categories, from the Polish intelligentsia to the Slav slave-laborers. In 1944-1945, the Soviet juggernaut returned, liberating certain categories of people while butchering, deporting or breaking others.

Dr. Richard C. Lukas has rendered a valuable service by showing that no one can properly analyze the fate of one ethnic community in occupied Poland without referring to the fates of others. In this sense, *The Forgotten Holocaust* is a powerful corrective. For the book was conceived at a time when official communist historiography in Poland ignored ethnic complications altogether, using the state censorship to enforce a highly selective view of the wartime occupation where all crimes were attributed to "Fascism" and all victims were described as "Polish citizens" or "people of various nationalities." There was no specific mention of either Jews or Catholics. By the same token, Holocaust studies in the West, which in the nature of things focused on the Jewish tragedy and hence on Fascist oppression, were giving an oversimplified, dialectical perception of wartime realities.

The main thing is that American readers should receive a comprehensive picture of occupied Poland, so that each and every one of the separate but interlinked tragedies can be fully understood. Lukas's book marks an important step in that direction. He chooses to concentrate on the impact of the German occupation on the inhabitants of western and central Poland in the early and middle years of the war, and on Polish-Jewish experiences in particular. It is not a complete picture, but it is much nearer to completeness than the great majority of English-language studies on occupied Poland. In addition, it effectively puts to rest those most harmful stereotypes about "Nazi murderers," "Jewish victims" and "Polish bystanders." In reality, the murderers were not just Nazis; the victims were not just Jews; and bystanding was one of the least representative of Polish wartime activities.

From time to time, it does no harm to indulge in what the Poles call *gdybologia*, "whatifery." Americans would find their bearings in wartime Poland more speedily by asking themselves what would have happened if a part of their country had been occupied for six years by foreign racists intent on reconstructing the racial makeup of, say, Chicago or New York. They would have to wonder in what racial category of subhuman they would have found themselves. They would have to search their consciences to guess how they would have reacted, if the invaders started murdering the black community, for example, or the Hispanics. They would then have to guess if they would have chosen to collaborate, to avoid trouble, or, at immense risk to themselves, their friends and their families, to resist. Finally, they would have to contemplate whether postwar historians should commemorate all America's dead, or not. The exercise is unhistorical. But it should help to illuminate some of the moral issues without which true historical understanding is impossible.

—Dr. Norman Davies, Oxford, 1997

CHAPTER ONE
THE GERMAN OCCUPATION OF POLAND

When Germany invaded Poland on September 1, 1939, the Poles became the first people in Europe to experience the Holocaust, for this was the inauguration of the German policies of systematic terror, enslavement, and extermination of civilians on an unprecedented scale. From the very moment German armies plunged across the vulnerable Polish frontier, it was apparent that they were not waging a conventional war, that is, a war against the Polish government and its armed forces. Instead, the Germans waged war against the Polish people, intent on destroying the Polish nation.

The Luftwaffe went out of its way to bomb and strafe civilians, repeatedly using incendiary bombs, releasing bombs among peasants working in fields, and hawking traffic along highways. No target was spared; sanitariums, apartment houses, and hospitals were attacked with the same ferocity as military targets. Even the defenseless village of Krzemieniec, where the American embassy was temporarily quartered after the invasion, suffered a severe bombardment.[1] The American ambassador to Poland, Anthony J. Drexel Biddle, Jr., who personally witnessed the killing of innocent civilians, reported to Washington that the German intention was "to terrorize the civilian population and to reduce the number of child bearing Poles irrespective of category."[2] The destruction to the country and especially to Warsaw was enormous. One prominent Polish official estimated that 95 percent of the capital's houses were damaged by bombs or fire; not a historical building or monument escaped total or serious damage.[3] A courier for the Polish underground recalled later how Warsaw looked after the September campaign: "The city resembled an overturned ant heap. The streets were full of rubble, already with pathways trodden through and over it by people hurrying in all directions. Everybody seemed to be engrossed in his own affairs, and all carried something: a rucksack, a basket with provisions, a suitcase."[4]

There was no way Poland could have been saved from destruction unless the British and French had launched an offensive on the western front. General Alfred Jodl said after the war that the Germans survived 1939 "only because the approximately 110 French and English divisions in the West, which during the campaign in Poland were facing 25 German divisions, remained completely inactive."[5]

The Polish army, poorly deployed and short of modern arms, was no match for the 65 German formations which numbered 1,850,000 men and were equipped with 10,000 guns and mortars, 2,800 tanks, and more than 2,000 airplanes. German mobility and firepower, the key to the *Blitzkrieg*, doomed the Polish defensive strategy, which counted on an Anglo-French offensive that never materialized. The Polish commander in chief, Marshal Edward Śmigły-Rydz, did not fully appreciate either the extent of German numerical and material superiority or the intervention of the Soviets into Poland following the Soviet-German Non-Aggression Pact.[6] The pact, signed on August 23, 1939, gave Hitler a free hand against Poland and made World War II inevitable. The Poles fought gallantly, beating off a German attempt to take Warsaw on September 9; this stout-hearted defense was organized by General Walerian Czuma and Warsaw's mayor, Stefan Starzyński, who, epitomizing the resistance of the Varsovians, encouraged his citizens by daily broadcasts and mobilized the city's human and material resources to collective defense.[7]

Warsaw finally fell on September 28, but some Polish units resisted until October 5. Though Polish losses were heavy—200,000 killed and wounded and 420,000 taken prisoner—the Germans lost 45,000 men, 697 airplanes, 993 tanks and armored cars, 370 guns and mortars, and 11,000 military vehicles. In conformity with the Soviet-German Pact, Germany and the Soviet Union each took its pound of flesh—the German slice followed a frontier closely resembling the prewar Curzon Line, netting the Reich 189,000 square kilometers with 21.8 million people, while the Kremlin digested 200,000 square kilometers inhabited by 13.2 million people.[8]

Even after Poland's surrender, the Wehrmacht continued to take seriously Hitler's admonition of August 22, 1939, when he authorized killing "without pity or mercy all men, women, and children of Polish descent or language. Only in this way can we obtain the living space we need."[9] During the Wehrmacht's administration of Poland, which went on until October 25, 1939, the German armed forces joined the Schutzstaffel (SS) and police in what Polish historians have described as "a merciless and systematic campaign of biological destruction."[10] During the period of military control of Poland, 531 towns and villages were burned; the provinces of Łódź and Warsaw suffered the heaviest losses. Various branches of the army and police carried out 714 executions, which took the lives of 16,376 people, most of whom were Polish Christians. The Wehrmacht committed approximately 60 percent of these crimes, with the police responsible for the remainder.[11] An English woman was an eyewitness to the criminal activities of the Germans in Bydgoszcz at this time:

> The first victims of the campaign were a number of Boy Scouts, from twelve to sixteen years of age, who were set up in the marketplace against a wall and shot. No reason was given. A devoted priest who rushed to administer the Last Sacrament was shot too. He received five wounds. A Pole said afterwards that the sight of those children lying dead was the most piteous of all the horrors he saw. That week the murders continued. Thirty-four of the leading tradespeople and merchants of the town were shot, and many other leading citizens. The square was surrounded by troops with machine-guns.
>
> Among the thirty-four was a man whom I knew was too ill to take any part in politics or public affairs. When the execution took place he was too weak to stand, and fell down; they beat him and dragged him again to his feet. Another of the first victims was a boy of seventeen, the only son of a well-known surgeon who had died a year before. The father had been greatly esteemed by all, and had treated the Poles and Germans with the same care and devotion. We never heard of what the poor lad was accused. . . .
>
> These are only a few examples of the indiscriminate murders which took place. The shooting was still going on when I left the town. At the beginning it was done by the soldiers, afterwards the Gestapo and the SS took it over, and exceeded the troops in cruelty.[12]

The Nazi theory of colonial empire in Poland was based on the denial of humanity to the Poles whom, next to the Jews, Hitler hated the most.

In persecuting the Jews, the two components of this hatred were combined. To the Nazis, the Poles were *Untermenschen* (subhumans) who occupied a land which was part of the *Lebensraum* (living space) coveted by the superior German race. Thus the Poles were to be subjected to a program of extermination and enslavement. As Hitler made clear even before the German invasion of Poland, "The destruction of Poland is our primary task. The aim is not the arrival at a certain line but the annihilation of living forces. . . . Be merciless! Be brutal. . . . It is necessary to proceed with maximum severity. . . . The war is to be a war of annihilation."[13] In the flood of directives, memoranda, and commentary by members of the Nazi hierarchy, the conclusion is inescapable that a racial war aimed at the destruction of the Polish people was the objective of the Third Reich. Heinrich Himmler, the man who implemented the German war on the Poles and other Slavs, echoed Hitler's will when he said that "all Poles will disappear from the world. . . . It is essential that the great German people should consider it as its major task to destroy all Poles."[14]

While the Germans intended to eliminate the Jews before the end of the war, most Poles would work as helots until they too ultimately shared the fate of the Jews. Extermination by outright execution was only one method in the Nazi arsenal; extermination by working the Poles to death had the advantage of deriving economic value from them before they died. Martin Bormann, who played an important role in the administration of the forced labor program and thus influenced Nazi policy concerning the Poles and other Slavs, suggested this when he said that "the Slavs are to work for us. Insofar as we don't need them, they may die."[15] Thus the economic value of the Poles was to be only temporary. After all, as one scholar has aptly pointed out, "The new Nazi society was not to indulge in the luxury of slave-holding but was supposed to gain its robust, healthy physical stamina by its own physical exertion."[16] Presumably the Poles who somehow managed to survive the horrific conditions imposed upon them would be deported beyond the pale of German *Lebensraum*. And who could be certain whether resettlement was to be a reality or a ruse? After all, as Czesław Madajczyk, the eminent Polish historian, has suggested, the so-called resettlement of Poles to Siberia could have been nothing more than another German subterfuge to liquidate the Poles after the Germans finished off the Jews.[17]

Nazi leaders recognized that the path to the extirpation of the Poles could be achieved by exterminating certain age groups. Or, as the Academy of German Law suggested, the Poles should be removed temporarily by the hundreds of thousands and employed for a few years in the old Reich; thereby their native biological propagation would be hampered.[18]

There was never any doubt among Nazi officials that Poland and the Polish people were sooner or later to be obliterated. Hans Frank, Hitler's viceroy in the General Government—the part of Poland not annexed by Germany but treated during the war as a gigantic labor camp—declared on September 12, 1940, that Hitler had "made it quite plain that this 'adjacent country' of the German Reich has a special mission to fulfill: to finish off the Poles at all cost." Two years later, Frank put it in grim facetious terms. Referring to the General Government, he said: "Constantly the necessity arises to recall the proverb: 'You must not kill the cow you want to milk.' However, the Reich wants to milk the cow and . . . kill it." In 1944, Frank reflected that when the war was over and Polish labor was not required, the remnants of the Polish people had a grim future. "As far as I am concerned," he declared, "the Poles and the Ukrainians and their like may be chopped into small pieces. Let it be, what should be." [19] For his part, Justice Minister Otto Thierack dolefully told Bormann that he was turning over criminal jurisdiction against Poles, other Slavs, and Jews to Himmler because "the administration of justice can make only a small contribution to the extermination of these peoples." [20]

Leading Wehrmacht and SS commanders were convinced that Poles and other Slavs were to share the same fate as the Jews, though the methods would be varied. General Heusinger, who headed the operations section of the Army High Command (*Oberkommando der Heeres*), said after the war that he believed "the treatment of the civilian population and the methods of anti-partisan warfare in operational areas presented the highest political and military leaders with a welcome opportunity of carrying out their plans, namely the systematic extermination of Slavism and Jewry." SS General Erich von dem Bach-Zelewski, Hitler's chief of antipartisan warfare who succeeded in quelling the Warsaw Uprising of 1944, said that if for years a doctrine is preached that Jews were not human and Slavs were inferior, "then an explosion of this sort is inevitable." [21]

Even Polish Jews who survived the war shared the conviction that the scale of Hitler's hatred and the logic of his wartime policies toward the Poles inevitably meant the Polish Christians would have been exterminated if the war had been prolonged. [22]

Thus the conclusion is inescapable that had the war continued, Poles would have been ultimately obliterated either by outright slaughter in gas chambers, as most Jews had perished, or by a continuation of the policies the Nazis had inaugurated in occupied Poland during the war—genocide by execution, forced labor, starvation, reduction of biological propagation, and Germanization.

Following the military phase of the occupation of Poland, Hitler for-

Poland, 1939-1944

mally annexed the territories of western and a part of central and southern Poland into the German Reich. The Germans formed the rump of conquered Poland into the General Government, to which they added eastern Galicia after the invasion of Russia in June 1941. The General Government consisted of 142,000 square kilometers and contained 16 million people. The incorporated areas, formed into Reichsgau Danzig-Westpreussen and Reichsgau Wartheland, covered 91,974 square kilometers and had a population of 10.1 million people of whom 8.9 million were Poles.[23]

Reichsgau Danzig-Westpreussen included principally the Polish province of Pomorże which had been a territorial bridge between East Prussia and the Reich. A Prussian province from the partitions of the eighteenth century until the rebirth of Poland in 1919, Pomorże had resisted Germanization efforts; the Germans who colonized the area concentrated in Danzig. During the interwar years (1919-39), the Poles attached great importance to this corridor, protecting it from German revisionism and building the port of Gdynia to serve as the center of Poland's maritime interests and a political lever against Danzig.

Reichsgau Wartheland included Poznań and part of Łódź. Poznań was not only a major agricultural and industrial center but also the center of the first Polish kingdom, with Gniezno as the original political and ecclesiastical capital of Poland. Łódź had been an important industrial center, boasting a textile manufacturing center in 1939 that employed 700,000 people. As for Upper Silesia, the Germans unified this rich industrial area that once sprawled over Poland, Germany, and Czechoslovakia and unified it with the Prussian province of Oberschlesien, and economically fused it with German Upper Silesia. Upper Silesia was a major center of industrial war production, especially synthetic oil and rubber and chemical plants.[24]

The General Government, which included the cities of Warsaw, Cracow, and Lublin, was unique among German-occupied territories in that it had no native or higher administrative body of any kind. Part of the reason for the exclusive German character of its administration was the fact that no prominent Poles were ever willing to collaborate with the Nazis. The zeal with which the Germans assumed direct control in the General Government was at least partially the result of their desire to establish a laboratory where they could experiment with methods of administration and exploitation that could be applied when German armies expanded *Lebensraum* in eastern Europe. In fact, when the Germans occupied the Baltic states and the Ukraine in 1941, a large number of the decrees promulgated in these areas were virtually identical to similar measures in force earlier in the General Government.

The relationship of the General Government to the Reich evolved as the war progressed. At first the area was seen as a kind of protectorate, originally called General Government of the Occupied Polish Areas (*General Gouvernement der Besetzten Polnischen Gebiete*). The accent was on "occupation" as opposed to "incorporation." In 1940, the *Frankfurter Zeitung* described the General Government as "an independent state . . . which, territorially, does not belong to the Reich, but which naturally has no foreign policy of its own." Two years later, the status of the area had obviously changed; now it was referred to as a *Nebenland*, or an adjunct to the Reich.[25] Even the new postal marking used to describe the status of the General Government—*Deutsches Reich-Generalgouvernement*—symbolized the evolution of the area in the direction of integration within the Reich. No doubt the German invasion of the Soviet Union in 1941 had something to do with the altered status of the area. Prior to the invasion, the area was seen as a buffer between Germany and the Soviet Union; afterward, it became a bridge between Germany and the newly acquired areas to the East.

To be sure, the ultimate aim of German policy in all Polish territory, whether the annexed areas or the General Government, was the same— enslavement and extermination. But the evolution from a protectorate toward an incorporated area revealed an increase in the German program of de-Polonization. After returning from a conference in March 1941, during which Hitler said he wanted the General Government to be free of Poles and Jews, Governor General Frank took a series of initiatives which sought to make the General Government as German as the Rhineland. As Frank said, "There is not a shadow of doubt that the territory of the General Government must be and will be colonized by Germans."[26] This despite the failure to accomplish the same objective in the annexed areas.

The German policy of destroying the Polish nation focused strongly, but not exclusively, upon eliminating anyone with even the least political and cultural prominence. Hitler gave the green light, placing responsibility for this campaign on Himmler's SS and police forces. The bespectacled Nazi leader told his officers, "You should hear this but also forget it again—to shoot thousands of leading Poles." Frank told his collaborators the same thing: "The Führer told me: 'what we have now recognized in Poland to be the elite must be liquidated; we must watch out for the seeds that begin to sprout again, so as to stamp them out again in good time.'"[27] Himmler was aware that psychologically the SS had to justify their horrible actions to themselves; this was suggested by the SS chief when he told an SS regiment which had participated in the French campaign that no less brave a task was being performed by their comrades in Poland: "In many cases it is much easier to go into battle with a company of infantry than it is to suppress an obstructive population of low cultural level or to carry out executions or to haul away people or to evict crying and hysterical women." Thus a special hardness was required to murder Poles by the thousands.[28]

The German definition of "elite" was so broad, however, that it embraced a major part of Polish society, including not only teachers, physicians, priests, officers, businessmen, landowners, and writers but also anyone who even attended secondary school.[29] The consequence was that millions of Poles were targeted for liquidation as Nazi dragnets swept the country determined to destroy the so-called harmful influence Hitler railed against.

The SS lost little time. In November 1939, they arrested almost 200 professors and fellows of the Jagiellonian University in Cracow—one of the oldest institutions of higher learning in Europe—and of the Polytechnic and sent them to Sachsenhausen. Many of them died. The episode shocked European public opinion. A short time later, in retribution for the killing of two policemen, 107 innocent men, mostly intellectuals, were killed, even though the offenders were known to the police.[30] In the last months of 1939 alone, there were more than 100 mass executions conducted in the General Government. Concerned about the difficulties incurred in dealing with the professors from Jagiellonian University in November 1939, Frank insisted that now Polish intellectuals would be dealt with "on the spot and we shall do so in the *simplest* way possible" (italics mine).[31] Taking advantage of the preoccupation of world opinion with military operations in the West in the spring of 1940, the Germans launched a massive program to exterminate the Polish intelligentsia in the General Government. Under the cryptonym A-B, *Ausserordentliche-Befriedungsaktion* (extraordinary pacification action), the Germans murdered at least 6,000 people; in addition, several thousand men who had been seized in roundups and searches were moved to Auschwitz concentration camp, where they later died.[32]

Pawiak and Palmiry became known to every Pole, not only in the district of Warsaw, where they were located, but also in the entire country, because these were the sites of frequent executions. Among the people of influence caught in the web of operation A-B were Maciej Rataj, a distinguished statesman who served as marshal in Poland's Sejm, Mieczysław Niedziałkowski, a prominent Socialist leader, Jan Poholski, deputy mayor of Warsaw, Jan Belcikowski, a distinguished writer, Maria Witkowska, a well-known artist, Janusz Kusociński, an Olympic 10,000-meter champion, and scores of other Polish notables.[33]

Although there were tactical shifts in the German campaign of extermination against the Polish elite, it never really eased during the war. The Nazis were so thorough in their grim work that when Dachau was liberated at the end of the war, there were only 50 Polish physicians, 100 lawyers, 50 engineers, and 100 teachers still alive there, in contrast to 5,000 farmers and 3,600 artisans.[34] Testimony of just how successful the Germans were in their resolve is revealed by the fact that during the war Poland lost 45 percent of her physicians and dentists, 57 percent of her attorneys, more than 15 percent of her teachers, 40 percent of her professors, 30 percent of her technicians, and more than 18 percent of her clergy. The majority of her journalists also disappeared—73 were murdered, 77 died in concentration camps and jails, 50 died in the ghetto, and 12 perished in the Warsaw Uprising.[35]

The intelligentsia who succeeded in evading death suffered physical and material decline because the Germans deprived them of a way to make a living. People in academe, and social, cultural, and professional workers joined writers, journalists, and artists in unemployment. Often they had to assume jobs they were unfamiliar with; they could be found everywhere: painting, trading, shopkeeping, and even operating rickshaws. For writers, all legal avenues of public expression were closed to them by the Germans, but those willing to assume the risk got involved with the illegal underground press; others worked in the offices of some of the wartime institutions, like the Central Welfare Council (*Rada Główna Opiekuńcza*), which provided at least a small salary but most of all protection from arrest and even execution. One report from Poland in 1941 said, "The intelligentsia grow increasingly poorer but are the most politically active and unsubmissive." By 1942, the situation improved for the intellectuals because manpower shortages forced German civil servants elsewhere, and their positions were sometimes made available to Poles. In addition, the Polish underground had expanded by then and served as an outlet for employment, even though a dangerous one. And, finally, charitable and relief organizations were able to offer material help.[36]

The extirpation of the Polish intelligentsia was part of a systematic program to destroy Polish culture. Education, the heart of a nation's culture, was singled out for elimination. "The Poles," Frank said, "do not need universities or secondary schools; the Polish lands are to be changed into an intellectual desert." The Germans denied Polish youth the right to a secondary and university education. Even elementary schools which used Polish as the language of instruction were closed in the annexed provinces, though a certain number were left open in the General Government. Nevertheless, the number of children attending elementary schools in the General Government in 1941 was not much more than 50 percent of what it had been before the war. In Warsaw there were 380 elementary schools in 1938; three years later, there were 175. In the annexed lands, Polish children were to go to work at age twelve, sometimes as early as ten, and if they attended school at all they were subjected to a process of Germanization. German teachers taught them only enough of the German language so the children could understand what orders to obey.[37]

Polish universities were often occupied by military and civil authorities, and their libraries and laboratories were pillaged. Before the war, Poland had an impressive collection of state, municipal, and ecclesiastical and private archives. Most of these archival collections were in Warsaw. Following the September campaign, the German authorities seized, dispersed, confiscated, and destroyed surviving collections. Berlin was anxious to acquire documents which either strengthened German claims to

Poland or emphasized German cultural influences in Polish society. For this reason, part of the records of the Polish Foreign Ministry and the Ministry of Internal Affairs were shipped to Germany. When Gestapo officials saw no German use for the records of the Polish Ministry of Religion and Public Education, they threw them into a courtyard where, thanks to the diligence of Polish archivists, the records were saved. The Germans confiscated some of the most treasured historical records, including seventy-four parchments of the former Polish Crown Archives, and sent them to Germany. Warsaw, where 75 percent of Polish archives were stored, suffered catastrophic losses.[38] According to one Polish account:

> Thus was concluded the work of destruction of the Warsaw archives during World War II. The Archives of the Age of Enlightenment, the Treasury and the Municipal Archives lost 100 percent of their records; the Archives of Recent Records—97 percent; the Central Archives of Earlier Records—90 percent; the Archives of Earlier Records—80 percent. All the Archives combined lost a total of 92.8 percent of their archive store. No Tartar invasion of the Middle Ages had resulted in such devastation.[39]

Polish art suffered equivalent losses. In six months, the Germans stripped major collections on the grounds "there was no such thing as Polish art." Hitler received thirty drawings by Dürer that had been stolen from the collections of Polish aristocrats. Among the great art works sent to Germany was the reredos of Witt Stwosz (Veit Stoss) in Cracow. By the end of 1942, Frank bragged that 90 percent of the art works in the General Government had been seized. Approximately 105 out of 175 public museums survived the war, but only 33 of these were in shape to open their doors to the public. Museums they did not pillage, the Germans sought to exploit for propaganda purposes to demonstrate alleged German influences on Polish culture. For example, in the Tatra Museum of Zakopane, the authorities used the collections to demonstrate the alleged separate nationality of the Polish highland people and their kinship to the Goths.[40]

The Germans closed all scientific, artistic, and literary institutions in both parts of Poland. Often their property and funds were plundered. The Polish press, which before the war boasted 2,000 periodicals in the Polish language and another 250 in other languages, was gutted and replaced by an extensive German press in the Polish language. Perhaps the most notable dailies printed by the Germans were the *Nowy Kurier Warszawski* (a name appropriated from the oldest Polish newspaper, the *Kurier War-*

szawski), the *Kurier Częstochowski, Nowy Głos Lubelski, Dziennik Radomski*, and the *Gazeta Lwówska*. These were official organs of Nazi policy which sought to emphasize the invincibility of German power and the inferiority of the Poles. At the outset, the Germans concentrated on defaming the Polish nationality and casting aspersions on the ability of the Poles to govern themselves. Somewhat later, the main thrust of German press propaganda was anti-Soviet and anti-Jewish. During the liquidation of the Jewish ghettos, the Germans even tried to convince the Jewish people that the Poles and not the Germans were responsible for killing them. The Polish resistance sought to boycott the German-run press, but people read it anyway, chiefly for the military news and the obituaries, one of the most avidly read sections of the press. Poles who read German could get more information from papers like *Das Reich, Deutsche Allgemeine Zeitung*, or the *Krakauer Zeitung*.[41]

In order to transform the Polish nation into a land of slaves, fit only for work or death, the Germans launched a concerted attack on Polish history. They confiscated history books and prohibited teachers to teach it. They removed monuments, busts, memorials, and inscriptions of Polish heroes, including Kościuszko, Chopin, and Piłsudski. In Warsaw the Germans even planned to erect a monument to the victory of the Third Reich in the exact place where the monument to King Zygmunt III was located.[42]

Hitler realized that the assault on Polish culture would be incomplete until Poland's cities were de-Polonized. Their names were changed— Gdynia became Gotenhafen, Łódź was now Litzmannstadt, Rzeszów was renamed Reichshof—along with street names. Hitler wanted Warsaw, the cultural hub of the country, reduced to a German provincial town with only 100,000-200,000 people. One of the few historic monuments to be spared from destruction was the Belvedere Palace which was to serve as Hitler's residence when he visited the city. Under the supervision of a German architect, the Germans reconstructed the palace in October 1941, trying to give it as magnificent an impression as possible by installing copper roofs outside and enlarging a large hall inside. But to achieve this, they destroyed some of the polychrome effects on the walls and chimney pieces. The great hall was decorated with a ceiling painted by inferior Viennese artists.

German plans for the Polish capital did not get too far because the demands of the war forced them to use their resources elsewhere. On the other hand, Cracow, as the center of the General Government, was a major German administrative and communications center with a large German population. The city boasted four German theaters and twenty-six German restaurants; in German eyes, Cracow had become a German city. In Lublin a major SS and police outpost in eastern Poland was slated for extensive Germanization, especially the area around Zamość where 100,000 Poles were evicted from their homes in the period 1942-44. Though Himmler had grandiose plans to make 40 percent of the people of Lublin German by 1944, he never succeeded.[43]

The Germanization of Poznań—Posen in German—was far more advanced than any other Polish city. After only a few short months of German control, one prominent member of the Polish resistance remarked, "Even I could hardly believe that it was the same city I had known before the war, so thoroughly had its face been remodeled."[44] A Scandinavian journalist observed that it was not so difficult to give Poznań a German character outwardly because the buildings proclaimed the language of German architects. "Posen has again a purely German face, provisionally sculptured," he said, "but its body is still Polish. Its brain and soul are German, but its arms are Polish." Deprived of an educated class, the Poles, he believed, were powerless to resist the fanatical de-Polonization campaign of the Germans. He predicted the next generation of Poles in the annexed lands would know German better than Polish.[45]

Polish nationalism was synonymous with Catholicism. The church had always provided the foundation of Polish nationalism, especially during periods of oppression. If the Nazi policy of exterminating the Polish nation were to have any chance of success, the Germans realized they had to destroy the organization and leadership of the church. Before the war the Polish church had been organized around six archbishoprics, an autonomous archbishopric, and eighteen suffragan dioceses. When the Nazis partitioned Poland into two sections—the annexed lands and the General Government—it wreaked havoc with the organizational structure of the church. The line between the annexed lands and the General Government separated metropolitan sees from their suffragans and capriciously cut many dioceses in half.[46] Thus weakened, the Polish church in the annexed territories lost most of its hierarchy and clergy. Out of six bishops in the Wartheland, only one—Bishop Walenty Dymek—remained; the others, like most of the clergy, were imprisoned. Significantly, only in Poland did the Nazis arrest and imprison clergy of episcopal rank. In 1939, 80 percent of the clergy had been deported from the Wartheland. In 1941, 500 priests from this area alone were in concentration camps. Predictably, the losses of clergy in the annexed lands were higher than those living in the General Government. In Wrocław, 49.2 percent of its clergy died; in

Chełmno, 47.8; in Łódź, 36.8; and in Poznań, 31.1. Out of a total of 10,017 secular clergy in Poland in 1939, 1,811 died during the war;[47] as a consequence, entire districts had no priests to serve the people. Poznań, which had a population of 200,000 people with thirty churches and forty-seven chapels before the war, had two churches available for Poles after the German occupation. Łódź, with a Polish population of 700,000, had only four churches open.[48] In addition to churches, the Germans also closed seminaries, monasteries, Catholic schools, and other church-related institutions.

Nuns shared the same fate as priests. It was reported that 400 nuns were imprisoned at a concentration camp at Bojanowo and that a large number were transferred from there to Germany for forced labor.[49] What happened to the congregation of the Sisters of the Resurrection of Our Lord was rather typical of what befell other religious orders. The Germans closed seven of their convents and seized their property. A large number of the nuns in Pomorże and Poznań had no choice but to live with their parents or to join thousands of Poles in forced labor. Out of 277 sisters, 37 died during the war. The nuns who survived cared for children, prisoners, and priests and aided the resistance movement.[50]

The Nazi Germanization of the Polish church in the annexed area was facilitated, unfortunately, by the abandonment of their dioceses by Polish bishops. Cardinal Augustus Hlond set the tone by abandoning the arch-diocese of Gniezno-Poznań, Bishop Stanisław Okoniewski gave up his diocese at Chełmno, and Bishop Karol Radonski left Wrocław. Hlond's departure understandably disappointed Polish Catholics, and when he turned up in Rome, Pope Pius XII showed his displeasure by not receiving him very enthusiastically. The cardinal later found his way to France so he would be near the seat of the Polish government-in-exile. But when France collapsed, Hlond was alone and isolated; he tried to return to Poland in 1943, but the Germans arrested and interned him. Anxious by then to get church support for their fight against the Soviet Union, the Germans offered Hlond his freedom if he sent a message to his countrymen to join the Germans in the fight against communism. Hlond refused.[51]

Nazi control of the church in Silesia was the easiest because the Polish bishop there, Stanisław Adamski, ordered the clergy and people to assume the status of *Volksdeutsch* (German national). Though criticized by the Polish resistance for trying to find a modus vivendi with the Germans, Adamski, who never declared himself a *Volksdeutsch*, believed this was a way to keep the Polish churches open and the casualty count of priests to a minimum. Although the Germans closed sixty convents and monasteries in Silesia, there were comparatively few casualties among the priests— forty-three died in concentration camps, two perished in resistance work, and thirteen were deported to the General Government, including, ironically, Adamski.[52]

German administrators of Polish dioceses could be extremely severe on the Poles, as illustrated by the example of Bishop K.M. Splett of Gdańsk, a German administrator who took over the diocese of Chełmno. Splett filled his diocese with *Volksdeutsch* priests and forbade the use of the Polish language in the churches, including the hearing of confessions in Polish. According to one report, two priests in Splett's diocese died in mysterious circumstances because they were guilty of hearing confessions in Polish. A fanatical Germanizer, Splett even ordered the removal of Polish inscriptions in cemeteries and their replacement in the German language.[53]

The clergy in the General Government was not persecuted as much as their confreres in the annexed lands. The reason for this was Hitler wanted to control, not obliterate, the church there. Besides, once he began the war with the Soviet Union, Hitler and his cronies sought but failed to get the support of the church to fight communism. During the first months of the German-Soviet war, German propaganda depicted the war as a struggle against the enemies of Christianity. The Germans exhibited posters with Christ and showed Bolsheviks trying to tear them down. Nevertheless, in the General Government the Germans killed several hundred Polish priests: in the diocese of Warsaw, 212 killed; Cracow, 30; Kielce, 13; Lwów, 81; Wilno, 92.[54] In general, however, 95 percent of the clergy in the General Government remained in the same parish in which they had resided before the war, and their general material situation was better than the clergy in the annexed lands.[55]

Most priests behaved with dignity in the face of the German occupation. The behavior of a few opportunistic bishops was questioned, but only Bishop Sokołowski of Podlasko-Siedlecka seemed to be considered a "black stain on the Polish episcopate."[56] Priests and nuns played an important role not only in charitable and humanitarian work on behalf of Christians and Jews but also in the resistance. Convents housed printing machines and became distribution centers for the underground press. In Cracow, three priests played a major role in creating depositories for money sent from abroad. The clergy frequently provided people, pursued by the Gestapo, with false baptismal records. In the remote mountain provinces on the Slovakian frontier, priests often concealed Polish underground agents passing to and from the country. Despite the risks, priests frequently made strong references in their sermons to the resurrection of Poland.[57]

Even in the General Government, the Germans interfered in church services. They limited church services and restricted singing to the priest and choir; and they prohibited some hymns which had patriotic meaning—"God Who Saved Poland" (*Boże Coś Polskę*) and "Tender Mother" (*Serdeczna Matko*). And specific sermons in German were mandated.[58] The Polish government gave an accurate description of what the church in Poland had to endure: "As a result of these persecutions church activities in Poland have been so harshly repressed by the German authorities that the Church can only accomplish its mission in a most restricted manner, reducing religious life to what it was at the time of the catacombs. In the western regions of Poland, illegally annexed to the Reich, all Church activity has been virtually suppressed."[59]

In face of the persecution of the church of Poland, the Vatican pursued a timid, reserved attitude. Pope Pius XII, who served as nuncio to Germany in the 1920s and was sentimental about the country, at no time made a clear, unequivocal statement in defense of the Polish church against the barbarities inflicted upon it by the Germans. Much has been said about the Pope's Germanophilism and his faith in diplomacy as factors in restraining him. The American representative to the Vatican speculated that the Pope feared a strong statement against the atrocities in Poland might result in even greater violence on the Poles; he also indicated that if the Pope denounced German atrocities directly, the papacy would be blamed later by the Germans for contributing to their defeat.[60] It was not until June 2, 1943, that the Pope expressed his hope for Poland's resurrection after the war. Although this speech was more explicit than others in referring "to the blows of fate" and "to the changing tides of the gigantic tragedy of war" that the Poles had to endure, the Pope shied away, as he had before, from directly condemning the Germans.[61]

The papal statement was an effort to respond to the widespread criticism that had developed in Poland among the clergy and toward the Vatican because of its reticence. Though there was a great outpouring of religious fervor among the Poles, papal leadership had been badly tarnished; some Polish voices called for severing relations with the Vatican.[62] Some Poles even walked out of church when they heard their priest defend the Pope. The Jesuits of Warsaw were so concerned about the situation that they published a leaflet which tried to show what the Vatican had done for the Poles.[63] In 1942, *WRN*, an underground organ of Polish Socialists, bitterly declared that the Vatican was "walking hand in hand with the Hitlerite . . . Fascists." *Głos Pracy*, another Polish underground newspaper, chided the Pope for shutting "himself up in the Vatican and does not bother to defend his own faithful." Stanisław Mikołajczyk, minister of interior of the Polish government, revealed on December 23, 1942, how impatient the Polish people were with the papacy and their own government: "The people would be relieved by official news about the protest of the Holy See and the Polish government, given the flagrant and never-hitherto-experienced persecution of the church in Poland."[64]

The Pope's speech of June 2, 1943, was warmly received by the Polish government-in-exile and quieted much, but not all, of the criticism of the papacy in Poland. After all, the Poles were interested not only in words but also in deeds. When Hlond fled to Rome, the country was left without a leader. The Pope, though displeased with Hlond, did not send him back home. Nor did he appoint, at least publicly, any other church official to lead the Polish church. The Pope did not make Archbishop Sapieha of Cracow a cardinal until after the war, nor did he appoint him head of the Polish church even on an interim basis. Such an action would have gone a long way to show the Poles in a concrete way that the papacy had not forgotten Poland and stood with the persecuted Polish church.

To be sure, the Vatican had some practical difficulties in maintaining official ties with the Polish government. The nuncio to Warsaw, Archbishop Filippo Cortesi, left the country when the war began. The Vatican appointed Monsignor Alfredo Pacini as chargé d'affaires to the Polish government-in-exile, which was then in France. When the Polish government moved to London after the French military collapse, the British did not allow Pacini to follow, on the grounds that England was at war with Italy and the chargé d'affaires was an Italian. The problem was resolved by the appointment of Archbishop William Godfrey, the apostolic delegate in London, to serve also as chargé d'affaires to the Polish government.

After Cortesi fled Poland, the Vatican was left without any representation on Polish soil. Hoping to get around that, the Vatican then extended the faculties of Archbishop Cesare Orsenigo, the nuncio in Berlin, to include Poland. But the German government never recognized the extension of Orsenigo's jurisdiction. Thus to the delight of the Nazis, the Polish church did not have a primate or a papal representative on Polish soil. Even though Orsenigo has been criticized by some Polish sources for being anti-Polish, it should be kept in mind that the Germans placed many limitations on him, and it was virtually impossible for the nuncio to do much for the Polish church from Berlin. As one historian has said: "It is certain that the Nazis were opposed to there being any Vatican representative in Poland. They feared not only that he would witness and report on their activities, but also that he would become a rallying point for the Polish church, which they preferred to keep in a subservient position."[65]

One of the major components of German policy toward Poland was the Germanization of the lands annexed to the Reich. The Germans even attempted an ambitious program of Germanizing a belt of land in the eastern part of the General Government, centered around Lublin. The importance Hitler attached to the Germanization of the annexed territories was revealed by his appointment of Heinrich Himmler, who already headed the SS and police establishments, to be Reich Commissioner for the Consolidation of German Nationhood. Germanization meant, of course, de-Polonization and was to be implemented by the colonization of Germans into the area. Approximately one million Poles were deported from the area, most of them transferred to the General Government or the Reich. The deportations, which reached a high point in 1940, were conducted under appalling conditions; people were forced into cattle cars and in the freezing weather of the winter of 1939-40 transferred to the General Government where they were unceremoniously dumped. Many died, especially children. Deportation meant despoiling the people because they were forced to leave, usually on short notice and at night, with only a few personal possessions, leaving most of their valuables and property behind. Expulsion also often meant separation of families; able-bodied members were frequently sent to Germany while the rest of the family was sent to the General Government.[66]

The Poles selected for deportation were classified according to their occupational status and to their attitude toward the Germans. The Polish intelligentsia and those who had worked for the Polish cause were among the primary candidates for expulsion. On the other hand, "neutrally inclined Poles" were considered candidates for Germanization while Polish agricultural laborers were to remain, at least temporarily, to assist German farmers. There were also other criteria which determined who should be deported from the annexed areas. Certain groups, like the Wasserpolen, Masurians, and Kashubes, were not deported because of their alleged racial closeness to the Germans. Geographical and strategic considerations sometimes outweighed other factors; for example, the Germans deported Poles from seaport cities like Gdynia and Orlowo and from the frontier area between the annexed lands and the General Government. In the latter case, the Germans intended to lock in the Poles in the region "which ultimately would close completely when the area became solidly German."[67]

While the Poles were being deported, Germans from foreign countries were simultaneously transferred to the Reich as colonists. Most of these German colonists came from areas annexed by the Soviet Union in 1939-40 and from other areas in eastern Europe—for example, Estonia, Latvia, Soviet-occupied Poland, Bessarabia, Bukovina, and the General Government.[68] A contemporary German source estimated that more than 650,000 colonists came from these countries to the Reich, most of whom were settled in the annexed lands.[69] But a Polish authority says that altogether about 750,000 Germans from the Reich and *Volksdeutsch* of various kinds were settled in the area.[70]

Despite the efforts to Germanize the annexed lands by the influx of German colonists and to Germanize the Poles who remained there, the Nazi program failed. German resettlement in the area fell in 1941 because of the exigencies of the German war with the Soviet Union. Approximately 125,000 ethnic Germans, who had been repatriated in 1939-40, were still living in transit camps in 1942. They complained to Himmler about their status, urging that the resettlement program be speeded up. Himmler bluntly told them that the supply needs of the German front outweighed in importance their resettlement.[71] Instead of being directed to their new homes in the annexed lands, German colonists remained in assembly camps where they were used as a labor force.[72] Most of the Germans from the Old Reich who had been transferred to the annexed lands were recruited for administrative reasons or were businessmen and craftsmen; their primary interest seems to have been to make huge profits from the enterprises the Poles were forced to abandon. Contrary to Nazi expectations, only a small number of German soldiers who had been injured in the war settled there too.[73] The reluctance of German teachers from the Reich to settle in these lands was so strong that many were forced to immigrate.[74] There was also a great deal of ignorance among prospective German colonists. For instance, many had no idea where Poznań or Toruń was. One trainload of Germans from Berlin refused to disembark in the Polish Corridor when they learned Poles still inhabited the area; understandably, they feared Polish retribution. The evacuees were sent on to East Prussia instead.[75]

Most German colonists from eastern Europe were on a lower intellectual level than the Poles they displaced and were unaccustomed to their new environment. Only the Germans from the Baltic states seem to have been on the same social level as the Poles in the area. In the *Ostdeutscher Beobachter* on December 8, 1940, a journalist described a visit to a German colonist who had been transferred from the East:

> At last we reached the gates of the courtyard. The peasant walked up to meet us.
>
> "Well, Comrade, how are things?" asked the SS officer who was acting as guide to the journalists.
>
> The peasant greeted us and expressed the opinion that he was better off now than before, but that his holdings were decidedly too large.
>
> "Too much land," he repeated, and looked mournfully around.

"What? Sixty acres too much for you? Surely not! You have enough horses and grown-up sons, and a strong wife—they can help you!" shouted the local peasant leader (Bauernfuhrer), who is also an officer of the SS.

In the stables I saw an amazing sight. Only two horses were there, and two cows instead of eight. When we went into the pigsty we found there only two sows and four young pigs.

"What did you do with the rest of the livestock?" asked the local Bauern-fuhrer, much surprised.

The peasant stared at the ground. "Well," he muttered, "I sold them; back in the east we never had more than this. I hadn't, nor my father or grandfather, but still it was enough to feed the whole family."[76]

Many of the younger colonists did not speak German, or they spoke it badly. Older peasants were often completely denationalized and had to be settled in central Germany and be "re-educated" in purely German surroundings. Despite indoctrination programs to which the newly settled colonists were subjected and the ever-present control of the Gestapo, German officials still feared that these racially pure colonies would be contaminated by the Polish people who lived in the vicinity. Arthur Greiser, a German official in the Wartheland, told the inhabitants of his Gau: "The dangers confronting the very essence of our German community are still overwhelming. Do not let your foreign and alien surroundings have the slightest influence on you." That was a major reason why the authorities settled German colonists from the East in compact settlements where they lived in the same groups and continued to be controlled and observed by the police.[77]

After two years of fanatical efforts, the percentage of Germans in this area increased only slightly. Little wonder, then, that German officials conceded failure by saying that real colonization efforts of Polish lands would not begin until after the war.[78]

Failure also greeted Nazi efforts to de-Polonize an area in the eastern part of the General Government. SS General Odilo Globocnik believed that the General Government should be cleared of Poles and in 1941, as a step in that direction, convinced Himmler to establish German settlements in the Lublin area. The plan envisaged a belt of German settlements extending northward to the Baltic states and southward to Transylvania. As one German report described it, Globocnik "wants to 'imprison' the remaining Poles in the western areas in between by way of settlement and gradually crush them economically and biologically." In other words, the Germans would expand from west to east out of the annexed Polish lands and exert pressure on the Poles from the north, south, east, and west from the Lublin area. Himmler liked the idea so much he personally visited the region and decided that the hub of the operation would center on the city of Zamość (southeast of Lublin), which was renamed Himmlerstadt.[79] Once the plan evolved, the Germans intended to expel Poles from the region in numbers substantial enough to accommodate 10,000 settlements, each comprising 50,000 Germans transferred from Bosnia, Bessarabia, the Soviet Union, and the Low Countries.[80] Himmler planned to Germanize completely the General Government within twenty years. Governor Frank lost out in the disputes concerning the competence of the SS and police in the General Government: Himmler ignored Frank's suggestion that the Germanization of the area be inaugurated only after the war.[81]

The expulsion of Poles began on November 28, 1942. SS, Gestapo, Wehrmacht, and Ukrainians in German service were responsible for the evacuation operation. Since Nazi racial principles of blood and land had to be considered, people were divided into four groups. The Germans placed Poles with desirable racial characteristics in the first two categories and sent them to Łódź for racial examination. Poles in the third category were sent to the Reich to work. Members of the fourth group were slated for Auschwitz and certain death. Children, especially those with racial value to the Germans, were forcibly taken from their parents and sent to the Reich for Germanization.

The deportation procedures used in the Zamość operation rivaled in fanaticism Greiser's expulsion of Poles from the Wartheland. The Poles had less than an hour to present themselves for deportation and were allowed to carry only a few personal belongings. The gendarmes forcibly evicted resisters and sometimes shot them.[82] One victim of the eviction remembered:

> They began to rap at the windows and the doors. Chattering in German proved that we were surrounded and there was no escape for us. At that moment I realized, though I was a child, the immensity of the horror and misfortune befalling us. . . . .I also had ready a package (in which I had a doll) but when the Germans rushed into the dwelling they gave us only five minutes to prepare and to take some things and immediately pushed us out of the house, disregarding the weeping of children and the requests of our parents. My parents thus took only bundles with bedding because it was already very cold.[83]

The people were then sent to transit camps where, due to the appalling conditions, the mortality rate was extremely high, especially among the children. One Polish peasant woman recalled seeing the Germans remove ten corpses of children every day from the camp.[84] Perhaps the most painful experiences were the abductions of children from their parents. One eyewitness remembered: "I saw children being taken from their mothers; some were even torn from the breast. It was a terrible sight: the agony of the mothers and fathers, the beating by the Germans, and the crying of the children."[85] In the rail cars carrying the adults and children to various destinations, many died of suffocation in the summer and cold in the winter. Packed into the cars like animals, they were given no food or drink.[86]

Once word spread through the country about the pitiful plight of the children—and there were approximately 30,000 of them expelled from the Zamość area[87]—the Polish people responded admirably. As the trains loaded with children moved westward across Poland, Polish women waited for hours at railroad stations in the hope of helping them. In Warsaw, residents reacted spontaneously and ransomed the emaciated and exhausted youngsters. In Kutno, the same thing happened. In Bydgoszcz and Gdynia, Poles bought children for forty Reichmarks.[88] Unfortunately, the children considered unfit for Germanization found their way to Auschwitz where, along with adults, they died. The Germans killed most of them by intracardiac injections of phenol. One Auschwitz inmate remembered the fate of forty-eight boys from the Zamość area: "The Germans started a rumour in the camp that the boys would be sent for training as bricklayers. As I found out, the Germans transferred these boys to the camp at Auschwitz to Block 13 where they remained two days, after which they were killed with injections and cremated. I cannot remember the name of the German doctor who killed the children."[89]

From November 1942 until March 1943, the Germans emptied 116 villages in the Lublin region, 47 of them in Zamość alone. In the period November 27 to December 31, 1942, the Germans hoped to seize almost 34,000 people from 60 villages, but in reality they grabbed only 9,771 residents; the remainder had escaped, mostly to the nearby woods. The Germans resumed the expulsions in June and July 1943, clearing 171 villages in the districts of Biłgoraj, Tomaszów, Zamość, and Hrubieszów. Altogether, by August 1943, 110,000 Poles had been expelled by the Germans, or 31 percent of the number of Poles who inhabited the Zamość region.[90] Pacification raids sometimes accompanied the expulsions, often resulting in fires that took the lives of many people. In the village of Kidów, the Polish resistance reported that 170 farmers were murdered.[91] The Germans cleared some areas so completely that only cattle were left wandering in the fields. Simultaneously with the expulsion in the Lublin-Zamość region, the Polish government reported mass deportations of the population from the district of Białystok in northeastern Poland. By the end of January 1943, the Poles claimed that more than 40,000 residents had been deported from that area. Six months later, the Poles reported that in the middle of July 1943, 500 prominent citizens were murdered in Bi-ałystok.[92]

The majority of Poles, panic stricken that they would be exterminated as the Jews had been in similar deportation operations, abandoned their homes and property and fled to the forests. In one village, only two people remained; the others had fled.[93] The Polish resistance army, known as the Home Army (*Armia Krajowa*—AK), had no partisan units yet in the region and could not immediately respond to the Germans. But the AK chief, General Stefan Grot-Rowecki, ordered a general increase in resistance activity, especially a widening of diversionary operations against the Germans. The Polish government-in-exile feared that these operations would get out of hand and lead to a premature uprising against the Germans, which was supposed to occur only when the enemy was at the point of imminent collapse on the eastern front. So the government urged restraint on the AK to limit its operations to the immediate locale. So cautious was the Polish government that a radio speech by Mikołajczyk from London was widely interpreted by the Poles to remain passive. Polish authorities in the homeland assured the government in London that military responses against the Germans would not be allowed to lead to an uprising.[94]

The Germans paid a heavy price for their Germanization efforts. Many people in the area burned their houses and destroyed their property before they fled to the woods, leaving only charred embers for the new German residents. Other Polish farmers actively resisted; one group attacked the German settlers in Cieszyn, killed 30 of them, and plundered their property. The raid on Cieszyn so enraged Himmler that he ordered the annihilation of entire Polish villages in reprisal.[95] In response to a German reprisal raid that took the lives of 280 Poles, the AK in June 1943, burned a German-colonized village in which 69 settlers perished. Retaliatory operations included attacks on railroad, military, and government targets. For example, on November 30, 1942, the AK attacked a railroad bridge at Łosiniec on the Lwów-Lublin line. On December 1, 1942, the People's Guard (*Gwardia Ludowa*—GL), the communist resistance military force, struck a railroad station at Terespol. On December 31, 1942, the AK conducted 60 different sabotage and diversionary operations in the Zamość area, destroying four bridges and two trains. The Peasant Battalions (*Bataliony Chłopskie*—BCh), which later became a part of the AK, also conducted successful attacks against the Germans in the area. These operations of the AK, GL, and BcH, combined with the German defeat at Kursk in the Soviet Union, forced the Germans to abandon further Germanization efforts in the General Government.[96]

As is well known, the Nazis tried to build a society on race. When they conquered the Poles and other people in eastern Europe, the Germans applied racial criteria to discover those with desirable traits for Germanization. As a group, Poles were considered racially alien and were in the same category as Jews, Gypsies, Belorussians, and Ukrainians. However, the Germans considered about 3 percent of the Poles in the annexed provinces good prospects for Germanization. The objectives were clear enough; as Himmler said on May 9, 1940, "It is, therefore, an absolute national-political necessity to screen the annexed Eastern territories and later also the General Government for such persons of Teutonic blood in order to make this lost German blood again available to our own people."[97] The Nazis not only wanted to increase the "racially desirable" growth of the German population but also prevent an increase of the Polish intelligentsia which, from the German point of view, had once been Germanic but had been Polonized over a period of time. There was the curious German notion that Polish resistance leaders had a considerable portion of Nordic blood which "enables them to be active in contrast to the fatalistic Slavonic elements."[98] Clearly, if these people were Germanized, the mass of Poles would be denied a dynamic leadership class.

The Nazis established an elaborate classification of persons considered to have German blood, and it contained provisions concerning the rights and duties of people in each classification. Called the Racial Register (*Volksliste*), the list classified people into four categories. Class I included Germans who before the war had promoted the Nazi cause. Class II were Germans who had been passive in the Nazi struggle but retained their German nationality. Class III included people of German extraction who had been previously connected with the Polish nation but were willing to submit to Germanization; this category also included Germans living in a mixed marriage—either with a Polish man or woman—and the children of these unions. Class IV were people of German descent who had become Polonized and resisted Germanization.[99] People who were eligible for classifiction on the *Volksliste* but refused inclusion were treated harshly. Usually they were deported to Germany or to a concentration camp. The case of Brunhilde Muszyński nee von Wattman, who married a Pole but rejected her German origins, disturbed her Nazi interrogator, who had met many such people. "As she gives a very bad example to the population owing to her position and mental capacities, it is proposed to transfer her immediately to Germany proper."[100]

The Nazis made efforts to Germanize entire groups of people, such as the Wasserpolen, Masurians, and Kashubes. Mass Germanization was easier on the people involved because it spared them the humiliations and indignities of investigations, checkups, and interrogations.[101] Much of the population of Silesia was Germanized in this way too. In Silesia it was simply accomplished by the individuals putting their finger prints on identity cards.[102] To be sure, it meant the complete suppression of Polish cultural life, but Polish communities in these areas were subjected to the same measures. The Polish underground did not consider these people to be traitors, because they became *Volksdeutsch* out of self-defense. But those Polish nationals who willingly registered, especially those in the General Government where most Poles were not forced to do so, were branded traitors, and the rules of resistance were applied against them.[103]

As the war progressed, the Nazis made greater efforts to expand the ranks of the *Volksdeutsch*, eventually abandoning their pompous pretentions to racial purity. The last chief of the Polish underground, Stefan Korboński, stated that in 1942, Polish men of military age in the annexed provinces were automatically placed on the *Volksliste* and drafted into the German army.[104] During the Zamość operation, the Germans forced into transports one-third of the Polish residents they seized and sent them to be Germanized. The racial farce would have been laughable if it did not have such tragic consequences on the unfortunate victims involved. One recent historical study aptly described the situation:

> Families who qualified for *Volksdeutsch* status might ask one relative to volunteer for the German list and another relative to refuse. In that way, they sought to get the best of both uncertain worlds. False papers, stolen ration cards, and spurious genealogies sprouted on all sides. Before long, the Nazi officials began to compete among themselves. Gauleiter Forster registered all the Poles in Danzig as Germans, just to spite the SS.[105]

As indicated earlier, the abduction and Germanization of Polish children was a major part of the Nazi program aimed at the biological reduction of the Polish nation and the corresponding increase in the strength of Germany. To be sure, the program centered in the annexed lands, but there were thousands of Polish youngsters, notably during the Zamość operation, who were deported to Germany and subjected to Germanization. Not only were children of ethnic Germans who met the criteria for inclusion in the *Volksliste* Germanized, but also children of Polish families were subjected to the process if they met Nazi racial criteria. On June 18, 1941, Himmler declared, "I would consider it right if small children of Polish families who show especially good racial characteristics were apprehended and educated by us in special institutions and children's homes which must not be too large."[106]

The campaign to abduct and Germanize Polish children started in the annexed lands, originally focusing on youngsters housed in Polish children's homes and later extended to include children raised by foster parents. After an initial period of Germanization, the authorities deported the children to the Old Reich.[107] In Silesia, where all the people were considered Germans, Germanization did not involve deportation, but it did include the abduction of children from parents or foster parents who refused to sign the *Volksliste*. Polish children born to women workers in Germany were also vulnerable to Germanization. The Nazis preferred to abort a pregnancy of a Slavic worker if it appeared the child would not meet their racial criteria. On the other hand, if the pregnancy promised a desirable result from the Nazi point of view, especially if the father were German, the woman had the baby and it was placed in the care of the National Socialist Public Welfare Association for adoption.

Sometimes the authorities forcibly removed a child from the family if the parents had been arrested, deported to a concentration camp, or forced to labor in Germany; in these cases, children were taken away even if they lived with relatives. The same thing happened to children whose parents had been executed.[108] And, as already seen, the Germans sent thousands of blue-eyed, blond Polish children from Zamość in the General Government to Germany for Teutonization. In that operation alone, 30,000 children were deported from Zamość; it has been estimated that 4,454 children between two and fourteen years of age were actually taken to the Reich for Germanization.[109] Another method to Germanize Polish youth was to send thousands of adolescent boys and girls to forced labor in Germany and in that way exploit them economically and racially.[110]

The fact that a child was sent to Germany did not mean that it would be Germanized. The Germans subjected the children to racial, medical, and psychological tests to determine the candidate's suitability. Ideally, the Nazi racial experts preferred to transnationalize children no older than eight to ten years of age, but even this criterion was watered down to include teenagers over seventeen years. During the racial selection process, the racial experts placed the children into three categories; they were considered to be either a desirable, a tolerable, or an undesirable increase to the population. The object of the tests was not to establish the German descent of the candidate so much as to select children with sound physical and mental qualities. Children selected for Germanization eventually found themselves in schools or institutions run by the *Lebensborn*, SS, or NSV. Everything was done to extinguish their Polish identity. They were forbidden to speak Polish; if they did, they were beaten or starved. If their parents were living, they could not see them. They were drafted into Nazi youth groups such as the *Hitlerjügend* or the *Bund Deutscher Mädel*. In order to totally extirpate their Polish origin, German names replaced their Polish ones and false birth certificates were issued. Often a number of the initial letters of the Polish name were preserved—Sosnowska became Sosemann, Mikołajczyk Micker, Witaszek Wittke; apparently the intention was to allow the two names to blend in the memory of the child so that the original name would be forgotten. Often the children got names which corresponded phonetically to their Polish names—Piątek became Pionteck, Jesionek Jeschonnek. Finally, some new names were German translations of the Polish ones—Ogrodowczyk was Gartner, Młynarczyk Muller.[111]

The evidence does not permit a precise figure concerning the number of Polish children subjected to the process of Germanization, but according to a source approximately 200,000 "were seized for purposes of Germanization."[112]

As the war progressed, the flow of people to the Reich to be Germanized dwindled, and, ironically, the Germans had to send thousands of their own children to Poland—many to Warsaw itself—to escape allied bombardment.[113] No doubt this was a disturbing development to the Nazi ideologues and activists who, obviously aware that their empire was collapsing around them, were probably more concerned about the dangers of racial contamination to their Teutonic children.

The German attempt to destroy Poland socially was accompanied by a policy of economic destruction. Matching the ruthless social and cultural policy toward the Poles in the annexed lands, the Germans were equally fanatical in exploiting the economy of the area. Through a plethora of bureaucratic agencies, they confiscated and administered Polish property. They took all the property of the Polish state and all private property considered necessary for strategic purposes or for Germanization. At first concentrating on large industrial and commercial enterprises, they then began to take over medium and even small Polish businesses. The Germans exploited Silesia so thoroughly that it was not operating by the end of 1940 at prewar capacity.[114] Not only did the former Polish steel combine *Wspólnota Interesów* fall into German hands, but Polish shops, hotels, cafes, restaurants, and scores of other enterprises also became Germanized. Out of 2,387 textile factories in Łódź, for example, 2,000 were held in trust by the *Treuhandstelle Ost*. According to official German statistics, this organization administered the following Polish enterprises as of February 1941: 264 industrial establishments, 9,000 medium-sized industrial concerns, 76,000 small industrial operations, 9,120 large commercial firms, 112,000 small commercial businesses. The scope of the confiscation was even larger than these figures indicate, because the *Treuhänder* transferred many enterprises to private German ownership, and once transferred they were no longer subject to its administration.

Even houses in the towns and cities of the incorporated territories that belonged to Poles and Jews were taken from their owners and placed in German hands. The plunder of personal property of Polish citizens not only affected property-owning classes but also people who earned a living by the work of their hands and brains. Poles expelled from the incorporated lands lost not only their homes and businesses but also most of their personal property.[115]

The plunder of personal property, including food and clothes, was so rampant that the Reich minister of justice became concerned not because the actions were illegal and immoral but because the "Polish inhabitant who has been left practically without the means after the extent of the confiscation has become very agitated, which might result in further expression of hate and acts of sabotage against Germans." Such plundering, of course, also existed in the General Government where house-to-house searches gave the SS, Gestapo, and military a license to steal personal possessions. The German army had not been immune to the lure of plunder that awaited them in Poland; as one journalist observed:

> The old German army usually respected private property. The Nazi army seems to regard plunder as normal. During the first days of occupation robbery was conducted under the pretense of searching for arms. All sharp instruments, razors, and even penknives, were seized. Watches, money, and other valuables were taken at the same time. In Warsaw and other large cities whole blocks of houses were surrounded by troops while a general search was carried out under the direction of Gestapo officers. Searches in Jewish quarters usually resulted in the expropriation of every kind of portable property—food was often taken as well as money.[116]

German expropriation in the General Government was somewhat milder than in the annexed lands. But Governor Frank's decree of January 24, 1940, made it clear that private property could be confiscated "if the public interest and more particularly the defense of the Reich or the affirmation of German doctrination demands it." From an economic point of view, the General Government existed simply to serve the needs of the Reich. Accordingly, enterprises "not absolutely needed for the meager maintenance of the bare existence of the population must be transferred to Germany," Hermann Goering declared on October 19, 1939.[117] The Germans stole the equipment from the Lublin Aircraft Factory (*Lubelska Fabryka Samolotów*), the Avia Precision Tool Works (*Wytwornia Maszyń Precyzyjnych Avia*) in Warsaw, and the Cegielski cultivator factory in Rzeszów, to name a few of the major industrial concerns plundered. In the field of trade, the Germans seized shops and warehouses, inflicting even heavier losses on Jewish establishments than Polish ones.[118]

In the General Government, the Germans concentrated wholesale and retail business and industrial activity in as few hands as possible, whereas in the annexed provinces they favored the protection of medium-sized and smaller units against larger commercial enterprises. This was to give the annexed provinces a German character by establishing as many German settlers there as possible. In the General Government, out of 195,000 commercial enterprises before the war, there were only 51,000 in October 1943.[119] After the outbreak of the German-Soviet war in June 1941, the Germans began to stop the dismantling and removal of the factories of the General Government, in order to keep the factories close to the eastern front. Besides, after the allied bombing raids began to inflict serious damage on German industrial plants in the Reich, it was prudent to move many of these enterprises to the East.[120]

A part of the economic exploitation of Poland was to ensure that the national currency, the złoty, was undervalued in relation to the mark. This enabled the Germans to get goods cheaply while it restricted purchases of German goods, preserving them for the citizens of the Reich. In order to prevent devaluation of the złoty, and thus reduce the advantage enjoyed by the mark, the Germans simply took over control of the Bank of Poland. In addition, fiscal exploitation involved raising taxes, introducing, for example, a special levy per head on every person in the country.[121] As one Polish report dolefully observed: "The country's income, seriously curtailed by the war, is mainly used for the upkeep of the German administration. Severe taxation compels the starving population to render ever increasing contributions to a system aiming at the destruction of its vital forces."[122]

Initially, the economic policy of the Germans toward the Polish peasantry was not to interfere with their land. Many farmers even thought conditions might improve for them compared to their situation under the *Sanacja*, the prewar Polish regime. And German benevolences—cancellation of farmers' debts to Jewish creditors, elimination of taxes, only a few quotas for compulsory food deliveries—did result in improving the economic condition of the peasantry.[123] But the honeymoon did not last long. Soon German demands for grain made life extremely difficult for the Polish peasant. In prewar days, the peasant considered a grain yield of twelve quintals from each hectare to be good; of that, the peasant maintained his family on eight quintals and sold the remainder. But the Germans insisted the peasant deliver six quintals per hectare. In the Cracow district, where peasants showed the least resistance, they refused to furnish more than 40 percent of the German demands. In some areas, Polish failure to supply the Germans with the requisite amounts of grain was not due to their inability to do so but to deliberate refusal, just as Polish peasants had slaughtered cattle for food rather than have the Germans take them. Villages that failed to furnish the food quotas had to face indiscriminate punishment by the Germans. If the arrest of the schoolmaster and head of the village did not elicit the cooperation of the peasants, the Gestapo burned down the buildings of the village. Once that had been done, the peasants were usually allowed to resume cultivating their land, since it was in German interest for them to produce foodstuffs for the Reich. On the other hand, there was sometimes extensive expropriation of Polish farmers when land was needed for war factories and airfields.[124]

The consequence of all these German policies was the pauperization of the Polish people. In 1940-41, the net income of the Poles fell below 40 percent of that in 1938,[125] and as the war progressed the Germans took larger chunks of the General Government's GNP. With skyrocketing prices and low wages, the average Pole lived in misery. In June 1941, a Warsaw worker earned 120 to 300 złotys monthly; yet it cost 1,568 złotys to feed a family of four.[126] The average daily food allotment to Varsovians (Warsaw residents) in 1941 was 669 calories to Poles, 184 to Jews, and 2,613 to Germans.[127] Next to the Jews, the Poles had one of the lowest food rations of any people in German-occupied countries. For example, the authorities each month rationed 4,300 grams of bread to the Poles and 9,000 grams to the Germans; 400 grams of flour, barley, and macaroni to the Poles and 2,000 grams to the Germans; 1 egg to Poles and 12 to Germans.[128] Soup kitchens sprouted in several cities to help the people. In Warsaw, 111,539 bowls of soup were fed to the hungry in July 1941; between September 1940 and March 1942, 3,377,497 dinners were made available by welfare agencies at little or no cost. One year after the occupation, Adam Ronikier, head of the Main Welfare Council of Poland, estimated that 20 to 25 percent of the people of the General Government could not support themselves without outside help.[129]

A German medical official told Governor Frank that in the General Government the "number of diseased Poles amounted today already to 40 percent."[130] Whether or not this estimate was accurate, Polish underground sources pointed up the increased deaths from tuberculosis, a disease tied most closely to poverty. The level of rickets among children increased to between 70 and 90 percent. In general, there was an increase over wartime levels of most infectious diseases.[131] When the former ambassador to Berlin, Alfred Wysocki, described the dreadful food situation to Governor Frank in December 1941, Frank promised not to export any more foodstuffs to the Reich. Yet, eight months later, in August 1942, he approved a six-fold increase of grain to Germany from the General Government for 1942-43. "The new demand," Frank declared, "will be fulfilled exclusively *at the expense of the foreign* population. It must be done cold-bloodedly and without pity" (italics mine).[132] This action was consistent with the Nazi view, expressed by Reichminister Ley, that since Poles were racially inferior, they "needed less food."[133]

To be sure, the Poles would have starved to death if they had to depend on the food rationed to them. They had to depend on the black market to bridge the gap between dying of starvation and surviving. Polish smugglers did their work so well, says Korboński, "that they deserve a monument to perpetuate their memory." They smuggled their goods not only at great expense but also risked arrest, deportation to a concentration camp, and even death. Despite the fact that the Germans maintained large forces of police in town and country to stamp out black market trade, they failed to make more than a dent in it. Even the Germans, if they did not learn any other Polish words, learned *na lewo* (illegal) from the black market trade that flourished in Poland. Warsaw had become the largest illegal commercial center of any area under German occupation.[134]

One smuggler managed to get a dead pig, dressed up as a peasant woman, into a railway compartment. When the dour police discovered the pig, even they exploded with laughter. The market women of Warsaw deserved a special tribute because they managed to provide meat and fresh bread to the Varsovians. "They moved like pillars, carrying and transporting by rail or carts tons of foodstuffs in little bags sewn into their underskirts and blouses. Never before have I seen such over-sized busts as in Poland at this time," Korboński related. He remembered seeing one of these motherly amazons hit a gendarme on the head with a basket of eggs because he tried to take it away from her; the gendarme ran away when he saw other hefty women coming to their friend's aid. "No one else would have dared to treat a gendarme in such a fashion," Korboński said.[135]

The clothing situation was no better than the food. Clothes were scarce and expensive. In Warsaw, a city of over one million people, only 17,000 items of clothing in 1941 and only 5,000 in 1942 were officially issued for sale.[136] There were many cases of Polish shopkeepers who ended up in prison for selling clothes without the proper coupons. Frequently shopkeepers collected unused coupons from friends and relatives and kept them in reserve at their stores, making them available to Poles who wanted clothes but had no coupons of their own. This enabled Polish purchasers to buy the clothing immediately when the goods came into the stores, while German shoppers found nothing when they came into the stores to buy. One woman who had been apprehended by the police received a fourteen-month sentence for hoarding twenty-three coupons.[137]

The shortage of shoes was even worse, since the Germans controlled all the stocks of leather and there was no rubber to resole shoes. As a consequence, Poles had to wear wooden clogs, even in winter.[138]

The extent of Nazi economic exploitation of Poland can be gleaned from the fact that during the period of German occupation Polish material losses were over 62 billion złotys.[139]

There had always been an unresolved conflict in Nazi minds about making the General Government, in Governor Frank's words, a "pure German colonized land" and keeping enough Poles alive to work until the Nazis won the war. Once the war was won, "mincemeat can be made of the Poles . . . it does not matter what happens," Frank declared.[140] In order to fulfill Goering's Four Year Plan, the marshal directed that at least one million agricultural and industrial workers be sent to the Reich to insure German agricultural production and remedy the labor shortages in the Reich.[141] Since the forced labor supply from the annexed areas was inadequate, the Nazis needed to exploit the vast labor reservoir available in the General Government. The Germans had problems recruiting Polish volunteers for labor in the Reich[142] and had to conscript workers by roundups and kidnappings. By the end of 1942, the head of the AK reported an increase in Nazi dragnets (*łapanki*) which netted Poles for work in Germany. The increased conscriptions of Polish labor in 1942 was intended to fill the shortages from Germans drafted into the army and the extermination of the Jews. Fritz Sauckel, the Nazi labor czar, explained on November 26, 1942, that Poles sent to the Reich would replace Jews in the German armament factories; the Jews were to work until they were relieved by the Poles. The unfortunate Jews would then be murdered.[143]

Anyone who looked healthy could be deported at any time. The Germans frequently caught Polish churchgoers and movie patrons and transported them to Germany. Not all Nazi leaders approved of this method of acquiring labor, because it undermined the people's willingness to work and strengthened the Polish resistance movement.[144]

Even with forced conscription, the flow of Polish workers to Germany was slow. In January 1941, there were 798,000 Poles working in the Reich. But a year later, this figure had only increased to slightly over one million. It wasn't until August 1943, that the number of Polish workers, most of whom came from the General Government, reached over 1.6 million; it showed only slight increases after that. In addition, the Germans used approximately 300,000 Polish prisoners of war who, along with regular Polish laborers, lived and worked in appalling conditions.[145]

Most factory and agricultural laborers had insufficient medical treatment. Young undernourished children were part of this labor force too; they lacked supervision and grew up illiterate. If a Pole were lucky, he might end up on a farm working for a decent German family who treated him kindly.[146]

Polish workers deported to the Reich had to wear a violet letter "P" on their clothing to distinguish them from the German population, which was admonished not to treat them too humanely or to have any social relations with them. Poles could not go to churches or movies, use public conveyances, or have sexual intercourse with women. "No remorse whatever should restrict such action," one directive said. Many Germans received stiff prison sentences for showing even a little kindness to Poles. Karl Lossin paid for a railway ticket for a Pole and attended a cinema with him; for that a German court sentenced him to nine months' imprisonment. For offering a box of cigarettes to a Pole, a forty-nine-year-old German at Halberstadt earned a month's prison term. When a middle-aged German enabled a Pole to correspond with his family, he went to prison for four months. One German appeal read: "Germans! The Poles can never be your comrades. Poles are beneath all Germans whether in the farm or in the factory. Be just, as all Germans must be, but never forget that you belong to the Master Race [*Herrenvolk*]."[147]

Poles could not have sexual intercourse even with Poles, but if a Pole had intercourse with a German, it called for the death penalty. In early 1941, Himmler directed the execution of 190 Polish agricultural workers who allegedly had sexual intercourse with German women. The Germans selected the youngest Polish prisoners at Buchenwald and forced them to administer the hangings of their kinsmen.[148]

As the war dragged on and German casualties mounted, the Germans forced thousands of Poles into the German army. Premier Władysław Sikorski estimated in June 1942, that there were 70,000 in Pomerania and 100,000 in Silesia. Most of these men served in auxiliary formations of the German army. Sikorski said, "The determined resistance to and the mass desertion from this press-gang conscription, unheard of in the 20th century, have already led to numerous death sentences in the home country." In 1943, the OSS reported Poles in German units in France and even on the eastern front.[149]

Every nation under enemy occupation during World War II experienced a reign of terror by the Nazis. But no nation suffered more than Poland. Poles were shot not only for resisting or fighting the Germans but also for simply being out after curfew or for selling black-market goods—or for merely being Polish. Even children under sixteen years of age were vulnerable to the death penalty for making anti-German statements or simply demonstrating what the Germans described as a "hostile mentality." A Pole could and often was shot for not making way on a sidewalk for a German approaching from the opposite direction, or for not taking off his hat when he passed a German.[150] Frenchmen and Belgians were not rounded up and shot in street roundups as Poles were for little or no reason. People lived in constant fear of arrest, torture, and death. No one could be certain when they left home in the morning that they would return in the evening.

Germans killed Poles for several reasons, including political repression, reprisals, and racial hatred. In no place in German-occupied Europe did one find the extensive machinery of repression the Nazis had in Poland. In the period October 1939 to September 1944, SS and police strength fluctuated between 50,000 and 80,000 men, supported by the Wehrmacht which rarely dropped below 400,000 troops and reached highs of 2,000,000 in June 1941 and 1,000,000 in September 1944.[151] Although Warsaw suffered the heaviest losses—35,000 to 40,000 deaths from November 1939 to July 1944—other cities like Radom, Lublin, Kielce, and Częstochowa had high losses also.[152]

As has been seen, the Germans indiscriminately killed civilians during the September campaign, then searched for and tried to destroy the intelligentsia and "political enemies." In the period 1939-41, Poles were even more exposed than Jews to arrest, deportation, and death. Most Jews during this period had been herded into ghettos. Emmanuel Ringelblum, a noted Jewish historian in Warsaw whose life had been prolonged due to the help of Poles, noted in his diary of May 8, 1940, that Polish people had been seized for deportation to Germany and Jewish barbers were used to shave their hair prior to transfer. Poles escaping the Nazi roundups, which resulted in either deportation or execution, discovered, as another Jewish historian noted, "an odd ally: the Jewish badge." Poles bought or borrowed these badges to escape their pursuers. Even Jews were screened at this time to make certain they were not camouflaged Poles. Prior to the deportation of the Jews to the death camps, an OSS informant reported that the treatment of Poles by the Germans was even worse than that of Jews.[153]

Governor Frank did not mince words when he stated that reprisals against Poles would not correspond to offenses. On January 19, 1940, he declared, "My relationship with the Poles is like the relationship between ant and plant louse. In cases where in spite of all these measures the performance does not increase, or where the slightest act gives me occasion to step in, I would not even hesitate to take the most draconic action."[154] The principle of collective responsibility was evident when the Nazis conducted their first atrocity in suburban Warsaw, the village of Zielonka. The Germans nabbed eleven people, but two escaped. The rest were killed; three of the victims were Polish Boy Scouts, sixteen and seventeen years old. The pretext for the murders was the appearance of a handmade poster with the words of the Polish writer Maria Konopnicka, "No German will spit in our faces or make Germans of our children."[155]

In the village of Wawer, outside Warsaw, the Germans took the lives of seventy-five people, one of whom was a forty-year-old official of the National Economy Bank of Warsaw, Daniel Gering, who was of German extraction. The authorities, astonished to find a namesake of Reich Marshal Goering, discovered that Gering insisted he was a Pole. "Do you realize what's involved?" they asked him. "Yes, but I am a Pole," Gering replied. They summoned him two times from the ranks, asking him simply to say he was a German. He refused. Because of his defiance, Gering was especially brutalized. According to one witness, when Gering insisted he was Polish, the Germans beat him to a pulp.[156]

Frank told a Nazi audience in Cracow in 1944, "I have not been hesitant in declaring that when a German is shot, up to 100 Poles shall be shot too."[157] Actually, the reprisals against Poles often exceeded the number of victims Frank had indicated. There were cases of 200-400 Poles being slaughtered for the death of one German. In Lublin, the Germans wiped out the village of Józefów for the death of one German family.[158] According to SS General Bach-Zelewski, any officer with the rank of captain or higher had the authority to kill 50-100 Poles for every German killed, without referring the matter to a higher authority.[159]

The Polish resistance reported an increase in the Nazi reign of terror toward the end of 1942 and in early 1943, characterized by roundups of Poles for forced labor and execution. On January 21, 1943, the head of the AK, General Rowecki, told Polish authorities in London, "A new wave of terror embraces the entire country."[160] And, indeed, Rowecki was correct—the manhunts conducted by the Nazis in the middle of January throughout the General Government was on a scale so large that Poles began to believe the Nazis intended to exterminate the entire Polish population just as they were in the process of doing to the Jews. One leftist underground newspaper urged Poles to prepare for the possibility of being caught: hide money on your person along with necessary tools in order to escape from a convoy taking Poles to their deaths. "When a manhunt threatens one should hide, taking into account local conditions, but cooperation and mutual help must be the order of the day for the nation and the community," *Gwardia Ludowa* admonished.[161]

The intensity of the terror campaign reached a high point in the autumn of 1943 when Frank introduced public executions in Warsaw. His decree carried a rider which allowed the police to kill anyone on the spot who even looked suspicious. The first street executions in Warsaw began on October 16, 1943, taking the lives of twenty-five people. After that, this type of execution occurred every few days until February 15, 1944, when following the killing of SS Brigadeführer Franz Kutschera, who headed the SS and police for the District of Warsaw, they were stopped. But secret executions continued to take place in the ruins of the Warsaw ghetto. Between October 16, 1943 and February 15, 1944, there were thirty-three street executions which took the lives of 1,528 innocent people.[162]

Those condemned to die in a public execution were handcuffed and blindfolded but, at first, not gagged. That enabled the victims to shout patriotic phrases, such as "Long Live Poland!" before the Germans shot them. After that, either their heads were tied up or their mouths were stuffed with rags saturated with narcotics. Somewhat later, their mouths were plastered up with plaster of paris and their lips sealed with adhesive tape. At first, the victims went to their deaths in their own clothes, but later the Germans stripped them to their underwear. Even their shoes were taken away from them. Sometimes they wore only prison overalls or paper trousers. Those who were still alive after being shot were finished off by a blow from a gun butt. After the executions, the Germans placed the bodies on trucks and took them to the ruins of the ghetto, where they were burned. After that, the street returned to normal.[163] At night, the Germans broadcast the names of the deceased. Some Poles were reluctant to listen to the hoarse impersonal voice of a German reciting the nightly litany of Polish victims, but they did anyway, if only because the name of a friend or relative might be mentioned.[164]

The principle of collective responsibility was applied in both the villages and the cities. But in the cities no one knew for certain who would be executed for the death of a German. All they knew was that there would be a roundup and several people would be indiscriminately killed. In the countryside, however, the Germans posted the names of prominent citizens, known to the entire community, who were held hostage for a period of three to four months; if the resistance killed a German in this period, these citizens would be killed in retribution.[165]

Much has been said about the killing of 192 men in the village of Lidice in Bohemia, executed in retaliation for the murder of SS General Reinhard Heydrich. But, as one Polish emissary observed, "We have thousands of Lidices in Poland."[166] According to a leading Polish authority, in 769 repressive actions which took the lives of at least ten victims in Polish villages, the Germans murdered 19,792 people in the years 1939-45; to be sure, there were countless other actions which have gone unreported or involved fewer than ten victims. The Nazis destroyed about 300 villages; some of the larger operations in which at least 100 people were killed included: Rajsk (140 killed), Krassowo-Czestiki (259), Michniów (203), Skłoby (215), Kulno (100), Cyców (111), Olszanka (103), Borów (232), Lazek (113), Szczecyń (368), Józefów (169), Sumin (118), Jamy (147), Kitów-Nawóz (174), Sochy (181), Milejów (150), Kaszyce (117), Wanajy (109), Mrozy (over 117), Krusze (148), Lipniak (370). In addition, some of the villages that had been bombed during pacification operations included Monty Dolne, Monty Górne, Pawłów, Tokary, Sochy, and Klew.[167]

The most dramatic evidence of German occupational and racial policies in Poland was the network of 2,000 concentration and allied camps that webbed the entire country. Camps built exclusively to exterminate people included Bełżec, Chełmno, Sobibor, and Treblinka. In addition, the Germans built three major concentration camps—Auschwitz-Birkenau, Majdanek, and Stutthof—which also served as extermination centers. Gross Rosen, located in western Poland today, was used primarily as a labor camp.[168] The Germans also built several camps in Germany; some of the most notorious included Dachau, Ravensbruck, Buchenwald, Sachsenhausen, and Mauthausen. But the major site of the German extermination program was Poland, an obvious choice because it was there that most of Hitler's primary victims, the Jews, already lived alongside the Poles, whom he also intended to annihilate.

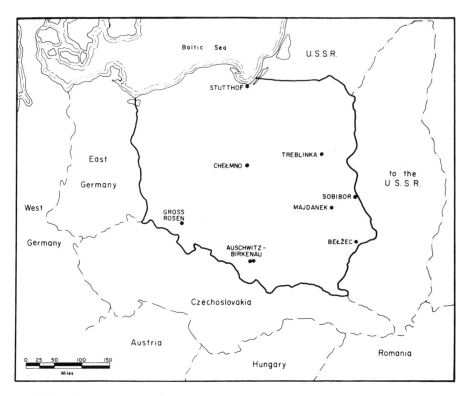

Major German camps in Poland

Unlike most Jews who died in gas chambers, most Poles perished in mass or individual executions and were starved or worked to death. However, many Poles died in the extermination camps too. The first non-German prisoners at Auschwitz were Poles, who constituted the largest number of inmates there until 1942, when the Jews became the largest group. Poles also numbered 90 percent of the inmates of Stutthof until 1942.[169] The first killing by poison gas at Auschwitz involved 300 Poles and 700 Soviet prisoners of war.[170] So many Poles were sent to concentration camps that virtually every Polish family had someone close to them who had been tortured or murdered there.[171] Over 35,000 Poles passed through Dachau; approximately 33,000 Polish women were imprisoned in Ravensbruck.[172] In Sachsenhausen, 20,000 Poles perished; in Mauthausen, 30,000; in Neuengamme, 17,000.[173]

As a result of almost six years of war, Poland lost 6,028,000 of its citizens, or 22 percent of its total population, the highest ratio of losses to population of any country in Europe. About 50 percent of these victims were Polish Christians and 50 percent were Polish Jews. Approximately 5,384,000, or 89.9 percent, of Polish war losses (Jews and Gentiles), were the victims of prisons, death camps, raids, executions, annihilation of ghettoes, epidemics, starvation, excessive work, and ill treatment.[174]

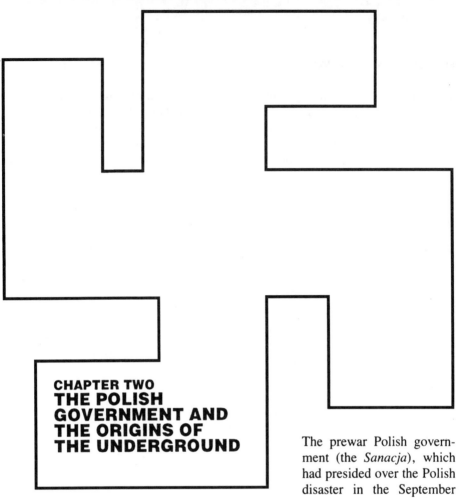

CHAPTER TWO
THE POLISH GOVERNMENT AND THE ORIGINS OF THE UNDERGROUND

The prewar Polish government (the *Sanacja*), which had presided over the Polish disaster in the September campaign, became totally discredited in the eyes of most Poles and fled to Romania. The void in political leadership that followed resulted in a struggle for power that was never entirely resolved, even after General Władysław Sikorski assumed the dual positions of commander in chief of Polish armed forces and premier of the Polish government-in-exile, which made its wartime home in London after the fall of France. Sikorski's difficulties in creating and maintaining a government of national unity among the Polish émigrés in England matched the problems he had in establishing political and military unity in Poland, where numerous military and political organizations existed and jealously guarded the independence they enjoyed within the underground movement. Sikorski presided over a political and military structure in England and Poland which enjoyed the support of the moderates but had to contend with the opposition of the right and left wings of the Polish political spectrum. In Poland the elements of disunity sometimes became blurred in the common struggle against the Nazis, but in the Polish émigré community they undermined the image and the effectiveness of the Polish government.

When the Polish government fled to Romania, the Polish president, Ignacy Mościcki, and other members of the government were interned there. Mościcki, who had the prerogative of appointing his own successor, toyed with the names of several possible candidates, including Cardinal Augustus Hlond and several members of the *Sanacja*—General Kazimierz Sosnkowski, a close follower of Piłsudski, August Zaleski, an experienced diplomat, and General Bolesław Wieniawa-Długoszowski (another Piłsudskiite), who served as ambassador to Rome. Mościcki favored Wieniawa-Długoszowski. But due to pressure from moderate and even conservative Poles within the exile community, combined with French displeasure with the nominee, the Polish president decided to appoint Władysław Raczkiewicz, who had not been too closely identified with the Piłsudskiites and therefore was a more acceptable nominee.[1]

Meanwhile, Sikorski, a bright, dynamic leader who had once served as chief of staff to the Polish armed forces and as premier during the years immediately following World War I, had arrived in France, where the Polish political community-in-exile first took shape. Sikorski, a severe critic of Piłsudski and the quasi-fascist regime he spawned, was one of the most prominent and best-known leaders in the democratic fight against the governments that had dominated Poland in the years 1926-1939. Sikorski became identified with the *Front Morges*, a group of reform-minded Poles who had within their company the eminent composer, pianist, and elder statesman, Ignacy Paderewski. Although Sikorski was appointed to lead the Polish army in France, a logical choice because he was well known to the French who had confidence in him, the question of who would be the premier revealed considerable political maneuvering among Polish leaders in France.

Raczkiewicz sought to deny the position to Sikorski and chose Stanisław Stroński. But Strónski, who though connected with the rightist National Democratic Party (*Stronnictwo Narodowe*) belonged to the moderate wing and was a collaborator of Sikorski's, renounced the nomination in favor of Sikorski. Therefore, in a matter of days Sikorski succeeded in pulling together the most important political and military positions the country offered. By early October 1939, Sikorski formed his cabinet and won the recognition of the Allied governments. A few months later, the National Council (*Rada Narodowa*), a kind of parliament, convened.[2] As one scholar aptly observed, although Sikorski's assumption of power "had all the trappings of a legal transfer of power, politically speaking it was tantamount to a *coup d'état*."[3]

Sikorski was always more popular in Poland than he was among the exiled Poles in Great Britain. His rise to the pinnacle of power was due not only to his own skills in political infighting but also to the realization among his opponents that the people in Poland would not accept a member of the discredited *Sanacja*, which was blamed for Poland's defeat at the hands of the Germans.[4] Sikorski's appointment was warmly received in Poland; soon Sikorski became a hero, a charismatic leader whom the Poles identified with ultimate victory against the Nazis. Often the Poles repeated the saying, "As the sun rises, Sikorski gets closer," or sang the ditty, "March, March, Sikorski from London to Poland." Despite the negative view of most Poles toward the *Sanacja*, the memory of Piłsudski still tugged the hearts of many Poles. Often people would say, "If Marshal Piłsudski lived, none of this would have happened." And, forgetting the deep rift between Piłsudski and Sikorski, they attempted to link the two men, claiming that the old marshal wanted Sikorski to succeed him in office.[5]

Despite his popularity in Poland, Sikorski's power base in London was tenuous. The supporters of the old prewar *Sanacja* regime were considerable in number, especially dominating the military and government bureaucracies; the two groups most critical of Sikorski—the *Sanacja* and the National Democrats—occupied perhaps three-quarters of the administrative posts in the Polish government-in-exile.[6] Sikorski's major strength came from the centrist political parties—the Peasant and Labor parties—and from moderate leaders of the National Democrats and the Socialists; but there were few such members in the exile community in England and fewer still in the government and military bureaucracies. Moreover, the Constitution of 1935 gave vast powers to President Raczkiewicz, who, as already seen, was no friend of Sikorski's.

In exchange for Raczkiewicz's pledge not to use his extraordinary powers except in close understanding with Sikorski's cabinet, the premier agreed to include in his cabinet two of his opponents, both moderate members of the *Sanacja*: Sosnkowski, who was designated successor to Raczkiewicz, was therefore an ex officio member of the cabinet; and Zaleski was made foreign minister.[7]

The focal point of much of the criticism toward Sikorski in Great Britain was the Polish army, which had strong links with the *Sanacja*. Disillusioned and bitter over the debacle in France, where the Poles had fought gallantly against the Germans, the Polish army was evacuated to Scotland where officers and men brooded about their fate. Some criticized Sikorski for not doing enough to save the entire Polish army in France; some men could not be withdrawn in time. Others resented their military assignments and expected something better. On his part, Sikorski tried to reduce the ratio of officers to enlisted men, which stood at four to one. And many of the officers who were his more severe critics Sikorski trundled off to exile on the remote Isle of Bute—dubbed the "Island of Snakes"—off the coast of Scotland. Despite these efforts, the military ranks continued to have an abundance of "irreconcilable Praetorians," as one Sikorski intimate described them, who remained his constant detractors. As a result, both Sikorski and his abrasive minister of interior, Stanisław Kot, often suspected the military in Great Britain and the underground army in Poland of conspiracy.[8]

The Polish army in Great Britain preferred General Sosnkowski over Sikorski to be its commander in chief. According to one estimate, only one out of four Polish generals in the Polish army in Scotland supported Sikorski. The consequence was that severe tension and strain characterized the relationship between Sikorski and Sosnkowski, despite the latter's efforts to prevent the establishment of a faction which centered on him against Sikorski. The premier tried to induce Sosnkowski to leave England and take a remote diplomatic post. But he refused. Almost every issue in the normal course of government business became a crisis of confidence between the two men.[9]

Little wonder then that Sikorski spent a good deal of his time beating back the fires of real and imagined opposition to him and his government. Although he went out of his way in making a show of working with his political opposition, he built up his own apparatus, a kind of cabal of trusted intimates, to conduct foreign policy and maintain contact with and control over the underground movement at home.[10] A few members, like Stefan Aubac, a Polish journalist with pro-Soviet leanings, and Dr. Józef Retinger, an *éminence grise* with wide contacts in England, especially in British Labor circles, were not even members of his cabinet.[11] On the other hand, Minister of Interior Kot, who later became ambassador to the Soviet Union, pursued Sikorski's opponents in Poland and in England with all the passion and intensity of a Savonarola. In the course of his activities, he constantly ran into difficulties with Sosnkowski, who headed for a time the Union for Armed Struggle (*Związek Walki Zbrojnej*—ZWZ), the Polish underground army established by Sikorski. Kot was also the zealous nemesis of Zaleski against whom he intrigued, seeking to get rid of him as the Polish foreign minister.[12]

After coming to power, Sikorski indulged both his vanity and dislike of his opposition when he established a commission to inquire into the reasons for Poland's defeat in the September campaign; what this amounted to was a witch hunt against people who had supported the Piłsudski government and its successors prior to World War II. The British,

French, and moderate Poles disapproved of the action. To be sure, the commission was not entirely motivated by personal vindictiveness; part of the reason also stemmed from Sikorski's conviction that he had to do something to placate the anger of his countrymen against the *Sanacja* and solidify his base of support in Poland.[13]

The suspicions, frictions, and quarrels between the supporters and opponents of Sikorski reached an apogee at the time of the military defeat of France and the initiative by Sikorski to probe the possibility of an understanding between Poland and the Soviet Union. Using the overture toward the Soviets as an excuse, Raczkiewicz dismissed Sikorski as premier and appointed Zaleski in his place. Sikorski's supporters rallied to his side: Colonel Tadeusz Klimecki, chief of the Polish General Staff, dramatically confronted Zaleski with the threat of using arms and demanded that he not accept the premiership. But the histrionics were not needed. Sosnkowski and other members of the armed forces, though they opposed Sikorski, recognized it would be a blunder to put the government in the hands of the *Sanacja*.[14] Sikorski had won. There was a hint of triumph when he later told the chief of the Polish underground, General Stefan Grot-Rowecki, "The intrigants had to become silent."[15]

Even though Zaleski was better known and at first even had greater support than Sikorski in English political circles, the British soon came around to agree with the judgment of a prominent Foreign Office official who said about Sikorski at the time of the attempt to oust him: "There is, in fact, no alternative to him, and we shall just have to bear with his idiosyncrasies. He is a public figure, and the Poles cannot easily do without him."[16]

Sikorski usually carried his cabinet on major issues, though, except for his closest followers, the support of some members was less than enthusiastic. The National Council, which ended up being an echo for conservative opinion,[17] was an advisory body whose primary activity was to consider the budget. The complexion of the government was essentially moderate; and from the standpoint of public opinion in the homeland, few of the men in the cabinet and the National Council were even known, much less admired. To them, only Sikorski stood out as their leader.[18]

Polish political life in England and, as will be seen later, in the underground in Poland revolved primarily around four political parties: Christian Democratic Labor Party (*Stronnictwo Pracy*), National Democratic Party (*Stronnictwo Narodowe*), Polish Socialist Party (*Polska Partia Socjalistyczna*), Polish Peasant Party (*Stronnictwo Ludowe*). The Labor

Party, cynically described as "a party of leaders without followers,"[19] was the smallest of the four but had a great deal of influence. It was democratic and progressive. Its leaders included Sikorski, Karol Popiel, Rev. Zygmunt Kaczyński, and General Józef Haller. The former mayor of Poznań, Cyryl Ratajski, became the first government delegate in the Polish underground state.

The National Democrats had been one of the strongest parties in prewar Poland. Urban, intellectual, and anti-Semitic, the party strongly opposed Piłsudski's coup d'état in 1926 and the subsequent regimes that dominated Poland until the outbreak of World War II. Once pro-Russian in outlook, most of the *Endeks*, as they were known, unlearned this part of the legacy of their founder, Roman Dmowski, and shared the anti-Russian attitude of the Polish Socialists. Moderate National Democrats, like Titus Komarnicki and Marian Seyda, the "Professors," who joined and supported the Sikorski government, were repudiated by their party.[20]

The Polish Socialists, like most Polish political groups, were badly split. Its right wing supported the *Sanacja* and opposed Sikorski; but the moderates, on the other hand, generally supported him. Left-wing socialists gravitated toward Moscow and at the end of the war cooperated with the Communists in establishing the Lublin regime, which became the cornerstone of Poland's postwar government. In domestic policy the Socialists often stood with the Polish Peasant Party for democratic and progressive legislation and, with them, claimed the support of a majority of the Polish population. Jan Stanczyk, Adam Ciołkosz, and Jan Kwapiński were associated with the Polish government-in-exile.

The Polish Peasant Party, the largest political party in prewar Poland, was democratic, was reformist, and supported the Sikorski government. In addition to Kot, Stanisław Mikołajczyk played a key role in the Sikorski cabinet and later succeeded the general as premier after his death in 1943. Polish Jews also had representation: Dr. Szmul Zygielbojm represented the Bund and after his tragic suicide was succeeded by Dr. Emmanuel Szerer. Dr. Ignacy Schwarzbart represented the Zionists.[21]

Sikorski had believed for a long time that a Russo-German conflict was inevitable; so when it occurred toward the end of June 1941, it did not come as a surprise to him. Sikorski, who was a realist, recognized that the sooner the Poles established relations with the Soviets, the better it would be for Polish interests. Placing Poland's future in British hands alone, he believed, was a serious mistake.[22] Accordingly, the day following the German invasion of the Soviet Union, Sikorski acted quickly: He spoke on the BBC and offered to improve relations with the Kremlin, provided the Soviet Union recognized the prewar Polish-Soviet frontier decided at Riga in 1921. He also asked for the release of thousands of Polish soldiers interned in Soviet prison camps. At first, the Soviets were unresponsive. But almost two weeks later, on July 4, 1941, Ivan Maisky, the Soviet ambassador, asked Anthony Eden, the British foreign minister, to act as an intermediary in Polish-Soviet negotiations. The British, who were moving themselves toward a treaty with their new-found ally, readily agreed.

The most controversial issue in the negotiations was the question of Poland's frontier with the Soviet Union. The Poles wanted the Kremlin to recognize the restoration of the Riga Line, violated by the Soviet pact with Germany in 1939. On the other hand, the Soviets, without committing themselves to a restoration of the Riga Line, would admit only that the agreements with Germany in 1939 affecting Poland's boundary with the Soviet Union were invalid. There were other issues, too: the release of Polish military and civilian personnel in the Soviet Union and the Sikorski proposal to establish a Polish army on Soviet soil to fight with the Russians against the Germans.

The Polish cabinet was divided; predictably, the strongest opposition came from members of the *Sanacja*. The Polish foreign minister warned that moral and legal considerations involving Poland would be transcended by military expediency. He, along with other members of the opposition, argued that the treaty should definitely spell out Soviet acceptance of the Riga Line.

Sikorski realized that although Britain was eager to solidify an alliance with the Soviets, the climate for the current Polish-Soviet negotiations was not favorable for Poland. Eden even bluntly told Sikorski at one point, "Whether you wish it or not, the treaty must be signed." The United States, by sending aid to the Soviets, had become a quasi-ally of the Soviet Union before Pearl Harbor. And public opinion in England and the United States began to move away from the hostility with which the Russians were viewed before June 1941.[23] There is no doubt that Sikorski wanted a treaty with the Soviets, but British pressure may have forced him to accept somewhat hastily what was a flawed document, as conflicting Polish and Soviet interpretations were soon to reveal.[24]

On July 27, 1941, the Polish cabinet approved the Polish-Soviet treaty which Sikorski and Maisky signed three days later. The treaty restored diplomatic relations between the two countries, annulled the Soviet-German Pact of 1939 without recognizing the Riga Line, provided for the establishment of a Polish army in the Soviet Union under a Polish commander, provided for mutual support against Germany, and attached a protocol which promised amnesty to Poles detained in the Soviet Union.[25]

The treaty precipitated a bitter crisis, resulting in the resignations of Minister of Justice Marian Seyda, who, however, returned six months later to collaborate with the government, Sosnkowski, and Zaleski. At the last moment, Raczkiewicz denied Sikorski the power to sign the agreement, but he signed it anyway.[26]

The reaction to the treaty in Poland was reserved. The Political Co-ordinating Committee, which represented the four major political parties in Poland, considered it "a positive act," though the committee had reservations concerning the question of Poland's eastern frontier. Attacked by his opponents in London, Sikorski considered this news from Poland "priceless."[27] Although the treaty provided an opportunity to secure the release of Poles from Soviet jails and prison camps, few Poles were really enthusiastic about the agreement, and some were more dissatisfied than the underground press reported. Of course, the diehard Russophobes, especially in the *Sanacja* and Socialist camps in Poland, were opposed to the treaty.[28]

One major casualty in the crisis over the treaty was Sosnkowski. He had resigned from the cabinet over the issue, and Sikorski used the opportunity to remove him from the high command of the ZWZ. Sikorski assumed the position himself. What followed was another crisis for Sikorski, only this time it was with the ZWZ in Poland. General Rowecki, who headed the underground army in the homeland, told Sikorski that Sosnkowski's dismissal had negative reactions in the ZWZ where the general was popular. Rowecki indicated that the rift between the two men would make it more difficult to consolidate the military aspect of the underground movement, and made a pointed reference to the fact that a number of officers in the ZWZ had been Piłsudski legionnaires and were loyal to Sosnkowski. In one of his messages to Sikorski, Rowecki somewhat tactlessly suggested that the issue served the propaganda interests of the Nazis. Sikorski was angry with what he considered Rowecki's meddling; in reacting to Rowecki's intervention, Sikorski shot back saying it was "at the least inappropriate." A little later, as if to make amends, he complimented Rowecki for his work in the ZWZ.[29] One of the reasons Sikorski assumed command of the ZWZ was his intention to end the friction that existed between it and political groups in Poland—some, like the Peasant Party, had strong misgivings about the ZWZ as a clique of the *Sanacja* and were reluctant to cooperate with it.[30]

While Sikorski sought to organize his government abroad, General Michał Tokarzewski-Karaszewicz, who had served as a corps commander in the army of General Tadeusz Kutrzeba in the September campaign, took the initiative in establishing the Service for Poland's Victory (*Służba Zwycięstwu Polski*—SZP), a clandestine military organization. Tokarzewski reached Warsaw on the night of September 20, 1939, and General Juliusz Rommel, the city's commandant, made him his deputy. Well aware that Poland's defeat was imminent, Tokarzewski presented a plan to Rommel for armed resistance during the German occupation. Rommel accepted it and transferred power to him. Tokarzewski tried to involve the indominable mayor of Warsaw, Stefan Starzyński, in the SZP, but he preferred to work with the people of Warsaw as long as the city held out against the Nazis. Highly intelligent and connected with the Socialists, Tokarzewski appealed to all the major political parties for their support.

The SZP was to be a unified military-political organization which gave wide powers—some said dictatorial—to Tokarzewski.[31] During the autumn, Tokarzewski toured the country, making contacts and extending the authority of his new organization. Meanwhile he sent to the "Commander in Chief" by courier the statute incorporating the SZP, without, unfortunately, specifying the recipient's name. The courier brought the document to Sikorski's predecessor, Marshal Edward Śmigły-Rydz, instead of Sikorski; Śmigły-Rydz later forwarded it on to Sikorski.[32]

The gaffe heightened Sikorski's distrust of Tokarzewski, whom he considered a dangerous rival and therefore unsuitable to head the military resistance in Poland. Sikorski was not alone in this assessment: Tadeusz Bór-Komorowski and Klemens Rudnicki, who had established a resistance group in Cracow and had made contact with the SZP, told Sikorski that Tokarzewski was unacceptable to lead the resistance, particularly indicating the opposition of the National Democrats whose support, they said, was essential. Other resistance groups that had sprouted up at this time were also suspicious of Tokarzewski's initiative, a few even labeling him an imposter.[33]

The SZP quickly gave way to the ZWZ, established by Sikorski in December 1939. Sikorski appointed Sosnkowski to head the ZWZ, an obvious ploy to satisfy his *Sanacja* critics in Poland and in exile. As originally established, the ZWZ was an organizational monstrosity, dividing the country into six regions, each with its own commanders. Tokarzewski was banished to Lwów (District III) where he had served as a military commander and was well known. According to one respected underground official, this "was tantamount to a sentence of death or imprisonment." General Rowecki, who had served as Tokarzewski's chief of staff, was put in charge of Warsaw (District I). Rowecki, who belonged to the intellectual elite of the army, came to Warsaw after the September defeat and planned to join the exodus of officers hoping to join the Polish army abroad. But Tokarzewski, who respected his gifts, convinced him to join the SZP.

It soon became apparent that the existence of six autonomous commanders with their own communication links to Polish authorities abroad exacerbated the chaos that already existed in the underground. To make matters worse, Sikorski set up a ministerial committee in London to supervise the conspiracy in Poland, but few of the members had any experience in it. Finally, the collapse of France in June 1940, removed expectations of an early end to the war, and the need to have a unified military organization in Poland was obvious. Sikorski put Rowecki in charge of ZWZ operations in the homeland, while Sosnkowski continued to serve as his superior in London, until Sosnkowski's removal shortly after the signing of the Polish-Soviet treaty in 1941.[34]

Sikorski's handling of the SZP and his original concept of the ZWZ betrayed his deep distrust of strong military leadership in Poland which might make a grab for political power when the war was over. He naturally feared that representatives of the *Sanacja* might try to infiltrate the ZWZ and use their position to political advantage. In view of his hope to establish a rapprochement with the Soviet Union, realized in July 1941, Sikorski knew his policy of long-term cooperation with the Soviets would likely not be supported by the ZWZ, especially one strongly influenced by the *Sanacja*.[35]

Sikorski's apprehensions about *Sanacja* influence in the ZWZ were probably exaggerated. The ZWZ denied there was extensive *Sanacja* influence in the organization, indicating that not more than a third of the officers had been Piłsudski's legionnaires; and in fact much of the new officer cadre came from worker and peasant backgrounds. Cyryl Ratajski, a Sikorski appointee, did not believe the *Sanacja* was a problem in the ZWZ, though he did worry about the drift of many young Poles toward right-wing groups.[36] And Rowecki himself was not a Piłsudskiite; he had liberal views about the kind of Poland that should be reborn after the war.[37] To be sure, there were *Sanacja* supporters within and outside the ZWZ. But the *Sanacja* had also experienced a diaspora in the aftermath of the defeat of Poland in September 1939—many were in prison, in internment camps in the Soviet Union, and in Great Britain.

Nevertheless, Sikorski and the ubiquitous Kot never entirely got over their suspicions about the *Sanacja* and its alleged attempts to infiltrate and influence the ZWZ. Rowecki had been directed not to include anyone in the ZWZ who had been identified with the prewar regime, but Kot continued to charge that there were disloyal elements in the ZWZ with *Sanacja* ties. Rowecki angrily denied the allegations, pointing out that former officers of Piłsudski's legions serving in the ZWZ did not automatically mean the same thing as the *Sanacja*. He specifically asked Kot for, but never received, the names of people in the ZWZ who were members of the *Sanacja*. Rowecki repeatedly denied political intrigues by the ZWZ which, he declared, was apolitical. He also highlighted the problem he had in building up a viable underground army at a time when German arrests and executions took a heavy toll of qualified people.[38] And he was correct. For example, after General Bór-Komorowski left Cracow to serve as Rowecki's deputy in Warsaw, all four of his successors were arrested and three of them murdered by the Gestapo.[39] Little wonder, then, that Rowecki told authorities in London that he could not get rid of good soldiers simply because someone had put a political label on them.[40]

However, one incident confirmed the existence of some *Sanacja* intrigue. In October 1941, when Marshal Śmigły-Rydz returned to Poland from Hungary where he had fled after Poland's defeat, his return was orchestrated by Julian Piasecki, a former *Sanacja* official. Piasecki used Śmigły-Rydz to establish political and military contacts with the *Sanacja* in Poland, especially elements gravitating toward the Camp of Fighting Poland (*Obóz Polski Walczącej*). Sikorski, learning from Polish sources in Hungary about the marshal's return, told Rowecki to inform Śmigły-Rydz that his presence in Poland was harmful to the country's best interests. He wanted him to leave Poland and make his way to Istanbul where he would be transported by the British to exile in South Africa. The hapless marshal lingered on in Warsaw for some weeks, dying there on December 1, 1941.[41]

The conflict between Sikorski and Rowecki concerning the complexion of the ZWZ was overshadowed by the larger question of subordinating the great number of military and paramilitary organizations which had sprung up following Poland's military defeat in September 1939. Sikorski and Rowecki agreed that in order for the ZWZ/AK to be effective, it had to be a unified organization. (The ZWZ became the Home Army [*Armia Krajowa*] after February 1942.) For five years, first Rowecki and then his successor, Bór-Komorowski, expended an enormous amount of time and energy trying to integrate disparate military organizations into the ZWZ/AK, for the landscape of the Polish underground movement was far less coherent, both militarily and politically, than has sometimes been depicted. Many military and political groups held their own counsel and pursued their own goals, often at variance with the ZWZ/AK and political authorities. No doubt this was an ironic expression of the freedom and independence they had acquired in the resistance movement that had been denied them in Poland during the dictatorship of the *Sanacja*. But it detracted from the ability of the ZWZ/AK and its political counterpart, the Government Delegacy, to function effectively.

If the war had ended by the summer of 1940, the plethora of organizations could have been used effectively against the Nazis. But as noted earlier, after the collapse of France, it was apparent that individual units, each pursuing its own activity, were detrimental to the long-range goals of the resistance. A larger, unified organization would offer its members more protection and pursue the myriad aspects of underground work more efficiently than smaller units. As one emissary of the Polish government pointed out, "If we were to continue large-scale activity and it was indeed impossible to retreat from the work to which we were committed, our survival and success demanded the co-ordinating of many individual units within one single, powerful, large-scale organization."[42] Finally, as was mentioned in Chapter 1 and will be dealt with in more detail later, once it was decided that Polish military strategy would be based on holding the ZWZ/AK in readiness for an eventual uprising to be launched only when the Germans were at the point of imminent collapse, it was imperative to have a unified command to prevent capricious and dangerous operations that might jeopardize this long-range objective.

It was quite natural that Poles throughout the country would organize various conspiratorial groups; after all, Poland had a long tradition of resistance. All kinds of organizations, both military and nonmilitary, grew up, sometimes under the leadership of teachers, priests, and foresters, and included a large number of young people, workers, and peasants. Some of the groups were based on prewar associations, including political parties, which had their own military units.

Rowecki's problem in trying to subordinate Major Henryk Dobrzański (Hubal) and his followers, considered by some to be the founder of the Polish partisan movement, was typical of the difficulties he experienced with other military units. Dobrzański organized a unit of peasants and workers which by February 1940 numbered 300 men. Their partisan activities provoked severe Nazi repressions. Despite Rowecki's order to cease operations, this colorful, fiercely independent leader stubbornly refused. Even a personal meeting with Rowecki, who appealed to the officer to submit to the ZWZ, did not deter him from continuing operations. The end of Dobrzański's unit came when he was killed in a battle against the

Germans on April 30, 1940. There were other self-styled mini-Bonapartes who led groups which clung to their independence and sometimes did foolish, dangerous, and unproductive things.[43]

Finally, on August 15, 1942, Sikorski ordered that all military groups operating in Poland subordinate themselves to the AK, and he forbade AK soldiers to serve in other military formations. As an inducement to these individualistic groups, Sikorski allowed them to retain some elements of their distinctive character, a grant of autonomy they could enjoy if they subordinated themselves to the ZWZ/AK. The August order was helpful to Rowecki and Bor, but progress was slow.[44]

The Voice of Poland (*Głos Polski*) was one of the first clandestine organizations to be founded following Poland's defeat in the war. Organized in Łódź by Tadeusz Kuropatwa, it stood for a free and democratic Poland. Like many other organizations in the annexed lands, the Gestapo broke it up. A similar fate befell the Legion of Liberation (*Legion Wyzwolenia*), which operated only two months in 1939. In the case of the Volunteer Army of the Western Lands (*Wojsko Ochotnicze Ziem Zachodnich*), the Gestapo gutted it, but a portion survived to join the ZWZ.

There were small groups which merged with each other. In Pomorze, a school teacher, Józef Dambka, organized the Kashubian Griffin (*Gryf Kaszubski*), which merged with several smaller organizations and became one of the major conspiratorial organizations of the region.

Even imaginative and courageous priests got involved in conspiracy. Father Józef Pradzyński was one of the leaders of Fatherland (*Ojczyzna*), a nonmilitary organization whose aims included informing the government of what was going on in the annexed lands, carrying out social welfare work, organizing secret classes for children, and fostering the spirit of independence among the Polish people.

Silesia had more than twenty conspiratorial groups. Toward Freedom (*Ku Wolności*) was one of these; mostly gymnasium students and workers belonged to it.

The Command of the Defenders of Poland (*Komenda Obrońcow Polski*), organized in Lublin in September-October 1939, eventually laced the entire country. Its newspaper, *Poland Lives* (*Polska Żyje*), admonished Poles: "Your obligation is to contribute your effort to regain [our] independence and destroy the enemies in our motherland." Suspicious of the ZWZ, this leftist organization eventually joined the People's Army (*Armia Ludowa*), the military arm of the Polish Worker's Party.

In 1939, the Union of the White Eagle (*Organizacja Orła Białego—OOB*) had a large following in Cracow, Kielce, Radom, and Częstochowa. When Tokarzewski organized the SZP, he made contact with

OOB, which later became part of the ZWZ; and one of OOB's units formed an important element of the sabotage-diversionary wing of the ZWZ.

Some groups in the General Government were organized by military men, including the Security Corps (*Korpus Bezpieczeństwa*—KB), the Secret Polish Army (*Tajna Armia Polska*), and the Secret Military Organization (*Tajna Organizacja Wojskowa*), all of which became part of the ZWZ/AK. The KB played a critical role in helping Jews during the Ghetto Uprising of 1943. The Secret Polish Army, a Catholic, nationalist group with fascist leanings, at first refused to subordinate itself to the ZWZ but did so in 1941. The Secret Military Organization, which specialized in sabotage-diversionary activity, subordinated itself in 1940 but apparently was not fully integrated until 1942-43.[45]

The Musketeers (*Muszkieterowie*), composed of young, aggressive people with political ambitions, was almost exclusively an intelligence organization. The leadership not only had direct access to the Polish High Command abroad, which subsidized it, but also sent their own couriers to the British. The value of the intelligence was mixed; and its leader, Stefan Witkowski, got involved in compromising intrigues with the enemy.[46]

The three major political parties fielded their own military groups and, except for the Socialists, who merged their Socialist Fighting Organization (*Socjalistyczna Organizacja Bojowa*), were unwilling at first to integrate their militias with the ZWZ/AK. The Peasant Party's Peasant Battalions (*Bataliony Chłopskie*—BCh) distrusted the ZWZ for its pro-*Sanacja* leanings and disagreed with ZWZ/AK strategy of delaying confrontations with the Germans until the Germans were at the point of collapse. The BcH nominally subordinated themselves to the AK early in 1943, adding approximately 50,000 men to the strength of the AK. The BcH were especially strong in the areas of Lublin, Warsaw, Cracow, and Radom.[47]

The National Democratic Party army, called the National Military Organization (*Narodowa Organizacja Wojskowa*—NOW), was strong in central Poland and merged with the AK in November 1942. NOW had approximately 70,000 men to add to the AK. But the merger caused a split in its ranks, resulting in the dissidents establishing their own military organization, the National Armed Forces (*Narodowe Siły Zbrojne*—NSZ).[48] The NSZ bragged that it numbered 100,000 men; in reality, its strength was smaller. One underground source put it as low as 15,000-18,000.[49] Under the command of Colonel Czesław Oziewicz, the NSZ operated independently of the AK against the enemy and frequently engaged in fratricidal warfare against Jews, Communists, and democratic elements of the AK. On June 19, 1943, an NSZ unit killed two officers of the AK High Command, Ludwik Widerszal and Jerzy Makowiecki, both of whom were Polish Jews who worked in the Bureau of Information and Propaganda (*Biuro Informacji i Propagandy*—BIP). A year later, the NSZ abducted two other workers of the BIP, Marceli Handelsman, another Polish Jew, and Halina Krahelska and turned them over to the Germans. On August 9, 1943, the NSZ attacked a Communist unit, the People's Guard (*Gwardia Ludowa*—GL), at Borowo and killed twenty-six soldiers and four peasants. Determined to rid the Polish underground movement of liberal elements and pave the way for its own assumption of power, the NSZ planned a Polish version of St. Bartholomew's Massacre, but nothing came of it.[50]

In a continuing effort to consolidate the resistance, the AK accepted part of the NSZ in March 1944. The group numbered only 10,000-15,000 soldiers, because many more members of the NSZ refused to become part of the AK. Some men came over to the AK during the Warsaw Uprising of 1944; others constituted themselves as the Holy Cross Brigade and with German protection migrated through Silesia to Czechoslovakia in early 1945.[51] The integration of even part of the NSZ into the AK was a serious mistake. Liberal Polish elements were understandably critical of the move. The addition of a few thousand men was a high price for the AK to pay in making itself vulnerable to moderate and left-wing charges that it was a reactionary organization.[52]

The Boy Scouts and Girl Scouts (*Szare Szeregi*) also played an important role in the work of the ZWZ/AK. Most of the 8,188 Scouts in Poland in 1944 served in the area comprising the General Government. Younger scouts served in noncombative roles, acting as couriers and gathering intelligence. Older scouts participated in "small sabotage" activities such as writing slogans on walls and distributing newspapers of the clandestine press. The oldest scouts served in combat against the Germans; two units of the AK which especially distinguished themselves were *Zośka* and *Parasol*.

Women too were very much part of the AK. Organized as the Women's Military Service (*Wojskowa Służba Kobiet*), women had the same rights and obligations as their male counterparts.[53] They could be found in many roles but seemed to be especially skilled in liaison work in which the life expectancy was little more than a few months. As one Polish resistance leader indicated, "Among all the resisters, their task was the most demanding, their sacrifices the greatest, and their work the least recognized. They were overloaded with work and doomed from the start."[54] Even prostitutes played an important role, especially in intelligence-gathering activity. German soldiers had standing orders to be wary of them. The last chief of the Polish underground paid a tribute to the women of the resistance when he said, "The part played by women in the underground organization is still waiting for its historian, but I am sure he will exhaust the whole vocabulary of superlatives when writing on the subject."[55]

Thus the ZWZ/AK was essentially a large umbrella organization which included numerous groups with varied political attitudes. Except for extreme right-wing diehards like the NSZ and the Communists on the left, all political shades of opinion were represented in the Polish underground army.

In subordinating various groups, the leaders of the ZWZ/AK allowed them to keep their identity. The process of integration evolved over a period of time, and it was not unusual to have leaders of these formerly independent organizations occupying positions of prominence in the High Command of the ZWZ/AK.[56]

The problems in hammering together a unified military structure in the Polish underground reflected the enormous political diversity that existed in Poland during the German occupation. Even when it was clear that the war would be a prolonged one and that it was sensible to cooperate for a long-term struggle against the Germans, this still did not mitigate severe political and personal conflicts in the underground that went on concurrently with resistance against the Germans. The political diversity in the Polish underground was a natural consequence of the collapse of the *Sanacja* in September 1939. Ironically, what occurred in the underground during the German occupation was a return to the plurality which had characterized the political life of Poland prior to the coup d'état of Piłsudski in 1926.

After the news of the fall of France and of the political intrigues among Polish leaders in the exile government reached Poland, political leaders in the homeland concluded that Poland's future would be decided in the homeland, not abroad. Consequently, the Polish emigration lost its importance in the minds of most Poles.[57] That is why when the Sikorski government demanded or instructed political leaders in Poland to take a certain action in internal affairs, they usually treated it as a recommendation; if the government's instructions differed from the practices of local political authorities, they were ignored. In foreign policy, however, underground political leaders accepted decisions of the government-in-exile as binding. As Korboński put it, "The government-in-exile ought to act as

Poland's ambassador to the world but the actual decision-making center ought to be in Poland."[58]

Both the Sikorski government and the ZWZ/AK resisted sharing power with political groups in Poland. Sikorski's initial reservations about strong political leadership in Poland even prompted charges from the homeland that the exile government was "motivated by the principle of *divide et impera*." The military component of the underground, the SZP/ZWZ/AK, preferred a political-military structure which gave more power to the military.[59] In the end, Sikorski favored the civilian-political component over the military largely because of his fear of *Sanacja* influence in the ZWZ/AK.

It is against this backdrop that Poland's major political parties—Peasant, Socialist, National Democrat, and Labor—which represented the vast majority of Poles, evolved a political structure alongside the ZWZ/AK during the German occupation. In December 1939, it was known as the Chief Political Council (*Głowna Rada Polityczna*), which, in February 1940, transformed itself into the Political Coordinating Committee (*Polityczny Komitet Porozumiewawczy*). Sikorski recognized the Political Coordinating Committee as constituting the political representation of the nation; even General Rowecki was a member of the body. The Political Coordinating Committee considered all areas of life in occupied Poland—political, military, social, and cultural. In an effort to gain more independence from the ZWZ, the Political Coordinating Committee formed itself into the Chief Political Committee (*Głowny Komitet Polityczny*) in June 1940. Further political evolution came with the establishment of a Government Delegacy (*Delegatura Rządu*) but not before major disagreements had been resolved between London and the homeland concerning the ephemeral life of the Collective Delegacy (*Delegatura Zbiorowa*). As finally established at the end of 1940, the Government Delegacy was headed by a delegate who was to cooperate with but remain independent of the ZWZ; the delegate even had control over the ZWZ budget. The Chief Political Committee later transformed itself into the National Political Representation (*Krajowa Reprezentacja Polityczna*) and in 1944 into the Council of National Unity (*Rada Jedności Narodowej*), to which the delegate and the commander of the AK were politically responsible.[60]

There were, of course, smaller political groups which did not recognize any of these political organizations. The Assembly of Organizations for Independence (*Konwent Organizacji Niepodległościowych*), headed by prominent Piłsudski followers, eventually assumed a position of opposition to the government and its agencies in Poland. Similarly, the Camp of Fighting Poland (*Obóz Polski Walczącej*), also composed of prewar government supporters, was another elitist group who opposed the government. On the left was the Polish Workers Party (*Polska Partia Robotnicza*).[61] Organized in January 1942, the Polish Workers Party was the successor to the Polish Communist Party which Stalin had ordered dissolved in 1938. The Polish Workers Party endorsement of Soviet policies and the party's criticism of the Polish government and its agencies in Poland militated against its becoming a party with a large mass following. Other left-wing opponents of the government and its agencies in Poland included the Workers Party of Polish Socialists (*Robotnicza Partia Polskich Socjalistow*), Polish Syndicalists, and other small groups.

Throughout the evolution of the civilian-political and military components of the Polish underground, there was a great deal of ambiguity as to where the real locus of authority in Poland was located. The average Pole, dazed by the array of political and military organizations which littered the Polish underground landscape, only saw chaos. The deep divisions within the major parties, the loss of skilled political leaders during the occupation, the suspicions of most political groups of the *Sanacja* and their influence in the ZWZ, the lack of clarity in what the Sikorski government wanted in the way of a viable political structure in Poland conspired for a long time to make a difficult situation even worse. All this had less to do with resisting the Germans than it did maneuvering for political advantage when the war ended and the political future of Poland would be at stake. But for all the confusion and divisiveness among these political groups, the average Pole was for the most part unaffected by what transpired on higher political levels. Unimpressed by all of it, the man in the street usually replied, "This is all very well, but first of all let's put an end to the Germans."[62]

The political division and confusion was not to the liking of either Rowecki or Sikorski. A year after the September catastrophe, Rowecki said, "We are still not ready to agree or make preparations to fight for independence." He severely criticized the confusion and conflict that existed in the political arena as different groups and individuals, some acting in the name of the government-in-exile, pursued conflicting goals and ambitions. Rowecki referred to the curious political activities of the Political Bureau (*Biuro Polityczne*) and the Central Committee of Organizations for Independence (*Centralny Komitet Organizacji Niepodleglościowych*—CKON), which for a time became the nucleus of political and military groups who were hostile to the ZWZ and to the Political Coordinating Committee and its successor, the Chief Political Committee. CKON, headed by Ryszard Świętochowski, an engineer by profession, received valuable support from the Polish representation in Hungary which consistently meddled in Polish underground politics. Even Sikorski's own political representative in Warsaw telegraphed him regarding this outside interference and asked for "a quick liquidation of this political nonsense." Świętochowski's activities didn't last long; he was arrested by the Germans in May 1940, and subsequently died in Auschwitz. CKON broke up in 1940, and though the Political Bureau limped along for some time, it ceased to be effective.

In the face of all this, Rowecki wondered disapprovingly if the slogans for Polish freedom and independence were "simply a subterfuge for the fighting for personal and political influence."[63] Two years after the Germans occupied Poland, Rowecki complained to the government delegate about political groups and their military units undermining confidence in the ZWZ/AK. "No one," he declared, "has the right to undermine always the spirit of the fighting soldier, to shake his confidence in his leaders, which is the most valued element in every army." He urged political groups to concentrate on unity or else doom Poland to catastrophe.[64]

Sikorski was equally concerned about what he perceived as unhealthy divisiveness in the homeland. At a meeting of his cabinet on February 11, 1943, he stressed the need for genuine unity, "not a paper declaration," among Poles at home and in exile. In a message to the government delegate one week earlier, Sikorski feared that the division in Poland might result in a revolution which would risk losing the country to the Soviets and thus the support of the western democracies.[65] "It will be difficult," opined one of Sikorski's confidants, "to find in Poland after the war some common language or political platform, especially in domestic and foreign affairs."[66]

The concerns of Rowecki and Sikorski were not entirely exaggerated. To be sure, there was considerable freedom and individualism that characterized political life in the underground. But the Poles paid a price for it in the deep cleavages and distrust that existed among various political groups. As one observer dolefully commented, "They don't want to sit at the same table." With the exception of the Peasant Party, the other major and several minor political parties were split into two or more factions. Even the Boy Scouts were divided. It was not uncommon for regional groups to refuse cooperation with parent political groups in Warsaw.[67]

Neither the Socialists nor the Peasant Party succeeded in developing a close relationship with the National Democrats, who favored more of a nationalist than a democratic state based upon the equality of all citizens, including minority groups. The Nationalists were in a strange political position; they functioned as a part of the political and military structure of the Polish underground, but their leadership in exile in London refused to become a part of the Sikorski government and disavowed National Democrats who agreed to sit in Sikorski's cabinet or in the *Rada Narodowa*.

Yet the connection between the Socialists and Peasant Party was affected by the serious split in the Socialist movement, which had divided into the Liberty, Equality, and Independence faction (*Wolność, Równość, Niepodległość*—WRN), and left-wing Socialists with popular front ideas of coalition with the Polish Workers Party, which they joined in 1944. To many in the Peasant Party the right-wing WRN was too close to the Piłsudskiites. By 1944, however, cooperation between the two groups improved enough to encourage one observer to remark optimistically that it "possibly might begin a new epic at home." Though the smallest of the four major parties, the Labor Party cast itself in "the role of watchman of the Big Four."[68]

Naturally, the divisiveness among the political parties raised the question of their political fitness to rule the country after the war. In a reference to the murders of officials in the AK's Bureau of Information and Propaganda by members of the National Armed Forces (NSZ), one commentator bemoaned the fact that people were shooting each other, "not waiting for a free Poland."[69] Others feared the Nationalists, in collaboration with right-wing elements of the AK, planned to seize the government by a coup d'état when the fight against the Germans was over. Or at least a civil war between the National Democrats and the leftists was feared.[70] Despite the profound political divisions and disagreements, most of the major and several democratically oriented smaller parties agreed that Poland should be a free democratic country with equal rights for minorities. Except for the Polish Communists and their allies, virtually all parties stressed that the Riga Line should be the postwar frontier between Poland and the Soviet Union.[71]

One major issue which Poles believed should be resolved in order to bring political order to the underground was the question of the Delegacy. Once it was finally decided to have one government delegate instead of three for the different portions of occupied Poland (the latter idea never very popular among the Poles anyway), many people believed that the confusing political situation in Poland would finally come to an end. But that proved to be an elusive goal.

Three months after Sikorski appointed Cyryl Ratajski on December 3, 1940 as the first government delegate, one observer noted that "we are in a situation today as if there were no delegate." One reporter wondered if the problem was the man who occupied the position or the negative attitude of the political parties in Poland toward him. Another report, testifying to the low standing of the Delegacy in Poland, noted that political groups not in contact with the Delegacy abandoned any efforts to establish contact during Ratajski's tenure.[72]

Ratajski had been appointed government delegate over the objections of two of the major parties—the Peasant Party and the Socialists—who had understood that the initiative for the appointment would come from Poland, not the government in London. Poland's choice for the job had been Jan Piekalkiewicz. Elderly and unfamiliar with the work of conspiracy, Ratajski was a well-intentioned man who was not a wise choice for the job.[73] He was unable to infuse the Delegacy with the prestige and authority the office demanded. Because he had a weaker personality than Rowecki, Ratajski seemed to be content with the duality of power between the civilian-political and military components of the underground in Poland. Tired of the internecine squabbling, including the criticisms of the Socialists, the Peasant Party, and Rowecki himself, Ratajski was dismissed and lost his job to Piekalkiewicz in September 1942. Though a stronger personality than Ratajski, neither Piekalkiewicz nor his successors were able to resolve satisfactorily the duality of power between the civilian-political and military branches of the underground.[74] On his part, Rowecki was reluctant to give up to the Delegacy established ZWZ/AK bailiwicks which clearly had political implications. For example, he did not want to give up the Bureau of Information and Propaganda, which, he claimed, was essential to the efficient operation of the underground army. On the other hand, Sikorski wanted all agencies whose functions were essentially political to be transferred to the Delegacy.[75]

Though some have emphasized the plurality rather than the fragmentation of the Polish underground,[76] it is clear that the political and military divisions in Poland drained energy and attention from the immediate task of resistance against the enemy and exacerbated fears that the Poles would not be in a strong political position to act in a unified way when the war finally ended. Yet, despite the lack of cohesion, the groups within the Polish underground movement had a common enemy and were able to score remarkable underground successes against the Germans during their occupation of Poland.

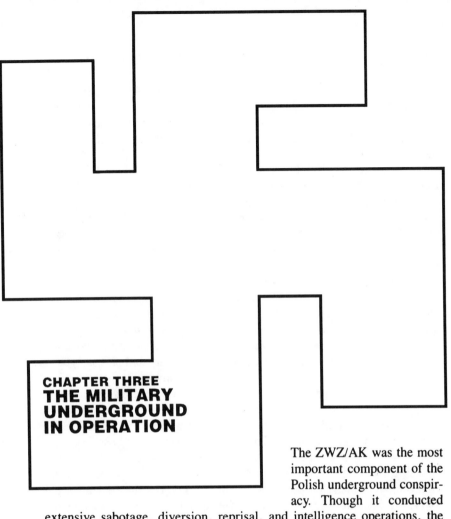

CHAPTER THREE
THE MILITARY
UNDERGROUND
IN OPERATION

The ZWZ/AK was the most important component of the Polish underground conspiracy. Though it conducted extensive sabotage, diversion, reprisal, and intelligence operations, the ZWZ/AK's primary role was to prepare itself for an eventual general uprising which would be launched when German power in the East crumbled and the Poles could assert their military and political authority over their own country.

As has been seen, the ZWZ/AK was a large military organization that had incorporated numerous military groups with different political views and attitudes. As late as the spring of 1944, General Bór-Komorowski described his organization as "a conglomeration of commanders and detachments, whose attitudes to one another are frequently undisguisedly hostile, and who are held together only by a badly frayed thread of formal discipline that may snap at the start of active operations."[1] Although these disparate groups associated with the ZWZ/AK showed a common hatred of the Germans, the men and officers who comprised these organizations were volunteers in the resistance, and often their loyalties focused more on the unit or group to which they belonged than on some distant command in Warsaw. That is why Polish resistance leaders, like those in other conspiracies in Europe, "had to work under the pure democratic law that they must win their authority by their words and deeds, day by day, situation by situation."[2] Whatever directives subordinate units received usually were flexibly interpreted to allow for independent initiative and local circumstances. Therefore, it should not be surprising that discipline in the ZWZ/AK was often a problem. From time to time individuals and groups within the AK followed their own impulses, sometimes challenging or disobeying their superiors. Often these initiatives were praiseworthy; others—and these did not loom large in number—were against the best interests of the Polish people.

After a decline in ZWZ/AK strength following the collapse of France, the AK swelled to approximately 380,175 officers and men by the first half of 1944.[3] They were organized into four types of units: full conspiratorial platoons, cadre conspiratorial platoons, sabotage-diversionary units, and partisan groups. The sabotage-diversionary and partisan groups conducted most of the operations against the enemy while the bulk of the AK was immobile. The average AK soldier carried out his daily routine of supporting his wife and family. Limited finances imposed limitations on the size and number of units in operation against the Nazis. "Large additions to the permanent strength [sabotage-diversion and partisan units] would soon bankrupt the GHQ finances," one report stated. Even if finances permitted, it still would not have been realistic to expect the full engagement of the AK against the enemy. During the Warsaw Uprising of 1944, for example, only forces from the capital and the surrounding area were involved against the Germans. The vast preponderance of weapons had been held in reserve by the high command for the future uprising that was to occur only when the Germans were at the point of collapse. At one point, only 10,000 out of 250,000 soldiers of the AK were armed to a reasonable degree. A high-ranking officer of the AK told British interrogators in early 1944 that an AK soldier considered himself well armed if he had a personal weapon of any sort; even a couple of hand grenades counted as a personal weapon.[4]

Since only a small portion of the ZWZ/AK was ever engaged at any time with the Germans, it is not difficult to understand why the organization limited itself to intelligence, sabotage-diversionary, and reprisal operations. It was not possible for the ZWZ/AK to undertake systematic operations to liberate large numbers of Poles and Jews from prisons and concentration camps. The AK, like the populace at large, was helpless in preventing the German roundups of Poles for forced labor, reprisals, and executions. If the ZWZ/AK could do little to prevent these tragedies from occurring to fellow Poles, it was even more at a loss to assist the Jews who, locked up in ghettos like caged animals, were difficult to contact, let alone liberate.

In the spring of 1940, Rowecki created the Union for Revenge (*Związek Odwetu*), which was responsible for conducting sabotage, diversionary, and reprisal operations against the Germans not only in the General Government but also in the Reich itself. Leaders of the Union for Revenge took a course which covered tactics, communications, mechanics, and even the chemical, bacteriological, and toxicological aspects of warfare. As of March 1942, approximately 100 operatives had taken the course.[5] Following the outbreak of the German-Soviet war in 1941, Fan (*Wachlarz*) came into existence; it was a unique sabotage-diversionary unit which operated on Soviet territory that the Germans occupied.

Later, in 1942, the AK organized the Directorate of Diversion (*Kedyw*), which absorbed the Union for Revenge and the remnants of the Fan, which had suffered major setbacks in its operations in the East. The Directorate of Diversion had units operating throughout Poland, relying heavily on young boys in the Grey Ranks who formed a discretionary element of the organization. Individual units of the Directorate of Diversion specialized in different operations, especially diversionary attacks on railroads, terror and reprisals against Germans, liquidation of traitors, and self-defense actions. Because of the growth of sabotage, diversionary, and partisan operations in Poland, Rowecki created the Directorate of Underground Resistance (*Kierownictwo Walki Konspiracyjnej*), which he himself headed to coordinate matters. Since the sphere of operations of the organization was similar to the existing Directorate of Civil Resistance (*Kierownictwo Walki Cywilnej*), the duality was resolved by combining the two organizations into the Directorate of Underground Struggle (*Kierownictwo Walki Podziemnej*).[6]

Although the primary goal of the ZWZ/AK was to prepare the country for an eventual uprising against the Germans, the military leadership could not be oblivious to the need to conduct sabotage, diversionary, and reprisal operations to impair German war potential and lower the enemy's morale. Moreover, these operations maintained the level of tension and readiness among the Poles, thus psychologically preparing them for the general uprising in the future.[7] No small part was also played by the negative influence of Polish Communists who criticized the ZWZ/AK for fighting "with their arms at their feet instead of actively engaging the enemy."[8] Polish Communist goals were really more political than military.

The ZWZ/AK had good reasons to minimize direct confrontations with the Germans, for ZWZ/AK actions often resulted in savage reprisals without seriously damaging the enemy's war machine. When the right moment finally came to attack the enemy with the full weight of the underground army in a general uprising, ZWZ/AK leaders feared that their forces would have been enfeebled by many repressive actions, too weak to be effective. Moreover, German reprisals for underground operations risked losing the support of the people and even played into the hands of those wanting to collaborate with the enemy.

Following the Polish defeat by the Germans in September 1939, Sikorski did not want the ZWZ to engage in any operations that invited Nazi repression. When Sosnkowski outlined possible activities for the ZWZ in January 1940, he gave priority to intelligence, followed by sabotage. Precisely because of the inherent risks of Nazi retribution, he gave a lower priority to retaliatory and diversionary attacks. Even when the ZWZ conducted sabotage, Sosnkowski directed Rowecki to do it in such a way as to minimize the repercussions from the Nazis; he suggested adding sugar or pitch to benzine and sand to the oil cans of freight cars, and infecting the grain of cows used by the military.[9]

By mid-March 1940, Rowecki reported on the successes of sabotage against the Germans. He correctly indicated that this type of operation could not be entirely executed by the ZWZ itself and that Polish railroad workers played a critical role because the major targets to be sabotaged were trains and related installations. Sharing the anxieties of top Polish military leaders in London about the risks involved in conducting diversionary attacks, Rowecki believed that if these operations were carefully planned and executed, preferably in the lands annexed by the Germans and by the Soviets instead of within the General Government, then Rowecki would approve them.[10] Of course, this did not preclude sabotage-diversionary operations in the General Government. The Union for Revenge, which Rowecki had created in April 1940, conducted a wide-ranging series of operations throughout different parts of Poland. In February 1941, as a result of the activities of the Union for Revenge, 43 percent of the locomotives in the General Government were inoperative.[11]

The Germans employed an estimated 30,000 Polish railroad workers in the General Government, a majority of whom were members of the Socialist Party. They played a major role in delaying and damaging German rail transports throughout Poland. As one Polish courier put it, "Not only the distribution of underground literature from Warsaw but also the whole program of sabotage and military intelligence relied to a large extent on them." Usually these workers added a chemical to the grease in the box of the railroad engine which disabled it. In 1940, an engine was damaged and out of commission on the average of fourteen hours; in 1942, with improved sabotage methods, the period was five days; in 1943, it had risen to fourteen days.[12]

The Union for Revenge made effective use of experts in bacteriology and toxicology for the conduct of bacterial sabotage. During the spring and summer of 1941, Rowecki reported that ninety-two people with bacteria had left Poland for Germany, and that thanks to bacterial sabotage, there were 178 known cases of typhus among German soldiers at the time of the German build-up in Poland. One Pole, called Jan, delighted in spreading contagious diseases among the Germans. Jan, who spoke German fluently, would visit bars, talk with German soldiers, and at the right time, drop from a little box a louse, bearing microbes and typhoid-bearing germs, behind the collar of his German acquaintance. The Poles became so proficient at this type of warfare that during the first four months of 1943, they succeeded in administering typhoid fever microbes and poison to over 600 Germans.[13]

Sikorski, reflecting his anxieties about the increase in Nazi retribution on the Polish people for sabotage-diversion actions, told Rowecki shortly after the German invasion of the Soviet Union to limit these operations to German territory and to the area directly behind the German front. However, he wanted the ZWZ to concentrate on building up its strength for the general uprising, which he predicted might occur sooner than anticipated.

Keenly aware of the possibilities of military cooperation between the Poles and the Soviets after the German invasion of the Soviet Union, Sikorski wanted Rowecki to explore the possibilities of Polish diversionary operations east of the Molotov-Ribbentrop Line which might eventually help to mellow the Soviets substantially enough whereby the Poles might gain "respectable concessions."[14] Clearly this was part of Sikorski's strategy of trying to build a comrade-in-arms relationship between Poles and Russians during their struggle against a common enemy. Whatever Sikorski had hoped would develop in the way of Polish-Soviet cooperation through the activities of the Polish sabotage-diversionary unit Fan, Rowecki reported that the Soviets themselves killed many of Fan's operatives. Although Fan hampered some German communications with the eastern front, the organization did not have the strength, the resources, or sufficient local support to sustain effective long-term military effort in the region. By the end of 1942, plagued with high casualties, Fan ceased to operate.[15]

By the end of 1942, the AK extended its diversionary operations to Warsaw itself where on October 8, six rail lines leading out of Warsaw had been cut. AK units, commanded by Captain Zbiegniew Lewandowski, executed Operation Wreath (*Wieniec*) and established a precedent by attacking German communication lines in Warsaw. The operation, responding to British requests to sever German railway lines with the Russian front, temporarily denied the Nazis the ability to send an urgent convoy to Stalingrad where the turning point of the war on the eastern front was being waged. In retribution for the losses, the Germans executed thirty-nine men and women.[16] AK attacks against German communications targets continued with impressive results during the period of the Battle of Stalingrad.[17]

As has been suggested, sabotage against the Germans was not limited to the ZWZ/AK. Virtually the entire Polish nation, mobilized first by the Directorate of Civil Resistance and later by the Directorate of Underground Struggle, sought to frustrate, delay, damage, or destroy whatever the Germans needed of economic value for their war economy. When it came to grain deliveries to the Germans, Polish peasants operated under the slogan, "As little, as late, and as bad as possible." Albrecht Tyburz was rather typical of Polish farmers who did not surrender milk from his cows to the Germans, declaring that the skimming station was too far and his cows were too old to give milk. The Directorate of Civil Resistance was behind the burning of documents on quota deliveries in the General Government. Once these documents, kept in village offices, were destroyed, the German authorities did not know who had made their quota deliveries.[18]

Economic sabotage extended to Poles forced to work in Germany. They were told by Polish broadcasts from the BBC: "A Pole in Servitude Works Slowly." (*Polak w Niewoli Pracuje Powoli.*) Some of these workers did even more; one agricultural worker set fire to harvested crops while another removed parts of a potato digging machine that resulted in ruining two wagonloads of potatoes that had to be left in the field to rot. Both of them paid with their lives.[19]

Almost every Pole employed in industry also engaged in sabotage to the extent of his ability. In the annexed lands, Polish workers burned down factories, mills, and ammunition dumps. The sabotage activities of ordinary Polish citizens were so extensive that, according to the chief of the Directorate of Civil Resistance, "If a balance sheet could be drawn up it would be found that it was worth at least several divisions fighting at the front."[20] The British, anxious to publicize Polish feats of sabotage, broadcast these achievements, sometimes with embellishment, over the BBC.

Rowecki, angry that these broadcasts sometimes resulted in hundreds of innocent Poles becoming Nazi victims, asked Polish authorities to stop them.[21]

German authorities in Poland grew progressively more nervous about the frequent attacks on German communication lines and supplies, especially in the important districts of Cracow, Warsaw, Lublin, and Radom. The Poles had escalated their attacks so much that by 1943, trains on many lines moved only at certain times under guard or not at all. By 1944, railroad sabotage increased to an average of ten explosions every day. In the first six months of 1944 alone, the Directorate of Diversion was responsible for 179 railroad disruptions which forced delays on various lines from 2 to 196 hours. General Haenicke admonished his forces in October 1943: "A large number of the Members of the Forces [sic] do not seem to have realized that when they find themselves in the Government-General area, they are not in the Fatherland, but in a region where the majority of the population is hostile to us and opposes us with violence."[22]

There is no complete tabulation of the sabotage-diversionary actions conducted by the Polish underground army during the entire period of German occupation. However, a report for the period January 1, 1941 to June 30, 1944 gives at least a partial indication of the extent of the damage and destruction the Poles inflicted upon the Germans:[23]

Locomotives damaged	6,930
Locomotives delayed in overhaul	803
Transports derailed	732
Railroad cars destroyed	979
Railroad cars damaged	19,058
Transports set on fire	443
Disruptions of electric power in Warsaw	638
Military vehicles damaged or destroyed	4,326
Railroad bridges blown up	38
Aircraft damaged	28
Aircraft engines destroyed	68
Gasoline storage tanks destroyed	1,167
Tons of gasoline destroyed	4,674
Oil shafts incapacitated	3
Carloads of wood burned	150
Military warehouses burned	122
Military food storage houses burned	8
Production in factories brought to halt	7
Factories burned	15

Defective parts for aircraft engines produced	4,710
Defective cannon barrels produced	203
Defective artillery shells produced	92,000
Defective aircraft radios produced	107
Defective capacitors produced for electronic industry	570,000
Defective lathes produced	1,700
Important plant machinery damaged	2,872
Various acts of sabotage	25,145
Attacks on Germans	5,733

In commenting on this list, General Bór-Komorowski observed, "This summary gives only the more characteristic acts of sabotage and is only half the picture of the scope of our activities."[24]

Despite the impressive armed action which the ZWZ/AK waged against the Germans, Polish military leaders in Warsaw and in London were not under any illusions that the primary objective of the underground army was to launch a general uprising to take control over Poland when the Germans were at the point of collapse. But Polish plans for an early uprising evaporated when France collapsed in June 1940. As early as January 1940, General Sosnkowski, reflecting on the size and purpose of the ZWZ and his preference for a small organization capable of conducting conspiracy but helping prepare the country for a massive action, warned that it "might be necessary to wait a long time." With the defeat of France, Sosnkowski's "long time" loomed large for everyone. "All logical basis for hopes of a German defeat had now gone," General Bór-Komorowski later observed. "We wondered how the people would react. In less than one year they had had to bear two very heavy blows."[25]

By the fall of 1940, Rowecki and Sikorski initiated an extensive correspondence (that went on until the summer of 1943) on the subject of the future Polish uprising. From the outset, it was clear that Rowecki's military thought was based on the "doctrine of the two enemies"—Germany and the Soviet Union, the two nations that had partitioned Poland by common agreement in 1939. Originally, Rowecki's plans anticipated a Polish uprising against the Germans only when German defeat was imminent and the Poles received major military assistance from the western allies, including Polish armored forces landing along the Baltic and parachute units being dropped in central Poland. Unfortunately, Rowecki had misinterpreted some early messages from Sosnkowski and Sikorski concerning the possibilities of western aid to the Polish underground.

Rowecki's plan even presupposed the contingency of a German-Russian conflict and speculated on what the Soviet position would be during the closing phase of the war. If the Germans weakened the Soviets to the point that their entire military-political structure was weakened, then the Poles would only have to worry about the Germans against whom they expected to launch their uprising when the western allies virtually defeated the Reich. Rowecki saw the ruin of Soviet strength by the Germans as an answer to the Russo-Polish boundary problem. On the other hand, Rowecki speculated on another possible scenario—namely, a German defeat by the Soviets and the entry of strong Soviet armies into Poland. In that eventuality, Rowecki recognized that the ZWZ/AK should maintain the underground apparatus and wait for a weakening of the Soviet system. But once the German army eventually collapsed, he still saw an opportunity for the Poles, supported by Polish forces from the West, not only to rise up against the Germans but also to conduct defensive operations against the Soviets. Drafted on February 5, 1941, Rowecki's plan did not reach Sikorski until after the Germans had in fact invaded the Soviet Union; thus a significant portion of the plan was already outdated.[26]

Sikorski had different views than Rowecki concerning the Soviet Union. As has been seen, a year before the Germans invaded the Soviet Union, Sikorski looked toward establishing some sort of rapprochement with the Soviets. He signed the Polish-Soviet treaty with the Soviets in July 1941, and hoped to mitigate the hostility between the two countries by fostering a Polish army, organized by General Władysław Anders, composed of officers and enlisted men who had been interned in Soviet camps during the years of Stalin's collaboration with Hitler. He had some of the same expectations for the work of Fan, the Polish sabotage-diversionary group that operated on Russian territory in 1941–42. Under no circumstances did Sikorski want to risk a confrontation with the Soviets; despite initial military setbacks in the fight against the Germans, the U.S.S.R. played a major role in the war and increasingly replaced Poland in Allied sympathies.

In early 1942, when it was clear the Soviets would not be defeated by the Germans, Sikorski told Rowecki to prepare a plan providing for the ZWZ/AK to seize control of the country at the time of a German military collapse and to impress the advancing Soviets with Polish strength. He wanted the Polish underground to assert Polish claims over Vilna and Lwów, key cities in the disputed boundary area between Poland and the Soviet Union. If the Soviets acted in an unfriendly way and refused to recognize Polish claims to eastern Poland, Sikorski did not want the Poles to become involved in hostilities with them. Sikorski placed his reliance on a politically and militarily unified Polish underground and Western Allied support to impress the Soviets substantially enough to deal with the Poles as allies and equals. More than once he emphasized the importance of Polish solidarity in the face of advancing Soviets, worrying that internal weakness and differences would provide an opportunity for the Communists to exploit the situation to the Kremlin's advantage. Despite the deterioration in Polish-Soviet relations since their treaty of July 1941, Sikorski still hoped that with British and American support the Polish government would eventually convince the Soviets of Polish territorial rights in the East. To take up arms against the Soviets, he told Rowecki on November 28, 1942, "would be madness."[27]

Sikorski was well aware throughout 1942 and early 1943 that the Western Allies had shown little disposition toward the idea of becoming involved in large scale supply and support operations to the Poles in an uprising against the Germans. Sikorski told Rowecki that aid to the Polish underground from the West at the time of such an uprising would be limited by strategic and logistical factors. Even getting the Polish Parachute Brigade from Britain to Poland depended on getting sufficient transport aircraft from the British and the Americans, and there was no certainty when these planes would become available. He also rejected the possibility of Polish land forces being able to get to Poland.[28]

Rowecki bluntly told Sikorski that there was a general awareness in the underground army that "Russia was and will be our enemy." By the end of 1942, Rowecki elaborated a plan for a general uprising which would go into effect when the Germans were at the point of imminent collapse but before the Soviets entered Poland in force. On the other hand, if the Russians beat the Germans and were in contact with them as they entered Poland, Rowecki agreed with Sikorski that it was pointless to resist the Soviets. But he did not agree that the AK should disclose itself to the Soviets, because he believed they would treat the Poles as enemies, not allies. Rowecki explained to Sikorski that for the Polish people to have confidence in the Soviets as friends, the Soviets would have to demonstrate some minimum loyalty to their Polish allies by directing their diversionary and partisan activity against the Germans and not against Polish interests.[29]

Rowecki's deep distrust of the Soviets was underscored in his early 1943 messages to Sikorski, when he proposed launching the Polish uprising against the Germans *before* the Germans collapsed, in order to ensure that the Poles take control of the major portions of the country prior to the arrival of the Soviets. In other words, Polish strategic thinking in the homeland now predicated the general uprising not on the state of dissolution of the Germans but on the entrance of the Russians into Poland. Rowecki hoped to accomplish this by getting military help from the United States and Britain, whose presence in Poland, he believed, would force the Soviets to act as loyal allies.[30]

Rowecki's continued unrealistic expectations of western military aid to the Polish underground or at least the deployment of Polish armed forces from Britain to Poland were disturbing to Sikorski, who had sought to draw a realistic picture of the situation for his commander in Poland. Rowecki's fanciful notions may well have been encouraged by certain military officers from Sikorski's staff when they were dispatched to Poland. Perhaps even more disturbing to Sikorski were the military implications of Rowecki's insistence that the Soviets were Poland's enemies and his doubts that this would ever really change. Accordingly, Sikorski told Rowecki that if relations with the Soviets worsened and they entered Poland as enemies, he wanted only the civil authorities of the Polish underground to reveal themselves while the AK withdrew to the interior of the country to avoid destruction.[31]

While admonishing Rowecki not to count on western military aid at the time of a Polish uprising, Sikorski, during his visit to Washington in December 1942, tried to influence American military planners to consider an Anglo-American invasion in the Balkans; "Poland," he said, "would be capable at the given moment to constitute a barrier against the retiring German troops into Germany proper and thereby hasten the occupation of Germany and safeguard Europe against upheaval." This strategy would anticipate the Soviets in the region and relieve the anxieties of the Poles. Sikorski explained to General George Marshall, the American chief of staff, that the "complete isolation of Germany and the rapid crossing by the Allies over the Central European bridge, between the Balkans and Poland, would considerably diminish that anxiety, by the immediate installment in this politically complicated area of sound conditions of security." He emphasized the military needs of the Polish underground, urging that the Polish uprising against the Germans was contingent on western aid, especially air force assistance, and that it would occur only "when there will be no peril of a long isolation."[32]

Despite Sikorski's hopes, American and British military planners were opposed to the Balkan scheme. They also opposed the idea of equipping the AK for a major uprising, because the Soviet Union would consider this an intrusion in its sphere of influence. Moreover, by fully equipping the Poles at the time when Polish-Russian relations had deteriorated during the spring of 1943, western planners feared that the AK might not only fight the Germans but also "would certainly be disposed to resist Russian encroachment within Poland's pre-1939 frontiers." But Anglo-American planners believed that sending a small amount of material to the Poles to continue their sabotage and diversionary operations probably would not "excite Russian susceptibilities."

Even before Anglo-American military planners had formally rejected Polish plans for extensive military aid to the AK prior to and during a Polish uprising against the Germans, Colonel Leon Mitkiewicz, who served as the Polish representative in Washington to the combined chiefs of staff, was convinced that the Americans would join the British in opposing the idea, because of their fears that the Poles would use their military strength against the Soviets.[33] Even a late desperate effort by Mitkiewicz to secure an Anglo-American pronouncement establishing their strategic responsibility over Poland failed.[34] Britain and the United States obviously did not want to interfere in an area that militarily they considered to be in the Soviet sphere of operations.

While Sikorski and Rowecki wrestled with the thorny question of the Polish uprising against the Germans and the policy of the AK toward the Soviets, Polish relations with the Kremlin worsened over such unresolved issues as the supply and recruitment of the Anders army, which was subsequently evacuated from the Soviet Union to the Middle East, the relief and evacuation of Polish refugees in the Soviet Union, and, most importantly, the boundary dispute between the two countries.[35] Finally, in April 1943, the Germans provided an issue which Stalin used as a pretext to sever diplomatic relations with the Sikorski government.

The story is well known. The Polish government had sought for a long time to find out what happened to 8,000 Polish officers who had been confined in 1940 in Soviet prisons. By 1942, when several Polish efforts to locate the missing men had failed, some Polish leaders came to the conclusion that the Soviets had murdered them. Polish suspicions about Soviet culpability were virtually confirmed in April 1943, when Berlin Radio announced the discovery of 3,000 corpses of Polish officers in the forest of Katyń and charged the Russians with the atrocity. The Kremlin denied the allegation, but the Sikorski government asked the International Red Cross to investigate the matter. When the Poles made that request, Stalin severed diplomatic relations with the Polish government-in-exile. To be sure, we now know that the Soviets were indeed responsible for the atrocity, but at the time no one in the West could be absolutely certain who was guilty; if anything, the British press blamed the Germans for the crime and thought the Poles "had slandered an ally and had acted with blatant political stupidity."[36]

The Katyń affair simply confirmed Rowecki's long-standing view that the Soviet Union was "nothing [more] than our enemy"—and he would continue to consider it that way in his military planning. In view of the state of Russo-Polish relations, Rowecki ordered the AK to concentrate its armed attacks against the Nazi administration in Poland instead of against the Wehrmacht and its communications to the Soviet front.[37] Though profoundly disturbed by the situation in Polish-Russian relations, on June 1, 1943, Sikorski directed the Polish underground to concentrate on the Germans as "enemy number one." Fearing that the Katyń affair might make it attractive for some to reach an accommodation with the Germans, Sikorski warned that any such efforts would undermine all that Poland had achieved. He told Rowecki that he would not tolerate Soviet interference in Polish internal affairs "either to mutilate Poland or worse to create of her a Soviet republic." On the other hand, he believed it still was in Polish interest to reach some military understanding with the Soviets concerning activities against the Germans.

Exactly what Sikorski intended to do politically with respect to the Kremlin is not entirely clear. In view of the claims of the Communist-dominated and Moscow-based Union of Polish Patriots to be the true spokesmen for Poland and their sponsorship of a Polish army—named after Tadeusz Kościuszko—to operate under the Soviet operational command, Sikorski could not allow the drift in Polish-Soviet relations to continue very long. According to one informed source, Sikorski was apparently willing to make concessions to the Soviets to prevent another government, a Communist one, from coming into existence.[38] He did not live long enough to guide or witness the outcome; he died in an airplane crash on July 4, 1943.

As we have noted, partisan operations under the aegis of the ZWZ/AK were not encouraged because of the obvious risks of Nazi retribution and of squandering valuable men and material needed for the eventual uprising against the Germans. Early initiatives in guerrilla warfare in eastern Poland were taken primarily by Communists and Jews who had escaped from nearby towns and villages. During most of the war, Polish partisans associated with various organizations—AK, BCh, NSZ, Jews, Communists—fought not only the Germans but also each other in an area characterized by anarchy. As already observed, Major Henryk Dobrzański's group was the best known of the early guerrilla organizations operating in Poland until the spring of 1940.[39] *Jędrusie* was another wildcat group that operated for several years in southeastern Poland, but it eventually subordinated itself to the AK. The name *Jędrusie* became so popular that in many places in Poland it became a synonym for partisans. It was not until the establishment of the Directorate of Underground Resistance, late in 1942, that the AK formally began to organize a partisan movement subject to its authority.

The Germans forced the issue in late 1942 by their deportation of thousands of Poles from the Zamość area.[40] The main burden of responding to this calamity fell to the Peasant Battalions (BCh), which fought the Germans in several major engagements early in 1943.[41] From that point on, AK-related guerrilla units grew; and operations expanded, especially, though not exclusively, in other parts of eastern Poland where the tasks of the AK partisans were not only to protect the Poles from German reprisals but also from the attacks of bandits, Communists, and Ukrainians. By the winter of 1943, the AK had the following partisan units, totaling over 3,000 men: four in Radom, eight in Cracow, four in Polesie, eleven in Lublin, eight in Nowogródek, two in Wilno, a few in Wołyn and Białystok, one in Łódź, and one in Rzeszów. Assorted units could be found in Pomerania and Silesia, too. The fighting strength of an AK partisan unit varied considerably but usually ranged between 30 and 100 men, from a platoon to a company.[42]

The partisan movement in eastern Poland not subordinated to the AK was tied directly or indirectly to the Communists. The AK and the Communists bitterly opposed each other on the issue of how and when to fight the Germans. The Communists branded the AK as fascists, tied to the *Sanacja* and capitalists, who preferred a strategy of hoarding arms and waiting. The Communists so convincingly argued against this unpopular view that many soldiers of the AK defected and joined the Communists. Echoing a patriotic line in which they urged the creation of a Peoples' Front that excluded "traitors and capitalists," the Communists argued for diversionary and partisan activity to help the Red Army, which was portrayed as the best guarantee to the life and freedom of the Polish people. Rowecki, concerned about the effectiveness of Communist propaganda, changed his position on the matter and urged Polish authorities in London to publicize AK armed actions to counter the image of the AK portrayed by the Communists.[43]

Rowecki complained how Communists encouraged bandit-type operations that had little or no value, created anarchy, and encouraged robbery—all of which resulted in harsh German repressive actions.[44] This approach, of course, collided with the AK view of coordinating its strategy in the West, husbanding its strength for the general uprising, and initiating only limited, calculated sabotage-diversionary assaults that would lessen chances of large-scale German retaliation.

To be sure, the differences between the AK and the Communists were not merely tactical. The AK and the Delegacy, loyal to the Polish government-in-exile, expected to fill the military and political void following the German collapse in the war. The Communists, on the other hand, hoped to prevent that from happening and wanted to pave the way for a Polish government favorable to Moscow. The struggle became increasingly bitter as the years went on, especially after the Katyń affair and the approach of Soviet armies to the prewar Polish frontier. Each side accused the other of killing its members. Though Sikorski denied the AK had been ordered to kill Communists and their allies, he admitted that "spontaneous incidents" had occurred.[45] The facts suggest that each side did attack the other.

There was an attempt early in 1943 by the Polish Communists to find some basis for cooperation with the Government Delegacy, then headed by Jan Piekalkiewicz of the Peasant Party. Piekalkiewicz was arrested by the Gestapo and was succeeded by Jan Jankowski, a member of the Labor Party. Władysław Gomułka represented the Communists in the talks. Rowecki, who played a major role in these negotiations, laid down conditions which the Polish Communists refused to accept. Rowecki wanted them to declare publicly that they were not foreign agents of the Comintern, that they supported a free independent Poland with the Riga Line as the Polish-Soviet boundary, and that they recognized the authority of the Polish government in London and its political and military representatives in Poland to which the Polish Communists would subordinate themselves. The Polish Communists would not go that far; they were willing to recognize the legality of the Polish government-in-exile as Poland's "external" representative, but they would not recognize the Riga Line. Also, Communist military subordination to the AK was made contingent upon an increase in armed actions against the Germans and the inclusion of the Communist People's Guard (GL) in the command structure of the AK.

To Rowecki, the Communist offer was a subterfuge to infiltrate the AK and secure a prominent role for itself in the resistance. While these discussions were conducted in Poland, official relations between the London Poles and the Kremlin had deteriorated and led to the April 26, 1943 Soviet severance of diplomatic relations with the Polish government over the Katyń affair. Two days later, Jankowski insisted that the Polish Communists agree to fight against the Soviet Union if it demanded changes in the Riga Line. The Polish Communists refused, and negotiations broke off. Even the probes of Soviet partisan groups toward the AK on the question of cooperating against the Germans in eastern Poland in 1943 collapsed over the refusal of Soviet groups to recognize the AK as the legal military authority in areas the AK considered an integral part of the Polish state.[46]

The leadership of the AK, keenly aware that many Poles were vulnerable to Communist political propaganda, urged the government to respond with promises of political and social reform to offset the Communist appeal. Within this context, Bór-Komorowski himself admitted that there was a tendency for many Poles to view the Soviets as saviors from the horrible terror of the Nazis.[47] Alarmed by the activities of the Polish Communists and their Soviet counterparts, which undermined the political and military leadership of the Polish government and its agencies in Poland, Rowecki established a special group called "Section K" of the Bureau of Information and Propaganda of the AK to counter communist propaganda.

Later, the anti-Communist program took on a broader aspect when the Government Delegacy, the Council of National Unity, and groups not connected with the Council, established the Civic Anticommunist Committee (*Społeczny Komitet AntyKomunistyczny-Antyk*). Virtually all Polish political parties and groups, except, of course, the Communists and their allies, were involved in its activities. The official Polish underground position was that the Communists were not really interested in fighting the Germans; rather, they were preparing the way for a Soviet seizure of power in Poland.[48]

By 1944, when Soviet armies had crossed the prewar Polish-Soviet frontier, both sides were keenly aware that the war was drawing to an end and the political stakes were closer to realization. Communists continued their propaganda barrages about the AK "traitors" and made special efforts to win over the poor peasants to their cause. By the spring of 1944, Bór-Komorowski revealed his concerns about conflicts between the left wing of the Peasant Battalions and the AK and efforts of the Communist People's Army (*Armia Ludowa*—AL) to draw some of the BCh into their ranks.[49] "One thing is certain," an OSS report observed at the time. "The Germans are helped by the lack of unity in the underground and by the basic fact that each side has other aims than fighting the Germans."[50]

The Communist-sponsored partisan movement originated in eastern Poland in 1941, when former Soviet prisoners of war joined Soviet paratroops and civilians, including a large number of Jews who had fled from ghettos to the countryside. As early as fall of 1941, Soviet paratroops with large amounts of money landed at various points in Poland and tried to organize partisan activities against the Germans. In Warsaw, an NKVD major, portraying himself as an intelligence officer, made contact with the Jewish Ghetto in September 1941. Two months later, a group of Polish and Jewish Communists, who had been indoctrinated by the Comintern, parachuted near Warsaw and, together with another group which landed later, established the Polish Workers Party on January 5, 1942, thus reviving the Communist party that had been dissolved four years earlier. Among the leaders was Pawel Finder, a Jew, who succeeded Marceli Nowotko as secretary of the party in November 1942.[51]

Jews had always played a major role in the Communist party in Poland. Prior to the dissolution of the party in 1938, Jews constituted 25 percent of the membership; in urban areas in central Poland, the percentage rose to 50 percent. The Jewish section of the Communist party in Poland was second only to the Jewish Bund in the number of adherents.[52] It was natural, then, that when Stalin decided to revive the party, the Warsaw Jews, who had been among the most dedicated Communists, would constitute the nucleus of the revived organization. Even Jewish Communists from other ghettos came to Warsaw to participate in the organization of the Polish Workers Party.

In March 1942, the Communists organized their military arm, the People's Guard, in which 30 percent of the members that year were partisans; later, in 1944, the organization became known as the People's Army. The Jewish leader Hanka Szapiro-Sawicka was the chief organizer and head of the Youth Struggle Organization (*Związek Walki Młodych*), which was an affiliate of the Polish Workers Party and provided it with most of the manpower for the GL/AL.[53] Significantly, in addition to Polish and Jewish Communists, there were approximately 5,000 Soviet members of the GL/AL in the period 1942-45.

Anxious to impress the Polish population that the Communists were the most militant of all underground groups in their opposition to the Germans, the GL began operations in May 1942. Though the military value, of the targets was often small—e.g., the GL bombed a German coffee house in October[54]—and casualties large, these operations popularized Communist activity and made the party a political factor that could not be ignored. Though deeply divided and unable to attract a popular following—there were probably only 1500-2000 members of the GL in 1942, and membership in the GL was larger than the party[55]—the Communists went on in December 1943 to establish the National Council of the Homeland (*Krajowa Rada Narodowa*), a challenge to the political legitimacy of the Polish government-in-exile and its representatives in Poland. It even asked for but did not receive diplomatic recognition from the United States. In July 1944, the Kremlin created the Polish Committee of National Liberation at Chełm, which later moved its activities to Lublin. Early in 1945, Stalin granted diplomatic recognition to the Lublin Committee, as it was popularly known, as the legal government of Poland.[56]

Jews were members of virtually all organizations of the Polish underground during World War II. That one found Jews within the various organizations comprising the ZWZ/AK should not be surprising since large numbers of them served in the Polish army before the outbreak of World War II; many held high positions in important units, the Polish General Staff, the Inspectorate General, and the War Ministry. Some held the rank of general. No accurate statistics are available for the number of Jews who were members of AK units, but it appears that the figure was at least several hundred. At the time of the Warsaw Uprising in 1944, it is estimated that 1,000 Jews fought with the AK against the Germans.[57] Moreover, several Jews occupied important leadership positions in the Bureau of Information and Propaganda of the AK. Indeed, there were so many Jews in that organization, it gave rise to criticism from some Poles.[58]

Jewish sources have tended to exaggerate anti-Semitism as a major factor to explain the lower numbers of Jewish personnel in the AK compared to those in the GL/AL and Soviet partisan units. Indeed, anti-Semitism existed in the AK, but it appears to have been far less common on higher command levels than in lower ranks. What one found in the way of anti-Semitic attitudes in the lower ranks would only mirror attitudes and opinions of the right-wing (but not the extreme wing, because it was not a part of the AK during most of the war). Right-wing sentiments constituted only a portion of the attitudes of Poles in the AK. After all, the AK included large numbers of men from the Peasant Party, the Socialists, the Labor Party, and other moderate groups who were quite sympathetic toward Jews. It was not unusual to find many individuals in the National Democratic Party who were loyal and sympathetic toward Jews, for the war brought about numerous changes among members of the National Democratic Party in their attitudes toward Jews. Moreover, there were many officers in the AK, some of high rank, who had no party affiliation but strongly believed in liberal values.[59]

Henryk Woliński, who headed the Jewish Bureau of the AK and was highly regarded by his Jewish contacts in and outside of the Warsaw Ghetto, related: "Never, not in the slightest way, did I come across signs of anti-Semitism, either from the side of the High Command of the Home Army or from the BIP [Bureau of Information and Propaganda]."[60] Woliński joined Korboński, who headed the underground's agency for civil resistance and was subsequently decorated by Yad Vashem for aiding Jews during the war, in affirming that the two men who headed the ZWZ/AK—Rowecki and Bór-Komorowski—were not anti-Semitic. If anything, Rowecki was pro-Jewish, as Woliński described him, a man who prevailed on the government delegate on two occasions in the spring or summer of 1942 to establish an organization to aid the Jews.[61]

In any case, the primary reason there were not more Jews in the AK had less to do with anti-Semitism than it did with the fact that most Jews were unassimilated—they did not know Polish well or at all—and their physiognomy gave them away. The vast majority of the members of the AK were civilians, subject only to mobilization, who went about their jobs and daily routines unnoticed. Most Jews could not function that way. If they managed to escape from the ghettos, they had to hide. The logical place to go was the forest. When Jews went there, they usually found and joined partisan units organized by the Soviets and the GL/AL, not the AK, because for a long time the AK did not place the priority on partisan warfare that it did later. Jews who lived in eastern Poland had some advantage over their kinsmen elsewhere, because it was easier to flee from a small town or village and find shelter in a nearby forest than it was to escape from the urban ghettos of Warsaw or Lodz where German control and separation from the Polish community was nearly absolute.

Thus most Jewish partisans could be found in the GL/AL rather than the AK. Although no reliable statistical data exist, one student of the subject estimates that as many as 5,000 Jewish partisans were in the GL/AL and the Peasant Battalions that operated in the General Government. Out of the first nine GL units operating in the Kielce area in the period 1942-43, three units were Jewish, one was predominantly Jewish, and Jews constituted a large proportion of the membership in two others. Large numbers of Jews could also be found in the ranks of Soviet partisans; ninety-two Soviet partisan formations had Jewish commanders, and hundreds of them received coveted decorations, such as the "Order of Lenin," for their bravery.[62] Although Jews could also be found in the AK, Peasant Battalions, and other Polish formations, the Jewish partisan movement, which numbered approximately thirty units,[63] was primarily linked with the Communists.

In view of the close association of Jews with Polish and Soviet Communists, who were regarded as traitors in the eyes of Poles loyal to the Polish government and its representatives in Poland, little wonder there was considerable hostility between Poles and Jews in the partisan movement. Even Shmuel Krakowski, a historian who is unabashedly pro-Jewish in his sympathies, comes close to implying this when he writes:

"In the beginning, the attitude of the local peasants to the [Jewish] partisans was fairly tolerant and they supplied the partisans with food and clothing. But a drastic change for the worse came about as early as July, 1943, when the local AK organizations began provoking the Jewish partisans and inciting the village population against them. This attitude can most likely be viewed as a result of the Home Army's decision not to tolerate a new partisan force connected to the People's Guard in an area that, until then, had been under its influence."[64] Long-standing Polish charges of Judeo-Communism were confirmed in the eyes of Poles who saw Jews collaborating with Poland's "other enemy," and this understandably revived anti-Semitic feelings in some Poles. Unfortunately, latter day commentators have failed to show the complexity of the situation and have been content, instead, to label, erroneously, the entire AK as an anti-Semitic organization.

To be sure, there were incidents of AK units attacking Jewish partisans, but most of these seem to have been motivated primarily by political rather than anti-Semitic reasons. It would seem implausible that in the ferocious partisan struggle between the AK and Communists that went on in eastern Poland (very much encouraged by the Germans), AK units would have the time or inclination to differentiate between Jewish and non-Jewish Communist partisans before they fired on them. Moreover, if AK authorities established that their units were involved in attacks against innocent Jews, the AK made an effort to bring the men to justice.[65] Naturally, this was a difficult task, considering the complexion and the problem of discipline that characterized partisan units in general, not only those affiliated with the AK. As Michael Borwicz, a Jew who commanded socialist fighting units in the AK, remarked:

> It should . . . be remembered that there were difficulties of control in those conditions of conspiracy, when, as sometimes occurred, some minor local leader would act as he saw fit and arbitrarily. It is true that they sometimes did punishable things, but this does not justify distorted generalizations, since what they did was not the result of orders they received. . . .
> To my great sorrow, similar punishable acts also occurred in the Communist "Popular Army," the AL (*Armia Ludowa*), but here, too, we should not succumb to distorted generalizations.[66]

Moreover, the number of alleged incidents of AK units against Jewish partisans seems to be greatly exaggerated in view of the fact that the AK had only a small partisan movement at the time when Jewish units flourished. By late 1943, when the AK partisan movement began to burgeon, most Jews had already been liquidated by the Nazis.

Finally, it is well known that the National Armed Forces (NSZ), a right-wing, anti-Semitic organization which operated in eastern Poland, was the primary enemy of Jewish partisans. The NSZ was not subordinated to the AK; only a portion of them were in March 1944, when Jewish partisan groups had already been exterminated by the Germans. The NSZ waged war not only against the Jews but also against Poles suspected by them of left-wing sympathies. There were numerous cases where members of the AK were charged with murdering Jews when, in reality, the culprits were probably the NSZ. Even individuals who were either personally involved in or knew of these tragic incidents were confused and uncertain concerning who, in fact, were responsible for killing Jews.[67] One wonders how many Andrzej Kielbasas there were in the underground. Kielbasa led an armed anti-Semitic group that had a brief affiliation with the AK before it became part of the NSZ.

Often people saw little difference between the AK and the communist AL, which made things even more confusing.[68] As Borwicz correctly pointed out, there were also cases of Jews being slaughtered by the GL/AL; for example, a Jewish partisan unit of over forty men was almost completely wiped out by the commander of a GL detachment. There were cases of Jews who questioned the propaganda indoctrination of the Communist unit to which they belonged and died for it. As one Jewish survivor of one of these Communist units pointed out to a Polish underground leader, "I survived because I kept my mouth shut."[69]

Life in the world of the partisans in eastern Poland was extremely cruel, perhaps the worst of any place in Europe. Human life had no value, and incidents of barbarity and betrayal were commonplace. Everyone, including the Jews who lived and operated in this bitter world, was affected by it. Jews were also involved in robbery, rape, and pillage. Often Poles were victims. Even Reuben Ainsztein, a Jewish apologist, admitted: "It was a barbarism that even some Jews, especially those with a criminal background, did not escape. Thus, in Galicia, where in the absence of an organized anti-German partisan movement groups of armed Jews simply tried to survive in the forests, there were cases of fratricidal murder motivated by the urge to obtain arms. In the Białystok region such a 'wild group' of Jews, as they were called, raped several Byelorussian peasant girls and stabbed to death two Jewish partisans of the Jewish Forois Detachment to get hold of their rifles."[70] In these circumstances, one wonders if it is historically justified to claim that the anti-Semitism of some Poles of the AK toward Jewish partisans was always without some foundation.[71]

The AK was keenly aware of its limitations in establishing a military presence in an area that was in a state of anarchy. Large-scale German

pacification operations coupled with internecine conflicts among antago-
nistic partisan groups who often robbed the local peasants made life unbearable for everyone in this region. Poles criticized the AK for not doing
enough to help the people in eastern Poland who were victimized by hostile partisans. One Polish critic claimed there was more contact between
Warsaw and London than between Warsaw and Lwów.

The consequence was that Poles in eastern Poland felt isolated and
forgotten by the people living in central Poland.[72] In Wołyń the situation
was especially bad; Ukrainian collaborators, well armed and supported by
the Germans, carried out an enormous slaughter of Poles. In Tarnopol
alone Ukrainians killed 43 Poles in August 1943, 61 in September, 93 in
October, 127 in November, 309 in December, 466 in January 1944. In
Nowogródek and Wilno, Communist bands made up of Belorussians,
Lithuanians, and Jews, robbed the Poles and sought to eliminate them
from the area. Despite the AK's efforts to check these outrages against the
Poles in eastern Poland, Bór-Komorowski reported in March 1944 that
"murders increase." The AK's inability to establish firmly its presence,
especially in southeastern Poland, played into the hands of the Communists, who argued that the local residents could not get along without them
and that the area, disputed between the Poles and Russians, should revert
to the Soviet Union.[73]

In an effort to demonstrate the concern of the AK and its military
presence in the area, General Bór-Komorowski attempted to curb the robbery and plunder of the peasants in which various bands, including Jews,
engaged. As he later described the "forest folk" who lived by plunder and
violence:

> They were wild bands of all sorts of refugees living by robbery, and were a
> terrible plague to people in the neighborhood, who were visited nearly every
> night by bandits, who gradually deprived them of their last belongings. The
> result was still another emigration to the forests of those who had been com-
> pletely stripped of their belongings. Many of them joined our partisan units.
> We could not, however, accept everybody in our ranks. We could certainly
> not accept those who had looting and violence on their conscience. It would
> indeed have been tantamount to the Home Army's acceptance of responsibil-
> ity for their deeds—a course which I had to avoid at all costs.[74]

It was a tragic situation. Many bandits were local people who had become
criminals after the Germans forced them from their homes. Others were
members of the criminal world. Frequently Jews joined these groups of
bandits or formed groups of their own. Conditions were so bad that one
village, Rossosz, had been assaulted by bandits 120 times before it was

secured by friendly partisans. The policy of the AK was to court-martial gang members; AK soldiers were treated the same as others found guilty of plunder and robbery.[75]

In a report to Polish headquarters in London on August 31, 1943, Bór revealed that he had directed that leaders of these bands—not the entire band—be eliminated. He clearly placed primary responsibility for much of the plunder and murder on Soviet bands, but he also mentioned the part played by Jews, especially Jewish women. Bór's order was interpreted by some to justify attacks against Communist partisans, not merely robber bandits. The Communists managed to get a copy of his directive and informed the West of its contents. Bór accused the NSZ of liquidating Communist partisans which, he said, was not the intention of his instructions. In December 1943, for example, he condemned the attack of the NSZ on AL units which had resulted in the death of twenty-six men.[76]

To most military officials in Britain and the United States, the most valued contribution of the ZWZ/AK to the war effort was the intelligence it provided to the Allies. The ZWZ/AK was responsible for informing the British about the German preparations for the invasion of the Soviet Union months before it occurred, the German drive toward the Caucasus oil fields in 1942, and the identification of the German rocket site at Peenemunde which the Allies bombed. The Poles even provided the British with parts of a V-2 weapon.

Polish authorities in London regarded the intelligence-gathering role of the ZWZ/AK as critically important. In a message to Rowecki in January 1940, Sosnkowski listed intelligence as the primary task of the military underground, a view he underscored again after the fall of France. The British were highly complimentary of Polish intelligence. After the war on the eastern front began, British intelligence agencies considered Polish intelligence regarding the German order of battle as "the best source of information," and also rated Polish information on the German wartime economy very highly.[77] In January 1943, the British Admiralty was impressed with the value of intelligence they received from the Poles concerning German naval installations and operations in the Gdynia area. The British Ministry of Aircraft Production in 1944 acknowledged: "Reports from Polish sources are considered as the most valuable of all we received. They contain entirely trustworthy information."[78] But the Germans themselves gave the Poles the supreme accolade. On December 31, 1942, Himmler wrote: "Within the framework of the entire enemy intelligence operations directed against Germany, the intelligence service of the

Polish resistance movement assumed major significance. The scope and importance of the operations of the Polish resistance movement, which was ramified down to the smallest splinter group and brilliantly organized, have been in (various sources) disclosed in connection with carrying out of major police security operations."[79]

As Himmler pointed out, the Poles had created a sophisticated intelligence network that not only webbed the General Government but also reached deeply into the Reich itself. Recruits came from all walks of life, and unlike other intelligence systems, the ZWZ/AK did not rely on or employ paid agents. Army officers held command positions in the structure, but often university professors and engineers handled special problems. Since one of the main sources of information was economic intelligence, the underground established two organizations to study and evaluate the reports which came from Polish agents concerning the location of factories, industrial production, and lines of communication.[80]

Since many of the prewar intelligence experts were in exile abroad, the ZWZ/AK had to train many new intelligence experts. Thanks to the establishment of an air shuttle between Britain and Poland in 1942, thirty-three intelligence officers who had been trained in Britain parachuted into Poland by the end of 1944. Despite the loss to the Gestapo of the first two AK intelligence chiefs and members of their staffs, Bór reported that the work of the organization had not been seriously compromised. On the contrary, he said, "under the direction of its third chief, it achieved its best results in the years 1943–44 and rendered valuable service to the Allies."[81]

One of the ways to get intelligence agents into the Reich was to have them volunteer for the periodic German demands for Polish labor in Germany. Since most Poles avoided volunteering for such work and regarded those who did as traitors, it was not an easy task for these agents; they risked injury, or even sometimes death, from their own kinsmen. Polish intelligence used all potential sources of information, including Polish officers and enlisted men in German prisons whom they contacted and provided with transmitters and receivers. Between March and August 1943, the number of informants in prisoner-of-war camps increased from 49 to 109.[82]

AK intelligence reports reached London by radio and courier. As will be seen later, the fall of France greatly complicated the lines of communication between Poland and the West, and alternative courier routes had to be developed. The AK sent more important reports by radio; beginning in the autumn of 1940, it sent weekly reports to London. During the period 1942-44, the volume of intelligence traffic reached 300 reports every month and constituted 40 to 50 percent of all the radio correspondence between Warsaw and London. Two times a day during the war, the Poles radioed London weather data, which, combined with what the British received from Stockholm and Istanbul, enabled air force meteorologists to forecast the weather over Germany and to plan more accurately missions over German-occupied Europe. The AK supplemented radio reports by sending couriers to the West; beginning in 1941, the AK dispatched one courier every month with a report on microfilm that averaged 150-200 pages.[83]

The AK gathered intelligence for its own use and for the western Allies. In view of the state of relations between Poland and the Soviet Union, especially after the Katyń affair in April 1943, the AK had no regular communication links with the Russians. Even when diplomatic relations existed between the two countries, the Poles were understandably reluctant to cooperate with the Soviets because they feared further NKVD penetration of the ZWZ/AK. Rowecki reported that the NKVD had infiltrated the high command of the ZWZ and were well informed about the structure and operations of the organization. The Soviets even knew one of Rowecki's pseudonyms—Rakoń. Major Emil Macieliński (Kornel), who ostensibly worked for the AK, was a top NKVD agent whom the AK condemned to death for his treachery.[84]

Despite Sikorski's intention to revive Polish-Soviet relations and to maintain them in the postwar period, even he opposed close intelligence contacts with the Soviets for the same reasons Rowecki did.[85] There was a brief period from April to July 1942, when the AK had radio liaison with the Russians, but even this limited contact ended when relations deteriorated over the question of training and equipping the Anders army in the Soviet Union.[86] Nonetheless, much of the intelligence that the AK provided the British subsequently was conveyed by them to the Soviets; one source was the British military mission in Moscow.

The flow of AK intelligence was to the British, who established close collaboration between their Special Operations Executive (SOE) and the Polish General Staff's Sixth Bureau (Intelligence), headed by General Sosnkowski. The Polish section of the SOE, created in the summer of 1940 and headed by Captain Harold Perkins, was to assist the Sixth Bureau in maintaining communications with Poland, training agents, and delivering supplies and personnel to Poland. In reality, the London Poles took charge of their own operations with Poland and were the only foreign nationals allowed to use their own cypher for radio liaison with Poland. "Until the very last days of the war," one British historian observed, "no British mission, as such, landed on Polish soil, and the operations technically organized by the SOE from Britain to Poland were essentially conducted by the London Poles acting as an independent power."[87]

Polish intelligence operatives were everywhere. Several worked for the British. One of the most effective rings was a Polish-Swedish connection, which was uncovered in 1942, resulting in the arrest and execution of fifty-one Poles. Swedes who had lived in Warsaw had great sympathy for the Poles; they usually smuggled out reports of the AK and returned with much needed money to finance AK operations. They also engaged in rescue work. The "Pesky Pole", described by Himmler as "the world's most dangerous espionage operative" because of the damage he did to German-Japanese relations, was Major Michał Rybikowski. Employed by the British, Rybikowski served "as a conduit to convey doctored intelligence to the Germans via the Japanese."[88]

Ladislas Farago also described a Polish staff officer who fought in Poland in 1939 and in France in 1940. After the French military collapse, Hubert, as he was known, organized one of the first underground groups in France. Though betrayed to the Germans, he made an arrangement with the *Abwehr* to work for the Germans in England. As soon as he reached London, he informed the British of the deal and ended up working for them under the code name Brutus. His mission, as Ladislas Farago described it, was "to persuade the Germans that the American army under Bradley would remain in England after the British forces of General Montgomery had landed in Normandy, to mount the main assault in the Pas de Calais area."[89]

Perhaps one of the most unappreciated Polish agents was Christine Granville, a bright young woman of Polish nobility, who collected intelligence and arranged for the escape from Poland of several Poles and British prisoners of war who had found their way to Poland after Dunkirk. She made several trips from Hungary to Poland over the Tatra Mountains and had special contacts with the Musketeers, a Polish intelligence organization with whom she had close ties. Granville also provided the British with German troop deployments and preparations prior to the invasion of the Soviet Union.[90]

The Poles made their greatest intelligence coup even before the war broke out. Polish cryptologists, Marian Rejewski, Jerzy Różycki, and Henryk Zygalski, who worked in the Intelligence Bureau of the Polish General Staff, succeeded in duplicating the German cipher machine, *Enigma*, thus enabling the Poles to begin reading German radiograms as early as 1932. The Polish feat was aided by the French, who had provided the Poles with critical German documentation. The Poles told the British and French intelligence agents how they broke *Enigma* and provided the representatives of both countries with duplicate machines before the war began. After the invasion of Poland, Polish cryptologists worked with their French counterparts on *Enigma* in France.[91] Based on the Allied reading of German radio messages enciphered on the *Enigma* machine during the war (information which came to light only within the last decade), a rewriting of the military history of the Second World War is necessary. When that is done, the Polish intelligence contribution to winning the war will play a critical, if not decisive, role, an ironic twist for a country which had been defeated by the Germans in the first month of World War II.

Among other notable accomplishments of Polish intelligence were the detailed reports it provided the British concerning German preparations for Operation Barbarossa, the code name for the invasion of the Soviet Union.[92] The British, in turn, sent the information to Stalin, who, oddly enough, did not alert his armed forces. The result was a Soviet debacle on the eastern front, enabling the German armies to drive deeply into the Soviet Union. On this occasion, declared Churchill, Stalin and his cronies were "the most completely outwitted bunglers of the Second World War." And in the post-Stalin era, even Soviet historians have come close to agreement with Churchill.[93] Polish intelligence expanded its operations on the eastern front in 1941 and correctly predicted, based on German troop deployments, that the Germans would make a major drive for the Caucasian oil fields in 1942.[94]

In response to the Allied air bombardment of Germany, Hitler intended to launch a decisive attack on England by hurling V-1 and V-2 rockets at the British. He gave top priority to the German rocket program. Thanks largely to intelligence received from Polish sources, the British got valuable information that enabled them, on August 17, 1943, to launch a massive air attack on Peenemunde, where the rockets were being tested.[95]

Undaunted, the Germans shifted their experimental station to Blizna, east of Cracow and out of bomber range of Anglo-American air forces. There in the Polish lowlands the Germans constructed a new testing area. To camouflage their activities in the area, the Germans placed wooden cows on the surrounding grazing grounds and dolls near empty cottages, and even hung clothes on lines in deserted cottage gardens.[96] None of this escaped the notice of Polish intelligence which kept the British informed of developments in the area. AK observers recorded the technicalities of every German test, General Bór said, "and a flying squad was detailed to gather the fragments after every explosion, having each time to win a race with special motorized teams employed to obliterate all tell-tale debris.

Although the Germans had motor-cars at their disposal, while our agents had only their legs to depend on, our patrols often got there ahead of the Germans."[97] After one German test, the AK managed to retrieve a rocket that had been hardly damaged. Polish experts dismounted, photographed, and described their find. On July 25, 1944, a Dakota aircraft from Brindisi, Italy, arrived in Poland, picked up Captain Jerzy Chmielewski of the AK, who had a detailed report from General Bór on the rocket and a bag of its undamaged parts which found their way to British intelligence. This was only the third time that an air bridge with Poland had been established and this was only possible because of the transfer of allied bases to Italy which enabled these secret air force missions to Poland to take place.[98]

The rocket affair was a major intelligence accomplishment. Without the intelligence and the bombing of Peenemunde, Hitler undoubtedly would have been able to bomb London and other targets in southern England sooner than he did. Meanwhile, the Allies had invaded France, overrun German rocket bases there, and forced the Germans to fire them from Holland, which seriously interfered with the accuracy of the weapon. General Dwight D. Eisenhower, who commanded the amphibious assault on France in June 1944, claimed that failure to interfere with the German rocket program would have made it difficult, "perhaps impossible," to launch the Allied invasion.[99]

The effectiveness of Polish intelligence would have been severely handicapped had the Polish underground not been able to establish regular radio and courier communications abroad. Radio contact between Poland and Polish authorities in Budapest, Bucharest, Istanbul, and Paris was established by the spring of 1940. After the fall of France and the transfer of the Polish government to London, radio contact between Warsaw and London was delayed until the autumn of 1940.[100] According to M.R.D. Foot, "Polish clandestine wireless was judged at the time to be 'outstandingly good,' in advance of any comparable service in the world, and at times as many as 100 sets were working at once out of Poland to bases in England and Italy."[101] The Poles produced many transmitters and receivers of their own; by 1943, they produced 6 to 8 transmitters monthly. Air drops from the West supplemented radio sets produced at home, but these never kept up with demand. Up to the Warsaw Uprising in 1944, the Poles trained over 300 wireless operators. Out of the 350 people parachuted into Poland from abroad, many of these were radio operators.[102]

Among the problems involved in communications work was the constant danger the Germans would discover the radio station; many operators met their deaths at their sets. In order to baffle the Germans, operators usually did not stay on the air longer than two hours, and changed their locations every few days. Receivers, less vulnerable than transmitters, could work in one place up to a month. Since most of the broadcasts centered in Warsaw, this only increased the intensity of German attempts to penetrate the system. Thus radio transmissions from Warsaw eventually had to be limited to twenty minutes. The vulnerability of the system to discovery by the Germans underscored the need to establish radio stations outside the capital; in March 1942, the AK established a radio station in Kielce. Early in 1942, a special radio station had been established for use by the government delegate, but it was less powerful than that used by the AK.[103]

In addition to the sophisticated radio network, the Polish underground had developed an impressive series of courier routes which were used with varying degrees of effectiveness and were vital to the communication links between Poland and the western allies. During the war, the Poles developed at least ten courier and postal routes to the West, but only seven of them were regularly used.[104] Prior to the fall of France in June 1940, the Poles used the route by way of Bucharest and Budapest through Italy, which was then neutral. At the same time, it had contacts through Kovno in Lithuania until June 1940.

After the defeat of France, the occupation of Lithuania by the Soviets, and the closer relationship between the Reich and Romania, the Poles had to look for other possibilities. The important Polish base in Hungary continued to operate, despite the formal break in Polish-Hungarian relations, testifying to the closeness that had existed between the two peoples for centuries. The communication link between Budapest and Warsaw was so safe that not a single emissary from Polish headquarters in London was arrested along this route. Budapest played a major role until the German occupation of Hungary in 1944. Alternative routes out of Warsaw relied on Berne, Switzerland, and Stockholm, Sweden, and thence to England. There was even a number of courier routes through the heart of the Reich—Berlin—and thence to France and the Iberian Peninsula to London. Until couriers from the West first parachuted into Poland in February 1941, they too had to use overland routes.[105] One courier left London in November 1940, and followed a route from Portugal across Africa, including Gambia, Sierra Leone, Nigeria, Belgian Congo, Sudan, Egypt, Palestine, Cyprus, Turkey, Yugoslavia, Hungary—and finally to Poland.[106]

Throughout the war, all westward-bound traffic had to follow one of the established land routes. While it took a courier seven to ten days to make it from Warsaw to Paris before the defeat of France, it took seven weeks to make the journey after that. Despite the obvious problems, the overland routes were used heavily. For example, the AK dispatched forty-four couriers and emissaries from Warsaw to Polish bases outside of Poland, including headquarters in London, from September 1942 to March 1943.[107]

Within Poland itself, the AK also used radio and courier communications. It was especially difficult to maintain regular courier contact with the area of Poland occupied by the Soviets, a difficulty that was exacerbated following the outbreak of German-Soviet hostilities. Prior to June 1941, for example, only sixteen out of eighty-six couriers dispatched to the area were able to complete the mission assigned to them.[108]

There were comical moments too. On one occasion, German guards became suspicious of a Polish courier who wore a German uniform in order to pass through an area. When the Germans demanded that the Pole strip to his underwear, they noticed that he did not have a military stamp on his shorts, thus revealing that he was not a German soldier. The Germans arrested and sent the Pole to prison from where he smuggled a message to AK authorities, telling them that in the future all couriers should have properly stamped underwear. The AK lost little time in issuing couriers properly stamped underwear. Meanwhile, German authorities were so convinced they had discovered a foolproof method of control, that they forced everyone, including bona fide German soldiers, to drop their pants for underwear checks, neglecting in the process other methods of spotting imposters. The result was AK couriers easily passing through German control points while German soldiers vented their anger over the indignity of being subjected to these embarrassing checks.[109]

Air drops from England to Poland never met with Polish expectations. The long distances, poor weather, inadequate aircraft, and other priorities conspired to keep these missions to a minimum. It was not until February 1941 that a flight in an adapted Whitley airplane made it to the annexed area of Poland, dropping three parachutists. Further flights were deferred because of light nights until the winter of 1941-42, when 9 out of 12 planes succeeded. There was improvement from August 1942 to April 1943, when 42 out of 65 flights succeeded in completing their missions. But from August 1943 to July 1944, 205 out of 381 planes completed their missions. Altogether, up to the Warsaw Uprising, the flights dropped over 300 tons of supplies, more than 300 parachutists, most of whom were soldiers, and considerable amounts of money to the underground. In the period from August 1944 to December 1944, most of the air operations were intended to aid directly the Polish insurgents during the Warsaw Uprising; 227 flights out of 400 succeeded in dropping 280 tons, almost as much as during the whole of the preceding three years.[110] Even though these numbers did not loom large compared to the needs that existed, one historian aptly observed, "Both psychologically and materially, the consciousness of support from the outside had decisive importance, for material support was also a psychological stimulus. One was not forgotten, and one had joined the struggle." General Bór-Komorowski's reaction to these air drops confirmed this: "These men brought with them the very breath of liberty."[111]

As the Germans increased their terrorization of the Polish population, there was a corresponding increase in reprisal operations by the AK. The AK launched so many reprisal attacks that the list of casualties of officials seriously alarmed Berlin. Only 3 out of the 123 German casualties reported from January 1 to July 31, 1943, were not employed in any official capacity. The AK considered members of the police, SS and SA, labor office, and railroad system among their primary targets. Because of the particular brutality of the police, the AK murdered 361 gendarmes in 1943, and in the first six months of 1944 killed 584 of them. By 1944, it was estimated that in Warsaw alone the Poles killed 10 Germans every day.[112] Some of the leading German casualties included the German mayor of Radom, Weigandt; the chief of police of Radom, Fruhbuss; and the director of the Warsaw Labor Office, Kurt Hoffmann.[113] It was quite common for Polish authorities in London to receive messages like these from Poland:

> October 11, 1943. Communique of the DUS [Directorate of Underground Struggle] No. 16. On October 1, 12:05 hours, in Warsaw, killed by shooting, SS-Sturmann, Ernst Wepels, the cruel oppressor and executioner in the Women's Prison in Pawiak.

> June 21, 1944. In the period June 2-10, by order of the DUS, 136 Gestapo agents and spies, including Willie Holtze, August Gering, and Kammertentz, were executed in the provinces of Warsaw, Lublin, and Kielce.[114]

The most spectacular murder was that of General Franz Kutschera, the SS and police leader in Warsaw, who was responsible for inaugurating the street executions in Warsaw. In the face of this massive terror, the government delegate and the heads of the major political parties considered whether the Poles should stop armed attacks against the Germans. Polish authorities unanimously decided to continue them because they feared that by doing otherwise the Nazis might interpret it to mean they had succeeded in breaking the morale of the Poles.[115] The AK slated Kutschera himself for elimination in December 1943. Colonel Emil Fieldorf, special operations chief of *Kedyw*, entrusted the operation to the Pegasus (*Pegaz*), a unit of the AK. On February 1, 1944, after weeks of planning, a platoon of Pegasus, commanded by twenty-year old Bronisław Pietraszkiewicz, attacked Kutschera's car on Ujazdowskie Avenue. In an operation lasting scarcely a minute, Kutschera and several other Germans were killed, but four of the attackers, including Pietraszkiewicz, were killed. The next day the Germans retaliated by executing 100 Poles on the site of the ambush on Ujazdowskie Avenue; another 200 were shot in the Ghetto, bringing the total number of victims on that day to 300. But Kutschera's execution did bring an end to the public executions in the Polish capital.[116]

German officials had every reason to be concerned about the growing insecurity for the German colony in the General Government. On December 7, 1942, Governor Ludwig Fischer of Warsaw, whom the Poles tried but failed to kill, complained about the deterioration of security in his district. German governors of other Polish districts echoed the same feeling. Secretary of State Kruger paid the Poles a grudging compliment in telling his cronies that the Polish people were brilliant conspirators who exploited every opportunity to press forward with their underground activities. But he could offer no encouragement that the situation would ever improve. "Poles were and will be enemies of Germans," he declared, predicting that the Polish resistance would solidify even more as the war lengthened and the food situation worsened.[117] Statistics of AK attacks on the German administration and its apparatus of terror supported Kruger's pessimistic view: From August to December 1942, the AK launched 87 such attacks; during the first four months of 1943, the AK increased these attacks to 514.[118] Little wonder that the German colony in Poland lived in their own neighborhoods and barricaded all of its most important buildings. Rarely if ever did one see a German walking alone on a Polish street. The situation so depressed some Germans that they did not expect to leave the country alive.[119]

The AK suffered heavy losses too. The Germans scored many successes in infiltrating and arresting key members of the AK. In 1941, the Germans arrested several high-ranking officers of the Union for Revenge (*Związek Odwetu*), including the chief of staff of the High Command of the ZWZ, Colonel Janusz Albrecht.[120] As has been seen, the ZWZ/AK lost its first two heads of Polish intelligence to the Gestapo. The Gestapo infiltrated the Sword and Plow (*Miecz i Pług*), a right-wing organization that had been subordinated to the ZWZ/AK, and the AK shot three of the organization's top leaders for being Gestapo agents.[121] Obviously, the arrests and executions of ZWZ/AK officers created shortages of people to fill leadership positions, a condition that Rowecki understandably deplored. Prior to the outbreak of the Warsaw Uprising in August 1944, the AK lost to the Germans an estimated 62,133 officers, noncommissioned officers, and enlisted men.[122] During the period from September 1, 1943 to February 29, 1944, Bór reported that 14,221 officers and enlisted men had been killed, arrested, and taken prisoner, representing a 119 percent increase in the number of officers and enlisted men lost to the Germans during the previous reporting period. Though the Polish resistance killed about 150,000 Germans, this did not come remotely close to the 5,384,000 Polish citizens killed by the Germans during the occupation.[123]

Among the greatest losses to the Poles was the arrest and subsequent execution of General Rowecki. On the morning of June 30, 1943, Rowecki had entered a home on Spiśka Street in Warsaw. A few minutes later the SS arrived, surrounded the home, and took Rowecki prisoner. The German success was due to the betrayal of Rowecki by Ludwik Kalkstein, who was an intelligence officer in the AK, Eugeniusz Świerczewski, his brother-in-law, and Blanka Kaczorowska, Świerczewski's fiancee. It was Świerczewski who finally betrayed Rowecki to the Gestapo and was the principal operative in the conspiracy. Before the AK had an opportunity to rescue Rowecki, the Gestapo whisked him off to Berlin for interrogation. While there, Himmler sought but failed to win over the resistance leader as a collaborator. In return for Rowecki's cooperation with the Germans against the Russians, the Germans promised to grant the Poles autonomy under the Reich. When his German interrogators tried to get him to talk about the AK, Rowecki replied with dignity, "I will not speak about that." In July 1943, the Germans moved Rowecki to Sachsenhausen.[124]

General Bór-Komorowski, who succeeded Rowecki as head of the AK, suggested that his predecessor be exchanged for a high-ranking German in allied captivity. The Polish ambassador to Britain, Edward Raczyński, suggested that the British intervene in the matter and offer the Germans an exchange of a German general for Rowecki, a proposal repeated later by Stanisław Mikołajczyk, the new Polish premier, to Churchill. At a minimum, Mikołajczyk wanted Churchill to secure assurances that Rowecki would be treated as a prisoner of war.[125]

Little did Mikołajczyk realize that Foreign Secretary Anthony Eden on the previous day had ruled out British intervention in the matter, on the technical grounds that under international law, Rowecki was not a prisoner of war but a *franc-tireur*. Churchill initially seemed to favor the idea of an exchange of Generals Jürgen von Arnim and Wilhelm von Thoma for

Rowecki, though he doubted the Germans would accept the proposal, because the Nazi leadership rarely showed interest in people no longer in its employ. The British did not consider the matter very long before Churchill told Mikołajczyk on August 1, 1943, "To our regret we have been forced to the conclusion that intervention on the lines you suggest is not possible."[126]

Despite Polish urgings and the endorsement of the Special Operations Executive, the British government did not make a serious proposal to the Germans for an exchange. Subsequent efforts of the Poles to move the British on the matter met with failure. The British took the position, as one Foreign Office official put it, "that the chances of the Germans agreeing to any such exchange are negligible." The British ruled out the idea without even trying, content in the belief that they simply had no inducements to offer the Germans to release the Polish military leader. Some Foreign Office officials seemed to be overly concerned with Soviet reactions to an arrangement involving an exchange between a Polish and a German general, and the precedent that such an exchange would establish which other exile governments in London might exploit to secure the release of some of their resistance leaders. Few seemed willing to acknowledge that the Rowecki case was indeed exceptional. As for the reactions of the Soviets, one British official, obviously echoing a minority view, bluntly stated: "Surely if we choose to effect such an exchange this is our business? I have never noticed the Russians are anxious not to run any danger that we might misunderstand some action of theirs."[127] Furious with the Poles for launching the Warsaw Uprising in August 1944, Himmler ordered Rowecki's execution.[128]

The Poles suffered another shock within a few days of the arrest of General Rowecki. On July 4, 1943, a B-24 carrying General Sikorski on his way back to England from a trip to the Near East crashed off the coast of Gibraltor. Following the crash, a court of inquiry went along with the claim of the pilot, Flight Lt. Edward Prchal, that the accident was caused by the jamming of the plane's elevator controls which made the aircraft uncontrollable. But based on the evidence presented, the court was unable to explain how those elevator controls had become jammed. A Polish investigating commission did not entirely rule out sabotage, a view held by many people ever since.[129]

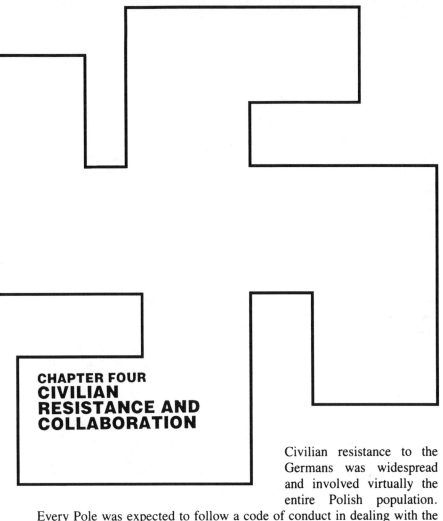

CHAPTER FOUR
CIVILIAN
RESISTANCE AND
COLLABORATION

Civilian resistance to the Germans was widespread and involved virtually the entire Polish population. Every Pole was expected to follow a code of conduct in dealing with the Germans, and underground authorities established an agency which institutionalized implacable hatred toward the occupier. Polish morale was maintained by many acts of resistance—both large and small—and by the piquant sense of humor of the Poles. In addition to economic sabotage, which Poles were encouraged to perform in factories, businesses, and farms, civilian resistance was also characterized by maintaining the entire fabric of Polish cultural life in the underground—schools, universities, theater, music, the press. This kind of resistance had less to do with damaging or destroying a particular aspect of the Nazi war machine than with expressing the individuality of the Poles. But it was no less damaging to the Nazi occupation than sabotage, diversionary, or reprisal operations because it defied the entire litany of Nazi laws and regulations which sought to extirpate the Polish nation. This kind of resistance could be

95

anything from a student attending a secret university class to an actress giving a reading from Henryk Sienkiewicz in a private home, from a youngster writing an anti-German slogan on a building to an elderly man helping to set type for a clandestine newspaper or a young girl secretly monitoring the latest broadcast on the BBC. It was all this and much more uniting the Poles against their hated enemy, and with it asserting their Polish identity.

All Poles were obliged to follow certain basic principles and rules of behavior during the German occupation—namely, to boycott all German orders or measures harmful to Poland, to conduct whenever possible sabotage against the Germans which would result in material and moral losses to Germany, and to obey Polish underground authorities, who represented the legal Polish government-in-exile. Based on these principles, a series of instructions, proclamations, and warnings were issued by the underground authorities through the underground press, the BBC, and the Polish radio station, SWIT. Because of the special situation in which the Poles in the annexed lands found themselves, few of these rules applied to them.[1]

In December 1942, Government Delegate Jan Piekalkiewicz established the Directorate of Civil Resistance, headed by Stefan Korboński, who served in that capacity throughout the existence of the organization. The Directorate of Civil Resistance was to see that Poles obeyed the rules of conduct during the occupation. It established a system of underground courts of justice, which heard major cases; and court commissions, a kind of people's court, which heard less serious infractions of the rules of civil resistance. The courts of justice were empowered, along with military courts, to administer capital punishment. The underground pronounced the first death sentences on Roman Leon Świecicki, an officer in the Blue Police who had taken part in street roundups of Poles and collaborated with a German police court that sentenced Poles to death, and Izydor Ossowski, an employee of the German Labor Office who pursued Poles seeking to avoid compulsory labor. There were also underground groups and individuals who usurped the authority of the Directorate and on their own liquidated people they considered guilty of some offense.

Court commissions could not pass the death sentence; instead, they reprimanded, censured, and pronounced judgments of infamy. Many Poles, including professionals, who were servile toward the Germans or who actively cooperated with them were censured and received sentences of infamy; in both cases, these were published in the underground press.

Often flogging was administered, especially in the countryside, to those who misappropriated Polish property; headshaving was meted out to women who socialized with Germans.[2]

Various political parties supplemented the injunctions and admonitions of the Directorate of Civil Resistance with those of their own. The Peasant Party, for example, came out with a series of recommendations to the peasants concerning their daily struggle under the occupation. Dubbed by one agent the "ten commandments" of resistance, these recommendations, which were printed in the underground press and even memorized by children, included: "Fight stubbornly for Poland's independence. . . . Serve your country honestly, for you are her nourisher. Sabotage the occupant's requisitions. . . . Be unyielding, cunning, and wise while dealing with the occupant. . . . Be merciless to traitors and provocateurs. . . . Have faith."[3]

The more intense the German terror became, the more it unified the Poles and strengthened their desire to resist. "The whole population in Poland is united in a hatred of the Germans whose intensity cannot be appreciated in this country," one British report stated; "the whole population is potentially resisting."[4] In addition to economic sabotage, already discussed, there were thousands of small incidents which occurred daily that testified to Polish hatred of the Germans and uplifted Polish morale: an old lady giving wrong directions to a German who wanted to get somewhere, a crooner singing anti-German songs in a streetcar to the delight of the Polish passengers, Polish school boys warning passengers in a bus of the approach of a German patrol in the vicinity, an old couple on opposite sides of a street warning pedestrians not to walk any further because of a German roundup ahead.[5] These were instinctive responses; it probably never even occurred to the people that what they did could have resulted in their own deaths.

Proof of Polish unity was dramatized by the support of the population for various boycotts. On September 1, 1940, the first anniversary of the outbreak of the war, the Poles in Warsaw emptied all cafes and restaurants between 2:00 and 4:00 P.M. and refused to buy German newspapers; instead, Poles went to church. At one point during the war, underground authorities forbade Poles to buy German newspapers on Fridays. Testimony to the confidence in and obedience toward their underground officials, Poles responded so well that the Germans had to curtail drastically the Friday edition of their newspapers. If a Pole disobeyed the boycott order, he was vulnerable to the ostracism of his neighbors: "An invisible hand might place a card on his back on which was written: 'This pig patronizes German trash.' On his house the next day, as if by magic, an inscription might appear in indelible paint: 'A fool lives here. A stupid, vile Pole who obeys the German gangsters instead of his own leaders.'"[6]

On November 11, 1941, Polish Independence Day, Varsovians observed a street boycott after 8:00 P.M. Underground units laid flowers on memorials and wrote pro-Polish and anti-German slogans on walls.[7] Most of these displays of "small sabotage" were conducted by *Wawer*, which carried out 150 such actions in the period 1941-43. Organized in December 1940 by Scout leaders, the group was made up of over 400 juveniles. The organization took its name from the village of Wawer where in December 1939, the Germans murdered scores of people; even though the Germans were responsible for countless other atrocities, Poles never forgot Wawer.[8] Members of the group threw acid bombs at Germans, placed Polish flags in conspicuous places, threw gas bombs in movie theaters frequented by Germans, and substituted the word *Verloren* (Lost) where the Germans had written *Victoria* (Won) to describe their military exploits.[9] On one occasion, *Wawer*'s boys rewrote a German propaganda poster that read "Germany conquers on all fronts" to read "Germany is prostrate on all fronts." These mischievous rascals, who did so much to maintain Polish morale and foster the spirit of resistance, unscrewed a tablet with German writing from a monument to Copernicus, and replaced it with one that read sardonically, "In retaliation for the destruction of the Kilinski statue [by the Germans], I order an extension of winter for six weeks. Nicholas Copernicus, astronomer." Bór remarked, "Strangely enough the winter that year did last much longer than usual and caused a severe setback to the German plans for a spring offensive on the eastern front."[10]

The Poles used their sharp sense of humor as an escape from the pain and suffering of their daily lives and as an act of resistance that revived hope against the occupier whom they scorned and laughed at. Some of the humor directly attacked Hitler: In the middle of Hitler's difficulties in conquering England, the Führer turned to a rabbi for help. The rabbi told him he needed the shepherd's crook that had parted the Red Sea for the Jews. "Fine!" the elated Hitler shouted, "And where do I find the crook?" The rabbi replied, "In the British Museum in London."[11]

The Poles unleashed their satire on the hated *Volksdeutsch* too. A piece from a German catechism was made to read: "Who are you?" "Sly German." "What is your sign?" "A broken cross." "Who gave you birth?" "A storm wind." "What awaits you?" "A dry branch."[12]

In reply to the question as to why there was a shortage of meat in

Poland, Poles answered: "Because the oxen have been sent to work in Germany, the horses have been sent to the front, the cows walk out with the Germans, and the swine spend their time in the cinemas."[13]

Since many Poles lived a life of conspiracy, when a person met a friend he had not seen for some time, it was likely the friend had been in hiding. This was assumed, sometimes too casually, as the following exchange between two men in a trolley illustrates:

> "Hello, Wisniewski," he shouts at the top of his voice, since he is wedged in between the other passengers. "What are you doing in Warsaw? Don't you live in Lwów any more?"
>
> "Hello Lesiński," the other shouts back in a voice equally stentorian. "It's good to see you. But stop calling me Wisniewski. I happen to be in *hiding*."[14]

A man who applied for a pass to travel to another area of Poland was asked by a German for his surname: "Schmidt," he answered. "First name?" "Henryk." "Place of birth?" "Berlin." "Are you a German?" "No, a Pole." "Where was your father born?" "In Berlin." "And your mother?" "In Berlin." "Then you are a German?" "Look," replied Schmidt, "If a hen lays an egg in a pig sty, does that necessarily make him a pig?"[15]

Poles chided themselves for the hope they shared in their eventual victory as seen in this doggerel:

They have no radios—but they know everything.
They don't have flour—but they eat pastries.
They have no army—but they'll win the war.
Who are they?—The Poles.[16]

The same hope in the future was reflected in the popular yarn: "God sent an angel to earth to learn the news. On his return the angel reported that everybody in Britain wears frock coats and sports clothes and talks about the war. In Germany everybody walks about in uniforms and talks about peace, but in Poland everybody is in concentration camps and prisons and shouts: 'We shall triumph!'"[17]

Polish attitudes about the outcome of the war fluctuated. Most Poles had expected the Germans to be quickly defeated when they invaded France. Polish morale plummetted after the French defeat, as demonstrated by a drop in recruits into the ZWZ. But Polish spirits picked up noticeably a year later when Hitler invaded the Soviet Union, reviving hope in a future allied victory over the Germans.[18] Many people hoped for a quick Soviet victory over the Germans; more thoughtful people hoped both sides would mutually exhaust themselves in the struggle.[19]

Poles paid close attention to the activities of their armed forces abroad. According to one Polish emissary who went from London to Poland, there was nothing that interested the average Pole more than the preparation of Polish soldiers in Britain for armed action against the Germans. Little did the Germans realize that when they published a photograph of the Polish army in Scotland, in the *Illustrierte Berliner Tageblatt*, it would become the most sought-after collector's item in Poland. When German authorities realized the positive impact the photograph had on the Poles, they confiscated the remnants of the issue and forbade it being sent to Poland.

The British were highly esteemed in Poland; there was even some discussion among some Poles that the Duke of Kent be considered a candidate for a postwar Polish monarchy.[20] At times, Polish faith in the western allies wavered, especially over the long delay in launching a major assault against the Germans. In May 1942, the government delegate warned the Polish government-in-exile about the impact of a prolonged war on the material and moral strength of the Polish people.[21] After the German defeat at Stalingrad, the inhabitants of Silesia in the annexed lands began to use Polish instead of German, dramatically telling the Germans how they felt toward them and expressing their confidence in an allied victory.[22] When Anglo-American forces invaded Italy and later Normandy, one report said, "Warsaw breathed, smiled, cried, and . . . got drunk."[23] By the summer of 1944, a Polish courier reported how the Poles were completely filled with the thought of an end to the nightmare they had to endure for so long. On the other hand, there was little thought to what would happen to the Poles when the Soviets replaced the Germans as the landlords of Poland.[24]

The German occupation had a demoralizing impact on the populace. The terror campaign against the Jews and Poles, the government delegate noted, increasingly deadened basic instincts of horror and pity because pain and tragedy had become so commonplace.[25] There was a decline in morals, especially in the cities. Some Polish youth indulged in Jew-baiting and in blackmailing Jews. Smuggling, practiced by virtually everyone, further contributed to the demoralization. The stress of living in a society where a person could never be certain whether he would survive until the next day wore heavily on the faces of the Poles, who appeared to one observer to be in a constant state of fatigue.[26] For those who labored in the underground, the stress was so intense that those who did not possess the physical or emotional resources to cope with it committed suicide.[27] For many, alcohol, or *bimber*, as the illegal product of stills was called, was a refuge. Alcoholism was such a problem that the Polish underground railed against it in several issues of the clandestine press and destroyed illicit stills. Obviously, alcoholism could not be tolerated among officers and officials of the ZWZ/AK and the underground political establishment, because people in responsible positions, when drunk, ended up blurting out information which could jeopardize the lives of others. But the problem was common within the ZWZ/AK and defied Bor's best efforts to deal with it.[28]

Poles had every reason to be pleased when the underground launched a widespread campaign, known as Action "N," to demoralize German soldiers and officials in Poland. The underground published newspapers and pamphlets—giving the impression they were printed by German anti-Nazi groups—which emphasized the hopelessness of the war with the Soviet Union and the inevitable defeat of the Germans. These publications urged a speedy return home of the German soldier. As the chief of Civil Resistance described the activities of Action "N," "It strove to disarm German soldiers spiritually; it endeavored to set them at loggerheads with the Nazi Party, whose members—it was claimed—'goldbricked' far from the front lines, enjoying luxuries at the expense of frontline soldiers and their families; it sought to drive a wedge between combat soldiers and the Gestapo, the gendarmerie, the SS formations—those legions of privileged praetorians, those uppity bastards, looking down their noses at frontline soldiers who froze and bled to death on the eastern front."[29]

Headed by Tadeusz Żenczykowski, Action "N" employed over 700 people in its psychological warfare against the Germans. Between July 1 and September 10, 1942, it published eighteen different items—three issues of *Der Frontkaempfer* for soldiers, two issues of *Durchbruch* for citizens of the Reich and the annexed lands, four issues of *Merkblatt für die Deutschen in Osten*, and several pamphlets and pieces aimed at destroying German confidence in the Nazi Party. There was even a brochure which pointed out the inconsistencies and contradictions contained in *Mein Kampf* and Hitler's speeches. The underground was so effective in distributing these publications that they reached from the French to the Soviet frontier.[30]

One pamphlet, printed in gothic, was signed by the *NSDAP erneuerungsbewegung* (Extraordinary Pacification Action). The group alleged that when he ordered the war on the Soviet Union, Hitler betrayed the ideals of National Socialism, loyally guarded by Rudolf Hess. Because Hess did not agree with Hitler, he fled to England. Hess, the pamphlet asserted, was the true führer, and it concluded with "Heil, Hess."

Action "N" dispirited Germans by sending them demoralizing letters and books with conspiratorial texts. Some of these letters were sent to Germans in prominent positions and contained at least some truth about commercial frauds or illicit love affairs in order to turn the Germans against each other.[31] The Poles also produced forgeries of orders, thus creating confusion among the Germans. Shortly after the German government announced the discovery of the graves of Polish soldiers at Katyń, the Poles printed thousands of posters similar in style and language to others posted by German authorities in Poland:

> Proclamation No. 35 of the Generalgouvernement Administration (Central Propaganda Office):
> At the suggestion of the Central Propaganda Office of the Generalgouvernement, a committee of representatives of the Polish public travelled to Smolensk on 11th April to see for themselves the bestialities perpetrated by the Soviet assassins of the Polish people. This was to prove to the Polish people the terrible fate awaiting them if the Soviets succeed in penetrating the Polish territories at present occupied by the Germans.

Up to this point the poster followed the lines of a routine Nazi proclamation. Then it diverged along sardonic lines:

> In this connection, the Generalgouvernement has ordered that a parallel excursion be organized to the concentration camp at Auschwitz for a committee of all ethnic groups living in Poland. The excursion is to prove how humanitarian, in comparison with the methods employed by the Bolsheviks, are the devices used to carry out the mass extermination of the Polish people. German science has performed marvels for European culture here; instead of a brutal massacre of the inconvenient populace, in Auschwitz one can see the gas and vapour chambers, electric plates, etc., whereby thousands of Poles can be assisted from life to death most rapidly, and in a manner which does honour to the whole German nation.
> It will suffice to indicate that the crematorium alone can handle 3,000 corpses every day. During the summer months excursions are also being planned by special train to the concentration camps at Mauthausen, Oranienburg, Dachau, Ravensbruck, and elsewhere.

Some German officials obediently posted the proclamation without even realizing it was a forgery.[32]

One of the most dramatic forgeries of Action "N" was the order of

February 1944, which purported to come from the chief of police of the General Government, directing all Germans to evacuate immediately from occupied Poland. Panic followed, but the Nazi authorities managed to avert a German exodus.[33]

Contrary to German expectations, the Nazi effort to blot out Polish culture, and with it to destroy national unity, produced opposite results. Governor Frank admitted to Hitler in 1943: "the paralysing of schooling and the considerable restriction on cultural activity results with increasing momentum in the strengthening of the Polish national unity under the leadership of the Polish intelligentsia conspiring against the Germans. What had not been possible during the course of Polish history and during the first years of German rule, namely the creation of national unity having a common aim and internally linked in life and death, is at present as a result of German action slowly but surely becoming a reality."[34]

Compensating for the enormous restriction on cultural activities, the Poles established an extensive and sophisticated underground culture. Teachers and parents established a system of elementary and secondary schools in the annexed lands where the Germans had prohibited them. In the General Government, since the Germans allowed some elementary schools, special attention had to be given to establishing secret secondary schools. Various organizations, such as the Secret Organization of Teachers (*Tajna Organizacja Nauczycielstwa*), cooperated in this work, and by 1941 the Government Delegacy created a Department of Education and Culture to supervise educational affairs. Czesław Wycech, a quiet, unobtrusive academician, played a key role in the establishment of the Polish underground educational system. By 1942-43, 5,252 teachers taught over 86,000 elementary school students, and over 5,600 teachers taught over 48,000 secondary school students in the General Government. In the annexed lands, where the difficulties in establishing secret schools were even greater than in the General Government, 1,434 Polish teachers taught 18,713 elementary school students, and 205 teachers taught 1,671 secondary school students in 1942-43.[35]

The Germans were unconvinced that underground schooling was as extensive as it really was; in consequence, they did not give major attention to cracking down on it, especially during the latter part of the war. Nevertheless, the Germans arrested and executed a large number of Polish teachers; in the latter part of 1942, the Germans arrested 367 teachers, most of whom were sent to Auschwitz, where they perished. Until the Germans embarked upon the systematic murder of the Jews, there were by 1942 twenty primary and secondary schools in which 7,000 students were enrolled in the Warsaw Ghetto. Even university classes were held. Polish educators connected with the Secret Organization of Teachers also cooperated with Jewish educational officials.[36]

Despite the closing of Polish universities and the arrest of professors, university-level classes began in the latter part of 1940 in the secret University of Warsaw. By 1944, 2,000 students were enrolled. In December 1940, professors and students deported from the University of Poznań established a secret University of the Western Lands in Warsaw. This unique institution, boasting about 250 teachers and over 2,000 students, even offered extension work in Częstochowa and Kielce. Because of the devastating loss of professors at the Jagiellonian University early in the occupation, secret university studies were delayed in Cracow. There were approximately 1,000 students who attended classes at the clandestine university for Cracow, Wilno, and Lwów.[37]

Students attended secret classes, took examinations, and received diplomas, usualy drawn up in code and signed by professors using pseudonyms. Sometimes a student received a calling card that could be exchanged for a diploma after the war. One of these cards read: "Thank you for your charming visit on September 19, 1942. I was *most* satisfied. You told me such *interesting* things. Bravo."[38] One former student remembered how in the middle of her examinations, the Gestapo broke into the room and arrested her instructors.[39] Despite the obvious difficulties of being denied access to libraries and laboratories, Polish scholars wrote and distributed 150 scientific books on various subjects, and graduate students wrote theses and dissertations in their specialties. One could find almost everything offered in the Polish university curriculum, except, for obvious reasons, German.[40]

One of the most amazing aspects of Polish higher education was the extensive program in medical studies centered in Warsaw. The Poles set up clandestine teaching departments in hospitals and held secret classes in the State Institute of Hygiene. About 500 teachers instructed 4,000 students enrolled in medical and pharmacy classes. There was also a less extensive program in legal studies; about 600 students attended the secret law school in Warsaw. Attendance at the universities was free, or, as in the case of the medical school, the cost was minimal.[41]

Germans permitted Poles to attend the cinemas, but these were often of low quality and usually propagandistic in nature. The underground tried to get the people to boycott the cinemas, but despite the slogan "Only Pigs

Sit in the Cinema" (*Tylko Świnie Siedzą w Kinie*) which appeared everywhere, Poles still attended them, undoubtedly because it provided respite from the grim and unpredictable life most Poles were forced to live. According to the Germans, nine million Poles patronized 200 movie houses in the General Government.[42]

German authorities allowed Poles to attend only third-rate theatrical productions, often pornographic in nature. Since the Union of Polish Stage Artists forbade its members to perform in German-controlled theaters, this meant that actors and actresses frequently became singers or gave recitations at coffee houses where people drank ersatz coffee and ate minuscule pastries. From time to time, some Polish actors violated the prohibition and appeared in performances that were propagandistic and anti-Polish; for this, the underground punished these offenders. The Nazis produced an anti-Semitic play, "Quarantine" (*Kwarantanna*), which the Poles boycotted; nowhere did this play gain "either recognition or spectators" among the Polish people.[43]

Amateur and professional actors on their own initiative presented secret theatrical productions in cities and villages. They offered a rich variety of performances of plays, readings, and songs. One of the phenomena of the underground theater was the flourishing theaters of puppetry. Their program was versatile, offering everything from satire to the drama of Shakespeare. The actors performed in private homes, cellars, shops, garages, factories, and churches. Usually twenty to fifty attended a performance, and hundreds of people attended a production presented by a theater school in Cracow. Amazingly, in the five years of Nazi occupation, the Gestapo failed to break up a single theatrical performance, despite the fact that these productions occurred hundreds of times.[44]

There were therefore hundreds of amateur and professional presentations of plays, including drama, comedy, musicals, and puppetry, performed in the open and underground theater during the occupation. Among the authors favored in these productions were Adam Mickiewicz, Juliusz Słowacki, Alexander Fredro, Jean-Baptiste Moliere, George Bernard Shaw, and Johann Schiller. Perhaps the most popular playwright was Fredro,[45] a comedic genius who produced some of the most enduring characters in Polish theater. No doubt some of the pain and anxiety of Polish life under the Germans was relieved by the satire and merriment offered by Fredro's plays.

Undaunted, Polish stage artists recited from the great writers and sang Polish and French ballads even in confinement at Auschwitz. As part of Governor Frank's "flexible course," aimed at easing some of the horrible repressions of Nazi rule in Poland, he allowed an improved repertoire in the German-sponsored Polish theater in late 1943 and early 1944. In March 1944, he even allowed Poles to join Germans to see a theatrical production in Cracow.[46] The Polish underground theater kept the Polish heritage alive, responded to the nationalistic yearnings of the people, and served to confirm the underground code of conduct of Poles in their relations with the Germans.

As in the theater, the Germans permitted only light, frivolous music to be played in the cabarets frequented by Poles. Serious music could be performed only in private homes. The Germans officially banned the music of Polish composers. On one rare occasion the Germans officially permitted someone to play Chopin only because the pianist claimed he was a Ukrainian.[47] Despite the German proscriptions, many survivors of the war heard the muted chords of a Chopin polonaise or mazurka emanating from an apartment in Warsaw or Cracow.[48]

Thus, German efforts to paralyze Polish cultural life were ineffectual. Cultural and artistic vitality flourished in the underground. The underground press unified men and women from all walks of life as perhaps nothing else did; it continually stressed the need to resist the Germans and to condemn collaboration. As early as 1940, there were about 250 secret publications in existence in Poland, a figure that rose in the following years. There were 1,257 confirmed titles of the Polish underground press, but one authority estimates there were probably as many as 1,400. Poland exceeded all other countries in the number of titles regularly published under German occupation.

Unlike France and the Netherlands, the Polish underground press grew at an even rate throughout the occupation. The achievement in Poland was especially remarkable because the Poles, unlike the French or Dutch, did not have a legal Polish press with which to cooperate and thereby enable them to print large quantities of an issue.[49] When an underground newspaper published 10,000 copies of an issue in Poland, this was considered quite good, though the *Information Bulletin* (*Biuletyn Informacyjny*), a popular weekly published by the ZWZ/AK beginning in November 1939, came close to 50,000 copies.[50] To be sure, Warsaw led other Polish cities in the number of titles produced—690; this was not surprising since Warsaw had at least 150 secret printing and duplicating establishments. Other cities and the number of clandestine titles they published included: Cracow, 113; Łódź, 49; Lwów, 33; Wilno, 15; Lublin, 17. In addition to periodicals, there were 1,075 other types of clandestine publications—brochures and books on many different subjects.[51] History was a favorite because of German proscriptions against the subject being taught, but books on poetry, justice, and theater were also popular. Czesław Miłosz, the future Nobel Laureate, edited an anthology of poetry during this period.

During the first days of the occupation, news sheets appeared. These were typed or even handwritten. For the most part the early publications emerged spontaneously, the result of local initiatives. Political and military groups especially took the initiative in printing underground newspapers. The first Warsaw-published newspaper was *Information Monitor* (*Monitor Informacyjny ZPN*), published on October 3, 1939. Two publications early in the occupation took the title *Poland Lives* (*Polska Żyje*), one in Warsaw and the other in Cracow.[52] There were eleven publications carrying the name *Reveille* (*Pobudka*) and ten with the title *Redoubt* (*Redut*); predictably, the ZWZ/AK published most of these. Nine publications had the word *Struggle* (*Walka*) in their title, and seven were entitled *Freedom* (*Wolność*). Surprisingly, only one publication was entitled *Independence* (*Niepodległość*). There was even one named after the Polish national anthem, *Poland is Not Yet Lost* (*Jeszcze Polska Nie Zginela*).[53]

Out of 1,095 titles, 780 newspapers were mimeographed, 332 printed, 69 typed, and 14 written by hand. More than half of the underground newspapers were organs of the four major political parties and the military and political agencies of the underground. The overwhelming majority of these publications were in the moderate-left category of the political spectrum and thus pro-Sikorski in attitude; in 1942, the British identified only eight publications which they categorized as conservative-reactionary.[54]

Various groups also published underground literary journals of high quality, including: *Art and Nation* (*Sztuka i Naród*), *Turning Point* (*Przełom*), *Education and Culture* (*Oświata i Kultura*), *Review of Cultural Affairs* (*Przegląd Spraw Kulturalnych*).[55]

The Polish clandestine press was also characterized by a variety that attempted to meet the specialized interests of its clientele, including military groups, women, physicians, teachers, even foreign prisoners interned in Poland. For example, the underground printed thirty titles for Scouts, twenty literary and cultural publications, and fourteen satirical periodicals. Chess players published a monthly, mountain climbers had their own annual yearbook, and there was even a special publication on puppetry, *Manikin* (*Latka*). In addition to fourteen titles published in German for diversionary purposes, there were fifty-six titles of the Jewish press that appeared in Warsaw in the period June 1940-July 1942 in the Yiddish, Hebrew, and Polish languages.[56]

The underground press had numerous sources of information. The major radio sources were the BBC and, later, the Voice of America. Radio broadcasts from neutral countries like Turkey and Switzerland were also important. Poles also monitored and gleaned information from Soviet stations named after Kościuszko and Szewczenko. Major press agencies from which editors of clandestine newspapers gathered information included Reuters, UPI, AP, TASS, PA (Press Association), and the ATS-SDA (*Agence Telegraphique Suisse-Schweizerische Depeschenagentur*).[57] There were 350 listening posts and 1,500 professional "listeners" who monitored foreign broadcasts and were the major source of foreign news.[58]

Even SWIT was a source of information. SWIT, code named *Anusia*, was a radio station operating near London but pretending to be broadcasting from Poland. Korboński, who headed the Directorate of Civil Resistance, fed information from Poland to SWIT each day, convincing Poles it was indeed an underground station in Poland. By receiving these up-to-date reports from the Polish underground and the German press, SWIT was able to comment on events in Poland and to broadcast directives and warnings from the Directorate of Civil Resistance transmitted earlier the same day from Warsaw to London. The people of Poland never knew about the secret of SWIT until after Sikorski's death; it was eventually revealed to the high command of the AK. SWIT confounded and harassed the Germans and gave a high degree of credibility to news that ostensibly was broadcast from Poland.[59]

It was difficult to publish and even more so to distribute newspapers of the clandestine press. No aspect of underground life was more ruthlessly pursued by the Germans than the search for the secret press. The death penalty was usually applied to those involved in publishing or distributing these newspapers. Despite the high risk and casual ties, there always was someone ready to fill the position of a person just arrested by the Gestapo. Once the Germans realized the Poles distributed the *Biuletyn Informacyjny* on Thursdays, they increased their patrols and forced the publisher to change the day of distribution. Faithfully, the AK sent Governor Fischer of Warsaw a copy of every issue.[60] Because of the particular difficulties in distributing the newspapers, most of the circulation was limited to the General Government. There were no underground papers, for example, that circulated regularly in Gdynia, and this was the reason people in Silesia and Pomorze were not as well informed as Poles in the General Government.[61]

Poles practiced a three-tiered system of distribution, and each distributor knew only the man who handed him the paper and the one for whom it was intended. In this way, the distributor caught by the Gestapo could reveal only two names. The system worked for wholesale circulation, but it was a different matter when it came to hawkers:

> Newsboys on the streets of Warsaw and Cracow sold the German local papers, *Krakauer Zeitung*, *Warschauer Zeitung*, or the *Ostdeutscher Beobachter* in Poznan, or Adolf Hitler's own *Voelkischer Beobachter* in every small and large Polish city. No Pole bought these papers, unless the boy smilingly said to him:
> "*Today* you have extraordinary news about German victories . . . Buy it," and handed him a copy.
> The passer-by knew the copy was worth buying, for it was stuffed. Between the pages full of German dispatches describing incredible successes of the swastika-bearing flag, he found a hidden copy of his underground paper.
> A butcher would say to a woman customer, while wrapping her steak:
> "Put it on ice *immediately* when you reach home, will you?"
> And she would know that the paper was wrapped inside.[62]

People eagerly sought out the clandestine press. They were so eager for news that sometimes a person snatched a copy from someone else's hands.[63] "Every item of more important news, or even rumour," Korboński observed, "was the talk of Warsaw after a few hours."[64] The quality of the Polish clandestine press varied; some were extremely polished, others were crude. But all attempted to slake Polish thirst for news. Newspapers usually offered information about the war, international relations, German occupation policies, Polish resistance efforts, and domestic politics.[65] At the outset, the political connections of the newspapers were not always apparent, but by 1943, political discussions and commentary about Poland's future were more common. The most influential newspapers included the *Information Bulletin* (*Biuletyn Informacyjny*), official press organ of the ZWZ/AK; *Polish Republic* (*Rzeczpospolita Polska*), the major publication of the government delegate; *WRN* (the title formed from the Polish equivalents of the words "liberty," "equality," and "independence"), the major publication of the Socialist party; *Through Fight to Victory* (*Przez Walkę Do Zwycięstwa*), the chief newspaper of the Peasant Party; *Struggle* (*Walka*), key publication of the National Democrats; *Voice of Warsaw* (*Głos Warszawy*), one of the major papers of the Labor Party; and *Tribune of Freedom* (*Trybuna Wolności*), the best-known paper of the Polish Workers Party.[66]

As one Pole observed, "The secret press sustained the Polish spirit." Korboński said it best when he wrote: "The underground press provided the mortar binding the structure of the Polish Underground State. It was the voice not only of this underground state, but also of the entire Polish nation throughout over five years of its struggle against the German occupier."[67]

During the early years of the German occupation of Poland, the Germans did not encourage Polish political collaboration. There were a few initiatives by isolated individuals on both sides, but nothing ever came of them. After the outbreak of the German-Soviet war in June 1941, German interest in winning over Polish leaders to the idea of collaboration quickened, largely because Germany wanted to secure the areas behind the Russo-German front and end the sabotage, diversionary, and reprisal activites of the ZWZ/AK.

The German war with the Soviets elicited mixed feelings from the Poles. Most Poles were either reserved toward the Soviets or hoped the Germans and Soviets would destroy each other to Poland's ultimate political advantage. There were a few Poles, convinced the western allies would be of little or no help to Poland, who believed that it was necessary to come to terms with the Reich. Sikorski was well aware of the flirtation of some Poles in the homeland and abroad with the idea of collaboration with the Germans; he deplored the idea, and to offset any surreptitious Polish initiatives that might be taken toward the Germans, he even exaggerated the extent of Anglo-American commitments to the postwar reconstruction of Poland within its prewar frontiers.[68]

After the Katyń revelations, the rupture in Polish-Russian relations, and the subsequent armed clashes in eastern Poland between the AK and Soviet units, a few German leaders led by Governor Frank made their most serious efforts of the war to win over the Polish people to a German anti-Bolshevik crusade in return for some mitigation of the terror against the Poles and for the promise of restricted Polish autonomy under German rule. Despite what the Soviets had done to the Poles by the summer of 1944, including establishing the Lublin Committee to challenge the legal authority of the Polish government-in-exile, the Poles were unresponsive to Frank's overtures. The facts suggest that Hitler and Himmler were unwilling to look upon Poland and its people in other than the crudest terms of exploitation. Thus the severity of German occupation policies in Poland, unquestionably the worst in Europe, prevented any Pole of political stature to collaborate. Poland was, therefore, unique in not producing a Polish Quisling.

In the months following the defeat of Poland in September 1939, there were isolated initiatives by Germans and Poles toward reaching some kind of a modus vivendi. In October 1939, the German embassy in Geneva reported to Berlin that a Polish exile circle in Switzerland, hostile to Sikorski's government, wanted to reach an understanding with the Germans aimed at creating a new Polish state. However, Joachim von Ribbentrop, the German foreign minister, ordered the contact between the Poles and Germans broken off.[69] There were right-wing Poles who had fled from Poland to Romania who wanted to reach an understanding with the Germans and combat communism.[70] After the defeat of France in June 1940, and the evacuation of the Polish army and government to Great Britain, there were many demoralized Poles, especially members of the aristocracy, gentry, and army, who had lost faith in victory and talked about reaching some political understanding with Hitler.[71]

In Poland there were also Poles who, if the Germans had been serious about cultivating them, would have been willing to collaborate. In January 1940, Władysław Studnicki, a strong proponent of Polish-German cooperation, went to Berlin and presented a memorandum criticizing German occupation policies in Poland and urging the reestablishment of a Polish state. Arrested by Dr. Joseph Goebbels, Studnicki was placed in a sanitarium but because of his pro-German views was released after the fall of France. He continued to maintain contacts with the Germans, often intervening on behalf of Poles arrested by the police. Nothing ever came of his plans of collaboration with the Germans. One Polish report even remarked on the pro-German sentiment that existed among some Polish peasants who, during the winter of 1939-40, had not yet felt the repression the Germans had meted out to Poles in the cities.[72] On two occasions prior to the summer of 1940, Prince Janusz Radziwiłł, who had been released earlier from a Soviet prison due to the intervention of Hermann Goering, was approached by the Germans concerning the creation of a Polish government subservient to the Reich. Radziwiłł refused to cooperate.[73]

The German invasion of the Soviet Union and subsequent discussions concerning a Polish-Russian treaty revived some interest in Polish and German circles concerning the prospect of a Polish-German rapprochement. There were Poles in the exile colonies in England and Italy, some of whom were connected with the Polish foreign ministry, who regarded the Germans as the lesser of the two evils facing Poland. To be sure, many of these were supporters of the prewar Polish regime and feared a social revolution in Poland if the Soviets defeated the Germans. As the Germans drove more deeply into Soviet territory in 1941, some of these Poles believed that in the face of imminent Soviet defeat and the inactivity of the western allies, the Poles should try to establish a modus vivendi with Germany.[74]

One Polish official in London told the British that he would not blame his countrymen accepting a German proposal that created a new Poland, based upon the General Government and part of western Russia—even as a Nazi puppet—because such a state would alleviate some of the terrible hardships the Poles had to endure and would keep alive the nucleus of a Poland for the future.[75] Leon Mitkiewicz noted in his diary on July 16, 1941, that the Germans made an offer to Stanisław Rostworowski, a Polish official in Hungary, proposing Polish acquisitions in the East at Soviet expense for what the Poles lost to the Germans in western Poland—on condition the Poles join the Germans in the war aginst the Soviet Union. The alleged offer was rejected. The Germans met similar rejections from Professor Bartel and Count Adolf Bniński.[76] A few months later, Rowecki reported on an overture to him from the Gestapo which proposed a quid pro quo: The ZWZ to stop its sabotage and diversionary activity against the Germans, the Germans to end repression of the ZWZ. Rowecki interpreted this "peace for peace" proposal as a sign of German weakness.[77]

Up to this point, there were no prominent Poles in Poland willing to collaborate with the Germans. One official noted the caliber of the few Poles who were responsive to German overtures: "They include a notorious anti-Semite priest, two third-class lawyers of Warsaw, and a Christian Democrat who was expelled from his party because of his unsavoury role on the board of the French-controlled Warsaw electric power station."[78]

Early in 1942, the Germans approached Alfred Wysocki, the former Polish envoy to Berlin and ambassador to Rome, to act as an intermediary with Polish authorities in the underground. The Germans proposed an end to Polish underground activites in return for the release of political prisoners and the creation of a Polish advisory body in the General Government. Wysocki withdrew from the discussions with the Germans because of the wave of mass murder of the Jews in eastern Poland.[79]

The Germans found a more responsive ear in Leon Kozłowski, a former Polish premier. Kozłowski, thanks to General Anders, had been released from a Soviet prison, deserted from the Polish army in the Soviet Union, and made contact with the Germans with whom he carried on negotiations. Kozłowski appears to have been offered an opportunity to head a puppet Polish government but imposed conditions the Germans would not accept—namely, the release of Poles from concentration camps. Compromised in the eyes of fellow Poles, Kozłowski remained in Berlin where he subsequently disappeared. The Germans also made an approach to Adam Ronikier, head of the Central Welfare Council (*Rada Główna Opiekuńcza*), but he rejected the idea of collaboration.[80]

Immediately after the Katyń affair, the Germans made more serious efforts to get Polish officials to cooperate with them. Capitalizing on their charges against the Bolsheviks for the murder of thousands of officers and enlisted men of the Polish army while in Soviet custody, the Germans unleashed a barrage of anti-Soviet and anti-Jewish propaganda. The Germans again approached Ronikier to try and encourage Polish leaders to cooperate with them; they even considered releasing some Polish prisoners who were known for their anti-communist activities. Frank made a pro-Polish gesture in placing one million złotys at the disposal of the Central Welfare Council.[81] Strikingly, the Germans did not couple their appeals with an end to their policy of terror against the Poles and the extermination of the Jews who had launched an uprising in the Warsaw Ghetto at this time.

Underground authorities admonished the Poles not to be deluded by German propaganda and to remember German criminality against the Polish and Jewish people.[82] The admonition was not needed; most Poles sympathized with the plight of the Jews in the ghettos, and many members of the AK and GL actively assisted them in their doomed struggle against the Germans.[83] Significantly, no prominent Poles in Poland responded to the post-Katyń German overtures. Rather, a former Polish finance minister, Wincenty Jastrębski, joined by a Warsaw academician, Tarlo Mazyński, approached the German embassy in Paris in May 1943 with an offer to establish a Polish National Committee to collaborate with Germany. Although the German Foreign Ministry ruled out this idea, the incident revealed that the Katyń affair produced at least some interest among a few Poles to collaborate with Germany.[84]

Despite the failures to win over even a significant minority of Poles to the German side in the immediate aftermath of the Katyń affair, Frank was convinced that Germany had to alter its policy of terror toward the Poles in order to succeed in securing their support "in the anti-Bolshevik resistance front." He seriously proposed organizing right-wing Polish groups, such as *Sword and Plow* (*Miecz i Pług*), against the Soviets. He told Hitler on June 19, 1943, that the Reich should abandon "useless ideology and falsely construed supremacies" in order to meet the needs confronting the German people. Frank believed that the Germans had to demonstrate to the Poles that Germany genuinely intended to change its policy toward the Poles. He favored improving Polish food rations, stopping the deportation of Poles and the confiscation of their property, ending public executions of women, children, and the elderly, and improving the treatment of Poles forced to work in the Reich and taking care of their families left behind in the General Government. Hitler was unresponsive to Frank's suggested new strategy toward the Poles and authorized Himmler to renew the German campaign against the partisans in Poland.[85]

Frank was not alone in the conviction that German policy had to change, a view underscored by the failures in late 1943 and early 1944 of the escalation of the Nazi terror campaign highlighted by public executions in Warsaw. Goebbels agreed with Frank that ideological matters should be subordinated to the primary goal of winning the war; he dubbed Himmler's colonization campaign as a "lot of political nonsense." As the situation worsened for the Germans, even security agencies like SIPO and the SD saw the need to come to terms with the AK, though they were not prepared to go as far as Frank in making concessions to the Poles. Frank continued to espouse his flexible strategy in 1944, but by then it was too late to salvage anything of substance from the wreckage of the Nazi empire. One wonders whether Frank saw an end to the war and wanted to establish an alibi for himself in any postwar war crimes trials by identifying himself with a more humanitarian policy toward the Poles.[86]

Despite the lack of support in Berlin for his policy, Frank initiated a few steps in trying to alter the image of the draconic Nazis and to persuade the Poles to support Germany against the Soviets. In October 1943, he allowed the opening of a Chopin museum.[87] The same month he made a fulsome speech to Polish peasants in which he said, "Dear Polish peasants, I thank, through you, all the decent husbandmen of the General Government for their conscientious and industrious labor." Frank's speech was part of a German press campaign that described German rule in Poland as "hard, but just" and the majority of Poles as loyal collaborators. At the same time the Germans attempted to mitigate their long-standing campaign to depict the Poles as a racially inferior people.[88] By early 1944, as a result of Frank's initiative, the Germans opened a Polish theater in Cracow, ended the requirement of passes for Poles using trains, and opened some seminaries that had been closed in 1939. They even contemplated opening secondary schools and a school of medicine in Cracow staffed by Polish professors for Polish medical students.[89]

Frank's modest initiatives were supplemented by a massive propaganda campaign to exploit Polish fears that the Communists intended to conquer Poland and that the United States and Great Britain had abdicated Poland to the Soviets. British pressures on the Polish government-in-exile to compromise with the Soviets on the Curzon Line seemed to confirm the Nazi propaganda line of a British betrayal of Poland. German propaganda depicted Germany as the only bulwark protecting Poland against the "Bolshevik menace." In view of the hostile line taken by the Soviets and by the Polish Communists toward the Polish government-in-exile, the Government Delegacy, and the AK, it was difficult for Polish authorities to counteract the German line.[90]

The Germans printed thirty-two million copies of different brochures and pamphlets to convince the Poles to side with them against the Soviets. This huge publishing effort was necessary because the Germans had earlier in the war forbidden the Poles to have radios—and now could not reach Polish audiences by broadcasts. With an eye on the past, Germans exploited the Piłsudski legacy, flooding the people with pamphlets and pictures of the Russophobic leader who had stopped the Bolshevik drive into Poland at Warsaw in 1920. Kurt von Burgsdorff, one of Frank's supporters who was district governor of Cracow, even staged a solemn ceremony commemorating the anniversary of the death of Polish soldiers in the 1939 campaign.[91]

The various artificial means to secure compulsory expressions of loyalty to Germany were actually designed more to sooth the anxieties of the Germans in Poland than to convert the Poles. The Germans forced various classes of people—tradesmen, businessmen, farmers, workers—to vote motions and sign declarations against the Soviet Union. Trade and professional associations were compelled to send anti-Soviet messages to Frank. The Germans ordered mayors of towns to hold anti-Soviet meetings and obtain statements from citizens that they would actively oppose the Communists. The Germans tried but failed to get pastoral letters of an anti-Soviet character that they could use for propaganda purposes. Burgsdorff's office failed, despite two attempts, to get the ailing Peasant Party leader, Wincenty Witos, to issue an anti-Bolshevik proclamation.[92]

The results of these clumsy and blatantly hypocritical efforts of the Germans were a failure, belying the apprehensions of British intelligence which believed there was "a strong possibility of some kind of Quisling Government being set up in Poland supported by . . . Warsaw degenerates . . .[or] genuinely patriotic Poles who passionately fear the Russian menace more than anything else in the world."[93] Repeated German offers to the government delegate and to the commander of the AK to suspend mutual hostilities and collaborate with the Germans were rejected without negotiation. German approaches through neutral channels to the Polish government in London suggesting negotations that would lead to collaboration met with the same result. Even desperate German promises to create an independent Poland did not induce top political or military leaders in the homeland or abroad to respond favorably. Several German proposals to get the AK and Polish prisoners of war to fight in anti-communist units fell on deaf ears.[94]

One of the few things the Germans managed to accomplish in 1944 was to interest Ronikier in acting as an intermediary between the Germans and the Polish government on a proposal, apparently authored by Ronikier and accepted by Himmler, which would have drastically changed German administration in Poland and given the Poles self-government. The government delegate opposed Ronikier's initiative, and Ronikier did not pursue the matter. The Germans succeeded in 1944 in getting a few Polish journalists to publish a pro-German newspaper, *Turning Point* (*Przełom*), in Cracow where the sentiment for some kind of detente with the Germans seemed to be stronger than elsewhere in Poland, and a journalist in Lwów to do the same thing with the *Gazeta Lwówska*. There were some members of the right-wing National Radical Camp (ONR) who responded to Nazi appeals, and a few isolated cases where AK units cooperated with the Germans against Soviet partisans in the region of Nowogródek.[95]

After the suppression of the two-month-long Warsaw Uprising in October 1944, another opportunity arose for the Germans to influence Polish opinion. The Germans gave generous surrender terms to the AK, which was accorded the status of a regular army protected by the rules of international law. Yet, members of the German security and police establishment, who had consistently sabotaged Frank's efforts to mitigate Nazi rule over the Poles, compensated for the AK generosity by imposing even greater suffering upon the civilian survivors of the uprising. They transported approximately 50,000 of them to the concentration camps of the Reich in October and November of 1944. In addition, a large part of the Polish population who lived west of the Vistula River was forced to work on German defenses against the approaching Soviet armies.[96]

Hitler and Himmler did not support major departures from the general policy of terror that had characterized German rule since 1939. Little wonder that most Poles regarded contemptuously the few puny concessions offered by Frank. Despite the fear and anxiety most Poles shared about their nation's fate as Soviet armies swept across it, they were unwilling to abandon their commitment to the allied alliance. Frank's flexible policy had had a chance of some success in 1939, but not in 1943-44 when Polish hatred of their persecutors far outweighed their apprehension of the Soviets.

Despite German failure to secure Polish political collaboration against the Soviets, some Poles during the war used German institutions against fellow Poles and Jews. Some people settled personal or political grudges by denouncing their enemies to the enemy; there were cases of Poles blackmailing and denouncing other Poles and Jews. Then there were those who voluntarily became *Volksdeutsch* for the personal advantages that status brought them. All this suggested the breakdown of social cohesion, a consequence, as one scholar put it, of "constant fear for one's life, the unpredictability of German terror, and finally, anarchy."[97]

To be sure, the Polish government and its civilian and military authorities in Poland continually admonished the population against the evils of collaboration, blackmailing, and denunciation. And in one of Sikorski's comments on the subject, he declared to the government delegate that anyone who "openly or secretly cooperated with the Germans automatically excluded themselves from the [Polish] body politic."[98]

No precise data exist concerning the number of Polish collaborators during the war, but the number does not appear to have loomed large in relation to the total population. Emmanuel Ringelblum, the famous Jewish chronicler who lived through much of this period, said that most of the denunciation and informing in wartime Poland was done by the *Volksdeutsch*, who were considered traitors by the overwhelming majority of Poles.[99] One report suggested that in the period January 1943 to June 1944, underground authorities pronounced 2,015 death sentences on informers and collaborators.[100] Postwar statistics of the Israeli War Crime Commission indicated that only 7,000 Poles out of a population of over twenty million ethnic Poles collaborated with the Nazis.[101]

Perhaps the most celebrated case of individual collaboration concerned Igo Sym, the well known manager of the Warsaw City Theater, who was condemned to death by the ZWZ. He was shot in his home on March 7, 1941. The consequence of his death was a flood of arrests and twenty-one executions of Polish hostages by the Germans. The assassinations of Sym and other well-known collaborators by the underground did not always meet with the approval of Polish officials in London, who believed that they were not worth the high cost of innocent Polish lives which the Germans took in reprisal.[102]

As suggested elsewhere, even the ZWZ/AK had its problems with Polish agents who worked for the Germans. Bór complained about the loss of 15 intelligence contacts of the AK in Germany because of the treasonable activites of Stefan Kasprzycki. Even worse were the consequences flowing from the treason of Kalkstein, Świerczewski, and Kaczorowska, who were responsible for betraying General Rowecki and 200 other people in the underground army.[103]

One of the most controversial aspects of Polish collaboration with the Germans concerns the people who blackmailed and denounced Jews and their Polish protectors. Most of these renegades were young Poles, incited by right-wing groups, who probably did not number more than 1,000 people in Warsaw; they could usually be found in the vicinity of the ghetto. Called *schmalzowniks*, they often hunted Jews in gangs, and sometimes even Polish Christians with Semitic features were molested by them. There were, of course, also incidents of blackmailing and informing in the Polish countryside, but the evidence also shows numerous cases of aid by Polish peasants to the Jews.[104]

The Polish Blue Police was another group which collaborated with the Germans in hunting down fellow Poles—Jews and non-Jews. The Blue Police was not so bad at the outset, "but in the course of time, many honest people were excluded from the force and were replaced by *Volksdeutsch*, criminals, and weak characters poisoned by anti-Semitic indoctrination."[105] Increasingly, the Nazis distrusted members of the Polish police, executed many of them for their pro-Semitic views, and relied more on auxiliaries from abroad. In May, 1943, the Directorate of Civil Resistance condemned thirty-eight members of the Blue Police for their behavior. The list was posted on trees and homes and caused considerable panic among Polish collaborators.[106]

Even Jews collaborated with the Germans and informed on each other. Jewish officials in the Warsaw Ghetto admitted that they needed Poles to instruct them in military matters prior to the Ghetto Uprising because the only ones with prewar military experience were members of the Jewish police, and they were not trustworthy. In one notorious case, a secret Jewish court in the Warsaw Ghetto executed fifty-nine Jewish collaborators connected with the *Zagiew*, a Nazi-sponsored Jewish militia to spy on the Jewish underground. During the Jewish armed action against the Germans in January 1943, many Jews told the Germans where the bunkers were located, prompting this stiff warning: "The Jewish Fighting Organization warns all low-lifes that if they do not stop their degenerate deeds immediately they will be executed!"[107]

The Polish underground tried to deal with the problem of blackmailing and denouncing Jews by making admonitions and warnings in the clandestine press. On September 17, 1942, the Directorate of Civil Resistance expressed sympathy for the Jews, condemned the atrocities against them, and promised that the executioners and "their henchmen will be held directly responsible for these crimes." The Directorate of Civil Resistance repeated its condemnation of blackmailers in more specific terms in *Rzeczpospolita Polska* in March 1943:

> The Polish community, although it is itself a victim of frightful terrorism, looks with horror and deep sympathy on the murder by the Germans of the remaining Jewish population of Poland. It has put on record a protest against this crime, which has been made known throughout the world, and it has given such considerable help to the Jews who have escaped from the ghetto

or the concentration camps that the occupant has published a decree, threatening with death Poles who help the Jews who are in hiding. Nevertheless, there exist individuals, devoid of feeling and conscience, who find a source of original income for themselves by blackmailing Poles who are hiding Jews, or the Jews themselves.

The Directorate of Civil Resistance gives warning that cases of blackmail of this are noted and will be punished with all the rigour of the law as far as it is possible in existing circumstances and in any case in the future.[108]

Again on March 18, 1943, in the *Biuletyn Informacyjny*, the Directorate of Civil Resistance repeated its condemnation of those who blackmailed Jews and Poles who helped them.[109] Throughout 1943 and 1944, articles in the liberal democratic press also attacked blackmailers.[110]

The Council for Aid to Jews (*Rada Pomocy Żydom*), which used the cryptonym *Żegota*, also appealed to underground authorities to do all they could to combat the problem and created a separate branch of its organization to propagandize against it. One of *Żegota*'s publications read: "Every Pole, who cooperates in their [German] murderous actions or blackmails or denounces Jews, or exploits their horrible situation or participates in plunder, commits a grave crime against the law of the Polish Republic and will be immediately punished, and if he manages to escape punishment, let him be assured that the time is near when he will be prosecuted before the court of justice of Reborn Poland." *Żegota* published several leaflets, even one in German for soldiers and officials in Poland, which reiterated allied warnings concerning the extermination of the Jews.[111]

Underground authorities followed up their warnings about blackmailing Jews and about Poles who aided them by executing the culprits and publicizing these executions in the Polish clandestine press. Witold Bieńkowski, the representative of the government delegate to *Żegota*, claimed that 220 people were executed for blackmailing Jews and that he personally signed 117 of the death sentences.[112] There are indications, however, that there were many surreptitious executions which have not been recorded.[113] In Cracow, for example, because of the stern measures meted out to informers and blackmailers, the problem did not assume significant proportions.[114] Testimony to the role of the underground in trying to combat the problem of blackmailers was revealed by Emmanuel Ringelblum's comment that "the *schmalzowniks* feel great respect for the Party [underground] and are in deadly fear of it." He knew of cases where people threatened with denunciation approached the Polish underground because of its protection afforded Jewish families.[115]

As indicated, the underground gave wide publicity to the executions of blackmailers in order to deter others from engaging in the contemptible practice. The issues of the *Biuletyn Informacyjny* and the *Rzeczpospolita Polska*, official organs of the civilian and military authorities of the Polish underground, were filled with notices publicizing the executions of these traitors.[116] For example, in the *Biuletyn Informacyjny* on December 9, 1943, the Directorate of Underground Struggle announced the execution of the notorious Tadeusz Karcz for betraying Jews to the Germans and of Antoni Pajor for denouncing Poles sheltering Jews. A leading official of Żegota noted that the execution of renegades like Karcz had a noticeable impact on the decline of blackmailing of Jews.[117] The problems that had to be overcome in investigating blackmailers and bringing them to justice were not easy:

> Investigating cases of blackmail was a highly complex process. The special courts needed evidence, and getting evidence was difficult, at times almost impossible. Agents could not work in the open; it was impossible to interrogate people accused of blackmail, or to confront them with evidence.
> When a blackmailer learned that he was being investigated he could place himself under German protection or betray the identity of the agents working on the case. Agents, therefore, had to be extremely cautious and discreet in their investigations. After they were sentenced, blackmailers often moved, disappeared, or changed their names to escape execution. Implementation of sentences, therefore, often had to be delayed or abandoned.[118]

The problem of informing on and blackmailing Jews and the Poles who helped Jewish people was a serious one, but it was only a part of the larger question of the social disorganization characteristic of a nation suffering incredible horrors during five years of German occupation. Polish underground authorities, who had many serious problems with which to deal, revealed a sensitivity to the problem and tried to deal with it. Their record in pursuing blackmailers of Jews compares favorably with what they tried to do in tracking down the blackmailers of Poles who helped Jews.

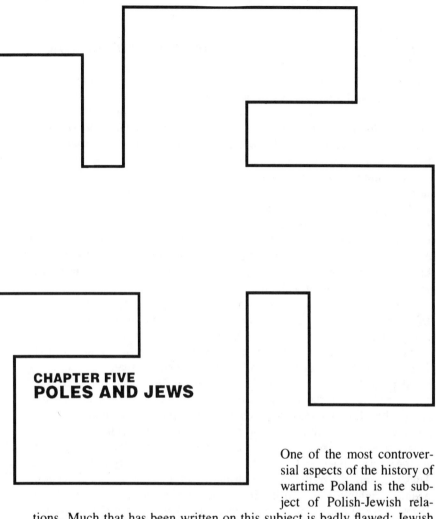

CHAPTER FIVE
POLES AND JEWS

One of the most controversial aspects of the history of wartime Poland is the subject of Polish-Jewish relations. Much that has been written on this subject is badly flawed: Jewish historians tend to make sweeping claims that label most Poles anti-Semites who did little to help the Jews against the Nazis; Polish writers tend to minimize Polish anti-Semitism and sometimes exaggerate the amount of assistance Poles gave the Jews. Anti-Semitism was less a factor in Polish-Jewish wartime relations than the reality of the Nazi terror, which was so overwhelming that the opportunities to assist the Jews were more limited in Poland than anywhere else in occupied Europe. When one considers the fact that most of the three million Jews who lived in Poland were unassimilated, the task of saving Jews was even more formidable.

Anti-Semitism did exist in wartime Poland, but it did not meet with a sympathetic response among the majority of people, who were preoccupied with their own survival during the German occupation. Further, a minority of Poles from various social classes, including former anti-Semites, risked their lives to aid Jews.

Poles and Jews lived side by side for centuries. One old Polish legend, underscoring this fact, told of a gathering of people at Gniezno to elect a ruler. Having reached a deadlock, the people decided to offer the crown to the first stranger who entered the city the following day. As it turned out, the first stranger was Abraham Prochownik, a Jew. Prochownik was offered the crown and given three days to make a decision. On the morning of the fourth day, a crowd gathered in front of Prochownik's door. One Pole, whose name was Piast, unable to control his impatience, broke open the door and demanded to know the Jew's decision. Prochownik said, "I cannot accept the crown—but I offer you a real king—this man Piast who has had the courage to break open the door when he saw the country was in danger of remaining without a ruler."[1]

While Jews were persecuted by Gentiles elsewhere in Europe in the Middle Ages, they found a home in Poland, where they benefited from many privileges granted by Polish kings and nobles, who welcomed them as a class of traders in a country that was primarily agricultural. In 1264, Bolesław the Pious signed the statute of Kalisz which guaranteed the Jews equal protection under the law.[2] This grant, underwritten by succeeding Polish rulers, was the first time in European history that the Jews had received such a guarantee of religious and communal autonomy. Though some writers have sought to read anti-Semitic discrimination into Polish practices toward Jews in prepartition Poland, one must not ascribe twentieth-century values and concepts to a period when they did not apply. Jews recognized that the system of that day was based on the concept of acquired rights for a small in-group. Most people, including the mass of Poles, were in a state of serfdom; therefore, Jews were not the only victims of discrimination. The Jews themselves applied the same exclusiveness in their dealings with other Jews and non-Jews: "Thus Jewish middlemen and agents were forbidden to put one Jewish businessman in contact with another or to bring a non-Jewish consumer into a non-Jewish store. Many warnings were issued to such agents against showing a non-Jew 'how to do business' or divulging Jewish business secrets to him."[3]

To be sure, in prepartition Poland the Jew encountered opposition from the Church, the burgher, and the artisan. But this cannot be glibly labeled anti-Semitism; "the opposition of the burgher or the artisans' guild member to the foreigner and the Jew . . . was for the most part no more immoral, according to the opinion of those times, than is present-day opposition by union members to the employment of nonorganized labor."[4]

Accounts of contemporary Jewish leaders, such as Rabbi Mozes Isserles, confirm that Poland offered the Jew much more than other European countries at that time: "It is better to have a dry morsel in peace in these regions of the Kingdom of Kraków where there is no such strong hatred against us as there is in German lands."[5] Almost 400 years later, the chief rabbi of the British Empire echoed similar sentiments: "As long as Poland was powerful, Polish Jewry enjoyed an inner autonomy and freedom equalled by no other contemporary Jewry. Furthermore, it cannot be too often repeated that to Poland belongs the priority among European peoples in religious and cultural toleration."[6]

When nationalistic trends developed by the nineteenth-century, nationalism affected Poles and Jews and inevitably led to tension and animosity between them. The Polish National Democrats, for example, wanted to create a "national" Poland; their appeal was to the growing Polish middle class, and they were anti-Semitic. Correspondingly, the extremist Zionists cared little for Poland, wanting their own national homeland instead. "The Zionists and the National Democrats were competing for influence on the same middle-class ground, and were offering diametrically opposed versions of the future—the one purely Jewish, the other purely Polish. In consequence, they regarded each other with undisguised hatred, the former complaining about 'anti-Semitism,' the latter about 'anit-Polonism.'"[7] The growth of political consciousness among Poles and Jews saw the creation of a rich variety of political groups by the turn of the century. In addition to extremists on the left and right, one also found Polish and Jewish groups, such as the Polish Socialists and Jewish Bundists, who cooperated. In the case of these socialists, they shared the common goal of working for socialism in Poland, not Palestine.

When Poland reappeared as an independent nation in 1919, one found two communities—Poles and Jews—who had lived together for centuries in the same country, the same city, the same village but maintained, for the most part, separate existences, lifestyles, and value systems. They tolerated each other, sometimes contemptuously. As one English observer in Poland noted, "the Jew despised the Pole for not understanding how to make money fructify; the Polish peasant despised the Jew for not being able to drive the plough or fell timber."[8]

The vast bulk of Polish Jews remained unassimilated. In the census of 1931, almost 80 percent of the Jews declared Yiddish to be their mother tongue, and a similar percentage considered themselves to be Jews by nationality.[9] Few Jews understood, let alone spoke, Polish. Approximately 40 percent of them were sympathetic with Zionist views.[10] In interwar Poland, there were 130 Yiddish and Hebrew periodicals and 15 Yiddish-language theaters. Before the outbreak of World War II, there were 266 elementary schools, 12 gymnasia, and 14 vocational schools using Yiddish or Hebrew in class.[11] "No Jew in America or France would have dreamed to send his children to similar schools," wrote one assimilated Jewish intellectual.[12]

These startling statistics reveal the sharp contrasts between the Jews of Poland and those in western Europe, who did not choose to remain a separate nation but instead became assimilated. The consequence was that during World War II, the Jews of western Europe were indistinguishable from other citizens of the country, and it was easier for them to avoid being caught by the Nazis and to receive aid from their Gentile friends and associates. In Poland, where contacts between Poles and Jews were so limited before the war, it would be unrealistic to assume that their relations during the war would be much different. Yet, as will be seen later, it is surprising that so many Poles responded to aid a people who were essentially strangers to them.

The tensions between Poles and Jews during the interwar period were largely the consequence of severe economic problems, exacerbated by the inability of the surplus population to emigrate because of the restrictive immigration laws in the United States, Great Britain, and other countries. The economic depression the Jews suffered during these years was also shared by the Poles themselves.

In the smaller provincial Polish towns, especially in eastern Poland, Jews often constituted 50 to 90 percent of the population. Practically all the shops were owned by Jews. The innkeeper was a Jew. In general, the Jews sold and the Poles either bought or worked for Jewish employers. It was in the 1930s that the Poles began to try to establish themselves in provincial towns not as taxi drivers and porters for Jewish employers but as shopkeepers and artisans. As one visitor to Poland observed, "In my experience the desire to resist and break the hold on trade in the country district rarely found expression in acts of violence against Jewish shopkeepers or their property: there were, however, in many places a growing tendency to 'buy Polish' if possible and this sometimes led to action on the part of the peasant community against persons who dealt with the Jews."[13]

Also, Jews discriminated against Poles. As they had done for centuries, Jews did business with each other and distrusted Jews who developed relationships with Polish Gentiles. One Polish Jew related: "It is true that the Poles did have the government on their side, which sometimes made things difficult for us. On the other hand, we had tradition on our side. In the big cities Jews tended to have significant trading advantages for the simple reason that they had been at it longer. . . . It is also true that though my father was assimilated, all the executives in his factory and ninety percent of his workers were Jewish. I remember once my mother, who was something of an intellectual, challenging him about this, telling him that he was being discriminatory. He said he felt easier working with Jews and that was all there was to it."[14]

Jews not only experienced competition for the first time from Poles in businesses they had traditionally monopolized but also witnessed efforts to reduce the percentage of Jews in the professions to levels that reflected their number in the total population. For example, even though Jews numbered 9.8 percent of the population, they comprised 21.5 percent of the country's professional class.[15] The economic well-being of Jews was aggravated by denying unassimilated Jews access to state employment, especially the army and the civil service.[16] A *numerus clausus* existed in some (but not all) Polish universities. There were also some laws that harassed the Jews—restricting the sale of Kosher meat (a law not enforced), depriving Jewish shopkeepers of Sunday as a trading day (in some areas), and so forth. The Jews were by no means the only minority which suffered from pressures and discriminations; in terms of wealth and social position, they were better off than the Ukrainian and White Russian minorities in Poland.[17]

The Jews in interwar Poland had to contend more with economic and bureaucratic discrimination than with physical attacks. American and British observers discredited western reports of widespread pogroms in the early years of the Polish Republic. For instance, an alleged pogrom in Lwów in 1918 was a military massacre in which more Christians than Jews perished. Another reported pogrom in Pińsk in 1919 was in reality the execution of thirty-five Bolshevik infiltrators, a judgment an American investigator considered justified in the circumstances. The brief internment of Jews in Jabłonna in 1920 did not result either in mistreatment or deaths. Moreover, in some places, as in Vilna in 1919 and 1920, the Jews put themselves in a vulnerable position by collaborating with Poland's enemies—Lithuanians and Bolsheviks.[18] There was a revival of incidents against Jews immediately prior to World War II. From 1935 to 1937, there were, according to a Jewish source, sixteen pogroms in which 118 Jews lost their lives.[19] Admittedly, these were quite regrettable, but they do not compare with the death of 2,000 Jews who lost their lives in a single pogrom in the city of Strasbourg in the Middle Ages or the millions who lost their lives during the German occupation.

During Piłsudski's political leadership in Poland, which dominated virtually half of the years of independence the Poles enjoyed between the wars, the government was not anti-Semitic. From the Jewish point of view, Piłsudski was more desirable than Admiral Horthy of Hungary and King Carol of Romania. Upon Piłsudski's death, Jews joined Poles in mourning the death of a man many Jews called "Father" (*Ojciec*).[20] Attempts by the post-Piłsudski regime, the *Sanacja*, to broaden its power base by appeals to anti-Semitism did not meet a responsive audience among most Poles. Poland's leading parties, the Socialists and the Peasant Party, rejected the *Sanacja*'s anti-Semitic program. The fact that the Peasant Party saw emigration for the Jews as a solution to the socioeconomic problem confronting Poland did not mean the party was anti-Semitic; after all, many Jews at the time endorsed the idea.[21] Only one major party in Poland was hostile to Jews—namely, the National Democrats; and according to one English historian, "they were no more rabid in their views on Jewry than on Germans, Ukrainians, socialists, or gipsies."[22] Even the anti-Semitism of the National Democrats had its limits compared to the right-wing fascist group, *Obóz Narodowo Radykalny-Falanga*, headed by Bolesław Piasecki, which had little popular support among the Poles.

Unlike other Central European countries, Poland did not enact Nuremberg-type laws against the Jews in the 1930s. Nor did it plan the destruction of the Jews as the Germans did. What happened to the Jews in Poland between the wars had nothing in common with what occurred to them under the Nazis during the Second World War. In fact, Poland was the exception among East Central European countries in the 1930s; Poland could boast major political opposition to the currents of extreme anti-Semitism that swirled around it.

It is impossible to generalize about Polish attitudes toward the Jews during the German occupation, because there was no uniformity. Despite German persecution of the Polish people, a small minority of Poles openly approved of German policies toward the Jews, and some actively aided the Nazis in their grim mission. But even the anti-Semitic National Democrats in Poland altered some of their traditional views toward the Jews as the bizarre logic of German racial policy became apparent in the extermination campaign; and some National Democrats personally aided Jews. Other Poles showed no outward pleasure at the removal of Jews from Polish offices, professions, and businesses but were not opposed to the economic expropriation involved. These people had anti-Semitic views which were economic, not racial, in character; if we can hazard any generalization at all, it is that to the extent there was anti-Semitism among some Poles, it reflected this *economic* anti-Semitic attitude. Still others quietly felt compassion for the Jewish people; they might be described, in

Philip Friedman's words, as "passive humanitarians." These people either feared becoming actively involved in aiding Jews because of the risk of the death penalty the Germans automatically imposed on Poles who helped Jews—Poland was the only occupied country where this was done—or were so pauperized by the war they simply could not afford to aid anyone without jeopardizing the survival of their own families. Then there was a very active group of Poles who were openly sympathetic toward the Jews, and many of these risked their lives to help Jews.[23]

Several factors had a negative impact on Polish attitudes toward Jews. Until at least the latter part of 1941, when the Germans began to exterminate the Jews, Poles felt that their situation was far worse than the Jews who lived in ghettos. They saw a big difference in Nazi aims toward the two groups; the Germans wanted to destroy the Poles politically, while they seemed to want only to cripple the Jews economically. After all, Jews as a group were not deported or executed as the Poles were in these early years. On the other hand, Jews in the ghettos tended to see only advantages that the Poles enjoyed on the Aryan side of the walls, while they alone experienced difficulties. Before the resistance efforts of the Jews developed later in the occupation, Poles perceived the Jews as being craven in their behavior toward the Germans, accepting without defiance the restrictions and persecutions imposed on them, collaborating with the Germans, and even denouncing Poles who hid them when the Germans discovered their hiding places outside the ghettos. By contrast, the Poles saw themselves as bearing their ordeal with pride and defiance. Poles were outraged by the active business the Jews conducted with the Germans, accused them of buying food which kept prices high, and saw many Jews preferring to have the Germans confiscate their goods rather than share them with Poles. On the other hand, those Poles who had economically benefitted from the move of the Jews to the ghettos by acquiring Jewish homes and businesses opposed the Polish government-in-exile's decree declaring all such actions under German occupation as illegal. "We will not return the shops and factories" was an all-too-familiar Polish cry.[24]

"We shall never forget their [Jewish] behavior toward the Bolsheviks"[25] was a familiar statement heard in Poland during the war, underscoring the negative behavior of many Jews during the Soviet occupation of eastern Poland beginning in September 1939. Some of these Jews were influenced by Soviet propaganda which promised them improvement in their social and economic status. Others were known to be sympathizers with the Soviet system and welcomed the opportunity that presented itself. No doubt there were also Jews who, unhappy with some of the discrimination that had existed in prewar Poland, believed their condition would improve under new landlords, a hope that soon proved illusory.

Jews in cities and towns displayed Red flags to welcome Soviet troops, helped to disarm Polish soldiers, and filled administrative positions in Soviet-occupied Poland. One report estimated that 75 percent of all the top administrative posts in the cities of Lwów, Białystok, and Łuck were in Jewish hands during the Soviet occupation. The Soviets with Jewish help shipped off the Polish intelligentsia to the depths of the Soviet Union. Some monasteries and convents were turned over to Jews.

The entire character of the University of Lwów changed during the Soviet occupation. Prior to the war, the percentage of students broke down as follows: Poles, 70 percent; Ukrainians, 15 percent; Jews, 15 percent. Under the Soviets, the percentage changed to 3 percent, 12 percent, and 85 percent, respectively. Students were so enthusiastic about the Soviet Union they wore pictures of Stalin on their breasts. In Lwów, even a memorial tablet commemorating the students who fell in defense of the city in 1918–19 was blotted out by Jews.[26]

Jewish collaboration with the Soviets, more than any other factor, was responsible for increasing anti-Semitism in Poland during the war. In these circumstances, many Poles did not understand and were even critical of the pro-Jewish declarations during these early years of the Polish government-in-exile. When the Germans invaded the Soviet Union in June 1941, the Polish government was understandably alarmed that once the Germans reoccupied eastern Poland, the Poles there would try to revenge themselves on the Jews.[27]

In the midst of the mutual antagonisms shared by Poles and Jews during the German occupation, the Germans launched a massive program of anti-Semitic propaganda through the media. They installed loudspeakers on street corners and in public places and published newspapers in Polish and German which continually spewed forth anti-Semitic themes. Wall posters, leaflets, illustrated brochures, and cinema programs, especially newsreels, were replete with anti-Semitic scenes. One *Stürmer*-type picture, which Nazis displayed, was a Jew with a louse crawling on his beard; the caption read, "Jews are crawling with the typhus." The Germans were responsible for burning a synogogue in Łódź and then blaming the Poles for doing it; the Germans explained that this was an angry Polish response to the alleged Jewish desecration earlier of a statue of Kościuszko. The Germans, of course, were really responsible for the destruction of the Kościuszko statue.[28] The entire incident was given wide publicity in the press. Michał Borwicz described the technique the Germans used to sow discord between Poles and Jews:

Anti-Semitism made use of a peculiar kind of "obligingness" in expectation of ignorance or lack of criticism on the part of the reader. At every opportunity ingenious quotations, historical examples, "facts", statistics, and so on were presented. The uncritical reader would grow hot under the collar at the Jews on the basis of examples dating back a few thousand years, although he would think it ridiculous to get excited against the English, the French, the Spanish, or the Swedes because of the behavior of their forebears.

The uncritical reader would grow incensed while reading quotations, mostly falsified anyway, from Jewish books thousands of years old, although no one experiences similar feelings toward other nations through the use of quotations from their medieval rubbish, tales, superstitions, and perversions.[29]

The violence of German propaganda against the Jews increased after Hitler's armies attacked the Soviet Union. The Germans continually sought to connect the fight against the Bolsheviks and the Jews, thus underscoring in Polish minds the link between the Jew and Bolshevik.[30] The destruction of the Warsaw Ghetto in 1943 was justified to the Varsovians at least partially because of the mass graves found in Katyń, implying Jewish-Bolshevik guilt.[31] The Germans also tried to divide the Polish people from its government-in-exile by emphasizing, falsely, Jewish influence in it.[32]

It would be difficult to determine to what extent German propaganda influenced Polish attitudes toward the Jews. There appears to have been a general repudiation by Poles of German anti-Semitic propaganda. This may have been due to the fact that Polish anti-Semitism was not racial in character; instead, as already seen, it grew out of economic circumstances and the competition of people in an overpopulated country. Sometimes it took on a sectarian character or even an anticapitalist reaction, but—except for the National Radical Camp (*Obóz Narodowo Radykalny*)—it did not take on racial attributes.[33]

In addition to the incidents of informing and blackmailing of Jews, discussed previously,[34] the most overt examples of anti-Semitism came during the early months of the occupation when the Germans encouraged gangs of young Polish hoodlums to attack Jews. Sometimes these criminals even attacked Poles. The pogroms against the Jews were not spontaneous; they usually were well-orchestrated by the Germans, who even conducted a course for members of anti-Semitic groups. The youngsters, often intoxicated, were paid by the Germans for their activity.[35] One Jewish eyewitness described the scene in Warsaw during the Passover pogrom in 1940:

The Passover pogrom continued about eight days. It began suddenly and stopped as suddenly. The pogrom was carried out by a crowd of youths, about 1,000 of them, who arrived suddenly in the Warsaw streets. Such types have never before been seen in the Warsaw streets. Clearly these were young ruffians specially brought from the suburbs. From the characteristic scenes of the pogrom I mention here a few: On the second day of Passover, at the corner of Wspólna and Marszałkowska Streets about 30 or 40 broke into and looted Jewish hat shops. German soldiers stood in the streets and filmed the scenes. . . .

The Polish youngsters acted alone, but there have been instances when such bands attacked the Jews with the assistance of German military. The attitude of the Polish intellectuals toward the Jews was clearly a friendly one, and against the pogrom. It is a known fact that at the corner of Nowogrodzka Street and Marszałkowska a Catholic priest attacked the youngsters participating in the pogrom, beat them and disappeared. These youngsters received two złotys daily from the Germans.[36]

Of course, anti-Semitic groups rejoiced at these attacks, but moderate and socialist opinion in Poland condemned them. The Socialists joined the government press in decrying the criminal behavior of some Poles. The Socialists went so far as to label any Pole a collaborator who was involved in the least anti-Semitic incident and thus an "enemy who should be exterminated with complete ruthlessness."[37] Even Emmanuel Ringelblum, who was often a severe critic of Polish behavior toward the Jews, admitted that the pogroms in Warsaw were limited to a small number of Poles: "No one will accuse the Polish nation of committing these constant pogroms and excesses against the Jewish population. The significant majority of the nation, its enlightened working-class, and the working intelligentsia, undoubtedly condemned these excesses, seeing in them a German instrument for weakening the unity of the Polish community and a lever to bring about collaboration with the Germans."[38]

Ironically, it was not so much the anti-Semitic incidents by Poles in the homeland that generated comment abroad as the charges of discrimination and racism in the Polish armed forces in Russia and in Great Britain. In the period 1942-44, at the height of the German extermination of the Jews of Europe, disproportionate attention was paid by the press and Jewish organizations abroad to this matter, which was exploited by left-wing Zionists for their own political reasons.

As has been seen, with the establishment of diplomatic relations in July 1941 between the Soviet Union and Poland, the Kremlin agreed to help form and supply a Polish army in the Soviet Union under the command of General Władysław Anders. In only a matter of weeks, Anders succeeded in organizing two divisions. Though officially committed to establish the Polish army in the Soviet Union, the Soviets threw up a series of roadblocks concerning the conscription of Polish citizens into the army and did not offer supplies in quantities substantial enough to enable the Anders army to become a fighting unit. Sikorski looked upon the Polish army in the Soviet Union as an important way to forge a closer relationship with the Russians, a goal not shared by his independent-minded commander, Anders, who was responsible for the initative that eventually resulted in evacuating the army and some civilians to the Middle East in 1942.[39]

One of the problems that disturbed Polish relations with the Soviets was the refusal of the Kremlin to allow Polish Jews, after November 1941, to enlist in the Anders army. The Soviets took the position that only ethnic Poles were Polish citizens, thus excluding Jews, Ukrainians, and White Russians, who had been citizens of Poland before the war. According to the Soviet interpretation, Jews, Ukrainians, and White Russians who lived in the lands occupied by the Soviet Union in 1939 were now Soviet citizens and thus eligible for conscription into the Red Army. Naturally, the Polish government protested the unilateral action of the Soviets, intended to underscore Soviet claims to eastern Poland. Until the Soviet policy was announced, however, a large number of Jews had enrolled in the Polish army, and some of them became recruits even later, despite the rigorous inspections conducted by Soviet officials.[40] Some Polish military units consisted of as many as 30 to 40 percent Jews. Polish anti-Semites in the army wanted but failed to get Anders to introduce a *numerus clausus*, while Zionists did not succeed in organizing separate Jewish detachments which, they hoped, would eventually find their way to Palestine instead.[41] In the first group of Jews who joined the Polish army, there were, in Polish Ambassador Kot's words, "many wretched elements arrested for smuggling and speculation," a view repeated by Sikorski to Stalin during their meeting in December 1941. Though Anders complained about Jewish desertion from his army while it was in the Soviet Union, the Polish commander of the Polish Fifth Division had no reservations about his Jewish soldiers.[42]

Sensitive to public opinion in the West, Anders agreed with Kot that there should not be a Jewish problem in his army and issued instructions to his commanders that Jewish soldiers were to be treated the same way as Polish soldiers. Jews in the Polish army, he said, had the same rights and responsibilities as Poles (*Do żyda w wojsku stosować będziemy to same prawa co i do Polaka*). And he specifically ordered his officers to combat all evidences of racism and anti-Semitism. Representatives of Polish Jews in the Soviet Union believed that Anders and Kot sought to restrain extremist elements in the army who wanted to divide Jews and Poles, and they applauded Anders's efforts to organize a single Polish army without distinction of race or religion. Isaac Schwarzbart, one of the Jewish representatives in the Polish government in London, discounted allegations of Polish discrimination against Jews in the Anders army. Following a conversation with Anders, Schwarzbart told him, "I was deeply impressed by this conversation and by your personality, general; in your hands now lies a great measure of responsibility for the advancement of Poland's cause."[43]

Later, after the Polish army had been evacuated to the Middle East, a Zionist publication alleged that Anders had indicated in an order to his commanders in November 1941, that he understood the reasons for some of the anti-Semitic incidents in the ranks because of the pro-Soviet behavior of many Jews in 1939 and 1940 when the Soviets occupied eastern Poland; but for political reasons, the troops should mitigate their anti-Semitism. The general categorically denied he had given such an order: "That order is a falsification from A to Z."[44] Whether or not the controversial order was a falsification, it is not difficult to understand why many Polish soldiers, especially those who came from eastern Poland, would resent Jews for their treasonable behavior in 1939-40. Those Jews who had pro-Soviet sympathies, however, rapidly became disabused of them because of the poor treatment they received from the Russians; they were soon, in Ambassador Kot's words, "frequently emphasizing their Polish citizenship."[45]

The American and Jewish press misrepresented Polish policy toward Jewish soldiers and civilians who comprised part of the exodus from the Soviet Union to the Middle East. They claimed the Poles were responsible for removing Jews from military units and replacing them with Poles so that a larger number of Poles would be evacuated from the Soviet Union. In reality, the Soviet authorities were responsible for excluding Jews from the evacuation on the grounds that they were Soviet, not Polish, citizens.[46]

Polish embassy officials tried to get Polish Jews out of Russia. They issued hundreds of passports and obtained transit visas from friendly countries, but the Soviets refused to give the Jews the exit visas—and they arrested representatives of the Polish embassy, charging them with being involved in intelligence activities. Several of these Polish Jews who were discriminated against by the Soviet Union addressed rabbis in the United States and Britain: "We want to open your eyes and those of the

Jewish public and make you see what we are going through here. The authorities of the USSR, contrary to all international laws, refuse to recognize our rights to Polish citizenship."[47] As one Polish military officer who was involved in the evacuation from the Soviet Union testified:

> The Soviet authorities forbade us most rigorously to include any Jewish families in our transports. If we attempted to bypass this order, the convoy would be stopped. After much bargaining, they agreed that the wives and children of Jewish soldiers on active service in our Division might be admitted in transports with their husbands or fathers. This was subject to a severe inspection of nominal rolls at the entrainment. Parents, or more remote relatives, were denied this opportunity, to which the families of non-Jewish soldiers were entitled. It was a new tragedy.

Once Jews in the Soviet Union heard of the evacuation, many of them flocked to where the army and selected civilians were entraining. Unfortunately, they had no relatives in the Polish army and were prohibited by the Soviets to leave. But Soviet officials gave the impression to these Jews that the Poles were guilty: "The Jews . . . cursing us and ascribing their tragedy to us. Our denials had no effect: they believed the Soviets. This was one of the most cunning and treacherous of the Soviet tricks, intended to smear the Poles throughout the world with the indictment that Polish soldiers were 'Fascist anti-Semites.'"[48] One Polish official wryly commented, "The locksmith was guilty but they hang the blacksmith." (*Ślusarz zawinił, a kowala wieszają*).[49]

Despite Soviet impediments, 3,500 to 4,000 Jews were evacuated from Russia to the Middle East during the summer of 1942. They included Jews in the ranks of the Polish army and their close families, a large number of Jewish orphans who had been housed in Jewish and Polish orphanages in the Soviet Union, and a number of people, among them several rabbis, who had no connection with the Polish army. The British concluded that Polish authorities had done their best to include as many Jews as possible in the evacuation.[50]

Once the Polish army got to the Middle East, a large number of Jews deserted from the ranks—for example, 236 out of 238 deserters from the Third Carpathian Division were Jews.[51] In succeeding months there were hundreds of additional Jews who deserted from the Polish army. Most of these desertions had less to do with anti-Semitism than with the influence and pressure of Zionists who wanted these men to remain in Palestine. No doubt there were Jews—Zionist and non-Zionist—who had had no intention of serving in the Polish army and deserted once they got to Palestine.

In Palestine, there were a number of anti-Polish Jews whom the Soviets exploited to spread Polonophobic and pro-Soviet propaganda to undermine the prestige and authority of the Polish government.[52]

The attacks against the Poles in the Soviet Union in 1941-42 also included allegations that Polish embassy officials discriminated against Polish Jews in the distribution of supplies. Ambassador Kot, who, like Sikorski, was a philo-Semite, exerted considerable energy and enterprise in trying to locate and meet the needs of Polish citizens, Gentiles and Jews, who were disbursed throughout the Soviet Union. Before the Soviets undermined the relief activities of the Polish embassy in the Soviet Union, the Polish embassy had established nineteen offices with 387 "men of confidence," among whom were 297 Poles, 82 Jews, and 8 Ukrainians or Byelorussians involved in the work.[53] The Soviets tried to prevent the Poles from appointing Polish Jews as "men of confidence." The difficulties for the Poles are revealed in a conversation between a Soviet and a Polish official in Russia regarding the status of two men, Rozencwaj and Lustgarten, whom the Polish government wanted to appoint as "men of confidence:"

> Soviet: "Are they Polish citizens of Polish origin?"
> Pole: "They are Polish citizens of Polish origin."
> Soviet: "Are their names Polish?"
>
> . . . .
>
> Soviet: "Aren't they Jews?"
> Pole: "They are not Jews, they are Poles."
> Soviet: "After all, there are Poles and Poles. When someone is called Smogorzewski, he is a Pole; but Rozencwaj and Lustgarten are, after all, Jews."[54]

By 1942, given the citizenship policy of the Kremlin, the Soviets forbade Jewish, Ukrainian, and Byelorussian citizens of Poland to receive assistance from the offices of the Polish embassy in the Soviet Union. Still, Kot and his staff continued to refuse to accept the Soviet distinction between Polish and Jewish citizens. "Here I represent all Polish citizens," Kot bluntly told a Soviet official.[55]

Prior to 1944, the question of anti-Semitism in the Polish army in Great Britain had attracted little public notice. There were some isolated anti-Semitic incidents in the Polish army, but the British foreign office considered the attitude of Polish authorities "was beyond reproach in this respect." This was made clear by Sikorski, who was probably the most philo-Semitic of all Polish leaders, when he issued an order-of-the-day stressing "that a soldier who has taken up arms for his country has thereby proved that he is a Pole without regard to his race or religion." He specifically prohibited any action which offended or abused soldiers of the Mosaic faith.[56] Professor Lewis Namier, a Zionist, confirmed the opinion held in British official circles by saying that the Polish government had behaved "very decently" on the Jewish question. Though Namier acknowledged there was anti-Semitic feeling among Poles, especially in the army, he did not believe it was reasonable to expect the Polish government to do more than it was already doing to deal with the problem. One member of the British Foreign Office, summing up his conversation with Namier, stated that the Polish government "could no more prevent occasional excesses on the part of individual N.C.O.'s than HMG could prevent occasional lapses in the treatment of internees."[57]

The conscription of Jews into the Polish army in Britain and the arrest of some Jewish recruits on charges of desertion gave rise to renewed charges of anti-Semitism. In truth Jews showed a reluctance to serve in the Polish army. According to one Jewish historian who sympathized with the Jewish soldiers, "There was a general reluctance among Polish Jews to serve under the Polish flag; the cause was not lack of anti-Fascist zeal, but a widespread suspicion that there existed among Polish soldiers and officers a certain sympathy with the anti-Jewish aims of the Nazis; the behaviour of the Polish troops to their Jewish comrades-in-arms often lent colour to these suspicions."[58] Polish authorities, on the other hand, believed that many Jews used their Polish citizenship to get passage from France to England without ever intending to meet their military responsibilities. Once in England, many denied their Polish citizenship. There were also cases of Jews who refused to serve in the Polish army because they allegedly preferred to serve with the British, but never enlisted with them. One eminent Jewish leader of the World Jewish Congress, Arie Tartakower, revealed the impact of Zionism when he told Sikorski that "if there were to be a choice of joining a Polish army or a Jewish army our place would naturally be in the Jewish army." To this, a Foreign Office official noted caustically, "And yet the Poles are expected to regard these people as 100% Polish citizens."[59]

Sensitive to evidences of anti-Semitism among the Poles, the British and American sections of the World Jewish Congress criticized the publication *I am a Pole* (*Jestem Polakiem*), a right-wing anti-Semitic newspaper that had been condemned many times by the Polish government. Despite the urging of Professor Namier to the Jewish press not to take the publication too seriously, Jews in Britain and the United States exaggerated its significance. In the words of one British official, "The altogether disproportionate attention paid to it . . . by the Jewish Congress seems . . . to me to show a complete lack of any sense of perspective."[60]

American Jews were no different. Before Sikorski's arrival in the United States on a state visit, an article in *Congress Weekly*, the organ of the American Jewish Congress, attacked the general: "Can we trust Sikorski, the proud, arrogant, aristocratic Polish general, more than we did Pilsudski . . . ?" *Der Wecher* saw no difference between the *Sanacja* and Sikorski. It said, "The Government of General Sikorski [is] an obstacle in the way of finding friends for a new and free Poland." A summary of an article in *Der Tog* stated, "In the opinion of the writer, all members of the Government are anti-Semites, hidden anti-Semites, and therefore more dangerous [than] the open ones." A delegation of American Jews presented Sikorski with a memorandum in which *Jestem Polakiem* was prominently featured as evidence of anti-Semitism in the Polish army. The lack of balance in the Jewish memorandum was cause for concern to a Polish writer who later said: "It is, however, appropriate to note that the suffering and persecution of Jews in Poland at that time were not mentioned, either in the memorandum or in the talks with General Sikorski. The Polish prime minister could certainly have been able to say a great deal about these subjects, yet the Jewish delegation did not ask about them."[61]

Judged by the number of reported cases of anti-Semitism and the number of desertions of Jews from the Polish army in Britain before 1944, it would seem that there was considerable harmony between Jewish and Polish soldiers. From September 1940 to May 1941, no cases of anti-Semitism came to the attention of the British government, which was well informed on these matters. Even more striking was the fact that from November 1940 to the winter of 1944, there were only seventeen Jews who had deserted from the Polish army in Britain.[62] No doubt the energetic efforts of Polish officials to encourage better relations between Poles and Jews in the Polish army had a great deal to do with it.

The Polish Ministry of Defense, headed by Marian Kukiel, launched an information campaign on Polish history, minorities, and the plight of Poland's Jews through discussions and the Polish military newspaper, *Soldier's Daily* (*Dziennik Żołnierza*). Kukiel established a rabbinical commission, headed by the chief rabbi in the Polish army, to deal with problems involving rabbis. He even created a special department in his ministry to look after Jewish soldiers and foster greater solidarity between Polish and Jewish soldiers. Kukiel's efforts were endorsed by Sosnkowski, who issued an order stating that all soldiers, regardless of their nationality, had the right to work in an atmosphere of collegiality, confidence, and unity in the Polish army. Even the Polish clergy was enlisted to educate Polish soldiers on the Polish question through homilies and discussions. In one order to the officers of the Polish army, Kukiel admitted the existence of anti-Semitic behavior in the Polish army which, he said, is exploited by Poland's enemies and undermines the confidence of the western allies in Poland, a point of view underscored by a resolution of the Polish National Council.[63]

Kukiel met regularly with representatives of the Jewish press in Britain, reaching a "gentlemen's agreement" with editors to inform him of any allegations concerning anti-Semitic incidents in the Polish army. The public relations effort produced results: There was a reduction in the number of unfriendly articles about Poland in the Jewish press in Britain.[64]

The apparent progress in creating greater solidarity between Jews and Poles dramatically ended in January 1944, when 79 Jews deserted from the Polish army. They were followed by 134 in February and 24 in March.[65] The deserters cited anti-Semitic remarks by Polish soldiers. A Polish commission of inquiry confirmed that there were men, mostly in the lower ranks, who were responsible for these remarks and were not disciplined sufficiently for these incidents. Specifically, Polish soldiers who had served in Russia and those who had been forced to serve in the German army were the sources of most of the anti-Semitic behavior. The commission found no anti-Semitic conspiracy in the army, but it did recommend that stiffer penalties be given to those found guilty of future incidents and that the military authorities foster a collegial spirit between Polish and Jewish soldiers. It also recommended that the principles of fairness be followed in granting promotions and advanced military training, one of the grievances of some of the Jewish soldiers.[66]

But the Polish commission also found that a sizable percentage of Jewish soldiers were unpatriotic and were motivated by personal ambition and politics in their desertions. The commission speculated that the desertions were orchestrated, significantly pointing out that almost all the January deserters came from the Polish First Armored Division, which had been placed on a military alert.[67] Significantly, there were no Jewish dissidents in General Stanisław Sosabowski's Polish Parachute Brigade, a fact which Jewish members of the unit confirmed.[68] Some Foreign Office officials agreed that the Jewish deserters were shirkers; one recalled the large number of Jews—Sosnkowski estimated 2,500—who had "waited until they got to Palestine and until the Polish army were just about to go into action, to desert."[69] Now with the upcoming plans to invade Normandy, it appeared all too coincidental to observers that many Jewish soldiers simply did not want to fight.

It is significant that most of these deserters were in contact with leftist members of Parliament—namely, Thomas Driberg, Michael Foot, and D. N. Pritt—who were anti-Polish and pro-Soviet in their views. Scotland Yard confirmed the suspicions of Professor Heitzman, a Polish Jew connected with the Polish Ministry of National Defense, who believed that the desertions had been planned and supported by English Jews. Heitzman believed that "Jewish nationalism was at the bottom of the trouble," not anti-Semitism.[70]

Since the outbreak of the war, Zionists tried to get the British to create a Jewish military force, which they hoped to use as leverage in creating Palestine as a Jewish home. The British were cool to the idea, but the Zionists continued their campaign in the United States to create a Palestinian army. Jeremiah Helpern and Lord Strabolgi were intimately involved in these Zionist schemes. In fact, Helpern even headed the Committee for a Jewish Army of Stateless Refugee and Palestine Jews. He took an active role in trying to convince the Foreign Office of widespread anti-Semitism in the Polish army and in championing the cause of the Jewish deserters he wanted to organize into separate Palestinian Jewish battalions. Helpern did not succeed in getting separate Jewish battalions, but the Poles, reluctant to discipline the deserters and prolong a crisis that undermined Poland's prestige, allowed the deserters in the first two groups to become members of the British Pioneer Corps, which were nonmobilized units.[71] To Zionist zealots like Helpern, this may have been viewed as a first, but important, step in reaching the cherished goal of getting separate Jewish units.

There was a curious convergence between the Zionist Revisionists and the right-wing National Radical Camp; both were extreme nationalists and used similar methods to achieve their objectives. Zionist agitation to get Jews to desert from the Polish army played into the hands of right-wing Poles who were delighted to see this Jewish exodus from the Polish army.[72] Polish authorities were reluctant to treat the third group of deserters as they had the first two groups because of fears that other soldiers, including Poles and Ukrainians, would begin to desert. They were so sensitive to allegations of anti-Semitism that some of them believed allowing the third group to serve in the Pioneer Corps would convince Jewish critics that the Poles deliberately intended to clear the Jews out of the Polish army. Polish authorities decided to go through the ritual of court-martialing Jews who had deserted in March 1944, but President Raczkiewicz signed an amnesty decree early in May 1944 for all Jewish soldiers who had left the ranks of the Polish army.[73]

The reaction of the British press to these incidents was shocking to

Poles who remembered a time when Poland had been treated sympathetically. Now the Poles were continually attacked for anti-Semitism, which
convinced Polish leaders that Soviet propaganda was behind the campaign, a view shared by Churchill, who declared, "I do not like people
who desert on the eve of battle, and I believe there has been some communist intrigue behind all this to discredit the Polish division."[74] Raczyński commented on the pro-Soviet line in the British press that had been
going on for some time: "Everything to do with the Soviet ally, and especially its relations with Poland, is enveloped in a dense fog of mendac-
ity."[75] Raczyński's criticism of the British press could also be applied to
the American press, which seemed intent on Americanizing the image of
the Soviet Union while treating the Polish government-in-exile less favorably.[76] As for the Jewish deserters, Raczyński wrote bitterly in his diary:
"No one ventures to suggest that our Jewish soldiers might be to blame
for deserting their units on the eve of battle. The press and public opinion
implicitly assume that the fault can only be on the side of our authorities."[77]

Jewish leaders and the Jewish press also joined in attacking the Poles.
Professor S. Brodetsky, president of the Board of Deputies of British
Jews, made the accusation: "Why should one of the armies of the United
Nations be permitted to carry out policies similar to those of the Nazis?"
The *Jewish Chronicle* published tendentious headlines such as "Anti-
Semitism in Polish Army: Shocking Revelations in Parliament: 3,000 Ex-
Hun Soldiers in Polish Ranks?"[78] Extremist Jewish and Polish groups pre-
dictably entered the crisis; some people describing themselves as Polish
Fascists threatened Driberg, while a group calling themselves *Irgun Zvai
Leumi* (Jewish National Military Organization) promised revenge for the
imprisonment of some of the soldiers who were part of the third group of
Jews to desert from the Polish army. Premier Mikołajczyk believed that
this same group was responsible for anonymously threatening him.[79]

News of the Jewish desertions caused indignation and outrage among
the Poles in Poland, especially among people who risked their lives to
hide Jews.[80] There was discussion of the issue in Polish underground
newspapers which were critical of the British press for exploiting the matter when there were so many more important issues, such as the slaughter
of millions of people by the Nazis, to be concerned about. *Przegląd Polityczny* saw the pious indignation toward the Poles in this matter as hypoc-
risy: Where, the newspaper asked, were the British when the Jews were
being slaughtered by the Nazis? Besides, it added pointedly, "Every single
Jew, who lives at this moment on Polish soil, owes his protection and help
only to the Poles. No one else will give it to him."[81] The British Political

Warfare Executive understood the sensitivity of the issue to the Poles and directed the BBC to play it down in its newscasts as much as possible: "We should always bear in mind that a very large number of Jews (all the Jews who still survive in Poland) are now existing under the protection of the Polish Underground Movement and of the general population, while the penalty for harbouring a Jew is death for the whole household. In broadcasting to Poland we should remember that any indignation aroused there at the action of Polish Jewish soldiers in this country might have repercussions on the fate of those Jews in Poland."[82]

To be sure, the desertions obscured the fact that many Jews in the Polish army served loyally. As one Jewish soldier pointed out in the midst of this crisis: "There are very many soldiers in the Polish army of Jewish origin or of Jewish religion only, who consider themselves as Poles . . . there is no doubt of the sincerity of their allegiance and that they are Poles in reality and not in name only."[83]

It is not known how many Poles actually aided Jews during the German occupation. For that reason, glib generalizations on the subject must be suspect. What is known, however, is that after the Germans ordered the Jews to live in ghettos, and especially after they unleashed the so-called "Final Solution," Poles increasingly responded to the Jewish plight not only as an expression of pity for the Jews but also as an action of resistance against the hated Germans. Poles of all classes gave a variety of assistance to the persecuted Jews; food, shelter, and false documents were some of the more common types of aid. Considering the utter barbarity of German rule in Poland and the continuing persecution of the Poles by the Germans, it is remarkable that so many Poles were involved in the aid efforts. The wonder is not how few but how many Jews were saved in Poland during the German occupation.

Jewish leaders at the time made clear their praise for those Poles who fought against anti-Semitism and extended aid to the Jews. The Jewish Bund, which had especially close ties with the Polish socialists, denied charges of widespread anti-Semitism among the Poles by commenting on how a majority of Polish people—workers and peasants—resisted anti-Semitic propaganda.[84] Szmul Zygielbojm, a respected Jewish member of the Polish National Council in London, gave a speech to the council, during which he read a statement from one of his kinsmen in Poland: "The Polish people showed the Jews much sympathy and gave considerable help in all these events." In the introduction to a pamphlet entitled *Stop*

Them Now: German Mass-Murders of Jews in Poland, published in 1942, Zygielbojm wrote: "I must mention here that the Polish population gives all possible help and sympathy to the Jews. . . . The walls of the ghetto have not really separated the Jewish population from the Poles. The Polish and Jewish masses continue to fight together for common aims, just as they have fought for so many years in the past."[85] His colleague in the Polish National Council, Schwarzbart, initiated a motion in the council in 1943 which praised Polish efforts to help save Jews and urged the Poles to continue their efforts. Adolf Berman, who was an important link between the Jewish and Polish underground, eloquently declared later: "Accounts of the martyrdom of Poland's Jews tend to emphasize their suffering at the hands of blackmailers and informers, the 'blue' police and other scum. Less is written, on the other hand, about the thousands of Poles who risked their lives to save the Jews. The flotsam and jetsam on the surface of a turbulent river is more visible than the pure stream running deep underneath, but that stream existed."[86]

Even Emmanuel Ringelblum, who often caustically criticized the Poles for not doing enough to help his kinsmen, said: "There are thousands [of idealists] like these in Warsaw and the whole country. . . . The names of the people who do this, and whom the Poland which shall be established should decorate with the 'Order of Humanitarianism,' will remain in our memory as the names of heroes who saved thousands of human beings from certain death by fighting against the greatest enemy the human race has ever known."[87] His own journal entries at the time confirm how Poles drew closer to the Jews after the September campaign. On September 9, 1940, he recorded how Poles voluntarily taxed themselves for Jewish causes. A month later, he noted "frequent occurrences where Christians take the side of Jews against attacks by hoodlums. That wasn't so before the war." About the same time, he wrote how he "heard many stories" of Polish customers who sent packages to Jewish merchants confined in the Łódź Ghetto. On November 19, 1940, he made this diary entry: "A Christian was killed today . . . for throwing a sack of bread over the wall." In May 1941, he recorded how "Catholics displayed a far-reaching tolerance" and how a Passover program "evoked great respect among the Polish populace."[88] And On July 11, 1941, he wrote: "This was a widespread phenomenon a month ago. Hundreds of beggars, including women and children, smuggled themselves out of the Ghetto to beg on the Other Side, where they were well received, well fed, and often given food to take back to the Ghetto with them. Although universally recognized as Jews from the Ghetto, perhaps they were given alms for that very reason. This was an interesting symptom of a deep transformation in Polish society."[89] In the latter part of 1942, Ringelblum recorded: "Polish organizations combatted and did away with blackmail."[90]

Adam Czerniaków, who headed the Warsaw *Judenrat* until his suicide in 1942, also kept a diary which reflected Polish sympathy for the Jews. On January 29, 1942, he revealed that a Polish Christian had financed repairs on one of the synagogues in the ghetto. On July 18, 1942, he recorded that a young Polish girl had been hiding a Jewish woman in her home.[91] Even extremely critical accounts of Poles by Jews who experienced the German occupation of Poland point up the complexity of Polish-Jewish wartime relations and the difficulty of making generalizations on the subject.[92]

In October, 1942, the *Rzeczpospolita Polska* claimed with some justification that Polish aid to the Jews was so conspicuous and spontaneous that the Germans felt compelled to order the imposition of the death penalty on all Poles who helped Jews, a sentence which was not typical of Nazi policy elsewhere in Europe. And the fact that the Germans continually repeated warnings to the Poles that they would be executed for helping Jews suggests that Polish people ignored the risks and continued to aid them.[93]

Perhaps the best evidence of the response of Poles to the plight of the Jews is revealed by the large number of Polish anti-Semites who, in Ringelblum's words, "grasped that . . . the Poles and Jews had a common enemy and that the Jews were excellent allies who would do all they possibly could to bring destruction on the Jews' greatest enemies." Even unreconstructed anti-Semites who had Jewish relatives helped them. "Polish anti-Semites did not apply racialism where relatives or friends were concerned," Ringelblum admitted. Many anti-Semitic Poles disliked Jews as abstractions. Once they got to know Jews, they had no personal animosity toward them and even developed genuine affection for them. Thus the truth of the old Polish maxim was confirmed: "Every Pole has his Jew" (*Każdy Polak ma swego Żyda*).[94]

Although more research needs to be done on the subject, it appears that Poles in some regions of the country were more responsive than those in others to the plight of the Jews. In addition to Warsaw, Poles seemed to be very sympathetic with the Jews in western and eastern Galicia. Cracow was the administrative center of the Nazi administration in the General Government, but Cracovians hid many Jews from the Germans.[95] Zygielbojm recalled when he was on his way to Cracow, he heard a Pole sermonizing on the Jews in the presence of other Poles, who remained silent. Finally, one of the Polish peasants who had heard enough of the anti-

Semitic diatribe asked the man, "And where did you learn to preach so well in German?" The anti-Semite tried to respond but was drowned out by the laughter of the pro-Jewish Poles. Zygielbojm wrote of the incident: "The peasant has not only lifted a stone from my heart, but I notice that the other passengers are relieved; now they openly criticize the fascist's remarks. The word—*Kanarek*—collaborator—is repeated several times. At first the man tries to defend himself, but no one listens to him; soon he sits dejectedly in his place and remains silent."[96]

The Polish Socialist Party alone managed to prepare about 150 hide-outs in Cracow for those wanted by the Nazis, no small achievement in a city innundated with the SS and Gestapo.[97] The same was true of other towns and cities in Galicia: In Nowy Sącz, a Pole claimed that thanks to Polish help, 1,200 Jews survived the Nazi terror; in Przemyśl, Dr. Józef Blech, a Jew, testified that 160 Jewish adults and orphans had been saved by the Poles.[98] Even one Jewish critic of the Poles admitted that Polish aid in the outlying areas of Galicia was so extensive that the Germans wiped out two Polish villages for helping Jews and partisans.[99] And, of course, there were other parts of the country where the Poles responded to the plight of the Jews, especially the area of Lublin and Chełmno. In Poznań, Ringelblum noted, the Poles tearfully accompanied the Jews when they were expelled from the city by the Germans.[100]

Poles who dared aid a Jew assumed risks that were largely unknown to western Europeans. As has been pointed out, the Poles automatically risked death. Since rescuing a Jew usually meant that more than one individual was involved in the effort, apprehension by the Germans often meant the execution of entire families or circles of people. A Polish historian estimated that to hide one Jew the cooperation of about ten people was required.[101] Based on testimonies made to me, I conclude that sometimes the number was even more than that. The Germans, in their zealous efforts to uncover Jews, constantly warned the Poles of retribution for hiding them and held committees responsible in each apartment complex for ferreting them out. It was not unusual for Jews to leave the home of their Polish protectors for fear of jeopardizing their lives; sometimes they chose suicide.

Occasionally, there were Poles who hid a number of Jews and were reluctant for obvious reasons to take in any more but were forced to do so under the threat of blackmail from those who desperately needed shelter.[102] The dangers were so great for the Poles that even the Polish Socialists were reluctant to aid their friends and colleagues in the ghetto. Poles were understandably reluctant to enter the Warsaw Ghetto, because it was not uncommon for them to be mistreated or even shot, even though they had legal passes. Thus to save a Jew in the conditions in Poland at that time represented the highest degree of heroism.[103]

Since the Poles had experienced progressive pauperization during the German occupation and lived in conditions of bare subsistence, most Poles could not offer assistance to Jewish refugees even if they wanted to. Therefore, when Jews gave money to Poles to keep them, it was not out of greed but out of poverty that it was accepted. "There are poor families who base their subsistence on the funds paid daily by the Jews to their Aryan landlords," Ringelblum wrote. "But is there enough money in the world to make up for the constant fear of exposure, fear of the neighbors, the porter and the manager of the block of flats, etc.?"[104]

One of the chief obstacles in rescuing Jews was the fact that the over-whelming majority of them were unassimilated. They did not know the Polish language, had few if any Polish friends, wore distinctive dress, and had been brought up in a pacifist tradition. Władysława Homsowa, who played an active role in saving Jews in the Lwów area, declared, "The greatest difficulty was the passivity of the Jews themselves."[105]

Prewar separation of the Polish and Jewish communities, along with earlier mutual animosities, sometimes got in the way of developing close relationships during the war. As one former Polish underground soldier remarked, "Before the war, they called me *goy, goy!* Now they wanted my help." He added, "Poles helped Jews, but do you realize how difficult it was to save a person who obviously looked Semitic? They had to be hidden all the time, because if they dared to venture out the Germans would pounce on them."[106]

According to one recent sociological study of rescuers throughout oc-cupied Europe, people who knew Jews before the war were more likely to help them than if the Jew was a stranger: "In many cases, perhaps over 75%, the rescued individuals reported that they were saved by some one whom they personally knew or by members of their respective families who knew each other."[107] In the case of Poland, it is important to under-stand that early in the war much of the Jewish intelligentsia, the most assimilated class of Polish Jews, had been executed along with their Polish counterparts. The Jews who remained came, for the most part, from the lower classes, were unassimilated, and had the fewest contacts with Polish Gentiles.

Finally, there was the enormous number of problems and difficulties involved in hiding a Jew—how to supply food, provide decent sanitary conditions, assure the person's security. It was difficult enough to provide these things for one refugee, let alone twenty-six Jews as Feliks Cywiński did:

In a flat where Jews were hiding, suitable hiding places had to be secured. Sometimes, we would set up a new wall in one of the rooms—so that people could hide behind it in case of danger; then I brought bricks home in my briefcase—not more than four at a time lest the neighbours suspect something; in the same way I brought lime and sand; other times we would conceal the last room in a large flat by covering the door with a wardrobe with a movable back wall.

The most difficult task was to procure food. Twenty-six people is quite a lot! Food had to be brought in small quantities so that no one should wonder why a single person needed so much food. I carried it in my briefcase, in small parcels, in pockets. In one day, I had to bring successive portions many times. The purchase and transport of food consumed much of my time.

Once it turned out that one of the women became ill. Later, the others got typhus. I contacted Dr. Jan Mocałło and asked him for assistance. The doctor came every day; he brought medicaments. Unfortunately, one of the women died. This is hard to understand today—but her death made the chances of survival very doubtful for all of us: the people under my care and myself who was giving help to Jews. We had no other way but to tie up the woman's corpse, put it in a sack and thus carry it out as a parcel containing food or, say papers. One of my friends drove up with a car; we crammed the body into the car and started towards the Jewish cemetery. I feared all the way that we might be stopped by a German patrol suspecting that the big parcel contained smuggled food. We reached the cemetery without any trouble, though. I attached a piece of paper to the sack with the name of the deceased and we threw the body over the wall. There was nothing more we could do.[108]

One Polish peasant, who had saved many Jews, remarked candidly that the penalty for hiding one or ten Jews was the same: death. He bluntly added, "The only difference being that it was harder to feed so many and clean away after them."[109]

As Jewish refugees themselves have observed, it was more difficult to hide Jewish people in the countryside than in towns and cities, because everyone knew one another, and any unusual thing—such as large purchases of food by a Pole—could give away the rescuer to an informer or to a loquacious friend whose remarks sometimes found their way back to the police. There were, of course, other major problems that made it difficult to hide a Jew—German house searches for grain and cattle not delivered by the peasant under the enforced quota system, frequent pacification operations by German police and regular troops, periodic roundups of young Poles trying to avoid deportation to forced labor in Germany.

Although this discussion has dwelt on Poles who provided Jews with shelter and security, there were thousands of Polish humanitarians who did a plethora of lesser but no less risky things that aided the Jews—smuggling food into the ghettos, conveying warnings about the death camps, providing false documents to enable especially non-Semitic-looking Jews to pass for Gentiles.

Smuggling food into the ghettos was a major part of Polish-Jewish cooperation. Children were especially active in the operation because they could slip through holes in the ghetto walls. "Jewish and Polish blood spilt together cries out for vengeance," wrote one Jewish chronicler about the smuggling effort. Another included in her diary Polish and Jewish smugglers in the "list of saints and heroes of our dark age," because without their activity the mass of Jews would have died of starvation. It was that keen realization that won the support of Jew and Gentile to smuggling operations.[110]

Polish railroad workers were the first Poles to warn Jews destined for Treblinka what really awaited them there. These men were the liaison between towns, informing people about the latest news concerning the deportation and persecution of Jews and maintaining contacts between Jewish families by carrying letters, money, and packages to them.[111]

The provision of documents was essential for a Jew to have any mobility. An old Russian saying about man consisting of three elements—a body, a soul, and a passport—applied with equal force to German-occupied Poland. To establish one's legal existence, several documents were necessary:

> To establish legal existence quite a number of documents were necessary. To begin with, a birth certificate or an extract from a register of births had to be shown. For married couples, a marriage certificate was required, as well as an extract from current registration lists and proof of registration. Only after obtaining these was one able to apply for a *Kennkarte* bearing a photograph and a thumbprint. Possession of a *Kennkarte* was obligatory. To complicate life even further, all persons below the age of sixty had to have an employment card as well, the so-called *Arbeitskarte*, stamped by the German *Arbeitsamt*, and indicating one's place of employment. To be absolutely safe, it was advisable to carry one's food ration cards too.[112]

There are many stories of extraordinary courage which form a part of the historical record of Polish-Jewish relations, and there are many others which have yet to be officially recorded and the heroes and heroines recognized for their uncommon acts. One story which is part of the record concerns the heroism of a mild-mannered, former carriage maker, Staszek Jackowski, who saved thirty-two out of sixty-six Jewish survivors in the city of Stanisławów. Jackowski searched for and brought his friends, Max and Gitya Saginur, to his home where he hid them behind his kitchen. The location was not satisfactory because every sound could be detected. Jackowski decided to build a small bunker in his cellar to house his friends. In time, thirty other Jews found their way to his enlarged "basket" (*Kosz*, a term that referred to a place where Jews were hiding) and were hidden in three bunkers, equipped with beds, stoves, plumbing, and electricity. Jackowski dug a well that provided fresh water for his guests, who could even take baths; ironically, his own family upstairs had no water. He had special cables to tap additional electricity without being metered through his home. Jackowski, who had a profound moral sense, believed that he had to do what he did. "After all," he said, "the Jews were human beings."[113]

Jackowski has been recognized by the Committee on the Righteous (Yad Vashem) for his heroism, but there are many Poles, such as the Kotkowski family, whose names and achievements are known only to a few people. Stanisław Kotkowski and his mother were responsible for hiding a young Jewish girl, Rachel Cymber, who jumped from a moving train on its way to Majdanek, near Lublin. "They were very good to me. I became a member of their family. I shall never forget them," Cymber stated. "There were many other Poles too who helped me in those dark days."[114]

The Poles were unique among the people under German occupation to form an underground organization which specifically aided Jews. In late September 1942, Zofia Kossak, chairman of the Front for Reborn Poland, and Wanda Krahelska-Filipowicz, an activist in the Socialist Party, had a major role in forming the Provisional Committee for Assistance to the Jews. During its brief existence, the committee helped hundreds of Jews in the Warsaw area. Three months later, it was replaced by the Council for Aid to Jews (*Rada Pomocy Żydom*), or *Żegota*, a cryptonym derived from the Polish word for Jew, *Żyd*. The executive board of *Żegota* represented the moderate-left of the Polish political spectrum: Julian Grobelny, a Socialist, was chairman; Tadeusz Rek, member of the Peasant Party, was vice-chairman; Dr. Leon Feiner, member of the Bund, was second vice-chairman; Dr. Adolf Berman, of the Jewish National Committee, was secretary; and Marek Arczyński of the Democratic Party was treasurer. The Front for Reborn Poland was represented at first by Ignacy Barski and later by Władysław Bartoszewski. Even Jews under the care of groups not represented on *Żegota*—the Polish Syndicalist Union and the Polish Workers Party—received help from it.[115] With headquarters in Warsaw, *Żegota* developed regional councils in Cracow and Lwów, and cooperated with councils in Lublin and Zamość. After the Warsaw Uprising, *Żegota* resumed operations out of Milanowek, near Warsaw, until January 1945.[116] The government delegate played a role in the organization of the Provisional Committee and later Żegota. The government's representative, who participated in the meetings of Żegota, also headed the Jewish department of the Government Delegacy.[117]

Żegota carried out an impressive program of aid that webbed the entire country. It was involved in trying to find shelter, provide food and medical assistance, and give proper documents to Jews under its care. It also carried out an active campaign against blackmailers, informers, and the anti-Semitic propaganda of the Nazis. Żegota never seemed to lack for personnel, including members of the AK, in its activities.[118]

One of the most critical aspects of Żegota's activities was the forging of documents which Jewish refugees needed. Using the printing presses of the Democratic Party, Żegota produced in time an average of 100 forged documents every day. In less than two years, Żegota was responsible for making available 50,000 documents, 80 percent of which reached Jews without any cost to them.[119]

The Polish government provided most of the funds for Żegota's operations. Until June 1943, Żegota also provided money to Jewish organizations involved in relief work. After that, a small amount of funds came to Żegota from the Jewish National Committee and Jewish organizations abroad. The government delegate's grant to Żegota amounted to 150,000 złotys in January 1943 and swelled to 900,000 złotys in April 1943, during the Ghetto Uprising. Monthly allocations leveled off to 550,000 złotys from June to October 1943, but by August 1944 reached 2,000,000 złotys and eventually went as high as 4,000,000 złotys.[120] The Polish government-in-exile, in response to western pressures to do more for the Jews, made additional extraordinary allocations; for example, in February 1944, the government instructed the delegate to make an outlay of 3,000,000 złotys above regular monthly allocations to Żegota and to help Jewish organizations involved in relief work.[121] The request came at a time when the Polish government-in-exile wanted to offset the negative publicity and charges of anti-Semitism stemming from the defection of Jewish soldiers from the Polish army in England. One Polish scholar estimates that the Polish government provided 37,000,000 złotys and $50,000 to Żegota. The World Jewish Congress seemed to be pleased with the financial allocations on behalf of Jewish relief spent by the Polish government at the time.[122]

To be sure, additional funds for Żegota would have helped it to expand its activities. What it received from the government delegate and Jewish organizations was inadequate to meet the tremendous needs.[123] But costs were so great they were beyond the budget capabilities of the Polish government alone to deal with the problem. One Polish leader actively involved in the work of Żegota estimated that it cost 5,000,000 złotys every month to maintain 10,000 Jewish orphans. To free one Jew from a camp, cost 6,000 to 15,000 złotys. On its part, the Jewish National Committee in Warsaw was critical of Jewish organizations abroad for not providing sufficient funds to save more Jews. In one message, it asked "does the American Joint no longer function? Why doesn't it send money?" In a letter to a friend, one Polish Jew echoed the sentiments of many Jews when he criticized the Jews in Great Britain and the United States for allowing the mass murder of their kinsmen in Poland.[124]

But budgetary limitations were obviously not the only, or even the most significant, problem facing Żegota and the Polish underground in saving Jews. German determination to kill the Jews with the apparatus of terror at their disposal was still the dominant factor that Jews themselves recognized in limiting Jewish survival. As top Jewish leaders of the Jewish underground told Jan Karski, a Polish emissary who in 1942 gave an eyewitness account to western statesmen concerning the plight of the Jews: "We want you to tell the Polish government, the Allied governments and great leaders of the Allies that we are helpless in the face of the German criminals. We cannot defend ourselves, and no one in Poland can defend us. The Polish underground authorities can save some of us, but they cannot save the masses. . . . We are being systematically murdered. . . . Our entire people will be destroyed. . . . This cannot be prevented by any force in Poland, neither the Polish nor the Jewish Underground. Place this responsibility on the shoulders of the Allies." Dr. Emmanuel Scherer, who represented the Bund on the Polish National Council after the suicide of Zygielbojm, echoed the same sentiments, "I fully realize that the main part of the work is beyond the limited possibilities of the Polish state."[125] Żegota officials recognized this and called for a general international effort to help save the remnants of European Jewry in 1943. "The needs are enormous," Żegota declared.[126] But there was, as is well known, no international action along the lines Żegota suggested.

Most of the Jews who survived the German occupation of Poland were saved by Poles who were not connected with Żegota. Recent estimates of the number of Jewish survivors range from 40,000-50,000 to 100,000-120,000,[127] though one estimate of the Polish underground at the time placed the figure at 200,000.[128] Tadeusz Bednarczyk, who was active in the Polish underground and had close contact with the Warsaw Ghetto, estimated that 300,000 Jews survived the Nazis in Poland. Władysław Zarski-Zajdler stated that at one point during the German occupation there were as many as 450,000 Jews sheltered by Poles, but not all of them survived the war.[129] As for Warsaw itself, it is speculated that there were 15,000 to 30,000 Jews hiding in Warsaw during the period 1942-1944 and that 4,000 of them were beneficiaries of the work of Żegota. Żegota officials boasted aiding 40,000 to 50,000 Jews throughout Poland.[130] As this study has suggested, it was the degree of Nazi control over Poland, not anti-Semitism, which was the decisive factor in influencing the number of Jews who survived the war. The Netherlands, which had few Jews and less anti-Semitism than Poland, experienced about the same percentage of Jewish losses as Poland. On the other hand, Romania, which had an anti-Semitic history, had a relatively low rate of Jewish losses.[131]

It is equally difficult to draw precise conclusions concerning the number of Poles actively involved in aiding Jews. Ringelblum estimated that in Warsaw alone 40,000 to 60,000 Poles were involved in hiding Jews. As Polish scholar Władysław Bartoszewski has pointed out, however, there were thousands of Poles who had been engaged in aiding Jews but, despite their best efforts, had been unable to save them. These people are not included in Ringelblum's guess. He estimates that "at least several hundred thousand Poles of either sex and of various ages participated in various ways and form in the rescue action."[132] More recent research on the subject suggests that 1,000,000 Poles were involved in sheltering Jews, but some authors are inclined to go as high as 3,000,000.[133] Thus a significant minority of Poles helped the Jews during the German occupation. Poles were no different from western Europeans, where only minorities—in much less threatening circumstances—aided Jewish refugees. The Polish record of aid to Jews was better than many Eastern Europeans—Romanians, Ukrainians, Lithuanians, Latvians—and, as Jewish historian Walter Laqueur has stated, "a comparison with France would be by no means unfavorable for Poland."[134]

There were large numbers of Poles who perished in their efforts to save Jews. Representative samples include the killing of 200 people in Berecz and Podiwanówka, 25 in Kłobuczyn, 43 in Bór Kunowski, 13 in Stoczek Węgrowski, 25 in Cisie, 22 in a village in Biłgoraj, and 23 in Stary Ciepielów. Especially significant is the claim that 1,000 Poles from Lwów were killed in the Bełżec concentration camp for aiding Jews.[135] Estimates of the number of Poles who perished for aiding Jews run the gamut from a few thousand to 50,000. According to one scholar who has researched the subject recently, "I succeeded to identify . . . a few thousand of them and every time I make a trip to Poland this number increases by 30 or 40."[136] It is doubtful that even a major portion of Poles who perished in trying to help the Jews will ever be known because of the lack of data and the fact that these Poles, like the Jews they aided, are no longer alive. And as Bartoszewski says correctly, "The postwar migration makes it very difficult to find witnesses of the events. A considerable part of the evidence collected in the archives of underground organizations had been destroyed in Warsaw during the 1944 uprising. Thus, we shall never know the full price of blood shed by Poles in efforts to save people that Nazism had condemned to death."[137]

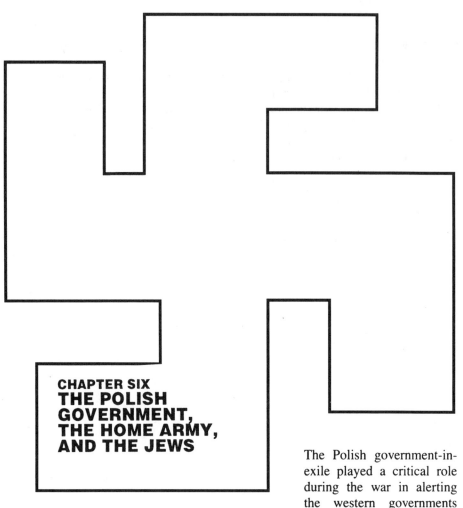

**CHAPTER SIX
THE POLISH
GOVERNMENT,
THE HOME ARMY,
AND THE JEWS**

The Polish government-in-exile played a critical role during the war in alerting the western governments and public opinion concerning the plight of the Jews. The London Poles conveyed from Polish sources in Poland the ghastly facts of the annihilation of the Jews and allowed its communication network to be used by Jews in Poland and in Switzerland to relay messages dealing with the Jewish plight. Once it became aware of the magnitude of German criminality against the Jews, the Polish government-in-exile used its diplomatic influence in London and in Washington to try to persuade the western democracies to launch major efforts to help the Jews. The Polish government in London was the first allied government to press for western reprisals against Germany. The London Poles were ahead of the western democracies and Jewish organizations in the West in appreciating the Nazi objective of annihilating the Jews of Europe. The Polish government also made available its diplomatic offices and financial resources in aiding Jewish refugees in Europe, Asia, and Africa. Unfortunately, a relationship of confidence never really developed between the Jewish community in England and the United States with the Polish government. Too often Jewish organizations had exaggerated expectancies of the power and resources of the Polish government to do more for the Jews than it could. And they were too prone to dredge up the anti-Semitic policies of the prewar Polish government in attacking the Sikorski government, which widened the gap between the Poles and Jews in the West and dissipated energies better spent elsewhere.

In 1940 and 1941, before the Nazis embarked upon the "Final Solution," the Polish government had informed public opinion in the West about the persecution of the Jews in Poland. In 1940, it published a pamphlet entitled *Persecution of Jews in German-Occupied Poland*. In a diplomatic note in May 1941, the Polish government drew the attention of western governments to German policy in Poland and the violence done to the Jews. In 1941 and 1942, the Polish government published several items, including the first edition of a *Black Book* in January 1942, which included the plight of the Jews with that of the Poles during the early years of the German occupation of Poland. The AK published the *Liquidation of the Warsaw Ghetto* by Antoni Szymanowski later in 1942, and parts of it were reprinted in the West.[1]

During two visits to Washington in March 1941 and again in March 1942, Sikorski asked for an American declaration against the Germans concerning their oppressive policies against the Poles and Jews. In March 1942, Sikorski especially emphasized the plight of the Jews and urged the United States to warn Hitler of reprisals if he continued his policy of exterminating entire groups of the Polish population.[2] At the same time in London, Polish officials received a negative reply to their request that the British launch a reprisal attack against the Germans in retaliation for the murder of 100 Poles in Warsaw, which was one of several incidents of terror to which Poles were subjected.[3]

Meanwhile, the Polish government was largely responsible for convening the interallied conference of nine countries that had been invaded and occupied by the Germans. On January 13, 1942, the conference, chaired by Premier Sikorski, met at St. James Palace and passed a unanimous resolution concerning the need to prosecute those Germans who had violated international law and committed violence against civilians in occupied countries. Though the Jews were not specifically mentioned, the interallied declaration, Sikorski explained, included the Jews. Neither the United States nor Britain signed the declaration, because they believed the reports of German war crimes had yet to be verified. Neither country wanted a repetition of the situation in World War I when everyone believed the atrocity stories and yet few were really true.[4]

Before the end of 1941, news of German massacres of Jews in eastern Poland was received in Warsaw. In January 1942, Warsaw received the first reports about the gassing of Jews in Chełmno. These reports of mass murder, conveyed to the London Poles by the AK, were confirmed by the government delegate in a message to London on April 8, 1942. Except for longer reports describing the situation in Poland which had to be sent abroad by courier, Polish military and civilian authorities sent shorter messages by radio which were usually deciphered in a matter of days. The Polish underground may not have given news of the Jews top priority, says historian Walter Laqueur, "but neither was such information suppressed." Once the information reached London, Jewish leaders in the Polish government were privy to it. Zygielbojm, perhaps the most vocal Polish-Jewish spokesman abroad, never complained that the information from Poland concerning the Jews "had ever been withheld from him, and he was not by nature the most trusting man."[5] The other Jewish representative in the Polish National Council, Schwarzbart, was also informed by the government concerning what was going on in Poland.

Then in May 1942, the Jewish socialists, the Bund, sent a message by Polish underground radio to the Polish government in London—Jews had unrestricted use of Polish underground communication channels with London—which went a long way toward revealing Hitler's plan to exterminate the Jews of Europe. The first sentence of the Bund Report read: "From the day the Russo-German war broke out, the Germans embarked on the physical extermination of the Jewish population on Polish soil." Then it proceeded to give a grim litany of the number of Jews who had perished in various places in eastern Poland: 30,000, Lwów; 15,000, Stanisławów; 5,000 Tarnopol; 50,000, Wilno; and on it went. The Bund estimated Jewish losses already at 700,000. These facts indicated, the Bund report continued, "without any doubt that the criminal German Government had begun to realize Hitler's prophecy that in the last five minutes of the war, whatever its outcome, he will kill all the Jews in Europe." The Bund asked the Polish government to influence the western governments "to apply the policy of retaliation against the Germans" (a request Sikorski had already made two months earlier to Roosevelt) and "against the fifth column living in the countries of the United Nations and their allies," a demand the western democracies could not, of course, implement.[6]

In June and July 1942, the British and American press publicized the

Bund report; the *Daily Telegraph* took the lead, while the *London Times* and *New York Times* followed hesitantly. The *New York Times* had a brief news item on June 27, 1942, and another on July 2, 1942. Yet, ironically, a few weeks earlier the *New York Times* had given front page coverage to the Nazi execution of 258 Jews in Berlin for an alleged plot to blow up an anti-Bolshevik exhibition at the Lustgarden.[7] Somehow the report of the massacre of hundreds of thousands of Jews did not seem quite as believable as the death of 258. The BBC broadcast parts of the report on June 2 and again on June 26.[8] These and other BBC broadcasts concerning the plight of the Jews broke a silence on the Jewish question for which Jews in Warsaw had erroneously blamed the Poles, claiming that Polish authorities kept the Jewish tragedy quiet, in Ringelblum's words, "so that *their* tragedy might not be thrown into the shade."[9] On July 1, 1942, the Polish Ministry of Information published in the *Polish Fortnightly Review* a detailed section on the murder of the Jews, the death camps, and the use of poison gas.[10]

The Polish government was responsible not only for publicizing the Bund report but also for making it clear that it was the first of the allied governments to accept the fact that the Germans indeed planned to massacre the Jews of Europe. On June 9, 1942, Sikorski warned that the Jews of Poland were "doomed to destruction in accordance with the Nazi pronouncements on destroying all the Jews regardless of the outcome of the war."[11]

A month later, the Polish National Council discussed the situation in Poland, especially the plight of the Jews, and passed a resolution by which it wanted its executive committee "to add to the proclamation of the National Council on June 10th to the Parliaments of all free nations the newly-revealed facts of the systematic destruction of the vital strength of the Polish Nation and the *planned slaughter of practically the whole Jewish population*." (italics mine) Responding to the request contained in the Bund report, the resolution also went on to record that especially in cooperation with the British and American governments, the Polish government "find all possibilities and means of paralising now, by adequate retaliation while the war is still on, the terror being carried out by the Germans." So intent on retribution were the members of the National Council that they recommended special air force groups to destroy an entire German city every day. And if the British and Americans demurred, the National Council wanted Polish air force units operating with the RAF to be withdrawn from British command and be authorized to undertake such retaliatory attacks on their own.[12] No allied government except the

Poles had given full credence to reports of the planned systematic murder of the Jews yet, let alone be prepared to launch retaliatory raids on the Germans as the Poles obviously were.

Immediately following the resolution of the Polish National Council, British Minister of Information Brendan Bracken chaired a press conference on July 9, 1942. Several members of the Polish government were present, including Stanisław Mikołajczyk, Polish minister of interior, Stanisław Stroński, Polish minister of information, and Zygielbojm and Schwarzbart from the Polish National Council. Mikołajczyk offered two reasons for the increase of Polish and Jewish victims at the hands of the Nazis: "First, the tremendous increase in terror applied to the Poles, and secondly, *the beginning of wholesale extermination of Jews*." (italics mine) He echoed the Polish belief that the Nazis intended to exterminate "the whole of the Polish population," implying that the Jewish fate would be shared by Polish Christians too. Then he appealed for the launching of a second front to bring a swift defeat to Germany; and, repeating the demand of the Polish National Council, he asked the Allies "to bring without delay retaliation against the German nation, a nation which only understands the language of immediate retribution for crime." Zygielbojm, focusing on the Jewish situation, confirmed Mikołajczyk's statement by saying, "There is no doubt that in Poland *a monstrous plan of extermination of all Jews is being ruthlessly executed*." (italics mine)[13]

On July 22, 1942, the Germans began the deportations of the Jews from the Warsaw Ghetto, the largest concentration of Jews in Europe, to the death camps of Treblinka. General Bór, General Rowecki's deputy at the time, stated that the AK sent daily reports on these deportations to London, but nothing was heard over the BBC on the matter.[14] Korboński, who headed the Directorate of Civil Resistance, said the same thing. Two of the cables sent by Korboński, which have eluded previous researchers, have been found and conclusively prove that Polish government officials in Warsaw did indeed inform London of the deportations of the city's Jews to German death camps. On July 26, Korboński sent the following message, using his pseudonym, "Nowak":

> The Germans have begun the slaughter of the Warsaw Ghetto. The order concerning the deportation of 6,000 people was posted. One is allowed to take 15 kg. of luggage and jewelry. So far two trainloads of people were taken away to meet certain death. Despair, suicides. Polish police [Blue police] have been removed, their place was taken by the *szaulisi*, Latvians [and] Ukrainians. Shootings on streets and in houses. Professor of Poznań University Raszeja was killed during a medical consultation, together with another physician and Jewish patients.[15]

On August 11, 1942, another message from Korboński read:

> From the Poznan Citadel Adolf Bniński disappeared without a trace. In Warsaw Chancellor [of the university] Tadeusz Pruszkowski was shot. From the ghetto, 7,000 [people] are taken away daily for slaughter. President of the Jewish Council, Czerniaków, committed suicide.[16]

Korboński's messages got to London, but it was a month before the BBC broadcast the news contained in them. Korboński learned later that the information in his messages was disbelieved: "Neither our Government nor the British would believe them," one Polish emissary told him.[17] However, this was an exaggeration. Though there were some skeptics in the Polish government—people who could not believe the Germans would eliminate the largest Jewish ghetto in Europe, a view many Jews also held—Sikorski and Mikołajczyk appear to have regarded Korboński's messages as a confirmation of what they already believed about Hitler's plans concerning the mass murder of Jews.

On July 27, 1942, the Jewish Telegraph Agency, obviously getting its information from Polish government sources, reported the Germans had begun the deportations from Warsaw to the death camps.[18] Two days later, the *New York Times* quoted the Polish government authorities that the Nazis planned to exterminate the entire Jewish population of Warsaw, estimated at 600,000 people. The *New York Times* story went on to repeat excatly what Korboński had radioed to Polish officials on July 26: It talked about the posting of notices to deport 6,000 from the ghetto, the departure of two train loads of people to their doom, the wave of despair and suicides among the Jewish people, and even the killing of Jewish physicians and patients.[19] It was the British who, until they received additional confirmation, thought the information was either unreliable or an exaggeration. "Thus," as Laqueur says, "those mainly responsible seem to have been some officials in the Foreign Office Intelligence Department." Jews had their skeptics too—Schwarzbart, for example, had warned about exaggerations of Jewish losses.[20] During the press conference arranged by Bracken on July 9, 1942,[21] he conspicuously avoided joining Zygielbojm in talking about the Nazi plan to murder all the Jews in Poland; and in November 1942, he gave a far more optimistic figure concerning Jewish survivors in the Warsaw Ghetto than the Polish government did.[22]

Despite the mounting evidence of the mass murder of Europe's Jews by the Germans, no one had up to this time any knowledge of a specific order for the total annihilation of the Jews. Dr. Gerhart Riegner, the World Jewish Congress representative in Geneva, had received information from a German industrialist—recently identified as Eduard Schulte—concerning a German plan to concentrate the Jews from Germany and German-occupied Europe in the East and murder them by prussic acid during the autumn of 1942. Riegner turned over the information to the American consulate in Switzerland and requested that a copy be sent to Rabbi Stephen Wise in New York; he also gave a copy of the draft cable to the British consulate for forwarding to Sydney Silverman, a member of Parliament and chairman of the British section of the World Jewish Congress. The American and British governments were skeptical about the news; it took the U.S. State Department until November to break its silence and reveal that the information was, indeed, true.[23]

Meanwhile, Isaac Sternbuch sent a message from Switzerland on September 3 to Jacob Rosenheim, president of the World Agudah Israel Organization in New York, through Polish diplomatic communications, informing him of the mass murders of the Jews in the Warsaw Ghetto, and warned that "a similar fate is awaiting the Jews deported to Poland from other Hitler-occupied countries." Rosenheim cabled this information to President Roosevelt, while the Polish ambassador to the United States, Jan Ciechanowski, conveyed the information to the State Department and to the British ambassador to the United States, Lord Halifax.[24] But this information was already dated, since the essence of Korboński's cable of July 26 had already become public knowledge. Nevertheless, the Sternbuch cable reinforced the truth of the deportations of the Jews from the Warsaw Ghetto. It was remarkable that it took the Americans and the British so long to confirm the truth of the Riegner message in view of the steady flow of messages and reports that had come from Poland, before and after the Riegner message, strongly suggesting the planned extermination of the Jews.

There should have been no doubt in the minds of western policymakers concerning the extermination of the Jews after the arrival of Jan Karski, a young, courageous courier of the Polish underground who had made several clandestine trips between Warsaw and London. Karski, a pseudonym for Kozielewski, met with Leon Feiner, leader of the Jewish Bund in Warsaw, and a Zionist leader whose identity has not definitely been established—it was either Adolf Berman or Menahem Kirschenbaum. Karski, at considerable personal risk to his own life, visited the Warsaw Ghetto on two occasions in October 1942, seeing first-hand the ghastly scenes of existence there, and managed to sneak into the Bełżec death camp where he masqueraded as an Estonian guard.

He left Poland and reported on his experiences, conveying the requests of the two Jewish leaders to officials in London and Washington.

The Jewish leaders wanted retribution: "The cities of Germany ought to be bombed mercilessly and with every bombing, leaflets should be dropped informing the Germans fully of the fate of the Polish Jews, and we ought to threaten the entire German nation with a similar fate both during and after the war," the Zionist leader told Karski. "Let the Allied governments, wherever their hand can reach, in America, England, and Africa, begin public executions of Germans, any they can get hold of. That is what we demand," he added. Other demands of the Jewish leaders, according to Karski's account, included the large-scale evacuation of Jewish refugees, especially women, the sick, and the old which might be worked out as an exchange or even for money.

Feiner urged Karski to tell Jewish leaders "that this is no case for politics or tactics. Tell them that the earth must be shaken to its foundations, the world must be aroused." These were unprecedented times, the Jews told Karski, and the West, including Jewish leaders and organizations, must take unprecedented steps to save the remnants of the Jewish community. Karski also transmitted a message to Sikorski from Jewish leaders in Warsaw which indicated that most Poles sympathized with the Jews but that there were criminals who blackmailed and denounced Jewish people in hiding. They asked that Polish underground authorities apply punitive measures, including executions, and publicize the identities and crimes of guilty Poles.[25]

Karski met with Polish, Jewish, and British leaders in London, and later, American and Jewish representatives in the United States. John W. Pehle, who directed the War Refugee Board, said later that "the Karski mission changed U.S. government policy from one of indifference at best to affirmative action." Thanks to Karski's revelation, Roosevelt ordered the creation of the War Refugee Board which, in Pehle's own words, "was too little, too late."[26] Karski's mission acted as a catalyst in mobilizing the British and American governments to admit officially on December 17, 1942, that the Germans were in fact annihilating the Jews of Europe.

Before Karski's arrival in London, Polish and Jewish labor leaders Zygielbojm and Adam Ciołkosz participated in several public meetings demanding that the Nazi criminals pay for their crimes, and convinced the British Labour Party to call for assurances that the Germans guilty of war crimes would be dealt with after the war. On October 29, 1942, Premier Sikorski in a speech at Albert Hall affirmed: "I warn the German torturers that they will not escape the deserved punishment for the mass crimes they have committed, primarily in our country which was and is the main centre of resistance against German barbarism."[27]

Karski's revelations galvanized the Polish government into action. On

November 27, 1942, the Polish National Council unanimously passed a resolution, initiated by Schwarzbart, appealing to the Allied nations to initiate immediately common action "against this trampling and profanation of all principles of morality and humanity by the Germans, and against the extermination of the Polish nation and other nations, an extermination the most appalling expression of which is provided by the mass-murders of the Jews in Poland and in the rest of Europe which Hitler has subjected." It used the word "retribution" two times and concluded with a stirring, "The day of victory and punishment is approaching." During this meeting, Deputy Premier Mikołajczyk conveyed the emotional protest of the Polish underground group, *Front Odrodzenia Polski,* which condemned the silence of the world to the massacre of Jews: "This silence can no longer be tolerated whatever the motive, it is abject. In the face of crime, it is not permissible to remain passive. He who is silent in the face of murder, becomes a collaborator to murder. He who does not condemn it, gives it his consent."[28]

On December 1, 1942, the entire issue of the *Polish Fortnightly Review* was given over to the matter of the extermination of the Jews, with special attention given to the liquidation of the Warsaw Ghetto.[29] The same day, Foreign Minister Raczyński, who exerted his considerable diplomatic skills to moving the British government out of its hesitancy concerning the Jewish question, met Foreign Secretary Eden and proposed an allied conference at St. James Palace to respond to the mass murder of the Jews. Eden agreed that something should be done but told Raczyński he wasn't sure what it should be. One influential member of the Foreign Office expressed reluctance for the British to associate with the proposed conference, even as observers, because it might commit the British to whatever representatives of the occupied countries resolved. Besides, he asserted (even at that late date), there is "no reliable evidence" of what the Germans are doing to the Jews. Then, annoyed with Polish initiatives on the matter, he took a swipe at the Poles, saying that they "are always glad of an opportunity . . . to make a splash as leader of the minor Allies and . . . to show that they are not anti-Semitic."[30]

The Polish government kept up the pressure. On December 9, 1942, Raczyński sent a diplomatic note to the Allies concerning the German aim to annihilate the Jews of Poland and those who had been deported there from other countries. He also pointed out the aid of the Poles to the Jews in his homeland. The Polish note asked not only that the Germans be condemned for their crimes but also that ways be found to restrain them from continuing to use their methods of mass extermination. The note was promptly published by the Polish government and received wide publicity in Britain's leading newspapers.[31]

Meanwhile, Premier Sikorski was in Washington exerting pressure on the American government.[32] Polish pressure played a critical role in removing the last doubts in London and Washington concerning the necessity for an Allied declaration. On December 17, 1942, eleven Allied governments and the French National Committee officially declared that the Germans "are now carrying into effect Hitler's oft-repeated intention to exterminate the Jewish people in Europe." The "bestial policy" of the Germans was condemned and the United Nations promised retribution on those responsible for the crimes and vowed "to press on with the practical measures to this end." Perhaps the most important aspect of the declaration emerged later: In the postwar war crimes trials, the crimes against the Jews constituted a specific part of the Allied indictment. One scholar has aptly observed: "The fact that such a declaration with its concomitant obligations upon its authors, was made at the end of the year [1942] in which the *Endlösung* programme was thoroughly organized in Germany and elsewhere says much for the nature of the underground networks, especially the Polish one, by which such information was sent out from occupied Europe."[33]

For a long time the Polish government appreciated the plight of the Jews. During the early years of the war, it shared the belief of the Polish people—and it was not entirely inaccurate—that the Jews were no worse off than the Poles. Pronouncements and publications of those years reflected this view. But when reports from Poland arrived in London that revealed Nazi determination to exterminate the Jews of Europe and it became clear that the Jewish situation was unique, a change developed in Polish thinking and the government was determined to deal with the Jewish situation. Since the Polish government represented the Polish people, not just a Jewish minority, it was understandable that the London Poles did not want the Allies to forget the tragedy that Christian Poles also experienced at the hands of the Nazis. When the Germans began the mass deportations and executions of Poles in the Zamość area late in 1942, it appeared to the Poles that the Germans intended to exterminate the Polish people even before they had finished off the Jews. The policies of the Sikorski government on behalf of the Jews took courage to balance between two criticisms: Some Poles in the emigration and in the homeland thought the London Poles paid too much attention to the Jews, while many western Jews, oblivious to the tragic experiences the Poles endured at the hands of the Nazis, believed the Polish government did not do enough for their kinsmen in Poland.

As has been seen, Premier Sikorski had appealed to Roosevelt in March 1942, to consider reprisals against the Germans if they did not stop their policies of extermination. Shortly after the murder of 250 people in the Czech village of Lidice in May 1942, Sikorski joined other ministers of exiled governments in proposing allied reprisals against Germany. Though not specifically mentioning the Jews, Sikorski protested in a broadcast what the Germans were doing in Poland: "Only by the announcement of retribution and the application of reprisals whenever possible can a stop be put to the rising tide of madness of these German assassins."[34] Churchill seriously considered a retaliatory attack for the Lidice massacre. Air Marshal A. T. Harris of the RAF Bomber Command told Churchill it could be done. "The justification of giving up one of our rare fine moonlight nights to this task can only be judged on political factors," Harris said. "The military-moral effect, though small, would not however be negligible."[35]

On June 22, 1942, Sikorski told Churchill that protests against German barbarism and threats of future retaliation did not do any good. He urged Britain to adopt the Inter-Allied Declaration of January 13, 1942, to take "drastic" measures against German citizens residing in Allied countries, and to launch "large scale" bombing of civilian targets in Germany. Less than a week later, Raczyński repeated to Eden the Polish demand for retaliation.[36] The Polish National Council made the strongest statement of any official Allied body when on July 7, 1942, it demanded retaliatory raids against the Germans by the Allies, and if they refused to do so, to withdraw the Polish Air Force from the Royal Air Force and to order it to launch the attacks itself.[37] All these appeals fell on deaf ears. A Foreign Office official tersely summed up the position of the British government on the matter: "Immediate retaliations and reprisals against civilians are not part of H.M.G.'s policy." Washington also refused to approve reprisal raids because, in Ambassador Ciechanowski's words, Roosevelt "did not think it advisable to start actual reprisals or bombing of German cities at a time when the Allies had not yet reached their full air power, and Germany might use this as a pretext for increased bombing and terrorism."[38]

The Polish people were unhappy with the silence of the world to the calamity in Poland, the government delegate told the Polish government in the latter part of 1942. He alluded to specific directives of Himmler in March and July 1942 which foresaw the final liquidation of the Jews and the pacification of the Poles. The Poles impatiently asked, What would be the benefit of liberation when most of the people of Poland had already perished? The Poles wanted immediate retaliation to restrain the Germans; they placed little faith in Allied promises of future retaliation.

The Polish underground press echoed these sentiments. On July 22, 1942, *Głos Polski* recommended that Britain and the United States turn over German nationals living in their countries to the Polish government-in-exile. For every Pole killed, 100 of these Germans would be eliminated. The newspaper, like most other Polish publications at the time, urged major air bombardment of German civilian centers to reduce them to rubble and "even to the ground." *Zywia i Bronia* concerning reprisals against the Germans, asked Polish authorities in London, "Why are you waiting?"[39] General Rowecki sent a message to London on September 30, 1942, describing how in the face of the silence of the world, the Poles observed the swift murder of millions of Jews and worried that this might lead to a premature insurrection from which the Communists might profit.[40] On December 5, 1942, the government delegate proposed a detailed list of diplomatic, propaganda, and military initiatives that the Polish government should take to stop "the furor teutonicus." Clearly, the annihilation of the Jews within the General Government and especially the beginning of the mass deportations and executions of Poles in eastern Poland had made its impact, convincing the government delegate that there would not be much left of the Polish nation at war's end unless the West initiated immediate reprisals against Germany.[41]

By the end of December 1942, Sikorski, reacting to Rowecki's earlier message, asked Churchill that the Polish Air Force, operating with the RAF, be permitted to have a major role in launching reprisal air assaults against German targets in eastern Poland. Sikorski believed this was the only way "to prevent [a] desperate attempt" by the AK against the Germans, "which can only result, at the present moment, in unnecessary bloodshed."[42] At the same time, Polish military representatives in Washington presented an *aide-mémoire* to the American chief of staff, George Marshall, asking the Army Air Forces to bomb German settlements in eastern Poland in retaliation for what was described as "the extermination" of Polish families in that area. The Poles explained that Poland was faced either with the premature destruction of its forces by an insurrection launched out of despair or the reduction of the strength of the AK by the Nazi policy "of the planned annihilation of the people."[43]

The Polish request about reprisal bombing was not favorably received either in London or in Washington. The British Foreign Office thought the Germans would massacre even more Jews if the Allies engaged in reprisal bombing. Eden suggested that the Germans could claim the Allies were morally bound to give up bombing German cities if they refrained from killing Jews and Poles. Air Chief Marshal Portal, chief of the Air Staff, raised other difficulties (with which Churchill agreed) militating against reprisal-type air raids:

> First, by labeling as a 'reprisal' any raid even on Berlin (particularly as there is no special feature or weapon that we can introduce into it) we would au-

tomatically abandon our previous position, which is that our attacks on cities are attacks on military objectives (including industry) and therefore 'lawful' and justifiable.

Alternatively, if we claimed that the raid had been an especially violent or effective one, should we not have the dilemma (a) 'Why not always do the same?' or (b) 'You are competing in brutality with the Germans?'

Then again, we should almost certainly be overwhelmed with requests from all the other Allies that we should also redress their grievances in the same way. This would result in nothing but a series of 'token' reprisals which would not only be completely ineffective as deterrents but would also destroy the last shreds of the cloak of legality which at present covers our operations.

Finally, we should make it much easier for the Germans to institute reprisals against our captured air crews.[44]

The American reply to the Poles was less convoluted: Marshall told Sikorski in March 1943, that the AAF could not undertake the proposed bombing operations "without serious dislocation to the United Nations' military effort in Europe and Africa. Other factors such as limitations of bomb carrying capacities at the range required also render these operations impracticable."[45]

On January 7, 1943, the Polish National Council added greater weight to the efforts of the Polish government by passing a unanimous resolution incorporating three motions proposed earlier by Zygielbojm—the subject of Polish initiatives in London and Washington—namely, to convene another interallied conference to protest and warn the Germans, to convince the British and Americans to prepare a plan of reprisals against Germany "to force it to cease carrying out mass executions of the civilian population and exterminating the entire Jewish population in Poland," and to inform the German population through leaflets which detailed "the monstrous crimes committed in Poland by the occupying authorities in the name of the German nation."[46]

The British agreed to drop leaflets over Germany, depicting German crimes in Poland, including those perpetuated against the Jews. The Poles, however, wanted these leaflets explicitly to say, after a heavy Allied air raid over Germany, that the raids were a sanction against the Germans for their crimes in Poland. The linkage between the Allied air raids over Germany and the leaflets depicting Nazi crimes in occupied Europe existed, but the British did not want it to be explicit. An article in *Dziennik Polski* on January 19, 1943 made it clear that British air raids over Berlin and German atrocities in Poland were linked in Polish minds:

> Considering how the Poles in Poland call with one voice for reprisals for German crimes it is desirable to underline this truth (i.e., the Allied air su-

periority) which is manifest in the glare of the recent raids on Berlin and London. The echo of the bombs which fell two nights running on Berlin had without any doubt sped through Poland with a breath of encouragement—the more so as the Poles are certainly thinking that in this way the Allies will punish the Germans and their latest crimes committed in Poland and her capital, Warsaw.[47]

Even though the British never formally approved of reprisal bombing by the RAF, Sikorski, apparently misinterpreting a speech by Labor leader Clement Attlee, in the House of Commons, told Eden on February 1, 1943, that General Rowecki was pleased to hear of "the announcement of eventual reprisal bombing on the part of the RAF against German targets in Poland." The British Foreign Office was stunned by Sikorski's message. One official pointed out that "we have repeatedly told the Poles, reprisals as such are ruled out." Another miffed official twitted, "The Poles are behaving very queerly these days." Eden suggested a compromise; he said the British were willing to drop leaflets over Poland, informing the people that Polish air force units participated in the RAF raids over Germany, which has treated Poland with such brutality. This proposed leaflet came close to depicting the air raids over Germany as reprisals; one section even described a Polish airman exclaiming after the bomb load was released during an operation over Germany: "That's for Poland! For our families! For our devastated towns!"[48]

Sikorski thought the leaflet idea inadequate; it was, after all, only the weaker half of the Poles' firm two-pronged recommendation. "Stronger arguments are needed," he told Eden and again urged reprisals. But the British refused to link the bombardment of German targets with German atrocities in Poland. One Foreign Office official said, "The Poles are being very irritating over this." Sikorski tried to put the best face on the leaflet missions by assuring Rowecki that during future bombardment of German cities, the Allied air forces would drop leaflets with photographs of the ruin of Warsaw and other cities, indicating the retributive character of the operations.[49] The reprisal matter lay dormant until the summer of 1943 when the Poles again revived it with the British and American governments, in connection with the mass deportations and executions of Poles in eastern Poland. The Allied governments made another declaration on German crimes in Poland on August 30, 1943, but said nothing about reprisal attacks on Germany.[50]

The Polish government-in-exile was the first official body to propose Allied bombing of railroad lines leading to and including the German death camps. The chief of the Polish Directorate of Civil Resistance declared: "The Polish underground leaders . . . requested regular bombing missions to destroy all railroad lines leading to extermination camps in order to prevent further transports from the ghettoes." Jewish leaders in the Warsaw Ghetto, Leon Feiner and Adolf Berman, made similar demands in their messages to London.[51] As has been seen, the AK conducted attacks against railroad lines to hamper German use of them in general, not specifically to delay transports to the death camps. AK attacks indirectly and temporarily benefitted the Jews by creating logjams in the transportation system: But the Germans were able to restore traffic in a matter of hours or days on these lines, and the AK did not have the resources to damage railroad lines substantially enough to make a real difference in stopping the transports to the concentration camps. That could only be done by unremitting attacks by the Allied air forces, which never happened. Allied air attacks were not blocked by lack of knowledge of the Polish railroad network because the Poles had made available to the Americans a map detailing all major railroad lines and their daily capacities in Poland.[52]

As early as January 1941, Sikorski had asked RAF officials to bomb Auschwitz in order to liberate the inmates there. This was well before the first group of Jews even arrived at Auschwitz. Air Marshal Sir Richard Peirse and Air Marshal Sir Charles Portal considered the Polish request but rejected it on the grounds that it was necessary to concentrate air force resources on German targets elsewhere in order to hasten an end to the war, a familiar argument which the British repeated with monotonous regularity throughout the war. Moreover, both men had grave doubts that an attack on Auschwitz would bring the desired result of liberating the inmates without their suffering serious casualties. But the Poles did not give up on an idea which took on greater urgency in 1942 and 1943 when it became known what a slaughter house Auschwitz had become. Throughout 1943, Polish leaders in London tried to convince the British to bomb Auschwitz during bombing runs on German factories in Silesia. On August 24, 1943, Polish officials in London told the government delegate that the British intended to bomb synthetic oil and rubber factories around Auschwitz. "For our part," they said, "we want to combine it with a massive liberation of prisoners from Oświęcim [Auschwitz]." The London Poles asked the AK to cooperate in preparing the prisoners for the liberation beforehand and in helping them after the raid.[53] Available British and Polish sources do not reveal what the British response was to this Polish proposal, but it can be assumed, based upon British reactions to Sikorski's proposal of January 1941 and their replies to similar proposals made in

1944 by Jewish officials, that bombing Auschwitz simply did not have priority in Allied military strategy.

The first report, made by an inmate, Witold Pilecki, about Auschwitz found its way to London early in 1941. But Jews had not been sent there until March 1942, and gassing did not begin until May 1942. Pilecki's later reports, however, described the death of Jews at Auschwitz.[54] Proposals for the bombing of Auschwitz were not resumed again until the summer of 1944; this time western Jews took the initiative and were supported by the Polish government.[55]

Much has already been said on this topic. As is well known, the British and Americans advanced reasons—the major one being diversion of resources from military operations—why they could not bomb the target, even though by 1944 it was technically feasible since Allied bombers had hit industrial areas just a few miles away from the gas chambers. If the Allies were concerned so much about killing the inmates in Auschwitz in such attacks—and this was one concern—it does seem they could have launched attacks on the rail lines leading to Auschwitz, which would have prevented further deportations to the gas chambers.

Beyond the diplomatic role of the London Poles, the Polish government carried out other services on behalf of the Jews. The Polish diplomatic mission in Switzerland, headed by Ambassador Alexander Ładoś, played a critical role in the success of the remarkable rescue activities of Recha and Isaac Sternbuch. Writing to Jacob Rosenheim, president of the Agudah Israel World Organization, the Sternbuchs admitted that it would have been virtually impossible to have rescued a single Jew in their operation without the help of Ładoś, whose office granted hundreds of passports which enabled Jews to obtain visas to the Americas, Africa, and Palestine. Other Jews were able to continue their stay in Switzerland. Ładoś also assumed a protective role over Jews in Swiss detention camps and tried to improve sometimes bitter relations between Polish and Jewish soldiers in a number of Polish army camps in Switzerland. "Jews involved in rescue work often asked Mr. Ładoś to intervene with Swiss Jews on behalf of fellow Jews in trouble," one recent study declared.[56]

One of the most significant contributions of the Polish embassy in Switzerland was to allow its communications network to be used to aid Jews in need and to link the Jews under Nazi rule with their kinsmen in the free world. Important information concerning the plight of the Jews in Poland found its way to Jewish organizations abroad through this Polish communication system. As already seen, the Sternbuch cable in September 1942, concerning the German deportation of Jews from the Warsaw Ghetto got to the Agudah Israel offices in New York through this channel. The transfer of funds to aid Jews as far away as Shanghai, China, was also facilitated through Polish sources.[57] The assistance of the Polish Consulate in New York, headed by Sylwin Strakacz, provided the same services on the other side of the Atlantic as Ładoś's embassy did in Switzerland. Messages, funds, and individual rescue efforts were also a major concern of Strakacz. Polish diplomatic missions aided Jewish organizations in attempting to rescue Slovak Jews in 1943, to save the internment camps at Vittel, France, and to send the trainload of Jews from Theresienstadt to Switzerland in 1945.[58]

The Polish government cooperated with various Jewish organizations in sending parcels of food and medicines through neutral states such as Portugal and Sweden to Jews in Poland. Much of the Polish relief budget went to help Polish and Jewish refugees abroad; this prompted criticism from Zygielbojm, who felt more funds should be expended on the welfare of Polish citizens in Poland. There were some charges, denied by Polish officials, that there was discrimination against Jews in dispensing relief, especially in Sweden, Switzerland, and Portugal.[59]

Finally, Polish authorities were involved in efforts to help Jews to escape from Poland to countries where they had a chance to survive. By 1944, Jewish sources estimated that 11,000 Jews had managed to flee Poland, and many of these had received help from the Polish government.[60]

One of the obstacles preventing the establishment of a relationship of confidence between the Polish government-in-exile and Jewish organizations abroad was the anti-Semitic orientation of prewar Polish governments. The past prevented genuine cooperation by most Jewish groups with the Sikorski and later the Mikołajczyk governments. Despite his philo-Semitic declarations and the moderate complexion of his government, Sikorski was astonished at Jewish circles in the United States who emphasized Polish anti-Semitism during the war—to the point that, in his judgment, they seemed oblivious to German murders of the Jews. Upon his return from a visit to the United States, Sikorski angrily criticized Zionists and Bundists, saying, "We can not tolerate this—we are not lambs earmarked for slaughter."[61] A few months earlier, Deputy Prime Minister Mikołajczyk had criticized the Jewish press who "cannot refrain from attacks on Poles and try to put the Poles in one line with the Nazis." He added, "No Pole is attempting to blame the Jewish Council of Warsaw [*Judenrat*] or the Jewish police whom the Nazi assassins, to their eternal shame, are using as a tool in exterminating the Jewish population."[62] It seemed incongruous that many Jews abroad in 1941 worried more about prewar Polish legislation interfering with the slaughter of animals for kosher purposes than they did with the murder of their kinsmen by the Germans.[63] One Jewish representative of the Bund in the United States observed to a colleague in Great Britain early in 1944 that among Jews "hardly a day passes without some new outbreak of anti-Polish sentiment."[64]

The Polish government did not always deal effectively with charges of anti-Semitism, with the consequence that its credibility was seriously affected in the minds of many Jews. There was a tendency for the Polish government to delay too long before it responded to allegations of anti-Semitism in the press. By the time it responded to some official charge, as one Polish official stated, "the truth [of the allegations] no longer is questioned." Polish government officials, including Sikorski himself, made numerous declarations during the war about the complexion of postwar Poland, which was to be democratic with equal rights to all citizens. These declarations would have been more effective had the Polish government repudiated specific prewar anti-Semitic policies of the *Sanacja*. Similarly, Polish concerns for the Jews during the war seemed to have slight impact on readers of the American press. To highlight the government's policy on behalf of the Jews in wartime Poland, one official argued that his government should advertize in ten major American newspapers its appeal to save "that segment of the Polish nation that was systematically exterminated." To increase Polish credibility on this matter, it probably would have been useful had the Polish government created, especially during the early stages of the war, a special undersecretary of state to deal with the question of German extermination of the Jews, a proposal once advanced by Zygielbojm. That would have dramatized the priority the Polish government did in fact give to the matter since the summer of 1942.[65] Moreover, the Polish government was unable to impress adequately upon some Polish political groups in England to pressure their constituents in Poland on the importance of adopting a more moderate position toward the Jewish question.

Sometimes Jewish charges were irresponsible. The Jewish *Morning Journal*, admitting the moderate complexion of the Polish government under Mikołajczyk, found it necessary to focus on a few National Democrats in the cabinet, though their influence was no greater than the moderate members of the government. Even Ludwik Grosfeld, a Polish Jew appointed minister of the treasury by Mikołajczyk, was attacked by some Jewish newspapers because he was an assimilationist.[66] Even Zygielbojm, who admitted the major role of the Polish government in informing and activating public opinion concerning the Jewish tragedy, sometimes made unsubstantiated charges that perpetuated notions of government-sanctioned anti-Semitic policies.[67] This only encouraged such groups as the Representation of Polish Jews in Tel Aviv, whose intemperate resolutions and declarations often repeated distortions about the Polish government and its efforts on behalf of the Jews. By war's end, the president of the American Federation of Polish Jews, Józef Tennenbaum, made the unsubstantiated claim that "tens of thousands" of Poles helped the Germans to exterminate Jews.[68]

To be sure, there were Jews who criticized their kinsmen for their attacks on the Poles. Rabbi Z. Babad, representing Polish Agudists in Great Britain, condemned the irresponsible generalizations about Polish actions toward Jews. Babad said that Jews, "the eternal victims of an artificially constructed idea of collective responsibility, must beware of such generalizations." In the name of the Federation of Polish Jews in Great Britain, Rabbi Etter loyally supported the Sikorski government and criticized foreign Jews, especially Zionists, for interfering in Polish internal affairs. To Etter, the answer to the Jewish question in Poland was found in supporting the Polish government rather than in pursuing partisan politics.[69]

The Poles themselves also contributed to the misunderstanding with the Jews. Although many Poles favored Jewish emigration from Poland after the war and major economic reforms to end the imbalances that had existed in prewar Poland, this did not suggest, except to right-wing groups, that most Poles supported forced emigration. General Sikorski revealed the policy of the Polish government on the matter when he said in August 1942: "The problem of Jewish emigration from Poland must be . . . [seen] as the right of the Jews to emigrate from Poland to their National Home, but never as a duty on the part of the Jews to do so, neither should that be taken as an intention on the part of the Poles to exert pressure in that direction."[70] However, right-wing groups did embarrass the government by their statements on such matters and undermined its credibility in Jewish eyes. The discussion in Polish and Jewish circles whether or not Jews should emigrate from postwar Poland had a strong note of tragic unreality because the Final Solution made it a moot question. Likewise, Polish and Jewish concerns over the postwar status of Jewish property confiscated by the Nazis, some of which Poles had acquired, were equally unrealistic; Poles who acquired such property resisted returning it, while Zionists agitated that property of deceased Polish Jews should be forfeited to the Jewish community.[71] As soon became evident, the question of the future of the Jews in Poland had less significance than the reality of reconstructing a devastated land.

One of the most controversial aspects of Polish-Jewish relations during World War II concerns the role of the AK prior to and during the Warsaw Ghetto uprising in April 1943. Prevailing historiography depicts the AK as a nest of anti-Semites reluctant to help the Jews and implies that had the AK given substantial assistance to them, the outcome of the struggle would have been different. As has been seen, the AK was a large umbrella organization housing numerous military organizations, reflecting, in political terms, a variety of attitudes. The extreme right-wing anti-Semites, the NSZ, were not members of the AK during the greater part of the war. The leadership of the AK, like the Polish government in London, was not anti-Semitic, and its decisions concerning the Jews of the Warsaw Ghetto were influenced by considerations that, unfortunately, have not been given the emphasis they deserve.

During the deportation of the Jews from the Warsaw Ghetto in the summer of 1942, the Polish underground press sympathetically chronicled the grim event. But the obvious passive acceptance of inevitable death by the Jews did little to inspire confidence among the Poles and especially the AK to initiate any kind of military operation on their behalf. "After all, how could the AK initiate operations without the knowledge and will of the Jews themselves?"[72] declared Henryk Woliński, a liberal humanitarian who headed the Jewish Bureau of the AK. Responsible Jewish leaders at the time, like Feiner and Berman, did not expect a military response by the AK during the Warsaw deportations. According to a Polish courier, Jerzy Lerski, "I heard no complaints against his [Rowecki] military inaction in the July-September 1942 period from any of the Jewish leaders whom I met in Poland in the 1943–44 period." He added: "And this was the case, because the alleged possibility of such 'military actions' in mid-1942, on the part of the Polish underground was non-existent."[73] The Polish Communists, who had strong contacts with Jewish groups that eventually decided to resist the Germans, urged the Jews on August 1, 1942, not to accept slaughter passively and "to save thousands and tens of thousands, though this will cost victims."[74]

There was substantial division among the Warsaw Jews themselves concerning what policy should be followed toward the Germans. Shortly before the deportations from Warsaw, Zionists—despite massacres that had occurred elsewhere—still believed it "unthinkable" that the Nazis would attempt to liquidate their ghetto, the largest in Poland. Bundists talked about maintaining a "psychological self-defense" and waiting for the Allied second front. "We should not be chauvinists—not only Jews suffer and perish," a Bund representative declared. "Thousands of Poles are also led to their deaths." The representative of the conservative Agudah Israel proclaimed faith as the solution to the Jewish problem. "I believe in God and in a miracle, God will not let his people be wiped out," he said. "War against the Germans is senseless. The Germans can put an end to us within a few days," he added. Even the leader of the General Zionists, Dr. Itzhok Szyper, believed that resistance would mean the destruction of the entire Warsaw Ghetto, while passivity would save at least a core of Jews from the Germans. Only the left-wing Jews—especially the left-wing Zionists and Communists—favored armed action against the Nazis.[75] Though the attitude of Jewish residents toward the idea of resistance changed somewhat after the deportations in the summer of 1942, even then, when Jewish resistance groups were organized, only 3 to 5 percent of the population of the Warsaw Ghetto participated actively in the uprising of April-May, 1943.[76] By then there should have been no doubt among Jews anywhere in Poland what their fate would be.

After the trauma of the deportations, the Jews in October 1942 organized the Jewish National Committee, which was under the influence of left-wing Zionists and Communists. That was the reason the Bund refused to join it. As a result, the committee and the Bund established a Coordinating Commission which later represented them in their dealings with the Polish underground. The Jewish Fighting Organization (ZOB), originally organized late in July 1942, was expanded on a broader political base in December 1942, and headed by Mordechai Anielewicz, a representative of the left-wing Zionist-Marxist group, *Hashomer-Hatzair*. There were several Jewish Communists on the staff of the Coordinating Commission and the Jewish Fighting Organization, including Michael Rosenfeld and Ephraim Fondaminski, who was the ghetto secretary of the Polish Workers Party. Immediately prior to the Ghetto Uprising in the spring of 1943, the Communists organized four or five combat units, about the same number the Bund put together. The remaining fourteen units were organized by the Zionists,[77] but many of these were also under Marxist influence. Little wonder the AK regarded the Jewish resistance groups with suspicion and questioned their loyalty; after all, left-wing Zionists and Communists had been less than friendly toward the Polish government and its representatives in Poland.

It was in these circumstances that the Jews sought to make contact with representatives of the AK. General Bór claimed in his book *Secret Army* in 1951, and again in an interview three years later, that "Wacław," one of several pseudonyms used by Henryk Woliński, had been sent by Rowecki in July 1942 to establish contacts with Jewish leaders in the ghetto and to offer AK support if the Jews decided to resist. The Jews refused the proffered help, said Bór, on the grounds that they did not believe the Nazis would deport and kill all the inhabitants of the Warsaw Ghetto. Woliński, on the other hand, has pointed out that he had no contact with Jewish representatives until October 1942.[78] This discrepancy, added to Bór's unconfirmed claim that Rowecki ordered an intensification of sabotage on German lines of communication to hamper or delay the deportations, has led several historians to conclude that Bór's claims were his own invention, made to improve the Polish image concerning wartime aid to the Jews.[79]

Woliński, however, does not deny that such a meeting between Polish and Jewish representatives may have taken place during the early stage of the deportations from Warsaw. In defense of Bór's claim, Woliński has suggested that the Jewish Bureau, the agency in the AK that he headed, was not the only source of information about the Jews available to the High Command of the AK, and that Bór had a wider range of information about the Jews than he did.[80] Furthermore, a courier of the AK confirmed Bór's claim in a statement that read: "In the initial stages of this appalling slaughter, the Commander of the Secret Army proposed, through his agents, immediate help to a number of outstanding representatives of the Jewish community, should they intend to take action in self-defense. This proposal was not accepted by the Jews at the time."[81] In view of the lack of unity among Jews themselves concerning resistance, a fact again dramatically illustrated shortly before the ghetto uprising when a member of the *Judenrat* approached AK authorities *not* to give the Jewish Fighting Organization weapons,[82] it seems that Bór's claim cannot be entirely ignored.

In any case, sometime during the Warsaw deportation action, a representative of the Bund contacted the Jewish Bureau, requesting that a cable be sent to Zygielbojm in London. The Bund simply requested that money be sent. The cable was dispatched and $5,000 was sent from London. It was not until October 1942 that Woliński met with Aryeh Wilner (known as "Jurek"), who represented the Jewish National Committee, and requested that contact between Jewish and Polish military and civilian representatives be established to coordinate their efforts and to secure Polish military help for the Jewish Fighting Organization (ZOB). It was during that meeting that Wilner said he had tried earlier—in August—to make contact with the AK, but that effort failed to produce results.[83] The reason it failed to materialize was, according to Woliński, not because AK authorities rejected the request but because Wilner "approached a person who was a civilian and that person didn't want to assume the task of putting him in contact with the A.K." Wilner's frustrated initial attempt to make personal contact with the AK was not regarded by Jewish leaders at the time as a major issue, and none of them—Wilner, Feiner, or Berman—made any allegations about the Poles to Woliński on this matter.[84]

On November 11, 1942, Rowecki took Jewish requests under advisement, praised the battle readiness of the ZOB, and authorized them to organize into units of five resistance fighters.[85] Polish cooperation initiated with the Jews was tentative and reserved. In December, the Poles gave only ten pistols and a small amount of ammunition to the Jews. In order not to deepen Polish suspicions about Communist influence in the Jewish resistance movement, Wilner submitted a code of regulations which included all Jewish organizations, except the Communists, that functioned under the Jewish political and military structure in the Warsaw ghetto.[86] Prior to January 18, 1943, when the Warsaw Jews initiated their first, if spontaneous, armed resistance against the Germans, the AK gave the Jews an additional ten pistols, instruction in diversionary actions, and directions to make Molotov cocktails. From the beginning of December 1942, members of the Jewish resistance regularly visited secret quarters of the AK on Marszałkowska Street, where they received military training:

> There, Captain "Szyna" himself was giving fighting-subversive training, aided by one of the devoted officers of the Sappers, Lieutenant "Gryf" (Leon Tarajkowicz). The men from the ghetto were handed various printed instructions on how to use the arms and explosives, studied the techniques of fighting in town, were acquainted on the spot with various anti-tank weapons effective at close range, and were initiated into the manufacture of typical incendiary materials, mines and grenades. The ZOB fighters showed tremendous ardour, lively interest, and a great deal of military ability, as confirmed many years later by the officers of the Home Army Sappers.[87]

The reserve of the AK in supplying the Jewish resistance with arms is pointedly brought out in Rowecki's message to London on January 1, 1943: "Jews from various groups, including Communists, turn to us for weapons as though we have full arsenals. I gave them a few pistols on trial but I have no idea whether they will use them. I will not give more arms because, as you know, we don't have them ourselves and are waiting for you to send them. Inform me what kind of contact local Jews have with London."[88]

After the armed resistance of the Jews during the period January 18–22, 1943, the attitude of the AK toward giving additional arms to the Jews changed. This change reflected the positive views of Poles who praised Jewish heroism and even inflated Jewish achievements against the Nazis.[89] According to the official Polish history of the AK, Rowecki's organization gave the following arms and supplies to the ZOB prior to the Ghetto Uprising of April 1943: 90 pistols with magazines and ammunition, 500 defensive hand grenades, 100 offensive grenades, 15 kilograms of explosives with fuses and detonators, 1 light machine gun, 1 submachine gun, and material to make Molotov cocktails and sabotage material such as time bombs and safety fuses.[90] The AK and its affiliates aided the ZOB in purchasing arms on the black market, a practice in which the AK also engaged. *Zegota* also allocated some of its funds for the purchase of arms for the Jewish resistance.[91]

In addition, two organizations, part of the AK—the Polish People's Independence Action (PLAN) and the Security Corps (KB)—gave the Jewish Military Union (ZZW), an independent Jewish resistance group, aid in acquiring arms and ammunition. According to Henryk Iwański, who distinguished himself along with other members of his unit, the KB provided the ZZW with 2 heavy machine guns, 4 light machine guns, 21 submachine guns, 30 rifles, 50 pistols, and over 400 grenades. The PLAN also managed to supply the ZZW with an assortment of pistols, rifles, ammunition, and on one occasion a case of 60 grenades. The aid of the People's Guard was the most modest: 25 rifles and 2 boxes of ammunition.[92] The Jews themselves produced a large number of Molotov cocktails, the primary weapon of the ZOB, and electronically detonated mines. Just how large Jewish production was came to light in 1964, when in the course of construction work on a street in the former ghetto, the workmen uncovered 100,000 detonators for Molotov cocktails.[93]

In comparison to the existing supply of arms in the AK, the amount of arms and ammunition given by the AK to the ZOB was small. In the city of Warsaw, the AK had immediately prior to the Ghetto Uprising 25 heavy machine guns, 62 light machine guns, 1182 rifles, 1099 pistols, and 51 submachine guns. But the AK had only a few anti-tank rifles and anti-tank guns in its arsenal in Warsaw,[94] and these were the types of weapons the Jews needed in order to prolong their struggle. Even Schwarzbart saw clearly that it was not merely a matter of giving the Jewish resistance more weapons. The critical problem for the Jews and the AK was the lack of heavy arms: "It is obvious that whatever the quantity of arms at their disposal, the Jewish fighters were doomed to be defeated eventually by the formidable war machine of the Germans. The only thing which could have been achieved by the possession of more and particularly of heavy arms would have been the inflicting of greater losses upon the German forces in the ghetto."[95]

It would have been unreasonable to have expected the AK to divest itself entirely of these few heavy weapons that it would obviously need for launching the long-planned general uprising when the Germans were at the point of military collapse. To be sure, the Poles could have given more pistols and rifles to the Jews, but smaller weapons of this type would not have altered the military situation in Jewish favor against the Germans. Moreover, it is not entirely clear how many of these guns were the personal weapons of members of the AK who, like soldiers anywhere, would have been reluctant to part with them.

Despite what appears to be impressive numbers of weapons in the AK in 1943–44, a large amount of these arms that had been buried after the September campaign were unusable. There were perennial shortages of ammunition in the AK, too. Air drops of arms and supplies had no appreciable impact on weapons shortages until 1943. As Bór said, "The quantity of weapons at our disposal was always a small amount in comparison with the number of men to be armed; so we had to supplement armed action by attacks on the enemy's morale which would not require dynamite or guns." As late as 1944, many of the AK's combat operations were at least partially intended to secure more arms and ammunition.[96] Finally, the extensive shortage of weapons in the AK was dramatized when it launched the Warsaw Uprising on August 1, 1944, more than a year after the ghetto insurgency: only 10 percent of its soldiers were properly armed.[97]

Although recent historians have been critical of the amount of AK aid to the Jews prior to the Ghetto Uprising, Wilner and Berman considered the help, in Woliński's words, "generous and honest," a view confirmed by General Bór's contacts with Jewish emissaries from the ghetto. Michael Borwicz, a Jew who fought in the AK, remarked later, "The cooperation of the AK was real and substantial even though it did not measure up to the enormity of the events."[98]

Responsible Jewish leaders in Warsaw were fully aware that by resisting the Germans, the Jews had no chance to survive if they remained in the ghetto. As Wilner told Woliński, "We do not wish to save our lives. None of us will come out alive. We wish to save our human dignity." Before Karski left on his mission to the West, Feiner told him that a defense of the Ghetto was to be "a demonstration and a reproach"; there were no Jewish illusions about defeating the Germans. Shortly after the uprising was launched in April 1943, Jewish representatives radioed Zygielbojm and Schwartzbart in London: "The result of the battle was decided from the outset. . . . We will fight to the last."[99]

At no time did responsible Jewish leaders of the Warsaw Ghetto, except perhaps Anielewicz, expect the AK to squander its strength and join the Jews in a suicidal uprising. Nor did they have the right to do so. As Woliński aptly suggested, any uprising by the AK at the time would have been "pointless."[100] This view was obviously shared by Sikorski, because as Poland's commander in chief he did not order major AK involvement in the Jewish insurgency. The only reasonable option open to the AK was to initiate diversionary attacks when the Jewish uprising began. Before the uprising began, the AK apprised the Jews of what it would do in this regard. To have attempted to do anything more would have unnecessarily eroded AK strength, depriving it of the men and resources they needed to take power in Poland at the time of German military collapse and before the Soviets took possession of the country. After all, the purpose of the Polish underground was not only to engage in anti-German conspiracy but also to help the Polish people survive the occupation into the postwar era.

Rowecki, apprehensive that a Jewish uprising in the ghetto might trigger a premature insurgency of the city of Warsaw, which would have invited a slaughter of the entire population, sought to get the agreement of the Jewish Fighting Organization (ZOB) to evacuate from the city with the help of the AK to eastern Poland where they had a better chance to survive than in the environs of the capital. It simply was not practical to absorb these Jewish units around Warsaw. Besides, it is possible that the AK preferred armed Jewish units not to be in a sensitive area where they could initiate an armed insurrection in close collaboration with the Communists; this would certainly be detrimental to the plans and interests of the AK and the supporters of the Polish government-in-exile.[101] In any case, the Jewish resistance fighters refused to leave the ghetto. Even after the Jewish uprising began and AK officials offered to get armed fighters out of the ghetto, Icchak Cukierman, who belatedly replaced Wilner as the Jewish liaison with the AK, replied, "The combat companies will not leave the ghetto as long as they have a single bullet left in [their] rifles to shoot themselves with."[102]

The fears of Rowecki and the High Command of the AK concerning a premature uprising in Warsaw in early 1943 were not without foundation. When the Poles finally decided to launch their own insurrection in Warsaw more than a year later in August 1944—a far larger enterprise that involved more people and resulted in greater casualties and destruction than the Jewish rising—they found that even in the more favorable circumstances of that time, the Germans could not be overcome without substantial Allied assistance, which never came.[103]

Prior to and during the Ghetto Uprising, there was understandable fear in AK circles concerning the extent of Communist influence in the Jewish resistance movement. As one AK spokesman allegedly told Cukierman: "We believe that the ghetto is no more than a base for Soviet Russia. A plan exists, and [we] Poles know what it is. The Russians were the ones who prepared the revolt in the Warsaw Ghetto, and you have far more weapons than you let on; and I am sure that on May 1, 1943 [May Day], they will land Dessant [sic] in the Warsaw ghetto." A well-known apologist for the Jews pointed up the problem when he wrote: "The direct relationship between the Communist ranks and the Jews in the ghetto was one of sincere comradeship and was free of the reserve and suspicion that marked the ties with the . . . AK." The exaggerated suspicion in official Polish circles that the Soviets were intimately involved in the Jewish insurgency is revealed by the query of the Polish minister of defense, Marian Kukiel, even after the Jews had been subdued: "Was the resistance of the Jews during the liquidation of the ghetto really led and organized by Soviet officers and noncommissioned officers parachuted into the ghetto, and were arms, ammunition, and anti-tank guns supplied in the same fashion?"[104]

The Ghetto Uprising that began on April 19, 1943, pitted 1,500 to 2,000 poorly armed Jewish fighters against approximately 2,100 enemy troops who had heavy weapons, including tanks, armored vehicles, and aircraft at their disposal. This struggle, in Ringelblum's words, was "between a fly and an elephant,"[105] and the result was a foregone conclusion. Estimates of the strength of the Jewish Fighting Organization (ZOB) and the Jewish Military Union (ZZW) vary: Gutman says there were 750 in the ranks of the ZOB and 250 in the ZZW, while Ainsztein estimates 600–800 in ZOB and 400 in the ZZW. The remainder of the armed Jews who participated in the struggle were wildcat groups which were not part of the ZOB or the ZZW. Estimates of their strength differ widely—from a few hundred to 2,000.[106] In any case, if one accepts the estimate that there were 70,000 Jews in the ghetto prior to the uprising, no more than 3 percent of the Jewish inhabitants actually took part in the struggle against the Germans. If one accepts the estimate of Gutman that there were as few as 40,000 Jews in the ghetto before the insurrection, then not more than 5 percent of the Jews participated in combat against the enemy.[107] Thus the overwhelming majority of Jews were not combatants during the uprising; most of them hid in bunkers and remained passive.

The heroic struggle of the Jews evoked sympathy and support among most Poles. The day the Jews launched their insurgency, Korboński immediately radioed London, informing Polish authorities there of what was going on and urging them to speak on the radio to the brave defenders. On April 30, 1943, the government delegate stated: "The Polish nation is right in showing compassion to the persecuted Jews and helping them. We should continue to help them." Sikorski was preoccupied with the Katyń affair, which resulted in Stalin's severing diplomatic relations with the London Poles shortly after the Jews rose up in revolt in Warsaw, but Sikorski declared in a radio broadcast on May 5, 1943: "The greatest crime in human history is being perpetuated. We know that you are helping the suffering Jews as best you can. I thank you on behalf of my government and myself. I beg you to give them all possible aid and to resist this terrifying barbarity."[108]

The Polish clandestine press gave thorough and compassionate coverage to the Ghetto Uprising. SWIT broadcast extensive and sympathetic accounts of the Jewish struggle. Mrs. Korbońska, who played a critical role with her husband in getting the information to London for broadcast to Poland, said dolefully at the time, "It will be easier for them [Jews] to die with the knowledge that the world hears how they are dying."[109] The Polish press was nothing more than a reflection of the prevailing views of most Poles.[110] Ringelblum was highly critical of Polish reactions.[111] But contrary to expressions by Ringelblum, who was the beneficiary of Polish aid that enabled him to live on the Aryan side before he and his Polish protectors were killed by the Nazis, other testimonies give a different impression of Poles who witnessed or heard of what went on in Warsaw in the spring of 1943. The picture is not only of fear and shock among most Poles, impressed by Nazi toughness in responding to the insurgency, but also of sympathy and friendship for the Jewish people.[112] Yes, there were anti-Semitic publications which delighted in the massacre of Jews, but these did not represent a predominant view.

During the uprising there were several combat actions undertaken by units of the AK and GL to help the beleaguered Jews. According to one account, there were twenty-six actions, including combat, supply, and evacuation actions, during the period extending from April 19 through May 10, 1943.[113] For example, on April 19, 1943, a unit of AK sappers, headed by Captain Józef Pszenny ("Chwacki"), tried to break through the ghetto wall on Bonifraterska and Sapieżyńska streets. Heavy enemy gunfire prevented the unit from destroying the walls. Two AK soldiers were killed and four were wounded. On April 23, 1943, AK units again attacked the Germans at several points. Four days later, an eighteen-man unit of the AK's Security Corps took part in fighting the Germans within the ghetto itself. Headed by Captain Henryk Iwański, the unit had entered the ghetto through a tunnel under Muranowski Square, which they also used to bring guns and ammunition to the fighters of the Jewish Military Union. Iwański's brother and two sons were killed, while Iwański was seriously wounded. There were also several operations initiated by the GL. For example, one unit eliminated a German heavy machine gun nest on April 20, and several units of the GL attacked the enemy near the ghetto walls on April 23.[114] SS General Juergen Stroop, who commanded the German forces against the Jews, referred several times to "Polish bandits" in his reports to headquarters. In one of his reports early in the insurrection, Stroop wrote: "It must be further stated that since yesterday, some of our formations have been repeatedly shot at from outside the Ghetto—i.e., from the Aryan part. Assault units immediately entered the area in question and in one case succeeded in apprehending 35 Polish bandits, Communists, who were liquidated at once. At executions, which became necessary today, bandits repeatedly collapsed shouting Long Live Poland! and Long Live Moscow!"[115]

The AK and GL also participated in several successful efforts to evacuate Jews from the ghetto. The AK gave Jews the plans of the municipal sewer network and put them in touch with Polish guides. According to one high-ranking officer of the AK, "Several dozen Z.O.B. fighters" were rescued by the AK through the sewers and later found refuge in nearby forests.[116] Iwański's unit helped evacuate thirty-four resistance fighters, about the same time that a GL unit rescued forty Jewish soldiers.[117] Thanks to units affiliated with the AK, as many as 140 ZZW fighters made it out of the ghetto to the Michalin Woods; unfortunately, about one-third of them died in combat later in a nearby forest.[118] There were uncounted numbers of Jews who made it to the Aryan side of the ghetto walls during these tragic days. Ringelblum noted: "Other Ghetto inhabitants besides the Ghetto combatants also escaped to the Aryan side, though those who were unarmed rarely succeeded. I was told as an authentic fact about a group of sixty Jews who made their way over to the Aryan side across the ruins of a block on Grzybowska Street through barbed wire. People living in this block saw the tragic scene and fortunately no one betrayed these Jews escaping from the Ghetto."[119] Żegota also played a role in moving a unit of ZOB fighters from Warsaw to Cracow and tried to link them up with partisans in the area.[120] Conspicuously absent was Soviet help to the Jews. Since there was an obvious Communist presence in the ghetto, one would have expected something more than an air attack by the Soviet Air

Force on the night of May 12, 1943, that ended up killing more Poles and Jews than Germans.[121]

Toward the end of May 1943, Stroop revealed that 56,065 Jews in the ghetto had been "apprehended"; of that number, 19,929 had died in the struggle. He claimed his own losses were only 16 killed and 85 wounded,[122] a likely downplaying for obvious reasons. But regardless, the Jews of the ghetto had embarrassed the Germans. As Rowecki wrote, "The continuation of the resistance for such a long time is viewed as a disgrace by certain German circles." More importantly, as one Jewish historian has aptly observed: "The Warsaw Ghetto Uprising had a real influence not only in stimulating the resistance in other ghettoes and camps, but also in encouraging the activity of the Polish underground."[123]

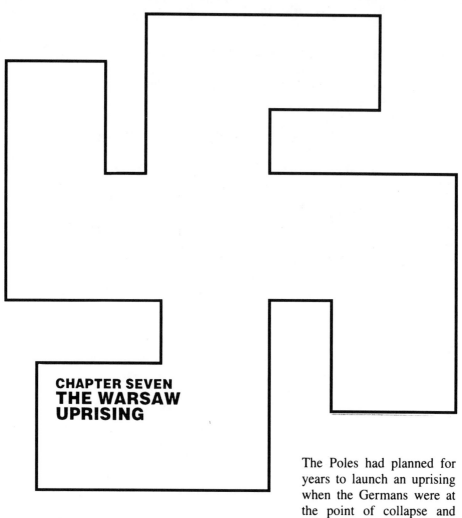

CHAPTER SEVEN
THE WARSAW UPRISING

The Poles had planned for years to launch an uprising when the Germans were at the point of collapse and there was a possibility of securing assistance from the western Allies. After the battle of Stalingrad, it was apparent that Poland's liberation would come from the East, not the West, and thus there was a great deal of discussion concerning what the policy of the AK should be toward the advancing Soviets. Polish authorities instructed Bór on October 27, 1943, that in the event Polish-Soviet relations were not restored, the AK should conduct sabotage-diversionary operations against the Germans (Operation Tempest—*Burza*) but remain under cover from the Soviets in order to avoid repression by them.[1] This advice from London was legalistic and impossible to implement; the AK was told, in effect, to attack the Germans but to retreat from the Russians.

Bór, who had more latitude in making military decisions than Rowecki because of the break in the unity of command in London following

A young Polish girl weeps over the body of her sister, killed by a German plane during the invasion of September 1939. Piłsudski Institute of America.

Above, a collecting point for persons stopped in street round-ups during the German occupation of Warsaw. Photo by AK Photographic Section. Polish Underground Study Trust, London. Below, German troops search the inhabitants of Gdynia for arms. General Sikorski Historical Institute.

Poles are executed in the prison courtyard at Tarnobrzeg by German military police in the autumn of 1939. Polish Underground Study Trust, London.

Bartosiak, an innkeeper, is hanged on the door of his inn during the massacre of Wawer, December 26–27, 1939. General Sikorski Historical Institute.

Polish women are taken to Palmiry for execution. General Sikorski Historical Institute.

Four Poles, one of them a priest, face a German firing squad. Photo by a member of the Gestapo. Polish Underground Study Trust, London.

Above, Poles are escorted to their execution, 1940. General Sikorski Historical Institute. Below, Polish victims are hanged from a balcony on Leszno Street, Warsaw, on February 10, 1944. General Sikorski Historical Institute.

The Polish Home Army
(AK) distributes weap-
ons dropped by the
Royal Air Force. Pił-
sudski Institute of
America.

AK soldiers in the streets of Warsaw during the uprising of 1944.
Piłsudski Institute of America.

Above, in front of the crematorium. Polish Association of Ex-Political Prisoners from German Prison and Concentration Camps. Below, the last execution in Auschwitz, 1945. Polish Underground Study Trust, London.

The bodies of Polish children from Zamość. Piłsudski Institute of America.

German soldiers captured by the AK during the Warsaw Uprising of 1944. Piłsudski Institute of America.

Sikorski's death, ignored the government's instructions and ordered his commanders that after they participated in combat against the Germans they should reveal themselves to the Soviets in order to show them who were the legal authorities in Poland, and should cooperate with them. To do otherwise, he argued, would create a vacuum that the Soviets would fill; besides, it was impossible to conceal the AK from the Soviets anyway. Bór authorized his units to defend themselves if the Soviets proved to be unfriendly toward the AK.[2] General Sosnkowski, the Polish commander in chief in London, had doubts about Bór's intention to reveal the AK to the Soviets without the existence of a Polish-Soviet political understanding. Despite Sosnkowski's reservations, the government approved Bór's plan on February 18, 1944.[3]

Although thousands of members of the AK participated in large-scale attacks (mostly against German communication targets) in eastern Poland during the early months of 1944, military cooperation by the AK with Soviet armed forces broke down, resulting in the dissolution of AK units by the Russians and the conscription of Polish soldiers into the Soviet army. There were also several instances of the Soviets killing Polish officers.[4] In the face of these Soviet actions against the Poles, Bór asked for a western Allied commission to be sent to Poland and witness what was going on there. Mikołajczyk raised the matter with Churchill, even arguing at one point that a British liaison officer dispatched to Wilno would at least help the AK in the region to function independently as the representative of the Polish government in London. Churchill demurred on the grounds that the Soviets would assume that any westerner there was a spy.[5] Early in July 1944, Mikołajczyk considered going to Poland with his cabinet in order to assert control over the country, a gesture opposed by the government delegate, who believed that the cabinet could do more good for Poland in London.[6] The situation was so bad for the AK that one British official remarked to Eden, "If only a tenth of it is true, it reveals a very disturbing situation."[7]

In view of the obvious failures of Operation Tempest concerning cooperation with the Soviets, Bór told his commanders on July 12, 1944: "We must co-operate with the Soviets only in the fight against the Germans. We must offer political resistance to the Soviets, constant and stubborn demonstrations of the autonomy of all forms of Polish organized life, including the problems of the Polish army and of the war. This resistance is in fact a manifestation of the whole nation's will to preserve its independent existence."[8] Meanwhile, as the Soviets advanced in eastern Poland, General Sosnkowski authorized the AK to broaden Tempest operations to include cities—Wilno, Lwów, and others; this revealed the intention of the Poles to seize these urban centers before the Soviets got there, thus confronting the Kremlin with political faits accompli.[9]

In late July 1944, General Bór and some of his lieutenants believed that the proximity of the Soviet armed forces to Warsaw presented an opportunity for the AK to include Warsaw within the scope of Operation Tempest. In that way, the AK and their civilian counterparts in Warsaw, who were loyal to the Polish government-in-exile, would become the de facto landlords of Poland's capital, a fact Bór thought the Soviet military and political authorities would have to recognize when they entered the city a few days later. It was to be a bold political statement by the Poles, who would find, to their tragic regret, that Stalin intended to make one of his own.

Warsaw, the last major city between the Soviet front and Berlin, was tenuously held by the Germans. The Soviet annihilation of twenty-five divisions of Army Group Center sent despair and panic among German civilians and soldiers in the Polish capital. On July 22, the German commandant of the Warsaw garrison ordered the evacuation of women and auxiliary service help from the city. Large numbers of soldiers and police were stripped from the capital for service elsewhere, leaving for a time only SA units.[10] The moment Varsovians had waited for for five years had finally arrived: the liberation of Warsaw.

German residents sold their possessions for almost nothing and clogged the roads leading westward to their own country. A German sergeant wanted to sell a Pole three truckloads of sheets and blankets on condition that he also take the trucks. When the Pole inquired why he wanted to get rid of the trucks too, the German told him that it gave him the excuse he needed to explain away to his superiors the disappearance of the sheets and blankets. He would simply report that the trucks had been bombed by enemy planes.[11] A baldheaded AK member, called "Staś," managed to get an entire lorry of vodka from a German soldier who desperately wanted to get rid of it cheaply and quickly. The vodka was subsequently stored in a cellar where Staś's friend operated a secret printing press for the AK.[12]

By July 31, the occupation newspapers, the *Nowy Kurjer Warszawski* and the *Warschauer Zeitung*, stopped publication. Even the German governor of the Warsaw district, Dr. Ludwig Fischer (who would be executed after the war for his crimes), panicked and scooted out of the city only to return a few days later, reprimanded by his superiors, with orders to help defend the Polish capital.[13] As Germans streamed out of the city, Poles were told, unconvincingly, not to believe the rumors that the Russians were at Warsaw's doorsteps and not to abandon their places of work.

Scared enemy patrols fired aimlessly at civilians. An elderly woman was hit in the hip by a bullet from an SS patrol which unloaded its bullets at a tram. On one of these days a tram conductor who made a living selling soap and cosmetics told his passengers: "Please, ladies and gentlemen, please hurry up, because the firm is departing, the firm is closing down and going into liquidation!" The passengers laughed and applauded.[14] It was a rare sight to hear people in Warsaw laughing and enjoying the difficulties besetting their hated enemies—difficulties that promised to give them back their beloved city.

Hitler was aware of the panic that gripped his people in Warsaw. Shaken and injured in the right arm by the attempt on his life at the Wolf's Lair at Rastenburg, the aging leader of the Germans had no intention of abandoning Warsaw, the loss of which would have been a major catastrophe in the continuing ability of the Wehrmacht to keep the Russians from the German homeland. Within a week of the assassination attempt, Hitler appointed an ascetic Austrian intellectual, General Reiner Stahel, to take charge of the defense of Warsaw. A courageous man with steellike nerves, Stahel's specialty was defending cities. "The Defender of Vilna," as he had been dubbed, would have liked even better the distinction of being called "The Defender of Warsaw." But this honor would elude him.[15] About the same time, on July 27, Governor Fischer issued an order calling for 100,000 people of Warsaw to begin fortifications the next day for the city's defense. The Poles did not respond, considering this an attack on their own underground units. But as they knew so well from experience, German reprisals might very well follow. On July 30, Himmler raised the summons to 200,000 people.[16]

In the last days of July there was a considerable increase in the number of arms dumps liquidated by the Gestapo; and, by the arrests of Poles responsible for organization, the Germans indicated preparations for an attack on Polish military formations. Machine-gun posts were simultaneously set up at various points in the streets, while at a few key points, like the Żoliborz Viaduct, tanks were drawn into position. These preparations supported claims that German authorities were on the verge, any day, of putting into execution their long-completed but hitherto not implemented plan for the wholesale removal of the male population from the capital.[17]

The quickening tempo of Polish political affairs received further acceleration on July 22 when the Russians sponsored the organization of the Committee of National Liberation in Lublin, composed of a group of little-known Polish Communists and left-wing sympathizers. Although Stalin did not formally recognize this body as the government of Poland for seven more months, it was obvious that a Stalinist fait accompli was in the offing when he turned over the administration of lands east of the Curzon Line, the much disputed boundary between the Kremlin and the. Polish government, to the Lublinites.

The Germans were well aware of an impending upheaval. The Poles openly advertised it, repeating to the Germans, *"Dzień się zbliża"* ("The day is coming").[18] Through its own network of informers, the Gestapo was apprised of AK plans and preparations.[19] In an effort to crush Polish hopes that they would be able to assist the Russians from within the city, the Germans went on a spree of arrests, deportations, and executions. And just a few days before the uprising actually occurred, the Germans found an AK cache of 40,000 grenades, which reduced by half the number available to units on the day of the upheaval.[20]

Most Poles, in anticipation of liberation, continued to train themselves in the use of weapons and ammunition. People who never had military experience gathered in private homes, six or seven to a group, once a week. And once a month they had maneuvers; in order not to cast suspicion of what they were up to, they left Warsaw for their practice. One man used to stand in front of a mirror for hours to see how he was demonstrating the use of a rifle; he did this repeatedly so he would be flawless in making a presentation to a group of neophytes.[21]

For some time prior to the summer of 1944, Moscow Radio urged the Poles to rise up against the Germans. In May 1944, the Union of Polish Patriots, the Communist Poles in the Soviet Union, repeated the same pleas and in the process criticized the AK for its alleged lack of action against the enemy. On May 9, General Zygmunt Berling, a member of the Union of Polish Patriots and the man who organized Polish units in Russia to fight with the Soviets, urged the Polish people "that freedom will not be gained waiting with a rifle on one's shoulder, but only on the road of armed deeds." Eleven days later, the chairman of the Union of Polish Patriots, Wanda Wasilewska, chimed: "Do not believe those who call you to idleness and inactivity. Our slogan is merciless, a deadly fight with the enemy at every doorstep."[22]

Although such pleas had been repeated with monotonous regularity for some time, those that came during the last days of July, when Soviet forces were at the Vistula, had special significance. On July 25, the Union of Polish Patriots, in a broadcast from Moscow, stated: "The Polish Army . . . calls on the thousands of brothers thirsting to fight, to smash the foe before he can recover from his defeat. . . . Every Polish homestead must become a stronghold in the struggle against the invaders. . . . Not a moment is to be lost."[23] At 8:15 P.M. on July 28, the day the Russians formally announced the shelling of Praga, a Warsaw suburb, Moscow Radio broadcast:

> Fight the Germans. No doubt Warsaw already hears the guns of the battle which is soon to bring her liberation. Those who have never bowed their heads to the Hitlerite power will again, as in 1939, join battle with the Germans, this time for the decisive action. The Polish Army now entering Polish territory, trained in the USSR is now joined to the People's Army to form the corps of the Polish Armed forces, the armed arm of our nation in its struggle for independence. Its ranks will be joined tomorrow by the sons of Warsaw. They will all, together with the Allied Army, pursue the enemy westward, wipe out the Hitlerite vermin from the Polish land, and strike a mortal blow at the beast of Prussian imperialism. For Warsaw, which did not yield, but fought on, the hour of action has already arrived . . . remember that in the flood of Hitlerites destruction all is lost that is not saved by active effort, that [by] direct active struggle in the streets of Warsaw, in its houses, factories and stores we not only hasten the moment of final liberation but also save the nation's property and the lives of our brethren.

Again the next day, another impassioned plea called the Poles to arms, repeated several times on the Russian-sponsored broadcasting station, "Kościuszko."[24]

The closeness of Soviet armies to Warsaw, the mood of the Poles in the capital, and the large political stakes involved convinced Bór and some of his key advisers that Warsaw was ripe for an uprising. Based on faulty intelligence information concerning the movement and strength of Soviet forces near Warsaw, Bór gave an order—authorized by Government Delegate Jankowski, who had been given plenipotentiary power in this matter—to launch an uprising in the capital on August 1, 1944.[25]

August 1, 1944 began cloudy and raining. It was unlike any other day in Warsaw. There was an electricity, a feeling of expectancy, that gripped the Poles. People streamed into the churches to hear Mass. Irena Orska, a nurse in the underground who suffered from heart trouble, went to hear Mass too. People prayed so hard, she said, you could almost hear them think. A small bird fluttered into the church. It was not a good omen.[26]

In another area of the city, Mrs. Gisted, a Swedish-born actress with ties to the Polish underground, ran a coffee house that once housed part of the British embassy. Ten unemployed actresses served as waitresses, a stage manager was the barman, and an elderly former actress sat at the cash desk. In one of several information leaks before the uprising, a major

in the Home Army had whispered to the Gisteds the day before it occurred
to close up early because there was a full-scale alarm. On August 1, a
German soldier came up to the part of the cafe where Mrs. Gisted had a
small circulating library. The German, who had always protested he was
not a Nazi, urged, "Close down; it's starting now." Mrs. Gisted ignored
the warning and routinely went about her business. When the uprising
finally came, her husband found her at the hairdresser. "It has begun.
Come!" he screamed, seizing her, wet hair and all.[27]

There was a great deal of activity on the streets before the upheaval.
Young boys crowded the trams and brashly occupied the front platforms
reserved for Germans. On the sidewalks women with bundles hurried
along, obviously carrying arms and ammunition to various assembly
points. On his way to a loft near Marszałkowska Street, where he would
establish a transmitting and receiving station to contact London, Korboński saw a young couple near a gate. The girl put her arms affectionately
around the boy and kissed him. The boy saw Korboński's top boots and
greeted him with a nod of his head. Korboński pointed to his watch and
whispered, "It's time." The couple kissed one more time, and then the
young Home Army soldier scurried away to his post. Not far away Korboński spotted a Jewish friend of his, walking unconcernedly down the
street. "Leave Warsaw at once," he warned; "in fifteen minutes a large
scale action is going to begin, and no one can foresee its outcome." The
Jew quickly parted from his friend and caught an electric train which
reached the outskirts of the city before the uprising began. The Germans
wanted to stop it immediately, but the train operator wisely pretended not
to see them and increased speed, saving the Jew's life. It was the last train
from Warsaw. Korboński met his friend after the war, and the Jew told him
how his whole family prayed that Korboński survive the ordeal.[28]

It was an enormous job to mobilize an army of approximately 25,000
to 28,000 men, to get personnel to their posts, to equip them with arms
and ammunition, and still try to maintain secrecy. Bór had selected 5:00
P.M. as the precise time of the uprising, believing it was the best hour to
surprise the Germans. At that time people would be returning from work,
and heavy traffic would make it easier to conceal the units moving to their
places. There would also be a few hours' daylight to take over enemy
positions before dusk.[29]

The AK looked like a motley bunch, dressed in all sorts of clothes,
some in prewar Polish military uniforms, others even in confiscated SS
outfits. The diversity in clothing was matched by an exotic collection of
hats—Polish, German, Russian, and French. The international flavor of
the apparel reflected a plethora of nationalities and religions in the Home

Army. In one battalion alone, after the uprising broke out, there were Catholics, Orthodox, Lutherans, Calvinists, and Hebrews of Polish, Ukrainian, Byelorussian, Great Russian, Georgian, Armenian, Azerbaidjani, and Spanish origin. There was even a Frenchman with a tricolor in his cap. But they all wore the red and white Polish armband, the only item of dress common to all Home Army soldiers.[30]

The moment the Poles had awaited for five years had arrived. "The last seconds seemed like an eternity." Bór remarked dolefully. "At five o'clock they would cease to be an underground resistance movement and would become once more Regular soldiers fighting in the open." The time had come.

> From all sides a hail of bullets struck passing Germans, riddling their buildings and their marching formations. In the twinkling of an eye, the remaining civilians disappeared from the streets. From the entrances of houses, our men streamed out and rushed to the attack. In fifteen minutes an entire city of a million inhabitants was engulfed in the fight. Every kind of traffic ceased. As a big communications centre where roads from north, south, east, and west converged, in the immediate rear of the German front, Warsaw ceased to exist. The battle for the city was on.[31]

The Home Army, launching the uprising with three divisions, had to take over six municipal districts of the city that included City Center, Żoliborz, Wola, Ochota, Mokotów, and Praga, not to mention outlying areas like Okęcie. The Eighth Infantry Division, named after Romuald Traugutt who was prime minister of the Polish Underground Government during the insurrection of 1863, was under the command of Colonel Mieczysław Niedzielski. The Tenth Infantry Division, named after the Peasant Party leader, Maciej Rataj, whom the Germans executed in 1940, was headed by Colonel Józef Rokicki. The Twenty-eighth Infantry Division, named after Stefan Okrzeja, a Socialist leader who led the Polish revolutionary movement against the czar in 1905, was commanded by Colonel Edward Pfeiffer.

This Warsaw Army Corps numbered approximately 25,000 men, although if one included civilians and reserves, the number was larger. But only about 2,500 soldiers were properly armed on August 1. Thus only a fraction of the AK could be used effectively against the Germans on "D" Day. The Germans, on the other hand, had 15,000 to 16,000 well-armed troops who were supplemented and strengthened as the uprising progressed.[32]

The results of the first day's fighting revealed that the Poles had seized most of the city, but it proved a Pyrrhic and ephemeral victory. Not only did the Poles lose more men than the Germans—2,000 against 500 casualties—but also they failed to take the kind of installations needed to prolong their ability to fight effectively and to facilitate the help that might come from the Russians and the West. It was not so much erroneous strategy; rather, it was the lack of properly armed personnel and poor tactical execution. Many of the key installations, such as the four Vistula bridges, remained in German hands. The Poles, ignoring the principle of mass concentration, tried to take all of them at once instead of concentrating on one or two, such as the Kierbedź and Poniatowski Bridges which were the main arteries across the Vistula.[33]

One Polish unit was to move from the area of the Royal Castle and take part of the Kierbedzia Bridge from the west while another group of Poles, advancing from the Praga side, was to take the other section of the span. Unfortunately for the Poles, a German engineer unit had been ordered to the pumping plant, which dominated the bridge, and it successfully defended the vital artery. And the situation with respect to the Poniatowski Bridge was even worse; the Poles had a small group of men assigned to take it, while the German defenders had strong artillery support from Praga where the Polish uprising was snuffed out before it really got started. As for the third major span, the Citadel Bridge, the Poles never even attempted to take it because of the strong German fire coming from the Citadel, the fortress dominating the bridge—and built, ironically, by the Russians after the Polish Uprising of 1830 to prevent another upheaval by the Varsovians.[34]

The failure to concentrate on fewer objectives with greater strength was repeated several times. The Seventh Regiment of Lublin Lancers, for example, was to attack the entire police district along Szucha Avenue, named "Strasse der Polizei" by the Germans. Though this in itself was too big a task for the unit, another objective was added at the last moment— the printing house on Marszałkowska Avenue where the *Nowy Kuryer Warszawski* was published. Out of a hundred attackers of this unit in the district, sixty-two were killed and eleven seriously wounded; the others who survived were also wounded, making this one of the highest casualty rates of any unit during the first day of the uprising.[35]

In Mokotów, in the south, the AK unit had at least ten major objectives to take from the Nazis. Most of them were in the northern part of the district, around Narbutt Avenue, where SS, police, and Gestapo units were housed. Some of the more important objectives in the southern part of the district included the race track at Służewiec, where there were 600 to 700 SS men along with aviators from nearby Okęcie; the Dominican monastery at Służew, where the Germans had a 300-man antiaircraft battery; and the Mokotów Fort, which housed the personnel and headquarters of the Luftwaffe—about 450 men—from the Okęcie airfield. It was impossible for the "Baszta" unit in Mokotów to take even half these objectives with the manpower and material it had, not to mention the fact that local commanders here and elsewhere in Warsaw were hopelessly confused as to the timing of the uprising. One unit commander believed that 5:00 P.M. was the hour his men were supposed to assemble rather than the time of the uprising itself.[36]

The same problem of timing occurred in attacks against the airports—Bielany in the north and Okęcie in the south. Not only was it important to deprive the enemy of nearby airfields from which they could bombard Warsaw but also to provide convenient bases for later allied landings and supply drops. Catastrophically, in the attempt to take Okęcie on August 1, some of the Polish units started the attack too soon, lost a large number of noncommissioned officers, and never got close to their objective. A similar attempt the next day to take Bielany resulted in Polish retreat. The consequence was that the Luftwaffe could with ease attack the Polish capital by air, which they did at 2:00 P.M. on August 4—the first German air attack since 1939.[37]

There was also a great deal of aimless and futile fighting by the naturally exuberant Poles on August 1. It was difficult at times to maintain discipline among the troops, a problem not confined to the Poles alone, and there was a great deal of administrative confusion with too many "colonels" without troops to command.[38] About 5,000 Home Army fighters, repulsed by the German defenders, followed their time-tested underground tactic of withdrawing into the adjoining forests—"do lasu"—not from cowardice but to regroup. Unfortunately, this was not a very wise tactic in trying to seize and hold a city, since it further weakened the strength of an already seriously weak insurgent force in the citadel. One authority estimated that these withdrawals, combined with losses by death and wounds, reduced the strength of the AK by half.[39]

It would be easy to label the operations during these first days a tactical nightmare played out by military amateurs, but that would be misleading. Although the Poles failed to take the bridges, airports, and key communications centers, they did acquire several important buildings, many of them housing military and police officers, that had a symbolic significance. This was not a small factor to a people oppressed for five years by Nazi occupation. Moreover, by the second day, several vital installations—gas, electric, and water works—were in Polish hands. The battle for the electric plant was especially fierce, but the building fell to the AK after a nineteen-hour fight; despite German shelling with 88mm guns, the plant operated until September 4, when air and artillery fire completely destroyed it. Costly though it was, the Poles did control the city and held the initiative—but only briefly.

In his hasty decision to order the uprising for August 1, Bór failed to take into account intelligence indicating German strength. This, plus Bór's faulty information (mentioned earlier) about the strength of Soviet forces near Warsaw, led him to underestimate the Germans' capabilities against both the Soviets[40] and the Polish uprising. The German response to the long, successful Soviet drive was counterattack, resulting in a temporary setback for the Soviets near Warsaw. After that, the Soviet government continued to claim, unconvincingly, that it was unable to give any military aid to the Poles and even refused to allow the United States to use Soviet airfields to aid the beleaguered Poles.

The Germans counterattacked the Poles on August 5. Nonetheless, during these days there was great euphoria, a feeling of identity among the people who helped their soldiers, an outpouring of emotion that had built up for five years, and a conviction—unsure and uncertain though it was—that the Polish people had somehow taken decisive action against the enemy. The history of the Poles in the Warsaw Uprising is in a sense a collection of individual biographies of men and women, young and old, many of whom did some incredibly brave, humane, and determined things. "The spirit of the Home Army and the people is magnificent," Bór telegraphed London on August 3. A few days later he said the Germans had technical superiority, but "we are on top spiritually."[41]

There is no doubt that the civilian population of Warsaw enthusiastically supported the AK when it launched the uprising against the hated Germans. It was not unusual to see women running into the streets, kissing the insurgents. Whatever occupation a civilian had, his skills could be used in some way by the AK. Technicians, plumbers, carpenters, masons, and other skilled workmen volunteered their services. A baker, so poor he did not even have a pair of shoes, volunteered to bake bread without pay for the AK.[42]

One of the most impressive and determined evidences of Polish determination to wrest their capital from the enemy was the postal service which flourished during the uprising. It was operated by young boys and girls, none of whom was older than fifteen, who were members of the scouting movement. These Boy and Girl Scouts, wearing the red and white armbands the soldiers wore, executed their responsibilities with dedication and promptness. Mailboxes, conveniently placed near hospitals and barricades, were emptied twice a day, and if material was addressed to a location in the same general area of the city, it would be delivered the same day. However, if the addressee lived in an area which enemy forces intervened, it took two or three days to deliver the material. In 1967, some undelivered letters stamped by the scouting postal service were discovered, and twenty-three years after the event many of those letters got to their destinations.[43]

People had nothing but praise for the members of the medical profession during the difficult days of the uprising. Since the Soviets had murdered many Polish physicians during the Katyń Massacre, there was a shortage of medical doctors. Medical students and nurses had to fill in the gap. It was not unusual for young men and women with only a few years of medical training to perform amputations and other complicated surgical techniques with amazing success. The demands made upon the physicians, nurses, and other medical personnel were enormous. Working in intolerable situations—frequently without water, toilet facilities, and even adequate nourishment—these dedicated people did an outstanding job to bring succor to the wounded soldiers and civilians of the city.[44]

"Warsaw will be wiped out," was Hitler's laconic reaction when he heard of the outbreak.[45] His order to destroy the Polish capital quickly filtered down to his henchmen. The Führer's new chief of staff, Heinz Guderian, quieted the serious concern of Dr. Hans Frank, the governor general of Poland, who once pompously remarked that "the whole Vistula shall be as German as the Rhine." Now he was not so sure, and he even contemplated moving his headquarters out of Cracow. Guderian reassured him on August 3 that the Polish uprising would be suppressed "with all means possible," and when it became clear which parts of the city were in German and Polish hands, the Luftwaffe would start its air bombardment.[46] A few days later the Poles were on the defensive, and Frank's morale had picked up. "The town of Warsaw is in flames in almost all parts. The burning down of the houses is the best means to prevent the rebels from using them as shelter," Frank declared to Reichminister Hans Lammers. "After this uprising and its suppression Warsaw will meet its deserved fate; it will be completely destroyed."[47] This kind of message was in character for the man who, we will recall, said in 1940, "If I were to have one poster hung up for every seven Poles who have been liquidated, all the forests in Poland could not supply enough paper."[48]

Meanwhile, Heinrich Himmler ordered Rowecki, who was in a German prison, shot to death. The former chicken farmer saw the Warsaw Uprising as a chance to annihilate the Poles. "My Führer," Himmler declared, "Warsaw . . . will be erased[;] this nation that has blocked our way to the East for the past 700 years and which has been a constant obstruction in our way since the first battle of Tannenberg. . . . Then, historically, the Polish problem will be no great problem at all, neither to our children nor to all those who will come after us, and not even to us."[49]

Then Himmler went to Posen, where he dispatched for Warsaw most of the police force of the city—some with artillery—together with the SS Brigade Dirlewanger and the SS Brigade Kamiński. All the units were under the command of SS Gruppenführer Heinz Reinefarth, who had the dual disability of lacking tactical training and despising the leaders of the SS brigades ostensibly subordinated to him. Reinefarth was a lawyer by education. He had moved through the ranks, and as an enlisted man won the coveted Knight's Cross for bravery. Whatever he lacked in tactical skill, he made up by personal courage which made him very popular with his men. Confident that the whole affair would be over swiftly, Himmler gave his units carte blanche—they were told to shoot everyone, including women and children, and they were permitted to loot. The order to raze Warsaw to the ground was given in writing and was, of course, Hitler's will.[50] In reference to the implementation of Hitler's order, Himmler later told a group of generals, "At the same time I have moreover given the order to destroy Warsaw completely. You may now think that I am a terrible barbarian, as you please. Yes, I am a barbarian when I must be. . . . The order was: to set fire to every block of houses and blow them up."[51]

Thus, from the outset, suppression of the insurrection was an SS and police affair. The Wehrmacht had its hands full in trying to stop the Russians at the Vistula. Field Marshal Walther Model, "the Führer's Fireman," did not want any part in the matter, advising that the Germans responsible for provoking the Poles—namely, Frank and his cronies—should handle it. His troops, Model sneered, were too good to quell insurrections.[52] Guderian, however, felt differently. He tried to have Warsaw included in the army's operational area, since it was on the front line. But Himmler beat him to the punch.[53]

The Germans discovered to their dismay that it was not going to be so easy to stop the upheaval. The German contingent in Warsaw, including SS, police, Wehrmacht, Luftwaffe, and auxiliary forces, were in a state of chaos. General Reiner Stahel, the commander of the Warsaw garrison, was cut off from his troops, completely isolated in his command post at the Palais Bruhl in the central part of the city.[54] He could not exercise the necessary leadership to clarify, among other things, the order of rank that resulted in subordinate commanders like Dirlewanger and Kamiński operating at will. The German troops, already suffering from low morale before August 1, frequently shot wildly and fought in isolated groups. No one knew always who was friend and who was foe. The reinforcements sent by Himmler contributed further to the chaos by their looting and indiscriminate killing. Warsaw had no battle lines during these days; the city was a shifting maze of people in a boiling cauldron.

One of the strangest questions of the war is why the Germans were so unprepared for an uprising they knew was coming. The imminent outbreak of the upheaval had been reported for weeks ahead by the police, and these reports were available to all top-ranking German officials. Dr. Ludwig Hahn, the German security chief, alleged he had the general plan for the uprising weeks before it happened. Ever since May, the Luftwaffe, in anticipation of an uprising in Warsaw, had made special provisions for landings in the airports near the capital. The German police in Warsaw even knew about Bór's alert order of July 25. On the following day, this notation appeared in the War Diary of the Ninth Army, "The Polish Resistance movement has ordered alarm readiness for their members. On the German side: strengthen guarding of objects." And at 7:00 P.M. that evening the Ninth Army notified its subordinate units of a possible uprising. Stahel knew of the reports yet took no pains to get to Warsaw earlier than July 31, one day before the uprising began. In at least two documented cases, and there probably were several more, Polish informers told German officials the night before the uprising of what was to occur the next afternoon.[55] Dr. Hahn reportedly learned of the exact time of the uprising at least five hours before it occurred. The explanation for the poor German showing at the outset of the uprising rests perhaps in the fact that they were dulled by the many warnings predicting the event. It seems to have been a matter of intelligence overkill, not unlike what happened to the Soviet Union when "Barbarossa" was launched in June 1941. Stalin had been repeatedly warned by Britain, the United States, and his own intelligence sources.

When the Germans saw they had a major crisis on their hands, they appointed General Erich von dem Bach-Zelewski, SS Obergruppenführer and General of the Waffen SS, to quell it. The twice-wounded World War I veteran, who joined the Nazi Party three years before Hitler's appointment to the chancellorship, was Chief of Anti-Partisan Combat Units. He was a reliable, political general, close to Himmler and to Hitler, who remarked fondly, "Bach-Zelewski is one of the cleverest persons. Even in the party I only used him for the most difficult things." Ever since the early days of the Nazi party, this bespectacled descendant of men who received their rank of nobility from King John Sobieski for the defense of Vienna and colonized Zelewo, Poland—hence the name Zelewski—was Hitler's troubleshooter. He was accused of killing Baron Anton von Hohberg during the Roehm affair in 1934.

When the Warsaw uprising broke out, Bach-Zelewski was at Sopot, not far from his birthplace, expediting the completion of the fortifications along the Vistula. "When I heard about the uprising over the radio," he observed with annoyance, "I wondered why I was not immediately called to take over." Irked by the oversight, he called Hitler's headquarters and talked with SS Gruppenführer, Hermann Fegelein, Eva Braun's brother-in-law, who served as Himmler's liaison at Hitler's headquarters. Bach-Zelewski told him that he was ready to assume command of German forces in Warsaw if Hitler would only give the order. Fegelein, indulging the naive notion shared by others in Hitler's headquarters that the Warsaw matter would be over quickly, said everything was under control. But a few days later, Fegelein telephoned him that the situation took a turn for the worse and asked that he take over immediately the supreme command against the Polish insurgents.[56]

Before Bach-Zelewski assumed command in Warsaw, Reinefarth and his men began to arrive on the outskirts of the city in the western districts of Wola and Ochota. On August 4, his forces numbered 1,000 men, but by the next day the SS, police, and Wehrmacht that had arrived in Warsaw swelled to 86 officers and 6,535 noncommissioned officers and men. They included:

Police Group (Posen): 45 officers; 2,695 NCOs and men.
Kamiński Brigade: 1,700 NCOs and men.
Dirlewanger Brigade: 16 officers; 865 NCOs and men.
Wehrmacht: 25 officers; 1,275 NCOs and men.

With this increment, German fighting strength in Warsaw doubled.[57]

At 8:00 A.M. on August 5, 2,300 men of Reinefarth's unit attacked Wola, defended by 1,650 soldiers of the elite Kedyw battalion. On his right flank, Kamiński's 1,700 men, bolstered by another 400 to 500 SS and police who were already operating in the vicinity, were to advance through the adjacent suburb of Ochota, defended by only 300 to 400 Home Army soldiers. Reinefarth intended to breach Polish defenses, advance through City Center, and reach the Kierbedź Bridge, thus establishing east-west communications.

The German counterattack began with a massive assault by the Luftwaffe, which dropped incendiary bombs. Shortly thereafter, men under the command of Dirlewanger and Colonel Wilhelm Schmidt, described as the "soul" of his unit, successfully advanced along Górczewska and Wolska streets. Other units attacked in the northern part of Wola, where the cemeteries were located, because AK control there prevented an effective

German drive into City Center. By the next day, Dirlewanger's men had darted through Chłodna and Elektoralna streets to the Brühl Palace, where General Stahel and his men were under siege. German relief arrived just in time because Stahel's men were half drunk and on the verge of surrendering to the Poles. By the evening of August 7, the Germans were in control of a key west-to-east artery from Wola into City Center, just a short distance from the Kierbedzia Bridge. Between ground and air action, houses were systematically leveled on both sides of the street, barricades were destroyed, and the entire area became an inferno.

Kamiński's unit, which began its assault at a more leisurely 9:30 A.M. on August 5, only advanced 300 yards. One reason for the slow progress of its attack stemmed from stubborn Polish defenders who were hopelessly outmanned and outarmed. Another reason, however, was the degeneration of the Kamiński counterattack into an orgy of murdering, looting, and raping—converting men into a mob of marauders more akin to Attila's hordes than to soldiers of a modern disciplined army. On August 5, the War Diary of the Ninth Army recorded sarcastically: "The 1st Regiment Kamiński . . . has drunken itself through by way of the Reichstrasse [Jerozolimskie] up to the Machorka Factory."[58] Most of the responsibility for the crimes in Warsaw has been leveled against the infamous Dirlewanger Brigade and the Russians in Kamiński's Brigade. Though this was true to a large extent, there were also regular, SS, and police formations who were involved in the degraded activities of these early August days.

Oskar Dirlewanger was one of those degenerates who, in saner days, would have been court-martialed out of the German army. Born in Wuerzburg in 1895, he served in the German army in World War I, after which he went on to earn a doctorate in economics. Though intelligent, he was a liar, an alcoholic, and a pervert who molested children. Convicted of a sexual assault upon a minor in 1935, he spent two years in prison. When released, he was arrested again on the same charge, but thanks to his mentor, Gottlob Berger, an SS general, he was released and served with the Condor Legion in Spain. In July 1940, he took over a unit of game poachers. Later, the group swelled to battalion strength and was sent to fight Polish partisans as the SS Special Battalion Dirlewanger. He was a sadist whose brutality was well known. He preferred to shoot two Poles too many to one too few. He was an ascetic-looking man who treated his own men as brutally as he treated the Poles. Beating them with clubs to maintain discipline was not uncommon. He even casually shot men he did not like. Little wonder that many of his soldiers deserted to the Russians when they had a chance. After 1942, hardened criminals were drafted into his unit, which gave and expected no quarter from the enemy. His battalion was very successful against Polish and Russian guerillas (allegedly wiping out 15,000 of them). For that success, Bach-Zelewski recommended him for a German Cross of Gold.[59]

Another criminal, Mieczysław Kamiński, commanded an SS brigade bearing his name, though he dubbed it the "Russian Popular Army of Liberation" (*Russkaia Osvoboditelnaia Narodnaia Armiia*). He was brought up a Russian, although his father was Polish and his mother German. Kamiński spent years in a Soviet labor camp and like most of them lived and worked in horrible conditions. He vowed never to return to one again. For a time, Soviet authorities forced him to live in exile in Lokot, near Briansk. Being a resourceful fellow, he became mayor of the city, and from that point on his career skyrocketed.

In return for providing the Nazis with food requisitions and maintaining the area against the Soviet partisans, Kamiński established a virtual dictatorship over Lokot. This latter day Cossack ataman built an army out of volunteers and conscripts from peasants, partisans, and prisoners of war. His army overlapped with a system of military settlements, manned by soldier-farmers not unlike those established by Alexander I early in the nineteenth century. The clever Kamiński cultivated his own popularity by pandering to the peoples' anti-Soviet feeling, allowing his soldiers freedom to loot and granting rapid promotion to anyone he liked. By 1943–44, the Kamiński force swelled to between 10,000 and 20,000 men, defending an area of 1,700,000 people. Unfortunately for the Germans, they did not strongly encourage movements which fed on the legitimate anti-Soviet and nationalistic feelings of Belorussians, Ukrainians, and Baltic peoples. Even after they made concessions to autonomous movements like Kamiński's, they treated most nationalities in the area they occupied contemptuously, unable or unwilling to dump their racist notions about *untermenschen* Slavs.

Unlike General Andrei Vlasov, whose anti-Stalinist movement had a firm ideological foundation, Kamiński was simply an opportunist, a power seeker. The colorful chieftain was so jealous of Vlasov that he did not want his name mentioned in his presence. Although Kamiński headed the Russian Nazi Party, he was no ideologue. His men looted Jew and Gentile alike. There were even some Jews in the Brigade itself.[60]

As German fortunes in Russia declined, Kamiński's people had to retreat westward with their patrons, else risk Soviet extermination. The exodus from Lokot took the refugees to Lepel in Byelorussia (one observer compared it to the Jews leaving Egypt), before they ended up in Upper Silesia—15,000 troops and 20,000 civilians—at the time of the uprising in Warsaw. Kamiński was now a brigadier general and his brigade the Twenty-ninth Division of the SS.

When Kamiński received the order to dispatch some of his troops to Warsaw, he demurred at first. But he was in no position to refuse an order from his patrons, especially now. He selected young unruly bachelors, who still wore Soviet uniforms, for the assignment. They were initially under the command of a colorless officer, Colonel Frolov of Kamiński's Operations Section.[61]

During the uprising, the Poles dubbed all enemy soldiers who spoke Russian as "Ukrainians," and Kamiński's men were incorrectly labelled "Vlasovs." Even those German units which comprised Asiatics, and there were several of them, were called "Kalmuks" by the Poles. The number of non-Germans operating in the SS and police units was very large: Belorussians and Ukrainians, for example, constituted more than fifty percent of some of them.[62]

The Kamiński and Dirlewanger brigades have the dubious distinction of perpetrating the worst crimes of any units in Warsaw. The Kamiński group, not composed of the hardened criminals that Dirlewanger had, went considerably beyond their actions elsewhere. Perhaps the men fatalistically concluded they were on the losing side and, with no future to anticipate except their own eventual demise, cast aside whatever scruples they still had and took the orgiastic descent into infamy.[63] What transpired in Wola and Ochota, the western and southwestern districts of Warsaw, during the early days of August must be considered one of the most horrendous tragedies in a tragedy-filled war. On August 5 alone, 10,000 civilians were murdered.[64] The plundering that went on so preoccupied the Kamiński group that the unit made virtually no progress in its advance through Ochota. The combination of atrocity and plunder conspired to prolong the struggle in the city, which probably could have ended sooner had professional, disciplined German troops been used from the outset.

The tragedy for Wola began in the morning of August 4, when Alexandra Kreczkiewicz and 500 of her neighbors on Górczewska Street were ordered to evacuate their apartments. Children and women cried. Several people were shot at the exit of the building. It was like the Jewish ghetto all over again. The Germans drove Kreczkiewicz and her friends to a potato field where everyone was told to lie down to lessen the chance for escape. A few moments later the group was told to get up, and it was driven under a nearby bridge. "There was no doubt about our fate," Kreczkiewicz related. When one woman asked where they were being taken, the grim answer came, "German women and children are perishing by your fault; therefore, all of you must perish." The SS men divided the people into ranks and one contingent of 70 people was separated and ordered to go behind the bridge. The remaining group, including Kreczkiewicz, was ordered against the wall between the barbed wire. Soon shots rang out. People died. "At a distance of five meters in front of us," she said, "one of the henchmen, very quietly loaded his machine gun; another was preparing his camera; they wanted to prolong the execution. . . . I fell down wounded and lost consciousness."

When she recovered her senses, Kreczkiewicz feigned death. The Germans left a guard over the corpses while they burned the houses in the neighborhood. Scorched by the heat and almost suffocated by the smoke, she thought only of how to get out of the hell in which she found herself. She crawled behind a basket of potatoes and inched her way forward when suddenly a cloud of smoke obscured the guard's vision of the area. She quickly got up and ran to a cellar of a house that was on fire. She met a few wounded people who were fortunate enough to have escaped from the pile of corpses. Despite the heat and smoke, the determined group of survivors tunneled their way to a nearby house untouched by fire. They were safe.[65]

The slaughter continued the next day in Wola. Between 11:00 A.M. and noon, the Germans ordered everyone out of building No. 18 Działdowska Street. A pregnant woman with three children was one of the last to leave the cellar where she had been hiding, hoping to spare herself and her family. The Germans escorted the inhabitants of the house to the Ursus factory on the corner of Wolska and Skierniewicka streets. There, in the factory yard, mass executions took place. The people who stood at the entrance were pushed inside in groups of twenty. A twelve-year-old boy, seeing the bodies of his parents and a little brother through the half-opened door, went hysterical. German soldiers promptly beat him.

Everyone knew what awaited them there. And the agonizing thing was the realization they could neither escape nor buy their lives. The pregnant woman came in last and hovered deliberately in the background, frantically hoping the SS would not kill someone who was about to have a baby. But such considerations did not apply to people like Kamiński's and Dirlewanger's men. They pushed her into the courtyard where she saw heaps of corpses at least three feet high. Bodies were everywhere. Then the Germans pushed her into a second, inner courtyard with a group of twenty people, many of whom were young children not much older than ten or twelve. There was a paralyzed old woman whose son-in-law had been carrying her all the time on his back. Her daughter was at her side. The Germans murdered the entire family. The old lady was literally killed on her son-in-law's back, and he along with her.

The Germans called out the people in groups of four and led them to the end of the second yard where there was a pile of bodies. There the Germans shot them through the back of their heads with revolvers. No sooner had one group been murdered than another group was escorted to the pile of corpses and liquidated. People screamed, begged for mercy, cried, and even attempted to escape.

The pregnant woman was in the last group of four. She begged the German soldiers to save her and her children, offering a large amount of gold to them to spare their lives. After they took the gold, she breathed easier, only to find that the officer supervising the execution would not allow her to go free. She and her children were pushed toward the place of execution, where she held her two younger children by one hand and the elder boy by the other. The children were crying and praying. Seeing the mass of bodies the elder boy cried out, "They are going to kill us!" The first shot hit him, the second one the mother, and the next two killed the two younger children. The mother fell to one side. The shot was not fatal; the bullet had penetrated the back of her head from the right side and gone through her cheek. She spat out several teeth; her body grew numb. But she was conscious and aware of the horror going on around her. There she lay as other men, women, and children were executed, their bodies falling on her. Late in the day when the orgy of executions finally stopped, she was able to crawl away to safety.[66]

The SS booted Maria Bukowska out of her home, which was burned. She, along with several hundred other women of the area, were pushed down the street. Anyone who looked back was immediately beaten. Kamiński's men took watches and jewelry from the hapless women, who were allowed to carry their suitcases a while longer. When the crowd reached the central market, even these items were taken from them and thrown on lorries which were quickly driven away. Then a car with SS officers drove up. The men ogled several pretty girls in the crowd and promptly seized them. The victims ended up in a church, used as a temporary detention center, where the SS took away the remainder of their belongings. All the young girls, some no more than twelve or thirteen, were left behind for the amusement of the men while the older women were put on a train for Pruszków, the camp set up by Bach-Zelewski to receive Polish civilians.[67]

The SS also followed a pattern of murdering, looting, and raping in Ochota, another western district of the city. On August 4, 50 of Kamiński's mob surrounded some houses on Grójecka Street. Under the pretext of looking for arms, they looted homes and then took 160 unarmed men, including twelve-year-olds, led them into a cellar, and shot them in the backs of their heads. They poured gasoline over the corpses, then threw grenades. The SS repeated the same grisly exhibition early the next morning at another house, this time killing 40 men and boys. The same morning on another street, Kamiński's men kicked 40 people into a cellar and machine gunned everyone. Only three survived.[68]

But the most hideous episode involving Kamiński's men began at 10:00 A.M. on August 5 at the Radium Institute. After invading the building, they robbed everyone—the nurses and the ninety patients. The Russians even stole hospital equipment, and what they could not cart off, they destroyed. A band of them tore apart the pharmacy and drank the rubbing alcohol until it ran out. Then they consumed ether. The orgy of plundering and drinking degenerated to raping not only the nurses but also the cancer patients, most of them elderly women. By Sunday, August 6, the men shot inmates and began to burn the hospital room by room. Some of the patients vainly tried to escape through the windows by tying sheets together. Thirty people died in the flaming rooms of the building or were shot that day. The others managed to save themselves by finding a place in the basement of the building and hiding there. The atrocities at the hospital did not end until the middle of the month.[69]

Those not murdered were herded to the "Zieleniak," a large area used as an assembly point on Grojecka Street where by August 6, 20,000 starving, thirsty people were forced to spend several days in the compound until they were evacuated to the internment camp at Pruszków. Among the casualties on August 6 was the well-known artist, eighty-two-year-old Victor Mazurowski, and his famous pianist wife, seventy-five-year-old Jadwiga Zalewska-Mazurowska. For not keeping up with the column of refugees streaming into the "Zieleniak," the distinguished couple were shot. Not far away on the same day, near the Mokotów fields, the well-known dramatic actor, Marius Maszyński, lost his life.[70] A short time later, Bach-Zelewski arrived at the "Zieleniak" where scores of women complained to him that his soldiers had raped them and stolen clothes and jewelry from them. As part of his effort to restore order among his troops and to extend a gesture of humanity, he ordered several hundred people transported out of the congested area.[71]

The murdering reached so feverish an intensity by August 7 that one eyewitness had the impression everyone in Warsaw would be decimated:

> When we passed No. 9 Gorczewska Street (a house which belonged to nuns), we were called into the house and ordered to carry out the corpses which were there. The courtyard was a dreadful sight. It was an execution place. Heaps of corpses were lying there; I think they must have been collecting there for some days, for some were already swollen and others quite freshly killed. There were bodies of men, women, and children, all shot through the backs of their heads. It is difficult to state exactly how many there were.

There must have been several layers carelessly heaped up. The men were ordered to carry away the bodies—we women to bury them. We put them in anti-tank trenches and then filled these up. In this way we filled up a number of such trenches in Gorczewska Street. I had the impression that during the first days of the Rising everybody was killed.[72]

The Poles fought savagely to stop the enemy in Ochota. They used grenades to stop the tanks massing in the area. In one section three ruined tanks testified to the ferocity of the fight. Near Słupecka and Barska streets, two tanks followed by a column of infantry steadily advanced until a Polish sergeant managed to knock a telephone pole down on one of the vehicles. German soldiers flew out of one of the tanks, shooting wildly, while the other vehicle and column of soldiers retreated. In the afternoon on another street, the Poles fended off three attacks by the SS Galizien unit, supported by two companies of Kamiński's men. The Polish positions held.[73]

Warsaw was subjected to one of the most systematic acts of plunder of any occupied city during the war. Before they got to Warsaw, the Kamiński and Dirlewanger units had won reputations for the property they confiscated. They even stole from the Wehrmacht, greatly pleasing the myopic Himmler, who was very jealous of the professional army. He spoke admiringly of the two brigades shortly before they left for Warsaw:

> They have come back with more weapons than they had before. I must find out from my German Leadership Staff how many cigar cases belonging to the General Staff the Russians have brought back as souvenirs. My units are never so well off for underwear as when such a breakthrough as this takes place. Why, another group of two or three thousand Russians under Lieutenant-Colonel Sickling of the SS and police arrived in absolutely new German uniforms, having plundered the clothing depots that the Wehrmacht had left behind.[74]

Although wounded in Warsaw, Kamiński was determined not to lose the opportunity to engage personally in wholesale looting. After one of his fleecing escapades, he sat on a Warsaw balcony, a girl on each knee, and drank champagne. Looting by Kamiński's men was ostensibly done for an unselfish cause—the nonexistent "Russian Liberation Fund."[75]

Beyond the wild plundering by these units, there were the planned and concerted activities supervised by Reinefarth's armed detachments who shipped an enormous amount of Polish property to Germans in Posen, and probably to Berlin. Special railway police were sent to Warsaw to insure more expeditious transport of the spoils. The Germans even dispatched an expert to supervise the loading of hospital equipment. In order that the property arrived safely in the Posen area, special inscriptions bearing the names of Reinefarth and the head of the Nazi Party in the Wartheland, A. Greiser, were put on the railroad cars—"Zur Verfügung von Gauleiter Greiser," and those that read "Kampfgruppe Reinefahrt-Polizeidienststelle." During the first ten days of August, about 7,000 railway cars loaded with property arrived in the Wartheland. Upon arrival there, the spoils—consisting of machinery, raw materials, food, clothing, medicine, and furniture—were placed at the disposal of Greiser, who distributed them among various German groups in the Posen area. Some of the goods went to shops which sold to German customers. Most probably some of the property ended up in Germany during the retreat from the Soviets.[76]

The major consequence of the atrocities committed during the early days in August was the determination that characterized the Polish defenders for the next two months. The horrors in Wola and Ochota helped to bind the AK even closer to the civilian population. Little wonder that the Poles distrusted subsequent German offers concerning evacuation of civilians and the initiation of surrender talks. On their part the Poles summarily executed all SS and police men. If an SS man knew he was fated to be taken prisoner, his only hope of survival was to change quickly into a Wehrmacht uniform. Not even the tearful pleas of a German mother, who came to Warsaw to plead for her son's life, helped spare an SS officer condemned to death by the AK.[77]

Motoring along the western rim of Warsaw on August 5 was a distinguished, impeccably-dressed officer in an SS uniform. He was General von dem Bach-Zelewski, the man appointed to quell the insurrection in Warsaw. As he drove by the cemeteries bordering the city, he saw a large pile of civilian bodies. German police were about to set fire to it. Standing nearby was a group of civilians who were to be executed then and there. Bach-Zelewski lurched from his seat, stopped the car, and ordered the executions to stop immediately. Then he repealed Himmler's standing orders. Bach's reasons were not so much humanitarian as they were practical: "a military force which loots and massacres, ceases to fight," he himself said. What's more, he was a realist about the limits of military pacification. "I divided my plan into a political and a military part," he asserted. "It was self-understood for me as a German that I would have to suppress the uprising by all military means. On the other side, however, from the first moment I had resolved if at all possible to put down the uprising by political means." Though he surely could have done so, he did not accept General Ritter von Greim's suggestion of evacuating German troops from Warsaw and allowing the Luftwaffe to bomb the Poles into submission. Bach-Zelewski's refusal was based on the realization that air attacks alone would not bring a Polish surrender, and like Stalingrad, Warsaw would have to be taken block by block and house by house. When he rescinded Himmler's orders, Bach-Zelewski claimed that he did so at considerable personal risk but that it was his "historic deed" for humanity.[78]

One of the first things Bach did was to try to restore order and discipline among the men who were a rabble, not an army. It was not easy to stop the tide of murder and looting loosed on August 4. It took time. However, Bach-Zelewski made a wise decision in appointing General Gunther Rohr to assume control over Kamiński's group, and as replacements arrived during the course of the Warsaw struggle, to withdraw formations of the brigade. Rohr, considered Bach's best commander, had the very rare ability of converting rabble into soldiers; he was an efficient officer who could be relied upon in difficult situations. Bach more than once commented on his good fortune in having Rohr under his command. Rohr had clearly been against the atrocities, and he even had several German tanks explicitly charged with the protection of Polish civilians.[79]

From the outset, Bach-Zelewski complained about the need for more soldiers and weapons to snuff out the uprising. His requests were avidly supported by the commander of the Ninth Army, Nicolaus von Vormann, who grossly exaggerated the situation in Warsaw to General Hans Krebs, head of Germany Army Group Middle. In a telephone conversation with Krebs on August 9, von Vormann painted a grim picture, arguing that only 3,000 to 4,000 Germans faced 1,500,000 Poles! With that kind of exaggeration little wonder a flood of new weapons streamed into Warsaw.[80]

Bach did not have too much difficulty getting rid of Kamiński after word of what his brigade had done in Warsaw got back to Hitler's headquarters. Apparently it was Fegelein who revealed to Jodl and Guderian what Kamiński's men had perpetrated in Warsaw. "Ten minutes later," General Alfred Jodl testified, "I reported this fact to the Führer and he immediately ordered the dissolution of this brigade." True, the atrocities did not disturb the man who had six million Jews murdered during the war. Rather, it was the inefficient and orgiastic way the Russians went about it. After all, there was a prescribed way for Nazis to commit murder. Fegelein's motives in squealing on one of Himmler's favorite brigades may have stemmed from his association with the Bormann-Kaltenbrunner cabal which wanted to reduce the SS chief's enormous influence. Or it may have been nothing more than a human gesture by a man who remembered his pleasant association with General Bór in the prewar international horse riding competitions.[81]

Bach arrested and sentenced Kamiński; the Gestapo in Łódź shot him in the back. A large quantity of loot—watches and jewelry—was found on his body. Kamiński's hoodlums had tried to get their commander released, but Bach-Żelewski put them off by saying he had gone to Cracow and would not be back until the following day. By then Kamiński was already dead. The official version of Kamiński's death was that the Poles had ambushed his car twenty miles from Warsaw and killed him, along with his chief of staff, doctor, and driver. But Kamiński's men refused to accept this version until they saw the exact spot where he died. It took ten days before the Germans permitted them to visit the alleged location of the murder. What they saw was Kamiński's car riddled with bullets and spattered with blood, but no bodies. The staged assassination scene, however, was apparently convincing enough for most of his men.[82]

The Kamiński Brigade itself, having lost 30 percent of its men in Ochota, was transferred first to Stawki and later to the Kampinos Forest area where it was supposed to help seal off Warsaw from the surrounding vicinity. It was there on the night of September 2 that a Polish unit led by Lieutenant Colonel Adolf Pilch took revenge for the atrocities committed by Kamiński's men. The Poles threw grenades into the cellars of buildings housing the headquarters of two of its battalions, virtually annihilating the unit. One hundred men were killed and two hundred wounded. Among the dead a great deal of jewelry, watches, and gold was found. After the uprising, what was left of the outfit returned to Częstochowa, joining that part of the unit which had taken no part in the suppression of Warsaw. Shortly thereafter, the group was disbanded and its soldiers incorporated, somewhat ironically, into General Andrei Vlasov's Second Division.[83]

But Dirlewanger escaped Kamiński's fate, and his unit continued to operate in the Polish capital. The sallow-faced commander continued to enjoy the patronage of influential Nazis, and not even Guderian's attempt to get rid of Dirlewanger's unit, along with the Russians, did any good. Nor did Fegelein's confirmation that Dirlewanger's group was as bad as Kamiński's: "It is true, my Führer, those men are real scoundrels."[84]

The German advance in the western part of the city came so close to Bór's headquarters in Wola that he had to move to Old Town on August 7. No sooner had he arrived there than he received some especially bad news: The Germans blasted a route to the Vistula at the Kierbedź

Bridge, establishing their vitally needed east-west communications and isolating Old Town and Bór from the rest of the city.

The Poles did not give ground easily. They furiously defended their positions; but in the process key units, such as the Kedyw, which defended the area around the cemeteries, were sacrificed. In the morning of August 9, the Poles lunged out against Fischer and his staff, who left the Brühl Palace and were on their way to safer quarters. Fischer was lucky to escape with his life; his deputy was killed, and several other assistants were either killed or wounded. The commander of the Ninth Army, von Vormann, was so concerned by the nature of Polish resistance and their capacity for offensive action that he told Himmler there was a real possibility that the situation for the German soldiers on the east bank facing the Russians might become "unbearable." There was also a chance, he warned, of the Poles cutting German supply lines through Modlin. That would have been a disaster. "The situation demands," he said, "a division of full strength with large quantities of armament."[85]

By August 11, the western part of Warsaw had been taken. Bach made it clear by then that his strategy was to clear Polish positions along the west bank of the Vistula to prevent the isolation of German troops on the other side of the river and a linkup of Russo-Polish forces. This meant Bach's battle group in the north under his industrious subordinate, Reinefarth, attacked Old Town while Rohr's battle group operated in Mokotów and Czerniaków in the south, eventually to join at Powiśle. Bach left City Center, the strongest fortified sector, and Żoliborz in the far north for the last. This strategy in effect virtually abdicated to the Poles the initiative in City Center, where the AK continued to acquire key installations throughout the month of August, while Bach-Zelewski concentrated on clearing the western banks of the Vistula. On the other hand, City Center became increasingly isolated from the other municipal districts which desperately needed its assistance as Bach gradually succeeded in splitting up and defeating them in isolated pockets.[86]

The situation for the AK grew more difficult as the days passed. When the decision was made to rise up, the AK had enough ammunition for only a few days, and not more than a week. Now two weeks into the battle with no prospect of Soviet relief, Bór kept sending his desperate messages to London, emphasizing his army's plight and asking for supply drops. Another possibility was to order units of the Home Army outside Warsaw into the capital to relieve their beleaguered comrades. He did this on August 14. Although some Poles got through to the Kampinos Forest, a haven for the AK for years, not all of them made it because of Soviet interference. A detachment from Cracow was disarmed as it advanced on the

Polish citadel. Another unit was disarmed in the Rzeszów area and forced into General Berling's army. In Lublin the NKVD arrested Polish soldiers. One of the few units of the AK that had enjoyed friendly relations with the Soviet Army—the Twenty-seventh Volhynian Infantry Division—was given permission to march to Warsaw with a Soviet corps. But they were drawn into an ambush.[87] The hostility of the Soviets to the AK was summed up in a Polish report of August 16: "Diversive activities helpful to the Soviets are continued in the Radom district. The attitude of the Soviets toward the Home Army is hostile. Part of our unit in Mińsk Mazowiecki has been arrested. In the district of Lwów 'voluntary' enlistment to the army under compulsion. . . ."[88]

Thanks to informers before the uprising, the Germans found a cache of 60,000 grenades, 600 flame throwers, and large amounts of explosive material in Mokotów. At the end of the spring in 1944, the Nazis discovered the depot of the AK High Command, bagging 78,000 grenades and 170 flame throwers. As a consequence, the resistance fighters on August 1 were simply not equipped for anything like a long-term struggle against the Germans. They had a total of 43,971 hand grenades, 3,846 pistols, 657 submachine guns, 30 flame throwers, 2 anti-panzer guns, 406 anti-panzer grenades, 12,000 incendiary bottles, 2,629 carbines, 6 mortars, 10 howitzers, and small amounts of ammunition and explosive material. Heavy weapons were nonexistent.[89] An ammunition shortage existed from the outset; yet Bór was reluctant to be too firm in ordering his men to use their ammunition sparingly because of its negative impact on their morale. With only 2,629 carbines, only about 6 percent of the soldiers could be armed with rifles.

Air drops by British and Polish fliers of the RAF particularly filled crucial gaps for the weapon- and ammunition-starved Home Army. The RAF sent ten supply missions to Warsaw during the uprising; and several other missions, intended for the Polish capital, dropped supplies outside the city. Casualty rates were very high: the Poles alone lost 16 crews. In all, 245 Poles, English, and South African airmen were shot down, and only 41 of them survived.[90]

The Piats, English-make anti-tank weapons, proved particularly useful against enemy tanks, along with homemade grenades. The Germans recognized early in the struggle the futility of using conventional tanks in city warfare. On the outskirts they performed better than in the central and older portions of the city where they were unable to maneuver easily. Narrow streets, rubble and debris, and death-defying young men and women with their gasoline bottles made the tanks easy targets for destruction. In fact, approximately 270 tanks were destroyed by the end of the uprising.[91]

As the level of fighting intensified and casualties mounted on both sides, the number of corpses in the streets made the entire city look like an open cemetery. The "gatherers," as the corpse collectors were euphemistically called, had the awful job of removing the bodies from the streets and buildings. Sometimes the corpses lay there for weeks, and when they were touched by hooked poles used for this purpose, they fell to pieces, often exposing swarms of rats who fed on the decayed flesh. For this dreadful work, the Germans, whenever they could, used Polish captives.[92]

The Germans quite by accident discovered the Poles were using the sewers. Early in September they started to dig a tunnel of their own from their positions in Saxony Park to the Polish stronghold in the Exchange Building, which they wanted to destroy. During their digging operations they found a sewer four feet in diameter. At first they simply took their own tunnel under it. But when they heard the sound of movement in the sewer, it dawned on them what was afoot. The Germans then immediately tried to stop Polish use of the subterranean maze by throwing grenades, mines, gas, and rubble into the passages. Even hand grenades without their pins were hung so that when an unsuspecting person hit one, he was blown to bits. There were full-scale battles below, as men fought hand-to-hand and drowned each other in excrement.[93]

Bach-Zelewski tried several ploys to get the Poles to stop fighting in August. Concerned that the uprising would spread throughout the country, he tried to offset the murderous image the Germans acquired earlier in the month in Wola and Ochota; he posed as a humane, gentle soldier anxious for the health and welfare of the people of Warsaw, an aspect he continued to foster even after the war when his life was at stake at Nuremberg. He ordered that leaflets be dropped over the city several times, calling for pauses in the fighting to enable the evacuation of civilians. This was a strong psychological impetus for many Poles who saw the hopelessness of their plight and were inclined to accept German offers of internment and good treatment. He also mixed these appeals with leaflets which argued that the Poles were helping the Russians by their insurrection. The first sentence of one of these propaganda messages read: "This Rising is a service to the Soviets."[94]

Bach was also in continual contact with the Polish Red Cross, asking it to act as mediator between the AK and the Germans. Countess Maria Tarnowska played a key role in some of these contacts. Bach-Zelewski allowed the Swiss Red Cross to inspect receiving camps, field hospitals, and kitchens. He even appealed to the Polish clergy to help him stop the bloodshed as fast as possible, and the Roman Catholic archbishop of the city tried to intercede between the two sides.[95] Late in August, contact with Bór's headquarters was made by the commander of the II Hungarian Reserve Corps, who knew many of the Polish generals when he served as military attaché in Warsaw before the war. He, along with most Hungarians, did not want to serve among the units charged with the suppression of Warsaw. But even these efforts to get the Poles to surrender were fruitless.[96]

The turning point of the uprising was the Polish defeat in Old Town, the centuries-old bastion of narrow winding streets and ancient timbered houses, which hugged the Vistula. The Germans had to eliminate the strong AK position there and follow it up by clearing the Poles out of the districts of Powiśle and Czerniaków. That way the German position in Praga would be less tenuous, and their forces could easily retire across the Vistula bridges if they were forced to do so by the Russians. Moreover, if the Germans held the Vistula embankment, they would prevent a possible link up between the AK and the Soviet Army.

The assault against Old Town began in earnest on August 19 and went on until September 2. The Germans attacked in a semicircle reaching from the Citadel in the north to Teatralny Square and Karowa Street in the south. They had one battalion of regular infantry, two battalions of engineers, three battalions of police troops, one company of Tiger tanks with 88mm guns, twenty 75mm assault guns, fifty Goliath tanks, six 150mm guns, two 280mm howitzers, two 380mm howitzers—the kind of weapon the Germans used to shell Dover—one 600mm mortar, one platoon of aerial minethrowers, several platoons of flame throwers, and also an armored train. This impressive mass of firepower made itself continuously felt on the Poles from morning until evening. The Luftwaffe, using Junkers and Stukas, began this attack by making ceaseless forays over the area. This was accompanied by heavy artillery bombardment which belched tons of steel daily by field and self-propelled artillery, tank guns, rocket mortars, and guns on railway platforms. One source estimated that during the two-week battle 3,500 to 4,500 tons of shells fell on an area three quarters of a square mile,[97] perhaps the largest amount of steel to be expended in so small an area during the war. The buildings of the sector soon became the collective graves of thousands of men and women who were buried alive. By the third day of the struggle, out of 1,100 buildings in Polish hands, 400 had been completely destroyed and 300 had been burned.[98]

There was only one way left for the 1,500 defenders of Old Town to get out. That was the sewer. There never had been anything but a small detachment which made the trek through the sewers before. And to evacuate the entire detachment would mean leaving Old Town totally undefended while the men retreated underground. To make matters worse, if the Germans discovered what was afoot, a few well-placed bombs would decimate the group. And how could the 1,500 men be concealed from the enemy when the manhole they had to use was only a few hundred yards from German positions? For Bór, it was one of the most difficult decisions he had to make during the uprising. On the night of September 1, 1,500 soldiers, 500 civilians, and 100 German prisoners began the 1,700-yard trek through the slime. Old Town was defenseless. If the Germans had attacked, there would have been no opposition.[99] Fortunately, the Germans did not enter the sector until the next day.

Although the AK lost more men than the enemy, the Poles took a heavy toll of German life. Writing to the commander of Army Group Center on August 29, Bach-Zelewski revealed that his casualties included 191 officers and 3,770 noncommissioned officers and troops. He complained that Warsaw could not be taken with the troops he had. Officially he reported that there were no signs of an early conclusion to the struggle,[100] though privately he was more optimistic about the ultimate suppression of the uprising, especially after the collapse of AK resistance in Old Town. To the commander of the Ninth Army, Bach asked for an experienced division to supplement the collection of troops he commanded.[101] The level of violence increased so much during the first two weeks of September that the Germans suffered 5,000 casualties, more than they sustained during the entire month of August, with particularly high losses among noncommissioned officers. Hitler was so shocked by these losses that he wanted his forces to use more mines and planes to destroy the Polish capital.[102]

While the defenders of Old Town had tried desperately to hold back the Germans, the Poles in City Center demonstrated that they were still capable of taking offensive action of their own. As a matter of fact, the AK in the central borough continued to win local successes against the Germans throughout early September. One of the most brutally contested buildings was the Branch Telephone Exchange, or "Little Pasta," as it was known. At the outset of the uprising, large numbers of Germans fled to the building and held it for the next three weeks. The swastika flying over the building was "a reproach to our conscience," one of the Polish soldiers solemnly declared. It was also an ever-present reminder of the vulnerability of the Polish position in the central borough if the Germans from the outside decided to launch a coordinated attack with their comrades inside the building. The stout-hearted German defenders repulsed many Polish attempts to take the building, but eventually the Poles took it.[103]

While the AK achieved local successes in City Center, Bach-Zelewski relentlessly followed his strategy of clearing the left bank of the river. His next objective was Powiśle, a key area situated between the Kierbedź Bridge in the north and the Poniatowski Bridge in the south. Again it was Reinefarth's forces, principally units of the infamous Dirlewanger brigade, which executed the major attack that began on September 6. By this time, despite some local setbacks, Bach-Zelewski privately admitted that if the Soviets did not attempt to link up with the Poles, he could quell the insurrection in a matter of days.[104] This was too sanguine an assessment, as the German general was soon to discover.

The atrocities returned. German soldiers used women as a screen for their advance into Powiśle. The defenders waited until they could get clear shots at the enemy, but it was too late; the Germans crossed the barricades. Panic-stricken refugees fled to City Center. There were reports that German soldiers ordered patients from the hospitals into bomb craters and then machine gunned them. Thirty-two-year-old Bronisław Dylak remembered the day when German soldiers ordered all nurses and inmates who could walk to leave his hospital, leaving only the badly wounded. Dylak stayed in his ward, which was in the cellar of the building. After the nurses left, the SS arrived and started to shoot. The patients who feverishly tried to get out of bed and make it to doors and staircases were shot immediately. Two murderers burst into Dylak's ward. But he and several other patients were saved because their beds were in the ward partitioned from the others. One of the soldiers went among the dead people and struck them in the faces with his gun. Then the building was set on fire. Dylak remembered:

> All other wards, as well as the staircase, were on fire; the smell of burning corpses, indescribable thirst; the wounded seized medicine bottles for lack of water, one of my neighbors mad from heat and thirst, seized a bottle of iodine and drank the contents, poisoning himself to death; for myself, together with some others, I moistened my lips with peroxide solution. So we lay until the morning of the following day when, with a superhuman effort, we managed to creep out from the burning ruins.[105]

Bór wanted to continue the struggle against the Germans, but this was becoming increasingly difficult to do. Members of the Council of National

Unity wanted him to begin surrender talks with the enemy. The population was now at the point of starvation. On September 3, Bór told Mikołajczyk that the uprising should stop. The president of the Polish Red Cross, Madame Tarnowska, made contacts with General Rohr, on September 4 and again on September 8. Rohr proposed that all civilians, as well as the sick and wounded, leave the city at agreed-upon points during a cease fire. He promised they would be cared for in German refugee camps. On September 8 and 9, several thousand Polish civilians responded, a small number of the total population. No doubt the fear of more German atrocities, especially the most recent ones in Powiśle, prevented many people from leaving the city. Red Cross contacts with the Germans paved the way for the surrender talks which began on September 9. By that time, Bór had departed somewhat from his policy of continued resistance. In the most desperate message he had sent London since the fall of Old Town, Bór made it unmistakeably clear that he was ready to surrender if powerful and immediate help did not come. "Without that," Bór declared, "We must capitulate." He explained: "The situation in the City Center is deteriorating. The soldiers' endurance is reaching the bounds of human possibility. A hopeless situation."[106]

The London Poles did not want Bór to continue the surrender talks. They hoped that recent British and American diplomatic pressures on Moscow might force the Soviet Army to roll again, or at least give the AAF permission to use Russian bases for the relief of Warsaw. Their policy of holding Bór back seemed to pay the desired dividends when late in the evening of September 9 an urgent message from London arrived in Warsaw: "Inform Government Plenipotentiary that today Marshal Stalin promised help for Warsaw."[107]

Meanwhile the Germans had presented their terms to the representatives of the AK, who promised to reply to them on the following day. The next morning, September 10, saw Soviet fighters instead of Stukas circling the city in pairs, confirming the recent news from London. Soon the Soviet silence across the Vistula was broken. The Russians attacked the German suburb of Praga.[108] Bór, who had despaired of Russian help ever coming, did not want to break off talks with the Germans prematurely before the Russian offensive got rolling. So he continued the parleys with Rohr, who wanted Bór's surrender by 4:00 P.M. that day. But Bór procrastinated and requested that the rights of the AK be guaranteed by no one less than the Commander of the Army Group Middle, Colonel General Georg-Hans Reinhardt, one of the best-known panzer generals in the German army, who saw service in Poland in September 1939. Rohr was furious, but he sent the request to Reinhardt, who saw through the Polish ruse. He declared firmly: "I have nothing to add to the conditions which have been made to you by Major General Rohr. In the event the capitulation is not made by September 11 at 1:00 P.M., the fighting will continue in sharpened form. This is my last word."[109] Ever since September 9, Bach-Zelewski substantially increased the artillery barrages to convince the Poles to capitulate. Seeing Soviet military activity increase steadily, the Poles allowed General Reinhardt's deadline to pass and opted to continue the struggle. Tasting political and military victory, the Poles—incredibly—put their faith in the Soviet Union for the second time in two months, and the bloodbath continued. It was to be August all over again.

The Russian offensive against Praga was successful. The key unit in the thrust was the First Polish Army, part of which had been taken from the Warka bridgehead. The Seventy-third Infantry Division retreated. Officers and men of the unit, humiliated by their failure to stop the Russians, lost any opportunity for leave or promotion; at one point German authorities even considered disbanding the unit. The poor German showing against the Polish and Russian troops was also blamed on the likeable but inept commander of the Ninth Army, von Vormann, who was replaced by a tank commander, General Smilo Freiherr von Luttwitz.[110]

By September 13, Polish-Soviet troops reached the Vistula bridges which the Germans, having previously wired for destruction in such an eventuality, destroyed, leaving the northernmost one open for the evacuation of the Nineteenth Panzer Division, commanded by the able tank leader, General Hans Kallner.[111] Accompanying the Soviet advance on that day were planes which dropped, somewhat ironically, American canned food to relieve the grave shortages of food and ammunition. The Soviet air drop beat the AAF to Warsaw, and the Soviets lost no time in propagandizing their assistance to the Poles. The air drops continued for the next four days, stopping on September 18. The Russians resumed them three days later, and continued the drops until the night of September 28. During the twelve nights of air operations over Warsaw, the Russians dropped about fifty to fifty-five tons of supplies, fifteen of which were food.[112] Unlike the RAF missions, the Russian planes—they used a plane called the *kukuruznik*—flew several times over the area but dropped their loads frequently without parachutes. The consequence was that the supplies were so damaged as to make much of them useless. The Soviet drops, however, came in time: Bór told London on September 13 that he would order on the following day the distribution of the last of the hunger rations. Two days later Bór credited the Russian drop with enabling the AK to continue further resistance against German attacks.[113]

The Red Army had the Germans on the run. By September 14, the

Ninth Army War Diary reported that Kallner's Nineteenth Panzer Division was pushed back in the northern part of Praga and that the Magnuszew bridgehead, one of the first the Russians had established, was firmly under the control of the Eighth Soviet Guards Army. It appeared that the Russians were ready to attack Warsaw from Praga, coupled with an encircling maneuver from the south. But this was not in the offing. Having established themselves in Praga, Berling's First Polish Army tried to force the Vistula, between September 15 and 19. The Poles, using artificial fog to mitigate the accuracy of German artillery, tried to cross to the western bank in several places, but their attempts were too weak and too forlorn. Instead of concentrating on Żoliborz, which constituted the largest stretch of land on the western side of the river in AK hands, the attack was initially made at Czerniaków, a far more difficult operation. The Ninth Army, moreover, considered Żoliborz a likely spot where the Russians would establish a bridgehead and were fearful they would do it while the Germans tried to squelch the Poles in the south. Though Berling's men eventually established a bridgehead 1,000 meters wide and 500 meters deep on the western side of the Vistula, Rokossovsky was conspicuous in doing nothing to expand and consolidate the dearly won position. In one of the more incomprehensible episodes of the Vistula debacle, a battalion of Berling's Second Infantry Division attempted a diversionary crossing near Marymount, two miles from insurgent positions, in order to allow a successful blow at the principal objective. No attempt to contact the Poles in Żoliborz had been made. The entire effort, allegedly undertaken at Berling's own initiative, failed, and the Polish general was relieved of his command and summoned to Moscow.[114]

The losses of Berling's troops in the Vistula crossings reached 2,000.[115] The series of attempts to cross the river in mid-September ring of Stalinist cynicism: He used Polish troops who were expendable in an operation that he probably never intended to support strongly enough by Soviet artillery and aircraft and by effective liaison with the AK. To Stalin, the crossings were a gesture only, not a genuine effort to take Warsaw from the Germans.

The Poles had made several attempts to establish liaison with the Russians. Before Berling's troops attempted to force the Vistula, Bór tried to coordinate efforts with Rokossovsky on September 11. No reply came. Colonel Antoni Chruściel, a member of the AK High Command, made at least two efforts on his own in succeeding days to establish liaison by sending patrols to the eastern bank of the Vistula. No one ever heard what happened to the first patrol, but the second one, which included Captain Konstanty Kalugin, an officer of the AL, did reach Berling's headquarters.

It was not until after the fiasco of the Vistula crossings that a Soviet artillery observer parachuted into City Center on September 21. In addition, between September 20 and 22, two Soviet liaison men landed in Żoliborz and two in Mokotów. The AK commander in Mokotów identified one of the Russians there as Alexander Chernukhyn, who curiously asked what the AK needed in the way of help—something the Poles had sought since August 1. But it took a few more days before the Soviet Army finally responded to repeated Polish calls for contact. That was on September 24, a week away from Polish defeat. During the few days that were left to the Polish resistance, the exchange of messages with the Russians ran ten per day, but these were confined to sightings for artillery fire and supply drops. The Russians again conspicuously avoided any discussion on matters of tactical cooperation with the AK.[116]

After repeated pleas from the Poles to the United States to aid them and Soviet refusals to allow the AAF to use their bases, which were essential for B-17s to drop supplies over Poland, Washington waited helplessly as the Germans relentlessly pounded the Varsovians. After Stalin's belated effort to aid the Poles early in September, he finally dropped his opposition to AAF use of Soviet bases, knowing by then that Polish surrender to the Germans was a certainty. At 5:30 A.M. on September 18, a massive air armada, consisting of 110 B-17s and three groups of P-51s, took off from English airfields. Eighty-six of the fighters escorted the air fleet only part of the way and returned to England while the remaining sixty-two P-51s stayed with the bombers all the way. The airmen spotted the flaming city forty miles away. The big planes, flying between 14,000 and 17,000 feet, dropped 1,284 containers with multicolored parachutes. Approximately 288 of them reached Polish hands. Out of 110 bombers, 105 arrived in Russia, three returned to base early, one was lost, and one was forced to land in Brest-Litovsk. Fifteen of the Flying Fortresses received major battle damage. Of the total number of fighters employed in the operation, the AAF lost four.[117]

The Germans believed that the West had sent paratroops to Warsaw. The German Sixth Air Fleet reported that 250 AAF bombers were on their way to drop the men over the city. This report came at the very time the Germans believed the Russians intended to press northward with their Forty-seventh Army and destroy the Fourth SS Panzer Corps and to link up with the 8,000 men in the Kampinos Forest. Bach-Zelewski believed he had every reason to be fearful that victory in Warsaw might elude him now. But his fears were exaggerted, since the AAF dropped supplies, not paratroops; the Russian pressure on the Fourth Panzer Corps was a local action, unrelated to Warsaw; and there were only 2,700 Poles who engaged the Germans in the Kampinos area, uncoordinated with the Russian action at the same time.[118]

After the fall of Mokotów, Bór met with his staff and the government delegate. Everyone agreed that the limit of endurance for the remaining soldiers and civilians was three to five days. "Either the enemy or hunger would overwhelm us in that time," Bór declared; "this was the time limit for the arrival of help from outside. Surrender was the only alternative." The next day Bór told London that if no Soviet assistance came by October 1, then the Home Army had to surrender. The horrible conditions already dictated an immediate surrender. The people had been on starvation rations for days. People searched vainly for the few remaining dogs to eat. Facilities of any kind—electricity, water, gas—were virtually nonexistent.[119] A glass of water sold for 500 złotys.[120] Warsaw resembled more a neolithic oddity than a center of western civilization.

German forces now concentrated on Żoliborz. The 8,000 German force massed against the 1,300 AK and 400 AL soldiers, monotonously repeating the bloody air and artillery attacks that converted this beautiful residential area into a pile of rubble, following the pattern of destruction begun two months earlier in Wola and Ochota. Zenon Kliszko, a young lieutenant in the AL destined to become a high-ranking leader in postwar Communist Poland, observed at the time: "We were waiting for a miracle, we were awaiting the forcing of the Vistula, a descent from the air. Calling for help all the time we came to realize more and more that nobody could help us any more. We knew this but our hearts and our hands went on with their work untiringly, carrying out every action accurately, and in some cases with great precision. People died unnoticed, dropping to the ground as though they wanted to rest for a while."[121]

Upon the suggestion of members of the AL, the commander of the AK in Żoliborz, Lieutenant Colonel Mieczysław Niedzielski ("Żywiciel"), dubbed by Bach-Zelewski a brave but fanatical man, apparently agreed to a retreat across the Vistula. The operation was predicated upon Soviet assistance, the promise of which had been made so many times before as to cause serious doubt in the minds of many of the defenders. On September 30, Berling's First Polish Army radioed that it would provide a fleet of boats for the defenders to cross the river. Shortly before the hour set for the retreat, Bór ordered Niedzielski to surrender. There was a substantial disagreement among the AK and AL soldiers whether to capitulate. But Kliszko and fifty others decided not to accept surrender and to cross the Vistula as planned. Only twenty-eight of them made it.[122]

In view of the hopeless situation in which the defenders found themselves, Bór could no longer trust the promises of assistance of Berling and

Russian authorities. Since no reply from Rokossovsky came to Bór's appeal of September 28, the Polish commander, probably anticipating another bloody debacle in Żoliborz that had occurred earlier to the Czerniaków defenders who awaited Soviet help, finally realized that it was all over. On September 29, Bór sent an envoy to the Germans with the object of discussing the evacuation of civilians. By September 30, Bór gave up hope of a reply from the Russians and ordered the surrender of Żoliborz. Meanwhile a cease fire was arranged, allowing the evacuation of civilians, beginning October 1. Finally, on that day, Bór told London: "Warsaw has no longer any chance of defence. I have decided to enter into negotiations for surrender with full combatant rights, which the Germans fully recognize. Negotiations tomorrow. I will arrange that the question of safety for the civilian population be linked with the question of surrender. I expect the surrender on October 3, 1944."[123]

On October 2, 1944, Polish representatives worked out the final surrender terms with Bach-Zelewski: AK soldiers were to be treated as prisoners of war in accordance with the rights of the Geneva Convention. Civilians were not to be persecuted, and their evacuation from Warsaw, demanded by the Germans, was supposed to be conducted in such a way to minimize suffering.[124] On October 5, Bór inspected his security platoon for the last time. There had been 128 of them on August 1. Now there were 36. By 9:15 A.M., the Home Army was ready to march out with their arms and surrender to the waiting Germans, just a few hundred yards away. A woman darted from the crowd and gave Bór a medal from the Polish insurrection of 1863. It was an emotional moment, heightened by the fact that Bór began to sing the Polish national anthem, *Jeszcze Polska Nie Zginęła* ("Poland is Not Yet Lost"), and was joined by the soldiers and civilians as the detachment proceeded down the street to the Germans. The crowd was in tears, and even the Germans seemed to have been touched as the words echoed across the street.

The Germans took Bór and his staff to Ożarów, where they boarded a train for their internment at Gansenstein. Bach-Zelewski, insistent that Bór and his staff be well treated, went out of his way to insure the safety and well-being of his Polish charges. Oddly enough, Himmler wanted to talk with Bór about the possibility of organizing a Polish national army under his leadership similar to the various ethnic units which had fought shoulder to shoulder with the Germans. Bór icily refused and the meeting never took place.[125] A few days later Hitler received Bach-Zelewski and commended him in the presence of Field Marshal Wilhelm Keitel, Martin Bormann, and Heinrich Himmler for his achievements in Warsaw. Hitler expressed the hope that his expert in antipartisan warfare would be equally successful in Hungary, his next assignment.[126]

No one knows for certain how many people perished in Warsaw during the two-month inferno that began on August 1. Various estimates abound. The official history of the Polish armed forces estimates that there were 21,600 military casualties in Warsaw—10,000 killed, 6,600 wounded, and 5,000 missing in action. The same source places German casualties at 26,000—10,000 killed, 9,000 wounded, and 7,000 missing in action.[127] Bach-Zelewski himself estimated German casualties at 20,000.[128] On the other hand, a respected German scholar estimated that the Germans suffered 11,000 casualties—2,000 killed and 9,000 wounded. Total losses, military and civilian, in Warsaw appear to have amounted to approximately 200,000.[129]

The Warsaw Uprising doomed the Poles in the capital to defeat and destroyed the heart of the political and military institutions of the Polish underground, a goal that Stalin needed to accomplish before his armies occupied Warsaw and installed his own political proteges as the rulers of Poland.

AFTERWORD

The word Holocaust suggests to most people the tragedy the Jews experienced under the Germans during World War II. From a psychological point of view, it is understandable why Jews today prefer that the term refer exclusively to the Jewish experience, thus emphasizing the distinctiveness of the wartime fate of the Jews. Yet, by excluding others from inclusion in the Holocaust, the horrors that Poles, other Slavs, and Gypsies endured at the hands of the Nazis are often ignored, if not forgotten.

From a historical point of view, no reasonable student of World War II can deny that Hitler's policy toward the Poles was also genocidal and that about as many Polish Christians as Polish Jews died as a result of Nazi terror. Without detracting from the particularity of the Jewish tragedy in which all Jews were victimized because they were Jews, it is time to speak about the forgotten Holocausts of World War II. By failing to broaden the scope of research on the Holocaust, we have allowed our perspective on it to become distorted, and this has led to simplistic and false conclusions about the subject.

Because of a lack of understanding of the Holocaust in its broadest terms, writers have perpetuated the stereotypical view of the anti-Semitic Pole as the primary or even the sole explanation for Polish attitudes and behavior toward the Jews during World War II. The famous writer and critic John Gardner is an excellent example of how desperate the need is to correct the still-flawed understanding of the Poles during the war. In a review of William Styron's *Sophie's Choice*, Gardner wrote: "Poland, occupied for centuries first by one cruel master, then another, pitifully devoted to both German culture and Nazi style anti-Semitism, . . . points to that ideal Edenic world that master musicians, the Poles and Germans, thought in their insanity they might create here on earth by getting rid of a few million 'defectives.'"[1] The stereotype is so ingrained in American consciousness that a reviewer of James Michener's novel *Poland* took issue with what he perceived as a lapse in the novel by asking, "But what of Polish anti-Semitism?"[2] Obviously Michener appreciated more than his reviewer that Polish-Jewish relations did not revolve exclusively around anti-Semitism, or in the Jewish case, Polonophobia, and that Poles and Jews lived more in harmony and mutual tolerance for a longer time in their shared history than is understood today.

Television has reinforced the negative image of the Poles too. In one installment of the television version of Herman Wouk's *Winds of War*, Heinrich Himmler informs Adolf Hitler that 3,000 men and officers of the *Einsatsgruppen* are ready to kill the Jews in Russia. They will be the organizers, says Himmler, but the local population will execute the job, and there are "plenty of volunteers" in Poland. The same impression was left with the NBC adaptation of Gerald Green's *Holocaust*, which focused almost exclusively on the Jewish tragedy and ignored the plight of the Poles, who, when depicted, were seen essentially in a negative light.

If novelists and publicists perpetuate distortions of the Poles and their history, one would at least hope for better in the writings of historians. Unfortunately, it is disquieting to read most writings on the Holocaust, because the subject of Polish-Jewish relations is treated so polemically. Preoccupied with the overwhelming tragedy of the Jews, Jewish historians, who are the major writers on the subject, rarely if ever attempt to qualify their condemnations of the Poles and their defense of the Jews. The result is tendentious writing that is often more reminiscent of propaganda than of history. Despite the scholarly pretensions of many of these works—and there is genuine scholarship in some of these books—they have contributed little to a better understanding of the complexity and paradox of Polish-Jewish wartime relations.

If a more objective and balanced view prevailed in the historiography on the Holocaust, there would be less said about Polish anti-Semitism and more about the problems that faced the Poles and their military and political leadership in dealing with the Germans. If the magnitude of the Polish tragedy were objectively presented, unrealistic and unhistorical judgments about the possibilities and opportunities available to the Poles to render greater aid than they did to the Jews would not be made. Ironically, many of the Jews themselves at the time understood this better than latter-day historians. The result has been a curious inversion of values in which co-victims of the Holocaust are placed in the position of defending themselves against these critics. The consequence is that instead of trying to understand the complexity of the Holocaust tragedy, too many writers and historians are primarily motivated by the search for scapegoats to explain the monumental Jewish losses of the war years. One must also wonder how much the postwar relations between Poland and Israel have influenced serious study of Polish-Jewish wartime relations.

There are serious methodological problems which have yet to be dealt with before convincing accounts of the Poles and Jews during the Holocaust can be produced. Some Jewish writers themselves have indicated part of the problem when they describe the manuscripts written at the time of the Holocaust and transmitted from the ghettos to the outside world as taking on the aura of holy writ and as such not subject to the same criticism as other sources that reach the scholar through normal channels of composition and publication.[3] The editors of Emmanuel Ringelblum's *Polish-Jewish Relations*, for example, do not subject the manuscript to critical analysis; yet, the manuscript is badly flawed because the author's generalizations are based on his own experiences, and his conclusions are often more emotional than factual. The editors not only accept uncritically Ringelblum's often-severe criticisms of the Poles but also expand on them in copious footnote commentary. Yet, not coincidentally, the editors choose to keep their commentary to a minimum in the author's chapter dealing with the Poles who aided the Jews during the German occupation.

The methodological problem goes even deeper: Holocaust writers have suggested that Jewish behavior at the time cannot be judged because, in the words of the *Encylopedia Judaica*, "standards of normal society did not obtain in the ghettoes and concentration camps."[4] Did such standards exist anywhere in occupied Poland? Is it reasonable to suggest, therefore, that historians should hold Jews to one standard of behavior and Poles to another? After all, Jew and Pole, saint and sinner, wanted only one thing—to survive.

Lucy Dawidowicz states that Jewish writers "are still mourning the loss of their past."[5] If that is true, it is doubtful that history is the genre for writers who are so overwhelmed by the Holocaust and yet want to describe it. It seems that some fictional form of expression may be more suitable than history for those who want to respond emotionally rather than historically to that great tragedy.

Philip Friedman, the father of Holocaust literature, said in 1957 that "the spirit of martyrology emanating from our literature on the Holocaust prevents a clear-cut view from a historical perspective." He added: "Our evaluation of the attitude of Christian neighbors to the Jewish tragedy should be one of differentiation and the finest distinction. The blurred and deficient picture we have in general—and unjustly so—of the Gentile friends, helpers, and rescuers of Jews during the Nazi era will also be decisively amended thereby."[6] A generation has passed, and unfortunately, with only a few exceptions, there has been, among historians and popularizers, little discernible change in the prevailing hagiographical approach to the Jews in the Holocaust and in the distorted picture of Poles and other victims.

It is my hope that this study has opened the door, if only a little, to a broader, more objective view of the cataclysm that engulfed so many so terribly for so long.

NOTES

ABBREVIATIONS

AKwD   Studium Polski Podziemnej. *Armia Krajowa w Dokumentach, 1939-1945.* Vol. 1: *Wrzesień 1939-Czerwiec
1941*; Vol. 2: *Czerwiec 1941-Kwiecień 1943*; Vol. 3:
Kwiecień 1943-Lipiec 1944.

BOD   Board of Deputies of British Jews. London, England.

DPSR   General Sikorski Historical Institute. *Documents on Polish-Soviet Relations, 1939-1945.*

FRUS   U.S. Department of State. *Foreign Relations of the
United States: Diplomatic Papers.*

GSHI   General Sikorski Historical Institute. London, England.

HI   Hoover Institution on War, Revolution, and Peace. Stanford, California.

IMT/NA   International Military Tribunal. National Archives.
Washington, D.C.

OSS/NA   Office of Strategic Services. National Archives. Washington, D.C.

PRO   Public Record Office. Kew, Richmond, England.

PSZ   Komisja Historyczna Polskiego Sztabu Głównego w
Londynie. *Polskie Siły Zbrojne w Drugiej Wojnie Światowej.*

PUST   Polish Underground Study Trust. London, England.

TWC   *Trials of War Criminals before the Nuernberg Military
Tribunals under Control Council Law No. 10, Nuern-
berg, October 1946-April 1949.*

WDGS   War Department General Staff. National Archives.
Washington, D.C.

YIVO   Zylberberg Collection. Institute for Jewish Research.
New York, New York.

Note: Full bibliographic information about works cited in the notes will be found
in the bibliography, beginning on page 273.

CHAPTER ONE

1. Anthony J. Drexel Biddle, Jr., "The Biddle Report," 17, 20, 36, 44, 53, 55, Franklin D. Roosevelt Library, Hyde Park, New York. Since I read the report at the Roosevelt Library several years ago, it has been edited and published. See Cannistraro, et al., *Poland and the Second World War.*

2. Message, Gunther to Secretary of State, 16 Sept. 1939, *FRUS*, 2:554-57.

3. Hanson, *Civilian Population and the Warsaw Uprising*, 5-6.

4. Nowak, *Courier from Warsaw*, 58.

5. Leslie, *History of Poland*, 209.

6. Ibid., 209-12.

7. Gross, *Polish Society under German Occupation*, 215ff.

8. Leslie, *History of Poland*, 212, 214.

9. Gumkowski and Leszczyński, *Poland under Nazi Occupation*, 59.

10. Ibid.

11. Duraczyński, *Wojna i Okupacja*, 36-38.

12. Quoted in Polish Ministry of Information, *Black Book of Poland*, 134. After October 1939, the Wehrmacht was used, sometimes extensively, in antipartisan and pacification operations. For example, in November 1943 Wehrmacht units participated in 100 antipartisan and pacification actions. See Madajczyk, *Polityka III Rzeszy w Okupowanej Polsce* 2:265-66. Yet there were some Wehrmacht generals, like Blaskowitz, who wanted to treat the Poles leniently, if for no other reason than to prevent the attacks of the Polish resistance in the rear of the Germany Army. Sprawozdanie Emisariusza Antoniego, Załącznik 24, 4/41, in PRM 46A/15, GSHI.

13. Duraczyński, *Wojna i Okupacja*, 17.

14. Pospieszalski, *Polska pod Niemieckim Prawem*, 189.

15. United States, Office of United States Chief of Counsel, *Nazi Conspiracy and Aggression*, 2:904.

16. Kamenetsky, *Secret Nazi Plans*, 140.

17. Madajczyk, *Polityka III Rzeszy w Okupowanej Polsce* 2:370.

18. Ibid.; U.S. Counsel, *Nazi Conspiracy and Aggression* 1:1027.

19. Central Commission, *German Crimes in Poland* 2:18, 21.

20. Quoted in Hilberg, *Destruction of the European Jews*, 644.

21. U.S. Counsel, *Nazi Conspiracy and Aggression* 6:435; *TWC* 4:494.

22. Hirszfeld, *Historia Jednego Życia*, 310; Interviews with Rachel and Karol Cymber, 18 July 1983.

23. Leslie, *History of Poland*, 214, 216.

24. Office of Strategic Services, Research and Analysis Branch, "German Military Government over Europe: Eastern Territories Incorporated in the Reich," 12 Feb. 1945, in OSS/NA.

25. Memoranda on Axis-Controlled Europe, 17 Aug. 1943, in FO371/34597, PRO.

26. Central Commission, *German Crimes in Poland* 2:33; Madajczyk, *Polityka III Rzeszy w Okupowanej Polsce* 1:125ff.

27. U.S. Counsel, *Nazi Conspiracy and Aggression* 1:1029; Poliakov, *Harvest of Hate*, 269.

28. Kren and Rappoport, *Holocaust and Human Behavior*, 55-56.

29. Bartoszewski, *Warsaw Death Ring*, 16.

30. Republic of Poland, *German Occupation of Poland*, 43, 213-14 (known as the *Polish White Book* and hereinafter cited that way); Duraczyński, *Wojna i Okupacja*, 56-58.

31. Bartoszewski, *Blood Shed Unites Us*, 24. See the extensive quotation from Frank's diary in Bartoszewski, *Warsaw Death Ring*, 38.

32. Duraczyński, *Wojna i Okupacja*, 61ff; Bartoszewski, *Blood Shed Unites Us*, 25; *TWC* 1:237.

33. Bartoszewski, *Warsaw Death Ring*, 66-67.

34. Domagala, *Ci, Którzy Przeszli Przez Dachau*, 22.

35. Duraczyński, *Wojna i Okupacja*, 58; Madajczyk, *Polityka III Rzeszy w Okupowanej Polsce* 2:168.

36. Hanson, *Civilian Population and the Warsaw Uprising*, 39-41. See photograph in Polish Ministry of Information, *Black Book of Poland*, opposite p. 315.

37. Polish Ministry of Information, *Black Book of Poland*, 444, 490-92; Central Commission, *German Crimes in Poland* 1:248.

38. *Polish Fortnightly Review*, 1 Aug. 1942, 5; Stebelski, *Fate of Polish Archives*, 5-34.

39. Ibid., 51.

40. Michel, *Shadow War*, 32; *Polish Fortnightly Review*, 1 Aug. 1942, 6; Madajczyk, *Polityka III Rzeszy w Okupowanej Polsce* 2:122-23.

41. Polish Ministry of Information, *Black Book of Poland*, 496-98; Madajczyk, *Polityka III Rzeszy w Okupowanej Polsce*, 2:166-70.

42. Polish Ministry of Information, *Black Book of Poland*, 492; Zarządzenie Niemieckie, 14 May 1941, in *AKwD* 2:197-98; Madajczyk, *Polityka III Rzeszy w Okupowanej Polsce* 1:341-42.

43. Madajczyk, *Polityka III Rzeszy w Okupowanej Polsce* 1:341:47; *Polish Fortnightly Review*, 1 Aug. 1942, 7.

44. Karski, *Story of a Secret State*, 79.

45. Press Extract, *Hufvudstadsbladet*, 18 Jan. 1941, in FO371/26723/52538 C3502/189/55, PRO.

46. Falconi, *The Silence of Pius XII*, 110.

47. Madajczyk, *Polityka III Rzeszy w Okupowanej Polsce* 2:182-83, 212.

48. Polish Ministry of Information, *Black Book of Poland*, 583.

49. U.S. Counsel, *Nazi Conspiracy and Aggression* 5:1018-31; *Polish Fortnightly Review*, 15 July 1942, 3.

50. Mistecka, *Zmartwychwstanki w Okupowanej Polsce, 1939-1945*, 59, 71, 119ff.

51. Madajczyk, *Polityka III Rzeszy w Okupowanej Polsce* 2:178, 193.

52. Ibid., 188-89.

53. Ibid., 178-80; Falconi, *Silence of Pius XII*, 177.

54. Madajczyk, *Polityka III Rzeszy w Okupowanej Polsce* 2:190-91, 212; memo, Savery to Roberts with reports, 26 Aug. 1941, in FO371/26727/5481 C9667/189/55, PRO. On 17 Feb. 1941, five Franciscan monks were arrested in Niepokalanów near Warsaw. Three of these men later died in concentration camps, including Father Maximilian Kolbe, who offered his life for another man. Kolbe died from an injection of phenol on 14 Aug. 1941. Kolbe was recently canonized a saint of the Roman Catholic Church.

55. Sprawozdanie Celta, 1944: Sytuacja Duchowieństwa w Okupowanej Polsce, in Kolekcja 25/9, GSHI.

56. Ibid.

57. Letter, Kennard to Eden, 14 Feb. 1941, in FO417/43 C1488/189/55, PRO.

58. Meldunek, Tokarzewski do Sosnkowskiego i Ogolny Raport Polityczno-Gospodarczy, 9 Jan. 1940, in *AKwD*, 1:41ff; Madajczyk, *Polityka III Rzeszy w Okupowanej Polsce* 2:190. At the end of 1941, the Germans even confiscated church bells in the General Government. *Polish Fortnightly Review*, 1 Aug. 1942, 8.

59. *Polish White Book*, 35.

60. Message, Tittman to Secretary of State, 6 Oct. 1942, in *FRUS*, 3:776-77.

61. Morely, *Vatican Diplomacy and the Jews*, 140, 305 n.79.

62. Dwa Lata Okupacji Niemieckiej w Polsce [1941], in PRM 45C/23, GSHI; letter, Savery to Roberts, with enclosures, 28 Feb. 1941, in FO371/26723/52538 C1827/189/55, PRO.

63. Falconi, *Silence of Pius XII*, 222; memo, Savery to Roberts with reports, 26 Aug. 1941, in FO371/26727/5481 C9667/189/55, PRO.

64. Quoted in Falconi, *Silence of Pius XII*, 228-29, 217.

65. Morley, *Vatican Diplomacy and the Jews*, 129-32.

66. Madajczyk, "Generalplan Ost" 3:399; *Polish White Book*, 23-25; Kozłowiecki, *Ucisk i Strapienie*, 76. Some estimates place the number of deported Poles at 1.5 million.

67. Kamenetsky, *Secret Nazi Plans*, 51-52.

68. Ibid., 55.

69. *Frankfurter Zeitung*, 3 Apr. 1942.

70. Madajczyk, *Polityka III Rzeszy w Okupowanej Polsce* 1:352; Madajczyk, "Generalplan Ost," 399.

71. Madajczyk, *Polityka III Rzeszy w Okupowanej Polsce* 1:353.

72. Polish Research Center, *German Failures in Poland*, 18.

73. Madajczyk, *Polityka III Rzeszy w Okupowanej Polsce* 1:352-53.

74. *Polish News Bulletin*, 27 Mar. 1942, in FO371/31092/52481 C520/520/55, PRO.

75. Office of Strategic Services, Report, 9 Mar. 1944, attached to #62067, in RG226, OSS/NA.

76. Polish Research Center, *German Failures in Poland*, 28.

77. Ibid., 13-15.

78. Ibid., 18.
79. *TWC* 4:864-65.
80. U.S. Counsel, *Nazi Conspiracy and Aggression* 2:641.
81. Madajczyk, "Generalplan Ost," 397, 399.
82. Duraczyński, *Wojna i Okupacja*, 393-96.
83. Hrabar, *Fate of Polish Children*, 51.
84. Gumkowski and Leszczyński, *Poland under Nazi Occupation*, 154.
85. Quoted in ibid.
86. Central Commission, *German Crimes in Poland* 2:81.
87. Ibid., 84.
88. Duraczyński, *Wojna i Okupacja*, 396; Office of Strategic Services, Appendix to Aide Mémoire of 5 Aug. 1943, #41746, RG226, in OSS/NA; Meldunek, Rowecki do Centrali, 12 Mar. 1941, and Depesza, Delegat Rządu i D-ca AK do N. W. i Min. Mikołajczyka, 3 Apr. 1941, in *AKwD* 2:479, 488.
89. Quoted in Gumkowski and Leszczyński, *Poland under Nazi Occupation*, 157.
90. Central Commission, *German Crimes in Poland* 2:70-73.
91. Depesza, Kierownictwo Walki Cywilnej do Mikołajczyka, 23 Dec. 1942, in *AKwD* 2:394.
92. Office of Strategic Services, Appendix to Aide Mémoire of 5 Aug. 1943.
93. U.S. Counsel, *Nazi Conspiracy and Aggression* 4:916; Meldunek Zbiorowy, Rowecki do Centrali, 21 Jan. 1943, in *AKwD* 2:405.
94. Depesza, Klimecki do Roweckiego, 25 Dec. 1942; Depesza od Roweckiego, 31 Dec. 1942; Specjalny Komunikat Radiowy Rządu R. P. do Kraju (n.d.); Instrukcja Rządu R. P. dla Delegata Rządu i Dowódcy, 8 Jan. 1943, in PRM 76/ 1 GSHI. Also see Posiedzenie Rady Ministrów, 7 Jan. 1943, in PRM-K 102/54A-J, and Depesza, Delegat do Mikołajczyka, 13 Jan. 1943, in PRM 105/4, GSHI.
95. Depesza, Rowecki do Centrali, 29 Jan. 1943, in *AKwD*, 2:407; *TWC* 4:871-72.
96. Komisja Historyczna, *PSZ* 3:478; Duraczyński, *Wojna i Okupacja*, 400-403. One underground newspaper declared: "If the bloodthirsty occupant intends to try on us the same experiments as on the Jews, he will first have to withdraw an army from the front. We shall not allow the cowardly Gestapo, the gendarmes or the Lithuanian mercenaries to exterminate us." *Żywią i Bronią*, Feb. 1943.
97. Quoted in *TWC* 4:762-64.
98. Ibid., 767.
99. Ibid., 715-16; U.S. Counsel, *Nazi Conspiracy and Aggression* 1:1031ff.
100. Quoted in *TWC* 4:740.
101. Kamenetsky, *Secret Nazi Plans*, 89.
102. Office of Strategic Services, Report, 31 May 1943, #38399, in RG226, OSS/NA.
103. Korboński, *Fighting Warsaw*, 135.
104. Korboński, *The Polish Underground State*, 1.
105. Davies, *God's Playground*, 2:446.
106. Quoted in *TWC* 5:103.

107. Ibid. 4:995-97; Gumkowski and Leszczyński, *Poland under Nazi Occupation*, 169-70.

108. *TWC* 5:109-110, 113; Gumkowski and Leszczyński, *Poland under Nazi Occupation*, 171.

109. Central Commission, *German Crimes in Poland* 2:84; Hrabar, *Fate of Polish Children*, 52.

110. Gumkowski and Leszczyński, *Poland under Nazi Occupation*, 172.

111. Ibid., 174-76; Hrabar, *Fate of Polish Children*, 135-37.

112. Hrabar, *Fate of Polish Children*, 206.

113. Depesza, Rowecki do Centrali, 12 Mar. 1943, in *AKwD* 2:481.

114. Polish Ministry of Information, *Black Book of Poland*, 267; Office of Strategic Services, "German Occupied Poland," 18 Mar. 1942, in OSS/NA.

115. Polish Ministry of Information, *Black Book of Poland*, 267-69; Office of Strategic Services, "German Occupied Poland," 18 Mar. 1942.

116. *TWC* 5:149; "The Nazi Army on Polish Soil," 213.

117. Polish Ministry of Information, *Black Book of Poland*, 271; Goering's directive is quoted in *TWC* 13:1952.

118. Polish Ministry of Information, *Black Book of Poland*, 272-73.

119. Duraczyński, *Wojna i Okupacja*, 67.

120. Davies, *God's Playground*, 454; Office of Strategic Services, "German Occupied Poland," 18 Mar. 1942.

121. Michel, *Shadow War*, 29-30.

122. Polish Ministry of Information, *Black Book of Poland*, 305.

123. Duraczyński, *Wojna i Okupacja*, 145,; Gross, *Polish Society under German Occupation*, 103-05.

124. Memo, Dormer to Eden, transmitting report by Savery, 6 Oct. 1941, in FO371/26727/5481 C9667/189/55, PRO.

125. Gross, *Polish Society under German Occupation*, 98.

126. Hanson, *Civilian Population and the Warsaw Uprising*, 22-23.

127. Duraczyński, *Wojna i Okupacja*, 69.

128. Hanson, *Civilian Population and the Warsaw Uprising*, 28.

129. Gross, *Polish Society under German Occupation*, 99-100.

130. U.S. Counsel, *Nazi Conspiracy and Aggression* 2:637.

131. Hanson, *Civilian Population and the Warsaw Uprising*, 32.

132. Gross, *Polish Society under German Occupation*, 102-103; Frank's statement can be found in U.S. Counsel, *Nazi Conspiracy and Aggression* 2:637-38. On 14 Dec. 1942, Frank bragged that the General Government had delivered 600,000 tons of grain to the Reich, at a time when there were food shortages throughout the country. See Central Commission, *German Crimes in Poland* 2:36.

133. *Polish White Book*, 2.

134. Korboński, *Fighting Warsaw*, 219-20.

135. Ibid.

136. Madajczyk, *Polityka III Rzeszy w Okupowanej Polsce* 2:84.

137. *Polish News Bulletin*, 7 Mar. 1942, in FO371/31092/52481 C520/520/ 55, PRO.

138. Hanson, *Civilian Population and the Warsaw Uprising*, 30.

139. Gross, *Polish Society under Nazi Occupation*, 97.

140. U.S. Counsel, *Nazi Conspiracy and Aggression* 2:632-33.

141. The Four-Year Plan can be found in Appendix 47, *Polish White Book*, 111ff.

142. For an idea of the difficulties incurred, see extracts of the fifth and eighth meetings of the General Council of the Four Year Plan in *TWC* 13:1952.

143. Meldunek Zbiorowy, Rowecki do Mikołajczyka, 20 Dec. 1942, in *AKwD* 2:382-84; U.S. Counsel, *Nazi Conspiracy and Aggression* 7:816-17.

144. See Dr. Hans Lammers's statement to Himmler on this subject in U.S. Counsel, *Nazi Conspiracy and Aggression* 1:879-80.

145. Madajczyk, *Polityka III Rzeszy w Okupowanej Polsce* 1:251. Dr. A. Gotowicki, a physician in the Polish Army, testified that Polish and Russian prisoners of war were beaten with rubber tubes, steel switches, and sticks at the Krupp works. Two people died daily by the end of 1941; three in four succumbed daily by the end of the following year. U.S. Counsel, *Nazi Conspiracy and Aggression*, 2:800.

146. U.S. Counsel, *Nazi Conspiracy and Aggression* 1:903-904; Staden, *Darkness over the Valley*, 39-40, 85, 98.

147. U.S. Counsel, *Nazi Conspiracy and Aggression* 1:905-06; Polish Ministry of Information, *Black Book of Poland*, 124-25, 427-28; the appeal can be found in Appendix 107 of the *Polish White Book*, 187-89.

148. Wytwycky, *The Other Holocaust*, 77-78.

149. Letter, Dormer to Eden with enclosures, 11 June 1942, in FO371/ 31097/52481 C5951/954/55, PRO; Office of Strategic Services, OB2813 and OB4123 of June 1943 and July 1943 in OSS/NA.

150. Korboński, *Polish Underground State*, 2; Haestrup, *European Resistance Movements*, 78. SS Brigadefuhrer Schöngarth admitted, "No other nation has ever been so oppressed as the Polish nation." Iranek-Osmecki, *He Who Saves One Life*, 179.

151. Madajczyk, *Polityka III Rzeszy w Okupowanej Polsce* 1:242.

152. Bartoszewski, *Warsaw Death Ring*, p. 454.

153. Letter, Savery to Roberts, 10 Apr. 1941, in FO371/26723/52538 C3396/189/55, PRO; Ringelblum, *Notes from the Warsaw Ghetto*, 38-39; Philip Friedman, *Their Brothers' Keepers*, 37; Office of Strategic Services, Report, Oct. 1942, #24128, RG 226, in OSS/NA.

154. U.S. Counsel, *Nazi Conspiracy and Aggression* 2:643.

155. Bartoszewski, *Warsaw Death Ring*, 28.

156. Ibid., 32.

157. U.S. Counsel, *Nazi Conspiracy and Aggression* 2:644.

158. Letter, Savery to Roberts, with enclosure, 22 June 1942, in FO371/ 31097/52481 C6260/954/55, PRO; Protokol, Posiedzenia Rady Narodowej R. P., 7 July 1942, in A. S. 2/32, GSHI; Central Commission, *German Crimes in Poland* 2:51.

159. Madajczyk, *Polityka III Rzeszy w Okupowanej Polsce* 1:177.

160. Meldunek Zbiorowy, Rowecki do N.W. i Mikołajczyka, 20 Dec. 1942, and Meldunek Zbiorowy, Rowecki do Centrali, 21 Jan. 1943, in *AKwD*, 2:382-87, 406.

161. *Gwardia Ludowa*, Feb. 1943.

162. Gumkowski and Leszczyński, *Poland under German Occupation*, 123-30.

163. Central Commission, *German Crimes in Poland* 1:178.

164. Zaremba, *Wojna i Konspiracja*, 132.

165. Karski, *Story of a Secret State*, 255.

166. Sprawozdanie Celta, 1944: Pierwsze Impresje-Roznice w Stosunku do r.1942, in Kol. 25/9, GSHI.

167. Madajczyk, *Hitlerowski Terror na Wsi Polskiej*, 9-10.

168. Madajczyk, *Polityka III Rzeszy w Okupowanej Polsce* 2:273; Central Commission, *German Crimes in Poland*, 1:21.

169. Wroński and Zwolakowa, *Polacy i Żydzi*, 66.

170. Gilbert, *Auschwitz and the Allies*, 16.

171. Protokol Posiedzenia Rady Narodowej R.P., 7 July 1942, in A.5.2/32, GSHI.

172. Domagala, *Ci, Którzy Przeszli Przez Dachau*, 21; Central Commission, *German Crimes in Poland*, 2:133.

173. Wroński and Zwolakowa, *Polacy i Żydzi*, 66.

174. Nurowski, *War Losses in Poland*, 44ff. Predictably, there is no agreement concerning the exact number of Polish Christians and Polish Jews who perished at the hands of the Nazis. Most informed estimates place the loss of Polish Christians at 2.8 to 3.1 million and Polish Jews at 2.9 to 3.2 million.

CHAPTER TWO

1. Duraczyński, *Wojna i Okupacja*, 109-10; Pobóg-Malinowski, *Najnowsza Historia Polityczna Polski* 3:72ff. Wieniawa-Długoszowski migrated to the United States where he was close to the Sikorski opposition there. When Sikorski later visited the United States, he tried to placate Długoszowski by offering him a Polish diplomatic post in the Caribbean. Mitkiewicz, *Z Gen. Sikorskim na Obczyźnie*, 132; Office of Strategic Services, Foreign Nationalities Branch, Report, 2 Apr. 1942, #16305, in RG 226, OSS/NA. Józef Piłsudski became head of state and commander-in-chief of the Polish Army in 1918. Regarded by many as the father of Polish independence after World War I, he played a critical role in defeating the Soviets at Warsaw in 1920 and in expanding Poland's eastern frontiers. After a brief retirement in the early 1920s, Piłsudski launched a *coup d' état* in 1926 and remained Poland's strong man until his death in 1935. His supporters, known as the *Sanacja* (Cleansing), continued in power until the outbreak of World War II.

2. Duraczyński, *Wojna i Okupacja*, 110-11.

3. Terry, *Poland's Place in Europe*, 175.

4. Dwa Lata Okupacji Niemieckiej w Polsce [1941], in PRM 45C/23, GSHI; Raczyński, *In Allied London*, 40. Even a severe critic of Sikorski saw that his appointment as commander-in-chief of the Polish army in France might overcome some of the bitterness the Poles felt toward the *Sanacja*. See Jędrzejewicz, *Diplomat in Paris*, 357-58.

5. Sprawozdanie z Kraju, 3 Mar. 1940, in PRM 24, and Dwa Lata Okupacji Niemieckiej w Polsce [1941], in GSHI.

6. Memo, Thwaites to Scott, 7 June 1944, in FO371/39447 C7931/119/55, PRO.

7. Terry, *Poland's Place in Europe*, 176-77.

8. Mitkiewicz, *Z Gen. Sikorskim na Obczyźnie*, 45, 70-77, 94-95, 97-99.

9. Minute by Roberts, 30 July 1940, in FO371/24474 C7639/252/55, PRO; Raczyński, *In Allied London*, 56; see Sikorski Diary, GSHI, which is replete with evidence concerning poor relations between the two men.

10. Raczyński, *In Allied London*, 60. Although Raczyński referred only to the matter of foreign policy, Sikorski was equally sensitive that he and his trusted men be in control of the situation in underground Poland. As a result of the crisis over the treaty with Russia, Sikorski wanted all messages from the Ministry of Foreign Affairs and from Sosnkowski to Poland to be cleared first by him. Notatka, Sikorski do Ministerstwa Spraw Zagraniczynych, 31 July 1941, and Notatka, Sikorski do Sosnkowskiego, 26 July 1941, in Kol. 1/24 (Sikorski Diary), GSHI.

11. See the list of advisers in Terry, *Poland's Place in Europe*, 196, n.115. As Terry says, Retinger was the most controversial of Sikorski's trusted confidants. She denies that he was a British agent, but W. W. Kulski, a respected Polish diplomat, recently stated that Retinger worked for British intelligence. See Kulski's review of Kacewicz, *Great Britain, the Soviet Union and the Polish Government-in-Exile*.

12. Mitkiewicz, *Z Gen. Sikorskim na Obczyźnie*, 103; minute by Roberts, 4 July 1940, and minute by Kennard, 6 July 1940, in FO371/24474 C7639/252/55, PRO. The conflict between the military and the interior branch of the government was not unique to the Poles; the Belgians, for instance, had similar problems. Foot, *Resistance*, 8.

13. Pobóg-Malinowski, *Najnowsza-Historia Polityczna Polski*, 97; Raczyński, *In Allied London*, 161; letter, Kennard to Halifax, 9 Jan. 1940; letter, Kennard to Strang, 26 Jan. 1940; letter, Kennard to Halifax, 11 Mar. 1940; letter, Kennard to Strang, 20 Mar. 1944; minute by Roberts, 20 July 1940, in FO371/24474, PRO.

14. Raczyński, *In Allied London*, 52-54; Mitkiewicz, *Z Gen. Sikorskim na Obczyźnie*, 79-80, 89; Komisja Historyczna, *PSZ* 3:223-25.

15. Sikorski Statement in Instrukcja Nr. 6, Sosnkowski do Roweckiego, 3 Nov. 1940, *AKwD* 1:315.

16. Minute by Strang, 20 July 1940, in FO371/24474 C7639/252/55, PRO.

17. Terry, *Poland's Place in Europe*, 177-78.

18. Sir Lewis Namier's comments regarding Sikorski were an accurate re-

flection of the attitude in Poland. See minute by Roberts, 19 July 1940, in FO371/24474 C7639/252/55, PRO. As for the responsibility of the National Council, see *Polish News Bulletin, Supplement*, no. 120, in FO371/31092/52481 C520/520/55, PRO.

19. Minute of conversation by Savery, 18 Aug. 1941, in FO371/26768 C9398/4598/55, PRO.

20. For the repudiation of Komarnicki and Seyda, see letter, Savery to Roberts, 26 Jan. 1942, in FO371/31094/52481 C1089/807/55, PRO. National Democrats who agreed to serve in the National Council were also repudiated. See letter, Dormer to Eden, 26 Feb. 1942, in FO371/31084/52481 C2149/807/55, PRO.

21. Agudah Israel, one of the largest prewar political parties of Polish Jews, was not represented. See letter, Savery to Roberts, 13 Apr. 1942, in FO317/31094/52481 C3937/807/55, PRO. For a cogent summary of the major political parties, see Polish Ministry of Information, *Polish Fortnightly Review*, 1 Dec. 1943.

22. Mitkiewicz, *Z Gen. Sikorskim na Obczyźnie*, 65, 74-75.

23. Lukas, *Strange Allies*, 7-9.

24. Ibid., 10; Mitkiewicz, *Z Gen. Sikorskim na Obczyźnie*, 167-78; Terry, on the other hand, suggests, "Thus in July 1941, it seems quite clear that he [Sikorski] exaggerated the level of Allied pressure on him in order to extract approval from a wavering Council of Ministers for what he believed to be the best Polish-Soviet agreement attainable." See Terry, *Poland's Place in Europe*, 197.

25. Lukas, *Strange Allies*, 9. Although Sikorski may have believed at this time that the Poles would have to compromise with the Soviets on their eastern frontier, he could not vent these views in public without risking his position. This is underscored by the fact that about one-third of the Polish army and one-half of the air force in England came from eastern Poland. Foreign Minister Eden had met with an emissary from Poland, who suggested that if Sikorski had ceded territory to the Soviets—in effect, agreed to something less than the Riga Line— he might have had to face the establishment of an alternative government in Poland. See memo, Sumner to Warner, 17 July 1941, in FO371/26756/52588 C8172/3226/55, PRO, and memo, Eden to War Cabinet, 17 Feb. 1943, in FO371/34550 C1943/34/G, PRO.

26. Raczyński, *In Allied London*, 95.

27. Depesza, Delegat Rządu do Centrali, 18 Aug. 1941; Depesza, Sikorski do Delegata Rządu, 25 Aug. 1941, in *AKwD* 2:42-43, 47.

28. Depesza, Sikorski do Andersa, 1 Sept. 1941, in *AKwD* 2:53-54; Dwa Lata Okupacji Niemieckiej w Polsce [1941]; Sprawozdanie Emisariusza L. o Sytuacji Politycznej Który Przebywal w Kraju od 1 do listopada, 1941 in PRM 46A.20, GSHI; Zaremba, *Wojna i Konspiracja*, 178-84.

29. List, Sosnkowski do Sikorskiego, 25 July 1941; List, Sikorski do Sosnkowskiego, 25 July 1941; List, Sosnkowski do Sikorskiego, 28 July 1941; Depesza, Rowecki do Sikorskiego, 15 Sept. 1941; Depesza, Sikorski do Roweckiego, 10 Oct. 1941; Meldunek, Rowecki do Sikorskiego, 26 Nov. 1941; Depesza, Sikorski do Roweckiego, 10 Feb. 1942, in *AKwD* 2:24-25, 70-71, 126, 161, 198.

30. Mitkiewicz, *Z Gen. Sikorskim na Obczyźnie*, 177-79.

31. Relacja Gen. Tokarzewskiego o Tworzeniu Armii Podziemnej; Janina Karas o Pierwszych Dniach Armii Podziemnej; Statut Służby Zwycięstwu Polski, in *AKwD* 1:1-4, 31ff; Korboński, *Polish Underground State*, 16-19. Tokarzewski's organization attempted to kill Hitler when he visited Warsaw on 5 Oct. 1939. The SZP placed explosives at the crossing of two main arteries, but they could not be detonated because the Germans cleared the streets of people before Hitler's arrival.

32. Duraczyński, *Wojna i Okupacja*, 163; Korboński, *Polish Underground State*, 21.

33. Report on the Situation in Poland, 9 Aug. 1940, in FO371/24474 C10589/252/55, PRO; Rudnicki, *Last of the War Horses*, 91-95. Because Bór-Komorowski had established close ties with the National Democrats in the Cracow area, some critics have suggested that he was anti-Semitic. There is no evidence to prove the allegation. See Chapter 3, note 61 below.

34. Decyzje Sikorskiego Dotyczące Kierownictwa Politycznego i Wojskowego Dla Kraju, 13 Nov. 1939; Instrukcja, Sosnkowski do Roweckiego, 4 Dec. 1939; Rozkaz Organizacyjny, 29 June 1940; Depesza, Sosnkowski do Roweckiego, 30 June 1940, in *AKwD* 1:4-5, 10-21, 261-63; Korboński, *Polish Underground State*, 22.

35. Mitkiewicz, *Z Gen. Sikorskim na Obczyźnie*, 104, 171, 176, 178.

36. Sprawozdanie Tymczasowego Delegata Kaczmarka, 15 Jan. 1941; in *AKwD* 1:409-11; List, Ratajski do Mikołajczyka, 3 Sept. 1942, in PRM 76/2 27, GSHI.

37. Zaremba, *Wojna i Konspiracja*, 189.

38. List, Sosnkowski do Roweckiego, 16 Feb. 1940; List, Sikorski do Sosnkowskiego, 4 Nov. 1940; List, Kot do Prezesa Rady Ministrów i Naczelnego Wodza, 26 Nov. 1940; Odpowiedź na Zarzuty min. Kota, 22 Apr. 1941, in *AKwD* 1:131, 324-25, 374-80, 391-95. One casualty in this matter was the removal of Major Tadeusz Kruk-Strzelecki from the Political Coordinating Committee.

39. Bór-Komorowski, *Secret Army*, 65.

40. Meldunek, Rowecki do Sosnkowskiego, 30 Nov. 1940, in *AKwD* 1:358ff.

41. Mitkiewicz, *Z Gen. Sikorskim na Obczyźnie*, 181-82; Garliński, *Polska w Drugiej Wojnie Światowej*, 172-73. Śmigły-Rydz was buried under the pseudonym Adam Zawisza.

42. Karski, *Story of a Secret State*, 232.

43. Duraczyński, *Wojna i Okupacja*, 227-29. Even the Germans had a grudging admiration for Dobrzański. See Rudnicki, *Last of the War Horses*, 103. Also see Rowecki's comments concerning the activities of Major Jan Mazurkiewicz, who headed an organization ostensibly subordinated to the ZWZ; yet his organization still conducted operations at variance with the guidelines of the ZWZ. Meldunek, Rowecki do Sosnkowskiego, 21 Nov. 1940, in *AKwD* 1:352.

44. Rozkaz Gen. Sikorskiego, 15 Aug. 1942, in *AKwD* 2:295-96.

45. Duraczyński, *Wojna i Okupacja*, 152-60; Komisja Historyczna, *PSZ* 3:162, 165.

46. Meldunek Organizacyjny, 1 Oct. 1941; Depesza, Smolenski do Roweckiego, 20 Oct. 1941, in *AKwD* 2:106, 129; Meldunek Specjalny, 2 June 1943, in ibid. 3:27-28.

47. Duraczyński, *Wojna i Okupacja*, 210-13; Depesza, Rowecki do Centrali, 17 Mar. 1943, in *AKwD* 2:482; Meldunek Organizacyjny, 1 Mar. 1944, in ibid. 3:334-45.

48. Duraczyński, *Wojna i Okupacja*, 364-65; Bór, *Secret Army*, 86; Meldunek Organizacyjny, 1 Mar. 1944, in *AKwD* 3:35. Krakowski is in error when he claims that 70,000 members of the NSZ joined the AK. NOW, not the NSZ, added its soldiers to the AK. The NSZ only came into existence *after* NOW merged with the AK. There was not only an organizational but also a political difference between the two groups, which recent critics of the policies of the AK toward the Jews ignore. See Krakowski, *War of the Doomed*, 7.

49. Sprawozdanie Celta, 1944, in Kol. 25/9, GSHI.

50. Depesza, Bór do Centrali, 21 June 1944 in *AKwD* 3:490; Korboński, *Polish Underground State*, 105-06.

51. Bór, *Secret Army*, 170; Korboński, *Polish Underground State*, 106.

52. Meldunek Specjalny, 22 May 1944, in *AKwD* 3:452.

53. Komisja Historyczna, *PSZ* 3:158-61, 236.

54. Karski, *Story of a Secret State*, 266.

55. Korboński, *Fighting Warsaw*, 172.

56. Leaders of the BCh and the KB, for example, held major positions in the High Command of the AK. Interview with Stefan Korboński, 7 June 1982. Sosnkowski had suggested that leaders of groups subordinated to the ZWZ should become officers in the High Command of the ZWZ. See Instrukcja, Sosnkowski do Roweckiego, 16 Jan. 1940, in *AKwD* 1:74-75.

57. Sprawozdanie Emisariusza Antoniego, Załącznik 23, Apr. 1941, in PRM 46A/15, GSHI.

58. Ibid., Załącznik 22; Korboński, *Polish Underground State*, 27-28.

59. Korboński, *Polish Underground State*, 32-33.

60. Hanson, *Civilian Population and the Warsaw Uprising*, 56ff.

61. Korboński, *Polish Underground State*, 101-103.

62. Sprawozdanie Celta, in Kol. 25/9; List, Jezierski do Sikorskiego 8 Sept. 1942, in PRM 76/2, 29; Dwa Lata Okupacji Niemieckiej w Polsce [1941], in PRM 45C/23, GSHI.

63. Sprawozdanie Emisariusza Antoniego, Załącznik 22, 4/41, in PRM 46A/15, GSHI; Meldunek, Rowecki do Sosnkowskiego, 21 Nov. 1940; Meldunek, Rowecki do Sosnkowskiego, 30 Nov. 1940; Depesza, Tymczasowy Delegat Rządu do Sikorskiego, 7 Sept. 1940, in *AKwD* 1:293-94, 350, 358ff.; Duraczyński, *Wojna i Okupacja*, 196-97.

64. Meldunek, Rowecki do Sikorskiego, 15 Dec. 1941, *AKwD* 2:164-69. See messages from Rowecki in the same source, for example, on pp. 254, 308.

65. Posiedzenie Rady Ministrów, 11 Feb. 1943, in PRM-K 102/55a, GSHI; Depesza, Sikorski do Delegata Rządu, 4 Feb. 1943, in *AKwD*, 2:411.

66. Mitkiewicz, *Z Gen. Sikorskim na Obczyźnie*, 177-79.

67. Sprawozdanie Celta, 1944, in Kol. 25/9, GSHI.
68. Ibid.; Zaremba, *Wojna i Konspiracja*, 166ff.
69. Sprawozdanie Celta, 1944, in Kol. 25/9, GSHI.
70. "WRN i Barykada Wolności," signed H.M., in PRM 76/1/19, GSHI; Meldunek, Rowecki do Centrali, 25 Aug. 1941, in *AKwD* 2:47-50.
71. For example, see Delegat Rządu do Mikołajczyka, 18 Mar. 1943, in *AKwD* 2:483-84, and Deklaracja Porozumienia Politycznego Czterech Stronnictw Reprezentacji Politycznej, 15 Aug. 1943, in ibid., 3:55ff.
72. Sprawozdanie Emisariusza Antoniego, Załącznik 22, 4/41, in PRM 46A/15; List, Wolski do Tygrysa, 3 July 1941, in PRM 46A/13; Raport (unsigned), 1 July 1941, in PRM 46A/12, GSHI.
73. Oświadczenie Stronnictwa Ludowego i Polskiej Partii Socjalistycznej w Związku z Nominacja Cyryla Ratajskiego Na Stanowisko Delegata Rządu, 14 Jan. 1941, in *AKwD* 1:404-05; Korboński, *Fighting Warsaw*, 52-55.
74. Garliński, *Polska w Drugiej Wojnie Światowej*, 174, 263. For Rowecki's criticisms of Ratajski and the latter's description of the cool state of their relations, see Depesza, Delegat Rządu do Sikorskiego, 25 Oct. 1941, and Meldunek, Rowecki do Sikorskiego, 2 Oct. 1942, in *AKwD* 2:130, 158.
75. Depesza, Rowecki do Ministerstwa Obrony Narodowej, 23 Dec. 1942; Depesza, Minister Obrony Narodowej do Roweckiego, 4 Jan. 1943, in PRM 106/12, GSHI.
76. Gross, *Polish Society under German Occupation*, 291.

CHAPTER THREE

1. Quoted in Ainsztein, *Jewish Resistance*, 402.
2. Haestrup, *European Resistance Movements*, 23.
3. Komisja Historyczna, *PSZ* 3:119. This included 10,756 officers, 7,506 cadet officers, and 87,886 noncommissioned officers.
4. Letter, Perkins to Alan with enclosures, 4 May 1944, in FO371/39425 C5397/61/55, PRO. This is an instructive report based on British interrogations of General Stanisław Tatar [pseud. Tabor], an emissary who had recently arrived in England from Poland.
5. Meldunek Organizacyjny, Rowecki do Centrali, 16 May 1942, in *AKwD* 2:237-38.
6. Komisja Historyczna, *PSZ* 3:458-64, 482-99. Also see the summary on p. 437. Rowecki directed that the letters "W.P." be inscribed when an act of diversion had been completed. The letters stood for "Fighting Poland" and were written in the style of an anchor.
7. Ibid., 436.
8. Interview with Korboński, 7 June 1982.
9. Instrukcja, Sosnkowski do Roweckiego, 4 Dec. 1939; Instrukcja, Sosnkowski do Roweckiego, 16 Jan. 1940; List, Sosnkowski do Roweckiego, 16 Feb. 1940, in *AKwD* 1:18, 75, 76, 131.

10. Instrukcja dla Łozinskiego, 11 Mar. 1940; Meldunek, Rowecki do Sosnkowskiego, 19 Mar. 1940, in ibid., 161, 178-83.

11. Komisja Historyczna, *PSZ* 3:441.

12. Office of Strategic Services, "Underground and Guerilla Warfare in Poland," in OSS/NA; Nowak, *Courier from Warsaw*, 82; Bór-Komorowski, *Secret Army*, 40. Many Jewish historians criticize the ZWZ/AK for not trying to prevent trains carrying Jews from reaching the death camps. As these figures indicate, the AK was strong enough only to delay, not stop, the transports. Massive diversionary attacks by the Polish underground on the rail transports would have squandered the strength of the ZWZ/AK without helping the Jews to any substantial degree. If anything, many Jews would have been killed in such attacks. These historians fail to realize that the primary purpose of the ZWZ/AK was to remain strong enough to deal effectively with the Germans in a general uprising to take place only when German strength in Poland was at the point of collapse. The only way to have interrupted the human traffic to Auschwitz and other camps was for the United States and Britain to have undertaken an enormous bombardment of the rail lines. The Allies thought the task too great even for them. Sir A. Sinclair told Eden on 15 July 1944, "I am advised that [interrupting the railways] is out of our power. It is only by an enormous concentration of bomber forces that we have been able to interrupt communications in Normandy; the distance of Silesia [Auschwitz] from our bases entirely rules out doing anything of the kind." Letter, Sinclair to Eden, 15 July 1944, in FO371/42809, PRO.

13. Meldunek, Rowecki do Centrali, 13 Aug. 1941, in *AKwD* 2:36; Karski, *Story of a Secret State*, 258. Also see CAB 122/923, PRO.

14. Depesza, Sikorski do Roweckiego, 24 Aug. 1941, in Kol. I/25 (Sikorski Diary), in GSHI.

15. Meldunek, Rowecki do Centrali, 15 Sept. 1942, in *AKwD* 2:342-45; Komisja Historyczna, *PSZ* 3:482-99. In the spring of 1942, Sikorski urged Rowecki to increase the scale of sabotage-diversionary activity *east* of the Polish frontier. See Depesza, Sikorski do Roweckiego, 27 Apr. 1942, in *AKwD* 2:221-22. Sikorski's strategy was rooted in the idea that by cooperating militarily with the Soviets against the Germans, Poland might be able to win its political objectives ("Atut współdziałania z wojskami sowieckimi potrafimy wygrać politycznie.") Depesza, Sikorski do Roweckiego, 4 Feb. 1943, in PRM 106/2, in GSHI. Also see Lukas, *Strange Allies*, 18.

16. Specjalny Meldunek Dywersyjny, Rowecki do Centrali, 20 Oct. 1942; letter, Selborne do Sikorskiego, 10 Nov. 1942, *AKwD* 2:350-53; Bartoszewski, *Warsaw Death Ring*, 139-40.

17. Komisja Historyczna, *PSZ* 3:467-68.

18. Korboński, *Fighting Warsaw*, 214, 216-17; Office of Strategic Services, "Examples of Resistance to the Germans in Poland," #28575, in RG 226, OSS/NA.

19. Message, FO to Washington, 1 July 1944, in FO371/39425 C5385/61/55, PRO; *Polish News Bulletin*, 7 Mar. 1942, in FO371/31092/52481, PRO.

20. Duraczyński, *Wojna i Okupacja*, 247; Korboński, *Fighting Warsaw*, 219.

21. Depesza, Rowecki do Sikorskiego, 25 Sept. 1941; Meldunek Zbiorowy, Rowecki do Centrali, 15 Nov. 1941, in *AKwD* 2:89-90, 133.

22. Haestrup, *European Resistance Movements*, 423; Komisja Historyczna, *PSZ* 3:468.

23. This summary is based upon the tabulation that appears in Komisja Historyczna, PSZ 3:482, and Zestawienia: Wyników Akcji Dywersyjno-Sabotażowych w Polsce, 1941-do Czerwca 1944, in 3.9.2.1.1.2., PUST.

24. Bór, *Secret Army*, 153.

25. Instrukcja, Sosnkowski do Roweckiego, 16 Jan. 1940, in *AKwD* 1:74-75; Bór, *Secret Army*, 49.

26. Depesza, Rowecki do Komendantów Obszarów, in *AKwD* 1:297ff; Meldunek Operacyjny (#54), Rowecki do Centrali, 5 Feb. 1941, in PUST. An appendix to this report can be found in *AKwD* 1:437-42.

27. Depesza, Sikorski do Roweckiego, 3 Mar. 1942; Instrukcja, Sikorski do Roweckiego, 8 Mar. 1942; Depesza, Sikorski do Roweckiego, 28 Nov. 1942, in *AKwD* 2:200-201, 202-07, 369-71.

28. Letter, Alan Brooke to Sikorski, 14 May 1942; Depesza, Sikorski do Roweckiego, 8 Mar. 1942, in *AKwD* 2:230-31, 202-07.

29. Raport Operacyjny (#154), Rowecki do Sikorskiego, 8 Sept. 1942; Depesza, Rowecki do Sikorskiego, 12 Jan. 1943, in *AKwD* 2:401-03.

30. Depesza, Rowecki do Sikorskiego, 12 Jan. 1943; Depesza, Rowecki do N.W., 26 Feb. 1943, in ibid., 403, 422-23.

31. Mitkiewicz, *Z Gen. Sikorskim Na Obczyźnie*, 328-29; Depesza, Sikorski do Roweckiego, 25 Mar. 1943, in *AKwD* 2:485-86. On 6 Feb. 1943, Sikorski told Rowecki that Poland during the war and in the future could not conduct a conflict "on two fronts," and that it was imperative to have an understanding with the Soviet Union. Depesza, Sikorski do Roweckiego, 6 Feb. 1943, in ibid., 412-14.

32. Memo, Nickerson to Wedemeyer, with enclosure, 17 Dec. 1942; letter, Sikorski to Marshall, with enclosure, 9 Dec. 1942 in RG 165, WDGS/NA.

33. Report by the Combined Intelligence Committee, 30 July 1943, in ibid.; Mitkiewicz, *Z Gen. Sikorskim Na Obczyźnie*, 353. The combined chiefs of staff did not formally reject the Polish plan for large-scale aid to the Poles until Sept. 1943, several months after Sikorski's death. Sikorski seems to have been hopeful that the western Allies might eventually endorse a southern strategy, enabling them to help the Poles in an uprising against the Germans and anticipate the Soviets in eastern Europe. Shortly before the premier's death, Mitkiewicz informed him of his own pessimistic views concerning Anglo-American help to the Poles.

34. Letter, Mitkiewicz to Combined Chiefs of Staff, 14 Oct. 1943, in RG 165, WDGS/NA; letter, Redman to Mitkiewicz, 20 Jan. 1944, in *AKwD* 3:256-57. The Poles originally placed conditions on the use of the Polish Parachute

Brigade's participation in the invasion of France because they hoped to dispatch it to Poland at the time of the uprising there; but General B. L. Montgomery refused to accept any such conditions. This forced the Poles, who obviously did not want to jeopardize their military and political standing with the Allies, to relinquish the brigade to the British, expressing the hope that the British chiefs of staff "will do all [in] their power to facilitate, at the right moment, the employment of the Brigade in support of the rising in Poland—particularly in securing of air transport for this purpose." See letter, Sosnkowski to Grasett, 1 May 1944; letter, Grasett to Sosnkowski, 21 May 1944; letter, Sosnkowski to Grasett, 6 June 1944, in *AkwD* 3:423-24, 449-50, 470-71.

35. See Lukas, *Strange Allies*, chapters 2 and 3.

36. Ibid.,37-38; Nowak, *Courier from Warsaw*, 131. According to one scholar, the Polish Communists openly admitted the murder of the Polish officers and men and justified it on the grounds that they were "Polish reactionaries." When the Soviets denied they had anything to do with the crime, the Polish Communists reversed themselves and accepted the Soviet explanation. Dziewanowski, *Communist Party of Poland*, 168.

37. Depesza, Rowecki do Sikorskiego, 19 June 1943; Depesza, Rowecki do Centrali, 29 Apr. 1943, in *AKwD* 3:28-32, 1.

38. Depesza, Sikorski do Roweckiego, 1 June 1943, in ibid., 24-25; Mitkiewicz, *Z Gen. Sikorskim Na Obczyźnie*, 359-60.

39. See Chapter 2 above.

40. See Chapter 1 above.

41. Komisja Historyczna, *PSZ* 3:518-20, 521-23.

42. Ibid.,524; Krakowski, *War of the Doomed*, 7.

43. Office of Strategic Services, "Underground and Guerilla Warfare in Poland"; Polpress, 11 July 1944, in FO371/39409 C10931/8/55, PRO; Depesza, Rowecki do N.W., 11 Mar. 1943, in *AKwD* 2:475ff; List, Kopański do Pana Prezydenta, 26 Nov. 1943, in A. 48.4/a III, GSHI.

44. Meldunek Specjalny, Rowecki do Centrali, 1 Apr. 1942; Meldunek Organizacyjny, Rowecki do Centrali, 16 May 1942; Depesza, Rowecki do Sikorskiego, 21 July 1942; Meldunek, Rowecki do Centrali, 1 Sept. 1942, in *AKwD* 2:209, 248, 288-89, 308.

45. Office of Strategic Services, "Underground and Guerilla Warfare in Poland." For Communist murders and betrayal of the AK to the Gestapo, see such representative messages as Depesza, Bór do Centrali, 30 Jan. 1944, and Meldunek Organizacyjny, Bór do N.W., 1 Mar. 1944, in *AKwD* 3:261-64, 326-27.

46. Depesza, Rowecki do N.W., 11 Mar. 1943, in *AKwD* 2:475-78; Meldunek Organizacyjny, 31 Aug. 1943, in ibid., 3:93-94; Korboński, *Polish Underground State*, 111; Leslie, *History of Poland since 1863*, 239-40.

47. Depesza, Bór do N. W., 30 Dec. 1943; Depesza, Bór do N.W., 31 Dec. 1943, in *AkwD*, 3:223, 225-26.

48. Meldunek Organizacyjny, Bór do N.W., 1 Mar. 1944, in *AKwD* 3:313; Korboński, *Polish Underground State*, 115.

49. Depesza, Bór do Centrali, 13 Apr. 1944; Depesza, Bór do Sosnkowskiego, 22 May 1944; Depesza, Bór do Centrali, 28 June 1944, in *AKwD*, 3:400-401, 453-54, 460, 494.

50. Office of Strategic Services, "Underground and Guerilla Warfare in Poland."

51. Depesza, Rowecki do Centrali, 6 Oct. 1941, in *AKwD*, 2:55; Ainsztein, *Jewish Resistance in Nazi-Occupied Europe*, 572.

52. Weydenthal, *Communists of Poland*, 26-27; Dawidowicz, *War against the Jews*, 263.

53. Ainsztein, *Jewish Resistance in Nazi-Occupied Europe*, 572; Duraczyński, *Wojna i Okupacja*, 368-69, 376; Krakowski, *War of the Doomed*, 150.

54. Duraczyński, *Wojna i Okupacja*, 376; Krakowski, *War of the Doomed*, 6; Weydenthal, *Communists of Poland*, 39.

55. Weydenthal, *Communists of Poland*, 43.

56. Lukas, *Strange Allies*, 60.

57. Iranek-Osmecki, *He Who Saves One Life*, 109-10; Krakowski, *War of the Doomed*, 154. Ainsztein, a tendentious critic of the Poles, says: "Only two cases are known of Jews being present in any numbers in partisan formations of the Home Army: about 200 Jews fought in the ranks of the 27th Volyn Division and several dozen in the 2nd Infantry Division in the Kielce Region." Ainsztein, *Jewish Resistance in Nazi-Occupied Europe*, 457.

58. See Chapter 2; Sprawozdanie Celta, 1944, in Kol. 25/9, GSHI.

59. Letter, Henryk Woliński to author, July 1984; Michael Borwicz, "Factors Influencing Relations between the General Polish Underground and the Jewish Underground," 360.

60. Letter, Woliński to author, July 1984.

61. Ibid.; interview with Korboński, 7 June 1982; letter, Raczyński to author, 21 June 1984; letter, Barbarska to author, 8 June 1984, containing replies from Ms. Lidia Ciołkosz to questions concerning General Rowecki and General Bór. Ms. Ciołkosz, who is Jewish, is the widow of the Polish Socialist leader, Adam Ciołkosz. She knew both generals, especially General Bór, and categorically denies that either man was anti-Semitic. In 1959, General Bór sued the *Manchester Guardian* for an article that alleged the High Command of the Home Army and he were anti-Semitic. General Bór won his case. See Iranek-Osmecki, *He Who Saves One Life*, 292-93. Some writers have implied rather than been explicit about Rowecki's alleged anti-Semitism. In the case of Bór, they have been most explicit. Ber Mark says that Bór was identified with the "reactionary anti-Semitic camp." See Mark, *Uprising in the Warsaw Ghetto*, 164. Ainsztein writes of "Bór-Komorowski, whose connections with the antisemitic National Party and sympathies for the National Armed Forces were well known." See Ainsztein, *Jewish Resistance in Nazi-Occupied Europe*, 672.

62. Ainsztein, *Jewish Resistance in Nazi-Occupied Europe*, 410ff., 428, 435; Elkins, *Forged in Fury* 182.

63. Krakowski, *War of the Doomed*, 3.

64. Ibid., 135.

65. Iranek-Osmecki, *He Who Saves One Life*, 262; interview with Korboń-ski, 7 June 1982.

66. Borwicz, "Factors Influencing the Relations," 360-61.

67. Interview with Karol and Rachel Cymber, 8 July 1982; interview with Korboński, 7 June 1982; interview with Pelagia Łukaszewska, 10 July 1983. Even Rashke, who is critical of Polish wartime attitudes toward the Jews, admits:"When the Jews report killings by Polish partisans, therefore, it is frequently difficult to determine whether the assassins were members of the Home Army (AK) or of the independent NSZ." See Rashke, *Escape from Sobibor*, 388. To be sure, distinctions between the NSZ and the AK are lost on writers like Ainsztein, who lumps the AK and NSZ together in such statements as: "The widespread antisemitism and general hostility of both the NSZ and the London-controlled underground." This failure to discriminate results in such factual errors as the claim that "The National Armed Forces [NSZ] separated from the Home Army [AK] only at the beginning of 1943." See Ainsztein, *Jewish Resistance in Nazi-Occupied Europe*, 419, 426.

68. Krakowski, *War of the Doomed*, 91; Bór, *Secret Army*, 170.

69. Ainsztein, *Jewish Resistance in Nazi-Occupied Europe*, 420; interview with Korboński, 7 June 1982.

70. Ainsztein, *Jewish Resistance in Nazi-Occupied Europe*, 305.

71. There is a great deal of ambiguity among Jewish writers on the question of Jewish affiliation or cooperation with the Communists as a major factor in Polish hostility toward the Jews. Anti-Semitic motivations of the Poles are stressed without referring to or emphasizing Jewish connections with the Communists. Krakowski's *War of the Doomed*, one of the most recent Jewish studies on the Jewish experience during the war, reflects this ambiguity. See Chapter 5 below.

72. Sprawozdanie Celta, 1944, in Kol. 25/9, GSHI.

73. Komisja Historyczna, *PSZ* 3:528-29; Depesza, Bór do Centrali, 23 Mar. 1944, and Meldunek Sytuacyjny, Dca AK do Centrali, 18 May 1944, in *AKwD* 3:346-47.

74. Bór, *Secret Army*, 172.

75. Duraczyński, *Wojna i Okupacja*, 78; Iranek-Osmecki, *He Who Saves One Life*, 259-61. AK reports indicated that 231 bandits were eliminated in 1943 and that 695 were liquidated in the period January-June, 1944. The AK executed AK soldiers who were found guilty of plunder and robbery. See Komisja Historyczna, *PSZ* 3:474.

76. Meldunek Organizacyjny, Bór do N.W., 31 Aug. 1943, and Depesza, Bór do N.W., 18 Dec. 1943, in *AKwD* 3:92, 215; Komisja Historyczna, *PSZ* 3:531-32; Leslie, *History of Poland since 1863*, 250; Jurewicz, *Zbrodnia Czy Początek Wojny Domowej*, 51-54, 62, 68-69. References are made to Bór's order no. 116 of 15 Sept. 1943. The order was anticipated in Bór's report in Aug. 1943, cited above. Krakowski in one of his articles makes the claim that Bór's order was primarily intended to eliminate Jews, thus suggesting the general was an anti-

Semite. See also note 61, above. In his book, the same author erroneously suggests that Bór's order placed armed Jewish units on the same level as gangs of robbers who, he admits, were composed of Jews and were large in number. Krakowski makes the strange observation that the Polish underground, which did not control the situation in eastern Poland, "could have easily solved the problem of feeding ten or twenty thousand Jews who were left in the forests." See Krakowski, "Slaughter of Polish Jewry," 19; Krakowski, *War of the Doomed*, 15-16. The same lack of appreciation for the anarchy in eastern Poland where Jewish fugitives fled is apparent in the editorial commentary made in Ringelblum, *Polish-Jewish Relations*, 132. Interestingly enough, one of the editors of this work is Shmuel Krakowski. In this book, on pp. 219-20, the editors give the following inaccurate and tendentious description of Bór's order: "On 15 September 1943, General Bór-Komorowski, Commander-In-Chief of the Home Army, issued Order no. 116 to the units under his command directing them to take active measures against the Jews in the forests." And they add, "in fact the Order in question was a weapon aimed at the Jews in the first place."

77. Instrukcja, Sosnkowski do Roweckiego, 16 Jan. 1940, and Depesza, Sosnkowski do Roweckiego, 11 Oct. 1940, in *AKwD* 1:75, 294-95; Depesza, Sikorski do Roweckiego, 5 Aug. 1942, in ibid., 2:293-95.

78. Duraczyński, *Wojna i Okupacja*, 420; Bór, *Secret Army*, 151.

79. Quoted in Lewandowski, *Swedish Contribution to the Polish Resistance Movement*, 8.

80. Komisja Historyczna, *PSZ* 3:296ff.; Bór *Secret Army*, 150; Garliński, *Hitler's Last Weapons*, 48.

81. Komisja Historyczna, *PSZ* 3:300-301; Bór, *Secret Army*, 150.

82. Meldunek Organizacyjny, Rowecki do Centrali, 16 May 1942, in *AKwD* 2:234-35; Meldunek Organizacyjny, Bór do N.W., 31 Aug. 1943, in ibid., 3:73-75.

83. Komisja Historyczna, *PSZ* 3:297-98, 304-05; Foot, *Resistance*, 27.

84. Meldunek Sytuacyjny, Okulicki do Centrali, 10 Sept. 1941; Depesza, Rowecki do Centrali, 23 Sept. 1941; Meldunek Organizacyjny, Rowecki do Centrali, 1 Oct. 1941, in *AKwD* 2:62-67, 87-88, 111ff.

85. Depesza, Smolenski do Roweckiego, 9 Sept. 1941; Depesza, Sikorski do Roweckiego, 10 Oct. 1941, in *AKwD* 2:57, 124-25.

86. Komisja Historyczna, *PSZ* 3:303.

87. Masson, *Christine*, 150, 217.

88. Farago, *Game of the Foxes*, 663-64; Lewandowski, *Swedish Contribution to the Polish Resistance Movement*, 32, 59, 61-62. Farago was unable to identify the "Pesky Pole" by name but Lewandowski did.

89. Farago, *Game of the Foxes*, 788-89.

90. Masson, *Christine*, 7-11, 50-53, 61, 68, 82-83, 103, 106.

91. Garliński, *Hitler's Last Weapons*, 116ff.; Foot, *Resistance*, 292; Woytak and Kasparek, "Top Secret of World War II," 98-103.

92. List, Sosnkowski do Brytyjskiego Ministra Informacji, 21 Apr. 1941, in *AKwD* 1:516ff.; Bór, *Secret Army*, 62.

93. Lukas, *Eagles East*, 8.

94. Depesza, Smoleński do Roweckiego, 9 Sept. 1941, in *AKwD* 2:57; Komisja Historyczna, *PSZ* 3:302-3.

95. Churchill, *Closing the Ring*, 230-33.

96. Piekalkiewicz, *Secret Agents, Spies, and Saboteurs*, 434.

97. Bór, *Secret Army*, 151.

98. Garliński, *Hitler's Last Weapons*, 161ff. Bór's detailed report on the V-2 can be found in Meldunek Specjalny, Bór do N.W., 12 July 1944, in *AKwD* 3:512-27.

99. Churchill, *Closing the Ring*, 234-35.

100. Komisja Historyczna, *PSZ* 3:226, 248-49.

101. Foot, *Resistance*, 295-96.

102. Komisja Historyczna, *PSZ* 3:246-48, 255; Haestrup, *European Resistance Movements*, 179.

103. Komisja Historyczna, *PSZ* 3:250-52. Korboński says this radio contact was established in Aug. 1941, not early 1942, as the *PSZ* states. See Korboński, *Fighting Warsaw*, 60ff.

104. Ibid., 234.

105. Ibid., 226-29, 230-37.

106. Garliński, *Polska w Drugiej Wojnie Światowej*, 131.

107. Komisja Historyczna, *PSZ* 3:229; Meldunek Organizacyjny, Rowecki do N.W., 1 Mar. 1943, in *AKwD* 2:438.

108. Komisja Historyczna, *PSZ* 3:221, 219.

109. Ibid., 221-22.

110. Ibid., 401-06.

111. Haestrup, *European Resistance Movements*, 35.

112. Memo on Axis Controlled Europe, 17 Aug. 1943, in FO371/34297/52538 C9900/551/55, PRO; Komisja Historyczna, *PSZ* 3:447; memo, Osborne to Calder, 10 Mar. 1944, in FO898/225, PRO.

113. Memo on Axis Controlled Europe, 17 Aug. 1943.

114. Quoted in Korboński, *Fighting Warsaw*, 292.

115. Zaremba, *Wojna i Konspiracja*, 133.

116. Bartoszewski, *Warsaw Death Ring*, 279-80; Michel, *Shadow War*, 222; Bór, *Secret Army*, 171.

117. Duraczyński, *Wojna i Okupacja*, 429-32.

118. Ibid., 432.

119. Sprawozdanie Celta, 1944, in Kol. 25/9, GSHI; Office of Strategic Services, Report, Oct. 1942, #24128, RG 226, in OSS/NA.

120. Meldunek Organizacyjny, Rowecki do Centrali, 1 Oct. 1941, in *AKwD* 2:99, 101. The ZWZ/AK suffered similar losses to the Soviets before June 1941. Rowecki reported in Nov. 1940 that the entire staff of the ZWZ in Wołyń had been arrested. Meldunek Organizacyjny, Rowecki do Sosnkowskiego, 21 Nov. 1940, in ibid. 1:351.

121. Madajczyk, *Polityka III Rzeszy w Okupowanej Polsce* 1:173 n.140.

122. Meldunek, Rowecki do Centrali, 23 June 1941, in *AKwD* 2:10; Komisja Historyczna, *PSZ* 3:124.

123. Meldunek Organizacyjny, Bór do N.W., 1 Mar. 1944, in *AKwD* 3:328-29; Leslie, *History of Poland since 1863*, 241.

124. Żenczykowski, *General Grot*, 10-11, 13, 15, 16-17, 19-24, 44.

125. Depesza, Bór do N.W., 13 June 1943; minute by Strang, 12 July 1943, in FO371/34553 C8277/34/G, PRO; letter, Mikołajczyk to Churchill, 20 July 1943, in *AKwD* 3:42, 43-45.

126. War Cabinet Meeting, 19 July 1943, in CAB65/35, PRO; Żenczykowski, *General Grot*, 27; letter, Churchill to Mikołajczyk, 1 Aug. 1943, in *AKwD* 3:52. If all other methods failed, the Poles were prepared to ransom Rowecki. Żenczykowski, *General Grot*, 29.

127. Minute by Strang, 12 July 1943, in FO371/34553 C8277/34/G; letter, Selborne to Eden, 12 Aug. 1943; letter, Law to Selborne, 30 Aug. 1943; minute by Cavendish-Bentinck, 23 Aug. 1943; minute by Allen, 26 Aug. 1943, in FO371/34551 C9479/34/G, PRO. Bór claims that the Germans asked the British to exchange Rudolf Hess for Rowecki, but the British did not agree to this. Available British documents do not support the claim. See Bór, *Secret Army*, 142.

128. Żenczykowski, *General Grot*, 79-80. There was some speculation that the Germans asked Rowecki to issue a declaration to the AK to stop the Warsaw Uprising. His refusal to do so allegedly resulted in his death.

129. Irving, *Accident: Death of General Sikorski*, 44ff., 106-07, 125ff., 131, 144, 167, 175-77; proceedings of Court of Inquiry of Investigation, 7 July 1943, Air 2/9234, PRO. Irving concludes: "Although there is no suggestion that Prchal staged the accident, the possibility that the crash was planned by somebody cannot be ruled out" (p. 174.) Sikorski's widow blamed the Russians. One author even placed responsibility on Anders, who did not get along with Sikorski. Rolf Hochhuth, the playwright, claimed that he had evidence to prove that British intelligence was responsible for Sikorski's death.

CHAPTER FOUR

1. Korboński, *Polish Underground State*, 71-72.

2. Ibid., 72-76.

3. Karski, *Secret State*, 256-57.

4. Memo, Osborne to Calder, 10 Mar. 1944, in FO898/225, PRO.

5. Sprawozdanie Celta, 1944, in Kol. 25/9, GSHI.

6. Hanson, *Civilian Population and the Warsaw Uprising*, 44; Karski, *Secret State*, 259.

7. Hanson, *Civilian Population and the Warsaw Uprising*, 44.

8. Duraczyński, *Wojna i Okupcja*, 247, 384; Bartoszewski, *Warsaw Death Ring*, 28-33.

9. Bartoszewski, *Warsaw Death Ring*, 151-54; Meldunek Organizacyjny, 16

May 1942, in *AKwD* 2:256; Office of Strategic Services, "Underground and Guerilla Warfare in Poland," in OSS/NA.

10. Duraczyński, *Wojna i Okupacja*, 384-85; Bór, *Secret Army*, 84.

11. Duraczyński, *Wojna i Okupacja*, 72.

12. Madajczyk, *Polityka Rzeszy w Okupowanej Polsce*, Vol.2.

13. *Polish Fortnightly Review*, 1 July 1942, 7.

14. Quoted in Karski, *Secret State*, 249.

15. Steven, *The Poles*, 10.

16. Dwa Lata Okupacji Niemieckiej w Polsce [1941], in PRM 45c/23, GSHI. A favorite ditty of the Poles repeated at the time of Hess's flight to England was: "The dog disappeared; his name was Hess."

17. *Polish Fortnightly Review*, 1 July 1942, 7.

18. Duraczyński, *Wojna i Okupacja*, 147; Office of Strategic Services, "German-Occupied Poland," in OSS/NA. Despite the Nazi terror and deportations, the OSS report related that Poles after the invasion of Russia said, "Yes, it is terrible, but now it is easier to endure, since we are certain the Germans are lost. We have a new basis for faith in the future." A year earlier, at the time of the French collapse, the Poles were shocked to learn of attempts by some Polish political and military officials to remove Sikorski from office. Sprawozdanie Emisariusza Antoniego, Załącznik 21, in PRM 46A/15, GSHI.

19. See Chapter 3 above.

20. Sprawozdanie Emisariusza Antoniego, Załącznik 21, in PRM 46A/15; Dwa Lata Okupacji Niemieckiej w Polsce [1941], in PRM 45C/23, GSHI.

21. Delegat Rządu, Uwagi Ogólne, 10 May 1942, in A48.4/a III.7, GSHI.

22. Duraczyński, *Wojna i Okupacja*, 404-05.

23. Sprawozdanie Celta, 1944, in Kol. 25/9, GSHI.

24. Nowak, *Courier from Warsaw*, 324.

25. Delegat Rządu, Uwagi Ogólne, 10 May 1942, in A48.4/ aII.7, GSHI.

26. Dwa Lata Okupacji Niemieckiej w Polsce [1941], in PRM 45c/23; Sprawozdanie Celta, 1944, in Kol. 25/9, GSHI.

27. Meldunek Organizacyjny, 16 May 1942, in *AKwD* 2:242-43.

28. Sprawozdanie Celta, 1944, in Kol. 25/9, GSHI. The Peasant Party exerted great efforts to deal with the problem among the peasants.

29. Korboński, *Polish Underground State*, 93.

30. Meldunek Organizacyjny, Rowecki do Centrali, 1 Sept. 1942; Meldunek, Rowecki do Centrali, 15 Oct. 1942, in *AKwd* 2:312, 348-50.

31. Meldunek, Rowecki do Centrali, 21 Sept. 1941, in ibid., 72-74; Nowak, *Courier from Warsaw*, 96. To demoralize the German soldiers' pride, the Poles circulated a pornographic cartoon "reminding German soldiers of the good time their wives were having during their absence." Michel, *Shadow War*, 79. The Poles were not unique in exploiting such tactics to demoralize the enemy. Tokyo Rose, known for her broadcasts to American troops, often suggested to them that their wives and sweethearts were unfaithful.

32. Quoted in Irving, *Accident*, 36-37.

33. Korboński, *Polish Underground State*, 95.

34. Quoted in Hanson, *Civilian Population and the Warsaw Uprising*, 44.

35. Duraczyński, *Wojna i Okupacja*, 234-37, 422-24.

36. Madajczyk, *Polityka III Rzeszy w Okupowanej Polsce* 2:160-62.

37. Garliński, *Polska w Drugiej Wojnie Swiatowej*, 225-26.

38. Karski, *Secret State*, 308; Michel, *Shadow War*, 144.

39. Pawelczyńska, *Values and Violence in Auschwitz*, xiv.

40. Michel, *Shadow War*, 144.

41. Ibid.; Rudowski and Zablotniak, "Clandestine Medical Studies in Poland," 240-50.

42. Dwa Lata Okupacji w Polsce [1941], in PRM 45c/23, GSHI; Madajczyk, *Polityka III Rzeszy w Okupowanej Polsce* 2:140-41.

43. Dwa Lata Okupacji w Polsce [1941], in PRM 45c/23, GSHI; Madajczyk, *Polityka III Rzeszy w Okupowanej Polsce* 2:135; Marczak-Oborski, *Teatr Czasu Wojny*, 63.

44. Marczak-Oborski, *Teatr Czasu Wojny*, 139-41.

45. Ibid., 271-309. Fredro was also a poet. One of his poems, often read during the occupation, was "Our Fatherland." One can readily see why it was popular:

On the long mountain ranges black firs tower high,
And murmur a dirge as the north wind sweeps by,
While down in the valley, below on the plain,
Billows an ocean of golden-speared grain:
An ocean, with islands of blossom-starred green,
Like vagabond sailing-ships dotting the scene.
Here and there little homes white and glittering stand—
    That's Poland, our Poland,
     Our fatherland!
. . . .
The country where naught can the race ever spoil,
The country that for its faith, language and soil
Stands ready its breast, heart and hand to lay bare
To the sword of the foeman, to wrong everywhere;
That, so long as life lasts, will not cease from the fight,
So long as it breathes will strive on for the right:
One man, with one sword, ever firmly will stand:
    That's Poland, our Poland,
     Our fatherland!

Quoted in Coleman, *Polish Land*, 5-6.

46. Marczak-Oborski, *Teatr Czasu Wojny*, 19, 33.

47. *Polish Fortnightly Review*, 1 Aug. 1942.

48. Interview with Pelagia Łukaszewska, 10 July 1983. She was a social

worker with the American Relief for Poland and was one of the few Americans to visit Poland in 1947. She interviewed many Poles during her visit and had many keen observations to make about wartime and early postwar Poland.

49. Lewandowska, *Polska Konspiracyjnej Prasa*, 43, 265; Dobroszycki, *Centralny Katalog Polskiej Prasy Konspiracyjnej*, 6-10.

50. Komisja Historyczna, *PSZ* 3:227. In contrast, the Dutch underground published *De Waarhied* in 100,000 copies and the French *Combat* boasted a publication run of 300,000. Dobroszycki, *Centralny Katalog*, 9.

51. Lewandowska, *Polska Konspiracyjna Prasa*, 215, 264-66. As one observer put it, "As never before and as never again, Warsaw under Hitler's occupation was a city of the clandestine press." Borowski, *This Way for the Gas*, 14.

52. Lewandowska, *Polska Konspiracyjna Prasa*, 35-36, 44.

53. Dobroszycki, *Centralny Katalog*, 10, 96, 135, 232-35, 254-56.

54. Lewandowska, *Polska Konspiracyjna Prasa*, 267; memo, Dormer to Eden, 13 Jan. 1942, in FO371/31092/52481 C520/520/55, PRO.

55. Madajczyk, *Polityka III Rzeszy w Okupowanej Polsce* 2:132-33; Marczak-Oborski, *Teatr Czasu Wojny*, 35-36.

56. Lewandowska, *Polska Konspiracyjna Prasa*, 145, 263; Borowski, *This Way for the Gas*, 14; Komisja Historyczna, *PSZ* 3:281. The AK in Lwów and Cracow printed publications dealing with women in the underground.

57. Lewandowska, *Polska Konspiracyjna Prasa*, 175-76. Karski also mentions Boston's WRUL and New York's WCBX as sources of information. Karski, *Secret State*, 265.

58. Office of Strategic Services, "Underground and Guerilla Warfare in Poland," in OSS/NA.

59. Korboński, *Polish Underground State*, 76-78; during the Warsaw Uprising, the Polish radio station Lightning (Błyskawica) broadcast from 8 Aug. to 4 Oct. 1944 in English and Polish. Several diversionary broadcasts in German were also made, urging the Germans to surrender to the Poles. See Komisja Historyczna, *PSZ* 3:286.

60. Komisja Historyczna, *PSZ* 3:296.

61. Memo, Press Reading Bureau to Political Intelligence Department, 13 Aug. 1943, in FO371/34553/52538 C9500/79/55; directive, Political Warfare Executive to BBC (Polish Services), 20 Apr. 1944, in FO371/39425 C5385/61/55, PRO.

62. Karski, *Secret State*, 270-71.

63. Duraczyński, *Wojna i Okupacja*, 421.

64. Korboński, *Fighting Poland*, 41.

65. Lewandowska, *Polska Konspiracyjna Prasa*, 339ff.

66. This is based on the author's analysis of the underground press.

67. Duraczyński, *Wojna i Okupacja*, 421; Korboński, *Polish Underground State*, 119.

68. Mitkiewicz, *Z Gen. Sikorskim na Obczyźnie*, 293.

69. Terry, *Poland's Place in Europe*, 187 n.87.

70. Letter, Rougetel to Halifax, 19 Aug. 1940, in FO371/24474 C10589/252/55, in PRO.

71. Mitkiewicz, *Z Gen. Sikorskim na Obczyźnie*, 73-75.

72. Dwa Lata Okupacji Niemieckiej w Polsce [1941], in PRM 45c/23, GSHI; Korboński, *Polish Underground State*, 141-42.

73. Minute by Savery, 30 July 1940, in FO371/24474, PRO; Rudnicki, *Last of the War Horses*, 100.

74. Memo, Savery to Roberts with reports, 26 Aug. 1941, in FO 371/26727/5481 C9667/189/55, PRO; Mitkiewicz, *Z Gen Sikorskim na Obczyźnie*, 74, 157-58, 180.

75. Memo, Sumner to Warner, 17 July 1941, in FO371/26756/52588 C8172/3226/55, PRO.

76. Mitkiewicz, *Z Gen. Sikorskim na Obzyźnie*, 153; letter, Sikorski to Churchill, 3 Oct. 1941, in PREM 3/351/7, PRO.

77. Depesza, Rowecki do Centrali, 19 Sept. 1941, in *AKwD* 2:71.

78. Letter, Wszelaki to Roberts, 10 Sept. 1941, in FO371/26727 C10208/189/55, PRO. Governor Frank got the cooperation of Wacław Krzeptowski, a former member of the Peasant Party, to organize the Polish mountaineers (*Gorals*) into a mountain nation (*Goralenvolk*). An underground court sentenced Krzeptowski and his accomplices to death. They were promptly executed, and Frank's scheme was aborted. Korboński, *Polish Underground State*, 142.

79. Depesza, Delegat Rządu do Centrali, in *AKwD* 2:210; Office of Strategic Services, "Underground and Guerilla Warfare in Poland," in OSS/NA.

80. Letter, Savery to Roberts, 5 Mar. 1942, in FO371/31098/52481 C2472/957/55, PRO; Rudnicki, *Last of the War Horses*, 211-13.

81. Depesza, Rowecki do Centrali, 13 May 1943; Meldunek Zbiorowy, Rowecki do Centrali, 28 May 1943, in *AKwD* 3:7-8, 16-17.

82. See, for example, the statement in *Rzeczpospolita Polska*, 6 May 1943.

83. See Chapter 5 below.

84. Irving, *Accident*, 39; 199 n.71.

85. Broszat, *Zweihundert Jahre deutsche Polenpolitik*, 241-42; Madajczyk, *Polityka III Rzeszy w Okupowanej Polsce* 1:171-77. *Miecz i Pług* had been infiltrated by the Gestapo, a source of grave concern to Rowecki and Bór.

86. Madajczyk, *Polityka III Rzeszy w Okupowanej Polsce* 1:172, 189-90, 192-93.

87. Ibid., 2:134.

88. Memo on Axis-Controlled Europe, 23 Nov. 1943, in FO371/34599/52538 C14153/551/55; message, Foreign Office to Washington, in FO371/39425 C5385/55, PRO.

89. Meldunek Sytuacyjny, Bór do Centrali, 23 Mar. 1944, in *AKwD* 3:382; Office of Strategic Services, Report, 24 Feb. 1944, #62067, in RG 226, OSS/NA. Despite all this, Bór wrote grimly, "The terror, however, continues."

90. Directive, Political Warfare Executive for BBC, Polish Services, 4 May 1944, in FO371/39425 C5385/61/55, PRO.

91. Madajczyk, *Polityka III Rzeszy w Okupowanej Polsce* 1:195, 203; 2:172-74.

92. Messages from Poland, 23 Mar. 1944, and 26 Mar. 1944, in FO371/39451 C584/131/55, PRO.

93. Letter, McLaren to Allen with enclosure, 10 Aug. 1943, in FO371/34551 C9658/34/G, PRO.

94. Depesza, Bór do N.W., 28 Feb. 1944; Meldunek Organizacyjny, Bór do N.W., 1 Mar. 1944, in *AKwD* 3:293, 305; Reuter Report, 23 Mar. 1944, in FO371/39510/52574 C2624/2624/55; minute by O'Malley, 3 Apr. 1944, in FO371/39510, PRO. The Germans were especially anxious to create a Polish anti-Bolshevik legion. See Bór's messages in Aug. 1943, to London, in *AKwD* 3:62, 74.

95. Sprawozdanie Celta, 1944, in Kol. 25/9, GSHI; Madajczyk, *Polityka III Rzeszy w Okupowanej Polsce* 1:194; Meldunek Organizacyjny, Bór do N.W., 1 Mar. 1944, in *AKwD* 3:344.

96. Broszat, *Zweihundert Jahre deutsche Polenpolitik*, 241-42. The British feared that after the abortive Warsaw Uprising the Poles would be especially vulnerable to renewed German efforts to win them over to collaboration. Memo, McLaren to Bowen, 11 Oct. 1944, in FO898/225, PRO. See Chapter 7 below.

97. Gross, *Polish Society under German Occupation*, 166.

98. Depesza, Sikorski do Delegata Rządu, 3 Feb. 1943, in Kol. 1/43.

99. Ringelblum, *Polish-Jewish Relations*, 226.

100. Komisja Polskiego Sztabu Głownego w Londynie, *PSZ* 3:473. It is not known how many of these sentences were executed. Korboński claims no more than 200 sentences of the underground courts were carried out. (Korboński, *Polish Underground State*, 74.) But it should be remembered that these courts were not established until December 1942, three years after the occupation of the country, and it is known that there were many executions of traitors, blackmailers, and informers before that time. Moreover, the Directorate of Civil Resistance only controlled civil underground courts; the ZWZ/AK also condemned people to death and executed a very large number of them. In addition, a large number of informers were liquidated by the Communists. *Gwardzista* announced that in the period 15 May 1942—15 Dec. 1943, the GL had liquidated 328 informers. *Gwardzista*, 25 Dec. 1943.

101. Kusielewicz, "Some Thoughts on the Teaching of the Holocaust," Insert D.

102. Letter, Kennard to Eden, 19 Mar. 1941, in FO371/26723/52538 C2763/189/55, PRO; Bartoszewski, *Warsaw Death Ring*, 77-80. Witold Wasilewski, a Polish judge who had collaborated with the Nazis, died in Cracow. Kennard remarked that the "mysterious circumstances (of this death) appear to be much the same as those attending the death of Igo Sym."

103. Meldunek Organizacyjny, Bór do N.W., 31 Aug. 1943, in *AKwD* 3:75; Żenczykowski, *General Grot*, 170-72.

104. Ringelblum, *Polish-Jewish Relations*, 124; Fein, *Accounting for Genocide*, 218. The figure of 1,000 *schmalzowniks* comes from an interview by Dr.

Wacław Zajączkowski of a former AK officer who had visited the Warsaw Ghetto regularly. I am indebted to Dr. Zajączkowski for this information. Letter, Zajączkowski to author, 5 June 1984. This figure corresponds with the estimates I received from several interviewees. See Chapter 5 below.

105. Ringelblum, *Polish-Jewish Relations*, 42 n.7.

106. Letter, Zajączkowski to author, 5 June 1984; Wroński and Zwolakowa, *Polacy i Żydzi*, 178.

107. Mark, *Powstanie w Getcie Warszawskim*, 28-29, 200, 218-19. Tadeusz Bednarczyk claimed that the Jews had more collaborators than the Poles. Dawidowicz, *Holocaust and the Historians*, 116. Dawidowicz asserts that no one has the right to judge Jewish behavior during the war; yet, strangely, she believes a stricter standard of judgment should be applied to the Poles.

108. Korboński, *Polish Underground State*, 125; *Rzeczpospolita Polska*, [2] Mar. 1943. (The date is placed in brackets because the copy I used was not entirely clear.)

109. *Biuletyn Informacyjny*, 18 Mar. 1943.

110. For example, *Głos Demokracji*, 4 Sept. 1943; *Nowa Droga*, 7 Feb. 1944, cited in Joseph Kermish, "The Activities of the Council for Aid to Jews (Żegota) in Occupied Poland," in *Rescue Attempts during the Holocaust: Proceedings of the Second Yad Vashem International Historical Conference* (Jerusalem: Yad Vashem, 1977), 380.

111. Arczyński and Balcerak, *Kryptonim Żegota*, 97ff.; Iranek-Osmecki, *He Who Saves One Life*, 255.

112. Kermish, "Activities of the Council for Aid to Jews." 368.

113. Statement by Rachel Auerbach in *Rescue Attempts during the Holocaust*, 459; Chciuk, *Saving the Jews in War-Torn Poland*, 53; Hirszfeld, *Historia Jednego Życia*, 407.

114. Bartoszewski and Lewin, *Samaritans*, 113.

115. Ringelblum, *Polish-Jewish Relations*, 125. He claimed that these were "rare cases," but based on oral testimonies given to this author, the number of interventions was substantial. Interview with Korboński, 7 June 1982; interview with Pelagia Łukaszewska, 10 July 1983.

116. See references, mostly to *Rzeczpospolita Polska*, in Iranek-Osmecki, *He Who Saves One Life*, 257-58. In addition, the issues of the *Biuletyn Informacyjny* on 2 Sept. 1943, 16 Sept. 1943, 9 Dec. 1943, 30 Mar. 1944, and 16 July 1944, contained notices of death sentences passed on Poles who betrayed Jews.

117. *Biuletyn Informacyjny*, 9 Dec. 1943; Arczyński and Balcerak, *Kryptonim Żegota*, 105. Joseph Kermish, like many other Jewish historians, takes the emotional rather than factual position that the Polish underground did little or nothing to combat the problem of blackmailers of Jews. Kermish, for example, claims that warnings against Polish blackmailers "remained on paper alone." Then he goes on to disregard existing evidence to the contrary by making the tendentious generalization: "The execution of death sentences against the blackmailers responsible for the deaths of *tens of thousands* of Jews and notices posted on walls as well in the underground press, would certainly have made an impression, but

this was *never* done" (italics mine). Nor does Kermish offer proof for his sweeping claim that "tens of thousands of Jews" were victimized by blackmailers. See Kermish, "Activities of the Council for Aid to Jews," 380. Kermish's lack of balance in dealing with the subject of Polish-Jewish relations is also revealed in the role he shared with Shmuel Krakowski in editing Ringelblum's *Polish-Jewish Relations during the Second World War* cited above. See "Afterword" for a commentary concerning the historiography on Polish-Jewish wartime relations.

118. Iranek-Osmecki, *He Who Saves One Life*, 259.

CHAPTER FIVE

1. Apenszlak, *Black Book of Polish Jewry*, 249.
2. Ibid., 250.
3. Weinryb, *Jews of Poland*, 157-59.
4. Ibid., 134.
5. Apenszlak, *Black Book of Polish Jewry*, 251.
6. Quoted in statement by Banaczyk at meeting of the Council for Rescue of the Jews in Poland, 25 May 1944, in C11/7/3c/8, BOD.
7. Davies, *God's Playground*, 255.
8. Memo, Savery to Allen, 17 July 1944, in FO371/39524 C9465/7711/55, PRO.
9. Mendelsohn, *Jews of East Central Europe*, 29-30.
10. Ainsztein, *Jewish Resistance in Nazi-Occupied Eastern Europe*, 187.
11. Bartoszewski and Lewin, *Samaritans* 1-2.
12. Hirszfeld, *Historia Jednego Życia*, 419. He talks about the split between the assimilated Jewish intelligentsia and the Jewish masses, with the former even manifesting an anti-Semitic character of their own in dissociating themselves from the poor Jewish masses.
13. Memo, Savery to Allen, 17 July 1944, in FO371/39524 C9465/7711/55, PRO.
14. Quoted in Steven, *Poles*, 313-14.
15. Heller, *On the Edge of Destruction*, 106.
16. There were a number of Jewish officers in the Polish army, including those who had reached the rank of general. General Bernard Mond, for example, had been a close collaborator of Marshal Piłsudski.
17. Steven, *Poles*, 313; Davies, *God's Playground*, 261. The *numerus clausus* was not applied, for example, at the Jagiellonian University. See Ciołkosz, *Walka o Prawde*, 245.
18. Davies, *God's Playground*, 261-62; Ciołkosz, *Walka o Prawde*, 243ff.; Mendelsohn, *Jews of East Central Europe*, 41. Like other Jewish writers, Mendelsohn exaggerates the violence to which Jews were subjected in Poland during the interwar years. Ciołkosz points out that the *Jewish Chronicle* reported on 6 Dec. 1918 that 3,200 Jews died in the Lwów pogrom; in reality, 73 perished. See Ciołkosz, *Walka o Prawde*, 243.
19. Bauer, *History of the Holocaust*, 143.

20. Interview with Karol and Rachel Cymber, 18 July 1983.

21. Wynot, "'A Necessary Cruelty,'" 1035-58.

22. Davies, *God's Playground*, 261-62.

23. This analysis is based on several sources. A few of the more helpful accounts include Sytuacja w Warszawie i w Generalnym Gubernatorstwie, 31 Dec. 1940, in PRM-K/86; Raport Specjalny, Kalski do premiera, 25 May 1944, in A.9 III.24/27, GHSI; Hirszfeld, *Historia Jednego Życia*, 356, 407; Iranek-Osmecki, *He Who Saves One Life*, 245-46; Friedman, *Their Brothers' Keepers*, 14; interview with Korboński, 7 June 1982; interview with Łukaszewska, 10 July 1983; letter, Barbarska to author, 8 June 1984. The difficulties in categorizing Polish attitudes are illustrated in the contrasts and contradictions in Ringelblum, *Polish-Jewish Relations*; see pp. 1-2, 246-47.

24. Z Placowki rzymsko-watykanskiej; Min. Inf. i Dok., 25 Nov. 1941, in PRM 45c/17; Dwa Lata Okupacja Niemieckiej w Polsce [1941], in PRM 45c/23; Sprawozdanie Celta, 1944, in Kol. 25/9, GSHI; Sprawozdanie za Okres 15 X-20 XI 1940, in YIVO; Ringelblum, *Notes from the Warsaw Ghetto*, 248.

25. Dwa Lata Okupacji Niemieckiej w Polsce (1941), in PRM 45c.23, GSHI.

26. Ministerstwo Spraw Wewnętrznych w Londynie, Sprawozdanie Sytuacyjne z Kraju, II, 1941-42; Rządy Rosji Sowieckiej we Wschodniej Polsce, 1939-41 in YIVO; report of conversation between Anders and representatives of Polish Jews in the USSR, 24 Oct. 1941, in Box 16, Mikołajczyk Papers, Hoover Institution.

27. Delegat do Rządu, (1944), Stosunek do Mniejszości Narodowych in YIVO; Depesza, Mitkiewicz do Mikołajczyka, 5 Dec. 1941, in A.48. 4/AI. 38, GSHI; Iranek-Osmecki, *He Who Saves One Life*, 185-86. For obvious reasons, Madajczyk made this understated comment about Jewish attitudes toward the Soviet occupation of Białystok in 1940: "Jewish society of Białystok adapted better than the Poles to the newly created conditions by Soviet authorities; it took an active part in its organization." Madajczyk, *Polityka III Rzeszy w Okupowanej Polsce* 1:209.

28. Ringelblum, *Notes from the Warsaw Ghetto*, 39, 135; Iranek-Osmecki, *He Who Saves One Life*, 24.

29. Quoted in Iranek-Osmecki, *He Who Saves One Life*, 24-25.

30. Polish Ministry of Interior, Reports on the Situation in Occupied Poland, 1 July-1 Dec. 1942, RG 226, OSS/NA.

31. Stroop, *Stroop Report*, 11.

32. Ministerstwo Spraw Wewnętrznych w Londynie, Sprawozdanie Sytuacyjne z Kraju, II, 1941-42, in YIVO.

33. Madajczyk, *Polityka III Rzeszy w Okupowanej Polsce* 2:171.

34. See Chapter 4 above.

35. *Biuletyn Informacyjny*, 19 July 1940; Hirszfeld, *Historia Jednego Życia*, 349; Ringelblum, *Polish-Jewish Relations*, 50-53. Ringelblum claims erroneously that there was no public expression by the Poles against these activities. There were statements made in churches and in the underground press against

such behavior; and as the following quotation in the text shows, there were Poles who tried to intervene and stop the hooligans. But it should be remembered that these gangs also attacked Poles (Ringelblum, *Notes from the Warsaw Ghetto*, 127), especially people who were philo-Semitic, and it was very risky for a decent Pole to try to stop one of these assaults, especially while the Germans protected the attackers. We are all aware of the number of assaults on individuals in the streets of our cities today in which few, if any, people are willing to risk their own safety in far less threatening circumstances. As for the ZWZ/AK intervening actively in these matters, the organization was weak and did not become an organized force until later in the war. By then, most Jews had already perished in the German gas chambers.

36. Apenszlak, *Black Book of Polish Jewry*, 30-31.

37. *Biuletyn Informacyjny*, 8 Nov. 1940; *Informator* (WRN), 8 Mar. 1940.

38. Ringelblum, *Polish-Jewish Relations*, 53.

39. Lukas, *Strange Allies*, 12ff.

40. Note, Polish Embassy to People's Commissariat for Foreign Affairs, 10 Nov. 1941, in *DPSR* 1:200-201; Kot, *Conversations with the Kremlin*, 182-86, 229-30. The Soviets were so zealous in trying to prevent Jews from joining the Polish army they even examined men for circumcision. For the dubious legal foundation of Soviet claims to eastern Poland, see Republic of Poland, *Polish-Soviet Relations*, 102-05.

41. Kot, *Conversations with the Kremlin*, 62, 182; report of conversation between Anders and representatives of Polish Jews in the USSR, 24 Oct. 1941, in Mikołajczyk papers, Box 16, HI. Yisrael Gutman erroneously claimed that the Poles imposed a *numerus clausus* on the number of Jews who could enlist in the Polish Army in Russia. See Borwicz, "Factors Influencing Relations," 356.

42. Kot, *Conversations with the Kremlin*, 182; minutes of meeting between Stalin and Sikorski, 3 Dec. 1941, in *DPSR*, I, 241.

43. Kot, *Conversations with the Kremlin*, 1; Rozkaz, Anders do dowódców, 14 Nov. 1941, in Mikołajczyk Papers, Box 16, HI; List, Blit, Fajnzylber and Oler do Sikorskiego, 9 Dec. 1941, in YIVO; Anders, *Army in Exile*, 77-78; translation of letter, Schwarzbart to Anders, 4 May 1942, in report, with enclosures by Lt. Col. Szymański, in RG 165, WDGS/NA.

44. See the correspondence on this question in the Ciechanowski Papers, Box 64, in HI; Depesza, Anders do Sosnkowskiego, 16 Aug. 1943, in YIVO.

45. Kot, *Conversations with the Kremlin*, 62.

46. Depesza, Besterman do Polskich Konsuli Generalnych, 9 Oct. 1942; Depesza, Zarski do Polskich Konsuli Generalnych, 29 Sept. 1942; List, Ciechanowski do Roppa, 14 July 1942, in Ciechanowski Papers, Box 64, HI; Anders, *Army in Exile*, 112. Kot described the secret arrangements that were required to get the first transport of Jewish children out of Russia. See Kot, *Conversations with the Kremlin*, 255.

47. Report with enclosures by Lt. Col. H. I. Szymański, in RG 165, WDGS/NA.

48. Rudnicki, *Last of the War Horses*, 248.

49. Depesza, Zarski do Polskich Konsuli Generalnych, 29 Sept. 1942; Depesza, Besterman do Polskich Konsuli Generalnych, 9 Oct. 1942, in Ciechanowski Papers, Box 64, HI.

50. Posiedzenie Rady Ministrów, 11 Feb. 1943, in PRM K.102/55a, GSHI; Anders, *Army in Exile*, 113; report with enclosures by Lt. Col. Szymański, in RG 165, WDGS/NA; British material can be found in FO371/32608, PRO.

51. Report with enclosures by Lt. Col. Szymański, in RG 165, WDGS/NA. One of the Jewish deserters from the Polish army in the Middle East was allegedly Menachem Begin, the future Israeli prime minister.

52. Office of Strategic Services, report 8 Nov. 1943, #50051; report, 21 May 1944, #76135, in RG 226, OSS/NA; Depesza, Zychon do Ministra Obrony Narodowej, 12 Aug. 1943, in YIVO. When the Polish army was evacuated to Palestine, Polish soldiers were instructed to avoid all possible incidents with Palestinian Jews. They were specifically forbidden to tell jokes with Jews as subjects. See Instrukcja od Rakowskiego, 1 Aug. 1943, in YIVO.

53. Note, #302, in *DPSR*, I, 608.

54. Depesza, Sprawa Żydów Obywateli Polskich, n.d., in Ciechanowski Papers, Box 64, HI.

55. Aide Mémoire, Polish Ministry of Foreign Affairs, 13 July 1942, presented to Sumner Welles; note, #302, in *DPSR*, I, 396-98, 608; Kot, *Conversations with the Kremlin*, 226. The Poles had testimonies from Jews in Russia that challenged allegations of Polish discrimination in the distribution of relief supplies to Jews. See memorandum (enclosure 1), in *DPSR*, I, 398-99. Since the Soviets denied claims that Jews in lands occupied by the Soviet Union in 1939 were Polish citizens, they resisted Polish efforts to locate and aid these Jews. Among the distinguished Jews the Polish embassy in the Soviet Union aided were Henryk Ehrlich and Wiktor Alter; Ehrlich was to be appointed a member of the Polish National Council in London, and Alter was to be appointed assistant at the Polish embassy in Kuibyshev involved in relief work. The Soviets executed both men on charges of subversion against the Soviet Union, which the Polish government strongly protested as soon as it learned about the executions. Note, Raczyński to Bogomolov, 8 Mar. 1943, in *DPSR*, I, 503-4.

56. Letter, Butler to Pritt, 27 July 1940, in FO371/24481/48 C5143/5143/55, PRO; Rozkaz, 5 Aug. 1940, in YIVO.

57. Minute by Roberts, May 1941, in FO371/26769, in PRO.

58. Wasserstein, *Britain and the Jews of Europe*, 125.

59. Przyczynek do Zagadnienia Żydowskiego w Armii Polskiej, 6 Aug. 1940, PRM 36.3, GSHI; letter, Tartakower to Schwarzbart, 25 Apr. 1941, in FO371/26769 C5410/4655/55, PRO.

60. Letter, Silverman to Eden, 1 May 1941, and minute by Roberts, 13 May 1941, FO371/26769 C4878/4655/55, PRO.

61. Iranek-Osmecki, *He Who Saves One Life*, 182-84; "Notes on Polish-Jewish Relations," in C11/7/3c/2 in BOD.

62. Minute by Roberts, 13 May 1941, FO371/26769 C4878/4655/55, PRO; *Times* (London), 29 Apr. 1944.

63. Rozdzielnik od Kukiela, 28 June 1943; Sprawozdanie z Konferencji 30 June 1943, Miejscowa prasa Zydowska; (unsigned statement referring to Kukiel's actions dated 9 Sept. 1943); Rozkaz do Sil Zbrojnych od Sosnkowskiego, 11 July 1943; Rozkaz Oficerski od Kukiela, 22 July 1943; List, Lunkiewicz do K.B., 6 Oct. 1943, in YIVO; Rezolucja Tajna, Rada Narodowa, 11 Sept. 1943, in A.5/15, GSHI.

64. Rozdzielnik od Kukiela, 9 July 1943; in A.XII. 1/65A, GSHI.

65. Depesza i Załącznik, Sosnkowski do Prezydenta, 4 July 1944, in A 48. 10a, GSHI. There are discrepancies in the accounts concerning the exact numbers of Jews who deserted.

66. Raport, Boruta-Spiechowicz do pana Ministra Obrony Narodowej, 25 Feb. 1944; Raport, Heitzman do Kukiela, 18 May 1944, in A.XII. 1.65B, GSHI.

67. Ibid.

68. Depesza, Sosnkowski do Kukiela, 8 June 1944; Raport, Heitzman do Ministra Obrony Narodowej, 18 May 1944; List, Kukiel do Sosabowskiego, 14 June 1944, in A.XII. 1/65B, GSHI.

69. Minute by Allen, 23, Feb. 1944; minute by Roberts, 23 Feb. 1944, in FO371/39480 C2643/918/55, PRO; Depesza i Załącznik, Sosnkowski do Prezydenta, 4 July 1944, in A48. 10a, GSHI.

70. Notatka, Ministerstwo Spraw Wewnętrzynych, 15 June 1944, in PRM 142.40, GSHI; minute by Allen, 13 Mar. 1944, in FO371/39480 C33331/918/55, PRO. Heitzman's speculation had greater credibility when it was learned that Jews also had deserted from the Czech armed forces, which had a reputation for being democratic. Notatka (unsigned), 24 Mar. 1944, in PRM 142.6, GSHI.

71. Penkower, *Jews Were Expendable*, 5-13; letter from Allen, 17 Feb. 1944, in FO371/39480 C1906/918/55, PRO; letter, Savery to Polish Government, 13 Apr. 1944, in A.XII. 1/65B, GSHI.

72. Notatka, Gorka dla Pana Ministra, 8 May 1944, in Sprawy Żydowskie-3E, GSHI.

73. Depesza, Heitzman do Bohuszewicza, 23 Mar. 1944, in A. XII. 1/65B, GSHI; press release, Polish Ministry of Information (1944), in Ciechanowski Papers, Box 64, HI; *Times* (London), 13 May 1944.

74. Mitkiewicz, *Z Gen. Sikorskim Na Obczyźnie*, 58; Raczyński, *In Allied London*, 201ff.; Wasserstein, *Britain and the Jews of Europe*, 129.

75. Raczyński, *In Allied London*, 183.

76. See Lukas, *Strange Allies*, chap. 5.

77. Raczyński, *In Allied London*, 213.

78. *Times* (London), 24 Apr. 1944; Wasserstein, *Britain and the Jews of Europe*, 129.

79. Raczyński, *In Allied London*, 203, 211.

80. Depesza od Korbońskiego, 20 June 1944, in PUST.

81. Excerpts from *S-OPW*, 21 May 1944, and *Przegląd Polityczny*, May 1944, in YIVO.

82. Directive, Political Warfare Executive to BBC, 27 Apr. 1944, in FO371/39425 C5385/61/55, PRO.

83. Open letter from Edward Warszawski (undated), in A. XII. 1/65B, GSHI.

84. List, Komitet Centralny Bundu do Rządu Rzeczpospolitej Polskiej, Apr. 1940, in YIVO.

85. Protokol, Posiedzenia Rady Narodowej, R.P., 7 July 1942, in A.5 2/32, GSHI; Bartoszewski and Lewin, *Samaritans*, 21.

86. Wniosek Nagły; Dr. I. Schwarzbart i Koledzy, Zgłoszony na Posiedzeniu Rady Narodowej R.P., 20 Dec. 1943, in GSHI; Bartoszewski and Lewin, *Samaritans*, 58.

87. Quoted in Kermish, "Activities of the Council for Aid to Jews," 395.

88. Ringelblum, *Notes from the Warsaw Ghetto*, 52, 67-68, 89, 170.

89. Ibid., 203.

90. Ibid., 322.

91. Hilberg, *The Warsaw Diary of Adam Czerniaków*, 320, 382.

92. Representative of this genre of writing is Pinkus, *House of Ashes*.

93. Wroński and Zwolakowa, *Polacy i Żydzi*, 113; Bartoszewski, *Blood Shed Unites Us*, 39-40.

94. Ringelblum, *Polish-Jewish Relations*, 24, 95. Jan Mosdorf, an anti-Semitic attorney before the war, had a change of heart when he was arrested and sent to Auschwitz. He distributed among Jewish inmates food parcels he had received from friends, and as an employee in the camp he warned Jews of selections for the gas chambers. Stanisław Piasecki, editor of the prewar anti-Semitic journal *Prosto z Mostu (Straight from the Shoulder)*, also underwent a change of attitude toward Jews during the early days of the occupation. Witold Rudnicki, a member of the National Democratic Party and commander of an AK unit, repudiated his earlier anti-Semitism and allowed his apartment to become a shelter for Jews who escaped from the Warsaw Ghetto. He also ordered the execution of four blackmailers who threatened to inform the Germans of Jews who were hidden in a village outside Warsaw. Dr. Franciszek Kowalski, an attorney from Zakopane, confided that "Hitler's bestiality toward the Jews changed me." Kowalski hid a young Jewish girl in his home. Friedman, *Their Brother's Keepers*, 114-16. During her travels in Poland in 1947, an American social worker talked with several former anti-Semites whose views changed as a result of German policy toward the Jews. Interview with Łukaszewska, 10 July 1982. One Jewish scholar has left a poignant account of her experiences in wartime Poland. She pointed out the discrepancy between the dislike of her Polish protectors for Jews as abstractions and their feelings for "real" Jews, who were "special and different, so they had no problems in treating us well." Tec, *Dry Tears*, 122.

95. Ringelblum, *Polish-Jewish Relations*, 139; Aleksandrowicz, *Kartk*, 22.

96. Ravel, *Faithful unto Death*, 108-9.

97. Bartoszewski and Lewin, *Samaritans*, 100.

98. Wroński and Zwolakowa, *Polacy i Żydzi*, 306-7, 349.

99. Ainsztein, *Jewish Resistance in Nazi-Occupied Eastern Europe*, 441.

100. Ringelblum, *Notes from the Warsaw Ghetto*, 45; Krakowski, *War of the Doomed*, 90; Ministerstwo Spraw Wewnętrznych w Londynie, Sprawozdanie Sy-

tuacyjne w Kraju, II, 1941-42, in YIVO. In contrast, Ringelblum claims the Poles in Kielce and Częstochowa were more anti-Semitic. See Ringelblum, *Polish-Jewish Relations*, 138.

101. Garliński, *Polska w Drugiej Wojnie Światowej*, 242.

102. Ministerstwo Spraw Wewnętrznych, Sprawozdanie, 4/43, in Ciechanowski Papers, Box 35, HI; Friedman, *Their Brothers' Keepers*, 18; interview with Staszek Jackowski, 30 July 1984.

103. Krakowski, *War of the Doomed*, 224; Polish Ministry of Interior, Situation in Poland from 1 July to 1 December 1942, #38092, in RG 226, OSS/-NA.

104. Bartoszewski and Lewin, *Samaritans*, 13; Bartoszewski, *Blood Shed Unites Us*, 85; Ringelblum, *Polish-Jewish Relations*, 226.

105. Wroński and Zwolakowa, *Polacy i Żydzi*, 258.

106. Interview with Stanisław Makuch, 17 Sept. 1984.

107. Oliner, "Unsung Heroes in Nazi-Occupied Europe," 134.

108. Bartoszewski, *Blood Shed Unites Us*, 208-09.

109. Bartoszewski and Lewin, *Samaritans*, 345.

110. Ringelblum, *Polish-Jewish Relations*, 79-82.

111. Wroński and Zwolakowa, *Polacy i Żydzi*, 298.

112. Iranek-Osmecki, *He Who Saves One Life*, 49. Jews who had the proper documentation and "passed" for Gentiles still ran the risk of a suspicious anti-Semitic Pole or German. Women suspected of being Jews were sometimes asked to recite the Lord's Prayer to prove they were Christians; men were subjected to physical checks for circumcision. Some Semitic-looking Jews had their noses reshaped and their penises uncircumcised to avoid discovery by the Germans. Bartoszewski and Lewin, *Samaritans*, 197-99.

113. Interview with Jackowski, 30 July 1984.

114. Interview with Rachel and Karol Cymber, 18 July 1983. The question of the objectivity of the chairman of the Committee on the Righteous (*Yad Vashem*), Moshe Bejski, was raised during a conference on "Faith in Humankind: Rescuers of Jews during the Holocaust" held in Washington, D.C., in September 1984. During Bejski's presentation at one of the plenary sessions, he cited examples of uncommon courage of Gentiles from various countries who saved Jews. When he got to Poland, he chose to confirm the prejudices of most Jews in his audience by telling a story of a Pole who refused to help him. Thus the judge allowed his personal experience to distort the historical record of which he was well aware—namely, approximately 25 percent of the Righteous Gentiles identified by Yad Vashem are Polish. Needless to say, Polish heroes and heroines who had been invited to this conference were outraged by Bejski's calculated insult.

115. Arczyński, *Kryptonim Żegota*, 76-80; Bartoszewski, *Warsaw Death Ring*, 362.

116. Bartoszewski, *Blood Shed Unites Us*, 89-106.

117. Raport Specjalny, Kalski do Premiera, 25 May 1944, in A.9 III. 24-27; Raport, Żegota, 12/42-10/43, in Sprawy Żydowskie-E, X-1, GSHI. Rather typical of the tendentious claims of some Jewish historians is the statement by Yisrael

Gutman who said that the support the Polish government gave *Żegota* was a calculated "gesture intended to absolve the Poles, in due course, from responsibility for the disaster which had befallen Polish Jewry." Shmuel Krakowski's charge that most of the leaders of the Polish government and underground saw *Żegota* as a "convenient front for their *real* policy toward the Jews" (italics mine) was sharply challenged by Miriam Peleg, who worked in the Cracow branch of Żegota. See Yisrael Gutman, "The Attitude of the Poles to the Mass Deportations of Jews from the Warsaw Ghetto in the summer of 1942," in *Rescue Attempts during the Holocaust*, 414. Also see pp. 452, 455 for Krakowski's statement and Peleg's rejoinder.

118. See Arczyński's account on the activities of *Żegota*. Arczyński, *Kryptonim Żegota*. A brief account is provided in Sprawozdanie w Działalności Rady Pomocy Żydom przy Pełnomocniku Rządu w Kraju za Czas od Grudnia 1942r.do Października 1943r. Włącznie. For some AK officers involved in *Żegota's* activities, see Bartoszewski and Lewin, *Samaritans*, 116-18.

119. Arczyński, *Kryptonim Żegota*, 87-88.

120. Ibid., 90, 136; Kermish, "Activities of the Council for Aid to Jews," 374.

121. Depesza, Orkan do Delegata, 23 Feb. 1944, in YIVO. Early in 1944, there was extensive correspondence between the Polish government-in-exile and the delegate concerning Dutch Jews. The Dutch government had given the Polish government $10,000 to help these Jews. The Polish government, sensitive to the bad press it received abroad about the desertions of Jewish soldiers from its army, noted to the delegate the propaganda value of helping the Dutch Jews; he was instructed to pay out this sum to *Żegota*. Depesza, Orkan do Delegata, 28 Feb. 1944; Depesza, Orkan do Delegata, 23 Mar. 1944; Depesza, Orkan do Delegata, 30 June 1944; Depesza, Orkan do Delegata, 25 Aug. 1944; List, Dentz do Serafinskiego, 11 Dec. 1944, in YIVO.

122. Ringelblum, *Polish-Jewish Relations*, 213 n.29; report, "The World Jewish Congress," Nov. 1944, quoting from "Report and Balance Sheet—Eighteen Months of Activity of the World Jewish Congress, November, 1943," in 37/6/4/11, Anglo-Jewish Archives.

123. Arczyński, *Kryptonim Żegota*, 182.

124. Ibid., 89, 182. See messages from the Jewish National Committee to Jewish leaders in London, especially depesza, ZKN do Schwarzbarta, 25 Oct. 1943, and undated, unsigned letter, in Delegata Rządu, 202/I and 202/XV-2, in Central Archives, Central Committee of the Polish United Workers Party, Warsaw, Poland.

125. Karski, *Story of a Secret State*, 323; statement by Scherer, 25 May 1944, in C11/7/36/8, BOD. Kermish apparently believes that money alone could have solved the problems facing *Żegota* during the German occupation. See Ringelblum, *Polish-Jewish Relations*, 301.

126. Depesza do Mikołajczyka, 8 Jan. 1943, in Sprawy Żydowskie-E III-9 in GSHI; Depesza, Rada Pomocy Żydom do Rządu, 22 July 1943, in T.78, PUST. The Polish government-in-exile organized the Council for the Rescue of

the Jewish Population in Poland in the spring of 1944. It was composed of Polish and Jewish representatives. Press communiqué by Polish Government, 11 May 1944, in C11/7/3c/8, BOD.

127. Heller, *On the Edge of Destruction*, 295; Bartoszewski and Lewin, *Samaritans*, 3; Wroński and Zwolakowa, *Polacy i Żydzi*, 258. Jewish historians tend to accept the lower figures, while Polish historians favor the higher ones.

128. Raport Specjalny, Kalski do Premiera, 25 May 1944, in A.9 III. 24/27, GSHI.

129. Dawidowicz, *Holocaust and the Historians*, 116; Zarski-Zajdler, *Martyrologia Ludności Żydowskiej i Pomoc Społeczeństwa Polskiego*, 16. I am indebted to Dr. Wacław Zajączkowski for calling my attention to the Zarski-Zajdler book.

130. Madajczyk, *Polityka Rzeszy w Okupowanej Polsce* 1:343, 2:337; Arczyński, *Kryptonim Żegota*, 95, 188; Bartoszewski, *Blood Shed Unites Us*, 100-101; Kermish, "Activities of the Council for Aid to Jews," 374, 394.

131. As Kren and Rappoport have pointed out, "SS domination was the most decisive factor in Jewish destruction." Kren and Rappoport, *Holocaust and the Crisis of Human Behavior*, 153 n.23.

132. Bartoszewski, *Blood Shed Unites Us*, 222.

133. Letter, Zajączkowski to author, 30 May 1984.

134. Laqueur, *Terrible Secret*, 106-07.

135. Wroński and Zwolakowa, *Polacy i Żydzi*, 262, 275-77, 361, 421, 423, 425, 445, 448; Duraczyński, *Wojna i Okupacja*, 413; Sytuacja w Polsce, 10/43, in Ciechanowski Papers, HI; Bartoszewski and Lewin, *Samaritans*, 119.

136. Letter, Zajączkowski to author, 30 May 1984.

137. Bartoszewski, *Blood Shed Unites Us*, 221-22.

CHAPTER SIX

1. Bartoszewski, *Blood Shed Unites Us*, 67, 171-72; Iranek-Osmecki, *He Who Saves One Life*, 181. The *Black Book* was published again in April 1942 and March 1943.

2. Ciechanowski, *Defeat in Victory*, 18, 101-02; memo of conversation of Welles, 25 March 1942, in *FRUS*, 3:130-31.

3. Depesza, Ministerstwo Spraw Zagranicznych do Szefa Sztabu N.W., 22 Apr. 1942, in *AKwD* 2:220-21.

4. Bartoszewski, *Blood Shed Unites Us*, 68; letter, Sikorski to Board of Deputies, 16 May 1942, in GSHI; Fox, "Jewish Factor in British War Crimes Policy," 87-88.

5. Laqueur, *Terrible Secret*, 109-12.

6. The Bund Report is reprinted in Bauer, "When Did They Know?" 57-58.

7. *New York Times*, 14 June 1942; 27 June 1942; 2 July 1942.

8. Bauer, "When Did They Know?" 52.

9. Ringelblum, *Notes from the Warsaw Ghetto*, 295.

10. *Polish Fortnightly Review*, 15 July 1942, 4-5.

11. General Sikorski's address, 9 June 1942, in FO371/31097/52481 C5951/ 954/55, PRO.

12. Protokol, Posiedzenia Rady Narodowej R.P., 7 July 1942, in A.5 2/32, GSHI; *Polish Fortnightly Review*, 15 July 1942, 3.

13. *Polish Fortnightly Review*, 15 July 1942, 4-8.

14. Bór-Komorowski, *Secret Army*, 101.

15. Depesza od N. [Korbońskiego], 26 July 1942, in A.9 III. 4/1, GSHI.

16. Depesza od N. [Korbońskiego], 11 Aug. 1942, in A.9 III. 4/2, GSHI. On 19 August 1942, Rowecki radioed military headquarters in London that the liquidation of the Warsaw Ghetto had resulted to that point in the deportation of 150,000 Jews, most of whom were murdered in Bełżec and Treblinka. Depesza, Rowecki do Centrali, 19 Aug. 1942, in *AKwD* 2:298.

17. Korboński, *Fighting Warsaw*, 253. Zaremba told a similar story: the killing of Jews in Tłuszcz was reported to London, and the Poles waited in vain for confirmation over the BBC. The story was disbelieved on the grounds that is was anti-Nazi propaganda. Zaremba, *Wojna i Konspiracja*, 127. Mikołajczyk addressed the same point in his memoirs: "As early as 1942 I had sent photographic evidence of the dead stacked like cordwood to the American and British press. They would not print the pictures. They could not believe them until their own men pressed into Dachau and Belsen." Mikołajczyk, *Rape of Poland*, 122.

18. Laqueur, *Terrible Secret*, 115.

19. *New York Times*, 29 July 1942. The release of the information to the Jewish Telegraphic Agency and the *New York Times* belies the claims of Gutman and Penkower that the Poles suppressed information concerning the deportation of Jews from the Warsaw Ghetto. For these erroneous claims, see Gutman, *Jews of Warsaw*, 266, 406-09; Penkower, *Jews Were Expendable*, 78.

20. Laqueur, *Terrible Secret*, 115-16.

21. *Polish Fortnightly Review*, 15 July 1942, 7-8.

22. Laqueur, *Terrible Secret*, 115.

23. Morse, *While Six Million Died*, 3ff.; Breitman and Kraut, "Who Was the Mysterious Stranger?" 44-47.

24. Letter, Cox to Ciechanowski with enclosures, 16 Sept. 1942; letter, Ciechanowski to Cox, 16 Sept. 1942, in Box 32, Ciechanowski Papers, HI. Also see Lewin, "Attempts at Rescuing European Jews," Part I, 3-23.

25. Karski, *Secret State*, 320ff.; Laqueur, *Terrible Secret*, 234.

26. *San Francisco Chronicle*, 29 Oct. 1981.

27. Ciołkosz, *Walka o Prawde*, 214-15; Sikorski's speech, 29 Oct. 1942, in A.XII.1/65A, GSHI.

28. Uchwała Rady Narodowej R.P. z 27 Listopada 1942r; Wniosek Nagły dr. I. Schwarcbarta in A.5/15 and 16; also see Przemowienie Wicepremiera Mikołajczyka na posiedzeniu Rady Narodowej Rz. P. w Londynie, GSHI; *Polish Fortnightly Review*, 1 Dec. 1942.

29. *Polish Fortnightly Review*, 1 Dec. 1942.

30. Notatka z Rozmowy Raczyńskiego z Ministrem w Edenem dnia 1 grudnia 1942, in A.12 49/14 PE I.10, GSHI; minutes by Roberts, 1 Dec. 1942, in FO371/30923/52481 C11923/61/18, PRO.

31. Letter, Razyński to Eden, 9 Dec. 1942, in FO371/30924/524/81 C/12313/61/18, PRO.

32. Letter, Sikorski to Welles, 12 Dec. 1942; letter, Welles to Sikorski, 18 Dec. 1942, in PRM. 161, GSHI.

33. Memo of conversation with attachment by Hull, 16 Dec. 1942, in RG 59, NA; Fox, "The Jewish Factor in British War Crimes Policy," 104. On 17 December and again on 20 December 1942, Raczyński gave two speeches condemning Nazi atrocities against the Jews. See Raczyński, *In Allied London*, 127. Premier Sikorski in a speech to the Overseas Press Club in New York said on 16 December 1942: "To realize the extent of the monstrous massacre of Jews, you must imagine the whole of Manhattan closed in by ghetto walls behind which all the Jews of the Western Hemisphere have been imprisoned and gradually and methodically exterminated in groups of several thousands daily by means of machine-gun shootings, or in lethal gas chambers or by electrocution." Address by Sikorski, 16 Dec. 1942, in PRM 89.32, GSHI.

34. *New York Times*, 12 June 1942; Gilbert, *Auschwitz and the Allies*, 50.

35. Memo, Harris to Churchill, 15 June 1942, in Air14/3507/52574, PRO.

36. Letter, Sikorski to Churchill, 22 June 1942, in PREM 4/100/13/52481; letter, Raczyński to Eden with enclosure, 27 June 1942, in FO371/31097/52481 C 6605/954/55, PRO.

37. Protokol, Posiedzenia Rady Narodowej R.P., 7 July 1942, in A.5.2.32, GSHI.

38. Letter, Raczyński to Eden with enclosure, 27 June 1942, in FO371/31097/52481 C6605/954/55, PRO; Ciechanowski, *Defeat in Victory*, 118. Garliński says that Flight Lieutenant S. Krol flew a plane to Poland on the night of 29 October 1942 with the objective of bombing Gestapo headquarters in Warsaw in revenge for Nazi terror against the Poles. He reached his target but did not release his payload for fear of killing innocent people. He dropped his bombs, instead, on Okęcie airfield. Garliński, *Poland, SOE, and the Allies*, 118-19.

39. Depesza, Delegat do Rządu w Londynie, [1942] in YIVO.

40. Depesza, Rowecki do N.W., 30 Sept. 1942, in Mark, *Powstanie w Getcie Warszawskim*, 190-91.

41. Message, Government Delegate to Polish Minister of Home Affairs (translation), 5 Dec. 1942, in FO371/31097, PRO.

42. Message, Sikorski to Churchill, 30 Dec. 1942, in FO371/34549 C34/34/G, PRO.

43. Aide Mémoire, Marecki to Marshall, 30 Dec. 1942, in RG 165, WDGS/NA.

44. Memo, Eden to Churchill, 2 Jan. 1943; memo, Portal to Churchill, 6 Jan. 1943, in PREM 3/351/4/52574, PRO.

45. Letter, Marshall to Sikorski, 31 Mar. 1943, in RG 165, WDGS/NA.

46. Quoted in Iranek-Osmecki, *He Who Saves One Life*, 208-09; letter by Zygielbojm, 7 Dec. 1942, in A.5/72, GSHI.

47. Quoted in letter, Dormer to Eden, 19 Jan. 1943, in FO371/34549 C728/34/55, PRO. The Poles submitted a leaflet to the British they wanted dropped over Berlin. It specifically referred to the mass murder of the Jews and the killing of Poles. The pamphlet made it clear that bombing of German targets was a reprisal for German crimes in Poland. One Foreign Office official sniffed; "Very amateurish." Since the British opposed the linkage between air bombardment of German targets and German crimes in Poland, Foreign Office officials marked through sections of the pamphlet that made this connection. Minute with copy of draft leaflet from Polish government, 9 Jan. 1943, in FO371/34549 C1149/34/G, PRO. By March 1943 the British dropped over Germany almost three million leaflets depicting German crimes in occupied countries. Minute by Roberts, 3 Mar. 1943, in FO371/24550, PRO.

48. Letter, Sikorski to Eden, 1 Feb. 1943; letter, Eden to Sikorski, 8 Feb. 1943; minute by Allen and Strang (attached); minute by Roberts with enclosure, 3 Feb. 1943, in FO371/34549 C1286/34/G and C1310/34/55, PRO.

49. Letter, Sikorski to Eden, 13 Feb. 1943; minute by Roberts, 18 Feb. 1943; letter, Eden to Sikorski, 27 Feb. 1943, in FO371/34549 C1797/34/G, PRO; Depesza, Sikorski do Roweckiego, 23 June 1943 in *AKwD* 3:34.

50. Aide Mémoire and annex, Polish Ministry of Foreign Affairs, 5 Aug. 1943; minute by Allen, 8 Aug. 1943, in FO371/34550 C8965/34/G55, PRO. The same aide mémoire was presented to the American government. See *FRUS*, 1943, 1:410-12. The declaration can be found in U.S. Department of State, *Bulletin* (4 Sept. 1943), 150.

51. Korboński, *Polish Underground State*, 130. The proposal to bomb the rail lines had been made several times by the Poles. Interview with Korboński, 7 June 1982.

52. Letter, with memo and maps, Marecki to Wedemeyer, 20 Feb. 1943, in RG 165, WDGS/NA.

53. Memorandum i załącznik, Zamoyski do Sikorskiego, 20 Jan. 1941. The enclosure is a letter, Peirse to Sikorski, 15 Jan. 1941; Depesza, Stem do Delegata, 20 Feb. 1943; Depesza, Orkan do Delegata, 24 Aug. 1943. in Teka Nr. 11, PUST.

54. Garliński, *Oświęcim Walczący*, 39ff. Laqueur says "the first more or less accurate report" of what was really happening at Auschwitz was published in September 1942. Laqueur, *Terrible Secret*, 111.

55. Wasserstein, *Britain and the Jews of Europe*, 309ff.; Penkower, *Jews Were Expendable*, 205. As in the case of attacks on railroad lines, the Polish underground did not have the resources to launch major attacks on prisons and camps on a scale vast enough to liberate even a fraction of the number of Jews and Poles housed in them. There were a number of escapes and rescues, but these were relatively small affairs. One GL unit is reputed to have freed 500 Jews from a camp at Janiszów. The AK rescued 348 Jews from a camp in Warsaw during the early days of the Warsaw Uprising of 1944. Wroński and Zwolakowa, *Polacy i Żydzi*, 143; Krakowski, *War of the Doomed*, 277.

56. Friedenson and Kranzler, *Heroine of Rescue*, 57-66.

57. Ibid., 66-68. Even before the war broke out, the Polish embassy in Vienna helped anti-Nazi Austrians and Jews to escape by issuing passports and visas. Woytak, *On the Border of War and Peace*, 14. Polish authorities even permitted personal messages, ordinarily forbidden in radio transmission, concerning the Jews. One representative message read: "Please find Esther Denenberg, recently at Rowne, ulica Legionów 7. If possible, smuggle her into Hungary." Iranek-Osmecki, *He Who Saves One Life*, 174.

58. Lewin, "Attempts at Rescuing European Jews," 4-7.

59. Depesza, Ullman do Szefa Kanc. Cywilnej Prezydenta R.P., 26 May 1942; List, Zaleski do Organizacji Rabinów Polskich w Tel Avivie, 29 May 1942; Posiedzenie Rady Narodowej, 22 Mar. 1943; Notataka w Sprawie Pomocy Krajowi, 3 June 1943, in A.18 10/C A.48. 4/2 II.24.A.5.3/57, GSHI; letter to Stephany, 11 Sept. 1942; letter, Schimitzek to Minister of Labor and Social Welfare, 30 Oct. 1943, in C11/7/3c/5 and C11/12/91, BOD; also see HO213/953, PRO.

60. Notatka, dla Gorkiego, 24 Jan. 1944; letter, Winter et al., to Midowicz, 18 Jan. 1944, in Sprawy Żydowskie-E, XI-4 and XI-8, GSHI.

61. Plenarne Posiedzenie Rady Narodowej, 1 Feb. 1943, in Kol. 1/43 (Sikorski Diary), GSHI.

62. *Polish Fortnightly Review*, 1 Dec. 1942.

63. This was one of the concerns of the American Jewish Congress to which the Polish government felt obliged to respond. List, Seyda do Sikorskiego, 7 June 1941, in PRM 57.3/11, GSHI.

64. Letter, Nowogrodsky to Scherer, 9 May 1944, in FO371/39524, C7711/7711/55, PRO.

65. Ze Sprawozdania Politycznego Delegatury M.P.K. w N. Yorku w dn. 15. XII. 1943, in PRM 142.2; Raport Specjalny, Kalski do Premiera, 25 May 1944, in A.9 III. 24/27, GSHI. The earliest statements about the democratic character of postwar Poland were made on 18 Dec. 1939 and 24 Feb. 1941. Even Schwarzbart pointed out the ineffectiveness of the Polish government in communicating its point of view to American Jews. Posiedzenie Rady Narodowej, 7 Jan. 1943, in A.5. 3/57, ibid.

66. Depesza dla Kukiela, 20 July 1943, in YIVO.

67. List, Zygielbojm do Raczkiewicza i Sikorskiego, 11 May 1943; Posiedzenie Rady Narodowej, 23 Dec. 1942, in A.5/72 and A.5.2/55, GSHI.

68. List, Teicher do Serafinskiego, 6 Sept. 1943, in Sprawy Żydowskie -E, XIII-3, GSHI; message, Representation of Polish Jewry in Tel Aviv to Schwarzbart, 26 July 1944, in FO371/39524 C11219/7711/55, PRO; Oświadczenie Doktora Jozefa Tennenbauma, 2 May 1945, in YIVO.

69. Statement of Rabbi Z. Babad on behalf of Polish Agudists in Great Britain, 25 May 1944, in C11/7/3c/8, BOD; Notatka, Romer dla Sikorskiego, 26 Aug. 1941, in Kol. 1/25 (Sikorski Diary), GSHI.

70. Statement by Sikorski, 16 Aug. 1942, in YIVO.

71. Memo, Knoll to Polish Government-in-Exile, Aug. 1943, quoted in Rin-

gelblum, *Polish-Jewish Relations*, 257; memo, Savery to Allen, 18 July 1944, in FO371/39524 C9465/7711/55, PRO. Savery observed: "The Amerian Jews are clearly out to keep all this property in Jewish hands. There is . . . no chance whatever that the Polish Government would agree to this suggestion, the result of which would certainly be to build up a state within a state in Poland."

72. Letter, Woliński to author, July 1984.

73. Letter, Lerski to author, 14 Dec. 1983.

74. Wroński and Zwolakowa, *Polacy i Żydzi*, 112.

75. Sprawozdanie Członka ZKN Mordechaja Tennenbauma o Utworzeniu Wiosna 1942 Bloku Antyfaszystowskiego w Getcie Warszawskim, in Mark, *Powstanie w Getcie Warszawskim*, 181-85.

76. These percentages are based on the estimated number of inhabitants in the Warsaw Ghetto before the uprising in the spring of 1943 and the number of Jewish resistance fighters. This suggests that even at this late date, the tradition of Jewish passivity still exerted a powerful influence among most Jews in Warsaw. See below. Ringelblum erroneously suggests that if the Jews had had the weapons at the time of the deportations "the Germans would have had to pay for the sea of Jewish blood shed." Ringelblum, *Polish-Jewish Relations*, 161. Even a strident critic of the Poles, Gutman, does not accept this view. He states that only after the deportations of the summer of 1942 did the attitude among Jewish inhabitants toward the idea of armed resistance change. See Gutman, *Jews of Warsaw*, 293.

77. Bartoszewski and Lewin, *Samaritans*, 16-17; letter, Barbarska to author, 8 June 1984; Mark, *Powstanie Getcie Warszawskim*, 196 n.1; Ainsztein, *Jewish Resistance in Nazi-Occupied Eastern Europe*, 602.

78. Bór, *Secret Army*, 99-100; Zakrzewski, "Przegląd Działalności Referatu Spraw Żydowskich, 12/44," in Mark, *Powstanie w Getcie Warszawskim*, 343; Wywiad-Rozmowa w Studium Polski Podziemnej, Miriam Nowicz z Gen. Bórem-Komorowskim w dniu 14 Maja 1954 roku, in YIVO. Zakrzewski was the nom de guerre of Woliński. Because the subject of AK aid to the Jews has become so highly politicized, I have used the above source in connection with the extensive letter Woliński sent to me in July 1984. There are several points in his letter that do not agree with the report published in Mark's work. Tadeusz Bednarczyk, connected with the Security Corps (KB) which was a part of the AK, alleged that leaders of the KB met Adam Czerniaków, head of the *Judenrat* in Warsaw, in January 1940, and tried to secure his support for Jewish armed resistance. The story has apparently not been confirmed. See Dawidowicz, *Holocaust and Historians*, 174 n.68.

79. Dawidowicz, *Holocaust and the Historians*, 121; Ainsztein, *Jewish Resistance in Nazi-Occupied Eastern Europe*, 584-91.

80. Letter, Woliński to author, July 1984.

81. Report, unsigned and undated, entitled "The Attitudde of the Secret Army Towards the Jews in Poland," in A. XII. 1/63, GSHI.

82. Kurzman, *The Bravest Battle*, 50.

83. Zakrzewski, "Przegląd Działalności Referatu Spraw Zydowskich, 12/44," in Mark, *Powstanie w Getcie Warszawskim*, 344.

84. Letter, Woliński to author, July 1984.

85. Zakrzewski, "Przegląd Działalności Refertau Spraw Żydowskich, 12/ 44," in Mark, *Powstanie Getcie Warszawskim*, 344.

86. Bartoszewski and Lewin, *Samaritans*, 31-32; Gutman, *Jews of Warsaw*, 298.

87. Bartoszewski and Lewin, *Samaritans*, 31-32; Bartoszewski, *Blood Shed Unites Us*, 120.

88. Depesza od Roweckiego, 7 Jan. 1943, in PUST. A spurious version of this message, which revealed an obvious tendentiousness, was published in Mark's *Powstanie w Getcie Warszawskim* and read: "Jews of various Communist groups turn to us for weapons."

89. Gutman, *Jews of Warsaw*, 320. Bartoszewski says the January 1943 resistance of the Jews "had a decisive effect" on increasing Polish material assistance to the ghetto. Bartoszewski, *Blood Shed Unites Us*, 124.

90. Komisja Historyczna Polskiego Sztabu Głownego w Londynie, *PSZ* 3:326-27. The list of arms and munitions of Major Stanisław Weber, chief of staff to the head of the AK in Warsaw, differs slightly from that contained in the *PSZ*. For example, Weber includes ten rifles but only fifty pistols. He also includes two Sten guns instead of one. Weber gives a more detailed account of other items. For example, he says the AK gave 30 kg. of plastic explosives of British manufacture, 15 kg. of plastic explosives in various bombs, 120 kg. of *szedyt* for the production of hand grenades, 400 detonators for grenades, 30 kg. of potassium for the manufacture of Molotov cocktails, and a large quantity of saltpeter for the production of black powder. Quoted in Iranek-Osmecki, *He Who Saves One Life*, 155.

91. Bartoszewski and Lewin, *Samaritans*, 31-32; Arczyński, *Kryptonim Żegota*, 144.

92. Wroński and Zwolakowa, *Polacy i Żydzi*, 165; Ainsztein, *Jewish Resistance in Nazi-Occupied Eastern Europe*, 613.

93. Ainsztein, *Jewish Resistance in Nazi-Occupied Eastern Europe*, 600.

94. Tabela Nr. V do Rozdziału F, Meldunek Organizacyjny, 1 Mar. 1943, in *AKwD* 2:450-51.

95. Schwarzbart, *Story of the Warsaw Ghetto Uprising*, 7.

96. Komisja Historyczna, *PSA* 3:323, 325, 479; Bór, *Secret Army*, 78.

97. Ciołkosz, "Broń dla getta Warszawy," 31.

98. Letter, Woliński to author, July 1984; Wywiad-Rozmowa w Studium Polski Podziemnej, Miriam Nowicz z Gen. Bórem-Komorowskim w dniu 14 Maja 1954 roku, in YIVO; Borwicz, "Factors Influencing the Relations," 347. Some sources refer to a controversial letter from the head of the Jewish Fighting Organization, Anielewicz, which scored Polish indifference and demanded large-scale aid to the ghetto before the April uprising. There are good grounds for suspecting the authenticity of the message. See List Anielewicza w Sprawie Broni Oraz Samoobronie Marcowej, 13 Mar. 1943, in Mark, *Powstanie w Getcie Warszawskim*, 222. For a discussion questioning its authenticity, see Iranek-Osmecki, *He Who Saves One Life*, 156-58.

99. Bartoszewski, *Blood Shed Unites Us*, 119; Karski, *Story of a Secret State*, 328-29; Radiogram do Londynu o Wybuchu Powstania w Getcie, 20 Apr. 1943, in Mark, *Powstanie w Getcie Warszawskim*, 315-16.

100. Mark suggests that Anielewicz did indeed hope the Jewish insurrection would result in a citywide insurrection in Warsaw. Mark, *Powstanie w Getcie Warszawskim*, 41; letter, Woliński to author, July 1984.

101. Ibid.; Zakrzewski, "Przegląd Działalności Referaty Spraw Żydowskich, 12/44," in Mark, *Powstanie w Getcie Warszawskim*, 346-47.

102. Gutman, *Jews of Warsaw*, 417.

103. See Chapter 7 below.

104. Gutman, *Jews of Warsaw*, 410-11, 417, 419.

105. Mark, *Powstanie w Getcie Warszawskim*, 41; Stroop, *Stroop Report*, 7.

106. Gutman, *Jews of Warsaw*, 365; Ainsztein, *Jewish Resistance*, 621. Polish sources at the time estimated that 1,500 Jews participated in armed action. Mark, *Powstanie w Getcie Warszawskim*, 286. Steinberg estimates that there were 2,000 Jewish combatants. See Steinberg, *The Jews against Hitler*, 194.

107. The 70,000 figure is accepted by Steinberg and Ainsztein. Steinberg, *Jews against Hitler*, 194; Ainsztein, *Jewish Resistance*, 621ff.; Gutman, *Jews of Warsaw*, 395. Bartoszewski estimates there were 60,000 Jews in the ghetto before the uprising. Bartoszewski, *Blood Shed Unites Us*, 128.

108. Depesza od Korbońskiego, 20 Apr. 1943, in PUST; Bartoszewski and Lewin, *Samaritans*, 41-42. Jewish critics, like Schwarzbart, have suggested that the reason for Sikorski's delay in making his statement was because he was apprehensive that it would meet with hostility from Poland's anti-Semitic population. Bór challenged Schwarzbart's claim, saying his explanation was "sucked out of his finger." Bór suggested that any public appeal to the Poles was dangerous because it made the Nazis more vigilant and made it more difficult for the Poles to maintain contact with the Jews in the ghetto. Schwarzbart, *Story of the Warsaw Ghetto Uprising*, 12. Bór's rejoinder can be found in Wywiad-Rozmowa w Studium Polski Podziemnej, Miriam Nowicz w Gen. Bórem-Komorowskim w dniu 14 Maja 1954 roku, in YIVO. Bór made a valid point since there was a substantial number of arrests and terrorization of the Poles by the Germans during the uprising. See Depesza, Rowecki do Centrali, 28 May 1943, in *AKwD* 3:24.

109. Korboński, *Fighting Warsaw*, 261-62.

110. Representative articles can be found in *Biuletyn Informacyjny*, 29 Apr. 1943; *Rzeczpospolita Polska*, 5 May 1943; *WRN*, 7 May 1943; *Nowe Drogi*, 20 June 1943.

111. Ringelblum, *Polish-Jewish Relations*, 184-85.

112. Interview with Korboński, 7 June 1982; interview with Pelagia Łukaszewska, 10 July 1983; Depesza Organizacji Żydowskich do Centrali, 4 May 1943, in *AKwD* 3:4; Radiogram do Londynu o Wybuchu Powstania w Getcie, 20 Apr. 1943; List b. komendanta OW AK Generala Antoniego Chruściela na temat Pomocy Walczącemu Gettu, 25 Jan. 1958, in Mark, *Powstanie w Getcie Warszawskim*, 274; Raport, Likwidacja Ghetta Warszawskiego, in A.48.4/2II.14, GSHI; message, Stroop to Krueger, 26 Apr. 1943 in *Stroop Report*.

113. Bednarczyk, "35 Rocznica Powstania w Getcie Warszawskim," 9.

114. Ibid.; Bartoszewski, *Blood Shed Unites Us*, 124ff.; Bartoszewski and Lewin, *Samaritans*, 39; Kurzman, *Bravest Battle*, 51ff.

115. Message, Stroop to Higher SS and Police Leader East, 23 Apr. 1943, in *Stroop Report*.

116. Iranek-Osmecki, *He Who Saves One Life*, 164.

117. Arczyński, *Kryptonim Żegota*, 154-55.

118. Ainsztein, *Jewish Resistance*, 660.

119. Ringelblum, *Polish-Jewish Relations*, 181.

120. Arczyński, *Kryptonim Żegota*, 155. Woliński coordinated and organized private assistance by members of the high command of the AK to Jewish survivors of the uprising. He reported that as of 1 Aug. 1944, there were 283 Jews sheltered by members of the AK. Letter, Woliński to author, July 1984. Jewish survivors of the uprising must have been favorably disposed toward the AK or they would not have supported the Poles against the Germans during the Warsaw Uprising of August-September 1944. See Depesza od Korbońskiego, 17 Aug. 1944, in T 13a, PUST.

121. Depesza, Rowecki do Centrali, 18 May 1943; Meldunek Zbiorowy, Rowecki do Centrali, 28 May 1943, in *AKwD* 3:13, 18-19. Jewish writers who are critical of the AK and the Polish government-in-exile noticeably avoid comment about the lack of Soviet assistance to the Jewish resistance.

122. Stroop, *Stroop Report*.

123. Krakowski, *War of the Doomed*, 213-14.

CHAPTER SEVEN

1. Instructions to Delegate of the Government in Poland and the Commander of the Home Army in General Sikorski Historical Institute, *DPSR* 2:68-71.

2. Depesza, Bór do N.W., 26 Nov. 1943, in *AKwD* 3:209-13.

3. Depesza, Sosnkowski do Komorowskiego, 12 Feb. 1944; Depesza, Sosnkowski do Komorowskiego, 20 Feb. 1944, in ibid., 278-79, 284-85.

4. Komisja Historyczna, *PSZ* 3:593-99, 601-28, 632-45.

5. Depesza, Bór do Sosnkowskiego, 30 Mar. 1944; Depesza, Mikołajczyk do Delegata Rządu, 12 Apr. 1944; message, Mikołajczyk to Churchill, 18 July 1944, in *AKwD* 3:386, 399-400, 563-64.

6. Depesza, Mikołajczyk do Delegata Rządu, 4 July 1944; Depesza, Delegat Rządu do Mikołajczyk, 12 July 1944, in ibid., 497, 527-28.

7. Letter, with enclosure, Williams to Eden, 5 Oct. 1944, in FO 371/39413/ 52538 C13829/8/55, PRO.

8. Order of Commander of Home Army to the Districts of the latter, 12 July 1944, in General Sikorski Historical Institute, *DPSR* 2:284.

9. Depesza, Sosnkowski do Komorowskiego, 7 July 1944 in *AKwD* 3:504-06.

10. Borkiewicz, *Powstanie Warszawskie*, 38-39.

11. Korboński, *Fighting Warsaw*, 346-47.

12. Zagorski, *Seventy Days*, 19.

13. Korboński, *Fighting Warsaw*, 350; Gunther Deschner, *Warsaw Uprising*, 22.

14. Korboński, *Fighting Warsaw*, 346-47; Bór, *Secret Army*, 207.

15. Krannhals, *Warschauer Aufstand*, 119.

16. Komisja Historyczna, *PSZ* 3:697-98; Krannhals, *Warschauer Aufstand*, 122-23.

17. *Biuletyn Informacyjny*, 25 Sept. 1944.

18. Ostaszewski, *Powstanie Warszawskie*, 36.

19. Sawicki, *Przed Polskim Prokuratorem*, 113.

20. Mikołajczyk, *Rape of Poland*, 68; Borkiewicz, *Powstanie Warszawskie*, 35.

21. Ostaszewski, *Powstanie Warszawskie*, 29-30.

22. Strzetelski, *Bitwa o Warszawe*, 16.

23. Duchess of Atholl, *Tragedy of Warsaw*, 9.

24. Transcripts of these radio broadcasts appear in translation in message, Winant to Secretary of State, 6 Sept. 1944, in DS/NA.

25. The circumstances surrounding the decision to rise up against the Germans is extensively treated in Ciechanowski, *Powstanie Warszawskie*.

26. Orska, *Silent Is the Vistula*, 1ff.

27. Taub, "Warsaw Tragedy," 17, 79.

28. Korboński, *Fighting Warsaw*, 352-53.

29. Bór, *Secret Army*, 215.

30. Ibid., 252; Zagorski, *Seventy Days*, 151.

31. Bór, *Secret Army*, 216.

32. Kirchmayer, *Powstanie Warszawskie*, 139, 166; Borkiewicz, *Powstanie Warszawskie*, 29-31, 37-41; Przygoński, *Z Problematyki Powstania Warszawskiego* 55-56; Krannhals, *Warschauer Afstand*, 120. Krannhals's figure of 12,000 German troops seems low. He does not count assorted units of the Bahnschutz, Werkschutz, etc. Neither does he count troops at other installations just as close to Warsaw as Bielany and Okęcie, which he does include in his calculations.

33. Krannhals, *Warschauer Aufstand*, 108-10.

34. Ibid., 108.

35. Bartelski, *Mokotów*, 229-33.

36. Ibid., 162-66.

37. Krannhals, *Warschauer Aufstand*, 109; Bór, *Secret Army*, 238-39; Bartelski, *Mokotów*, 75-76.

38. Podlewski, *Przemarsz Przez Piekło*, 120.

39. Krannhals, *Warschauer Aufstand*, 110.

40. Ciechanowski, *Powstanie Warszawskie*, 287-93, 306.

41. Pomian, *Warsaw Rising*, 2, 4.

42. Zawodny, *Nothing but Honour*, 155.

43. Ibid., 156-57.

44. Ibid., 165.

45. Krannhals, *Warschauer Aufstand*, 119.

46. Interrogation of General Erich von dem Bach-Zelewski in IMT/NA.

47. Ibid.

48. Deschner, *Warsaw Uprising*, 12.

49. Datner, "Destruction of Warsaw," 121.

50. Interrogation of Bach-Zelewski, IMT/NA.

51. Datner, "Destruction of Warsaw," 121.

52. Krannhals, *Warschauer Aufstand*, 124.

53. Interrogation of Bach-Zelewski, IMT/NA.

54. Krannhals, *Warschauer Aufstand*, 119; Kirchmayer, *Powstanie Warszawskie*, 165.

55. Krannhals, *Warschauer Aufstand*, 103-05; Kirchmayer, *Powstanie Warszawskie*, 158-59.

56. Interrogation of Bach-Zelewski, IMT/NA; Sawicki, *Przed Polskim Prokuratorem*, 68, 340, 342; Reitlinger, *SS: Alibi of a Nation*, 372-73, 377.

57. Krannhals, *Warshauer Aufstand*, 122-27.

58. Ibid., 131-32.

59. *TWC*, 13:514, 527-29, 537-38; Stein, *Waffen SS*, 266-69.

60. Dallin, "The Kamiński Brigade," 1-2.

61. Ibid., 48-49; interrogation of Bach-Zelewski, IMT/NA.

62. Iranek-Osmecki, "Przyczynki do Powstania Warszawskiego," 101-04.

63. Dallin, "Kamiński Brigade," 50.

64. Krannhals, *Warschauer Aufstand*, 134.

65. U.S. Counsel, *Nazi Conspiracy and Aggression, Supplement A, 800-801.*

66. *Harris, Tyranny on Trial*, 201-03.

67. U.S. Counsel, *Nazi Conspiracy and Aggression*, Supplement A, 803-04.

68. Wroniszewski, *Ochota*, 142, 149-50.

69. Ibid., 151, 165.

70. Ibid., 162-63, 166-67.

71. Interrogation of Bach-Zelewski, IMT/NA.

72. Quoted in Harris, *Tyranny on Trial*, 203-04.

73. Wroniszewski, *Ochota*, 134-41.

74. Reitlinger, *SS*, 375-76.

75. Dallin, "Kamiński Brigade," 51-52.

76. Luczak, "Aktion Warschau" 163-66.

77. Korboński, *Fighting Poland*, 373-74.

78. Interrogation of Bach-Zelewski, IMT/NA.

79. Ibid.

80. Krannhals, *Warschauer Aufstand*, 140.

81. *TWC* 15:298; Reitlinger, *SS*, 376.

82. Interrogation of Bach-Zelewski, IMT/NA; Dallin, "Kamiński Brigade," 57-58; Wroniszewski, *Ochota*, 238.

83. Wroniszewski, *Ochota*, 236-37; interrogation of Bach-Zelewski, IMT/NA.

84. Guderian, *Panzer Leader*, 256; Sawicki, *Przed Polskim Prokuratorem*,

106-07. Guderian, who disliked Bach-Zelewski, claimed that whatever restraint and humanity the Germans showed the Poles during the uprising was due to his influence, not Bach-Zelewski's.

85. Interrogation of Bach-Zelewski, IMT/NA; Kirchmayer, *Powstanie Warszawskie*, 284ff.

86. Ibid.

87. Bór, *Secret Army*, 279-80; Pomian, *Warsaw Rising*, 12, 19, 29; Bór-Komorowski, "The Unconquerables," 148.

88. General Sikorski Historical Institute, *DPSR* 2:360.

89. Borkiewicz, *Powstanie Warszawskie*, 33-35.

90. Lukas, "The RAF and the Warsaw Uprising," 192, 194.

91. Interrogation of Bach-Zelewski, IMT/NA; Pomian, *Warsaw Rising*, xi.

92. Borowy, *Okres Powstania 1944r. w. Bibliotece Uniwersyteckiej w Warszawie*, 11-12.

93. Bór, *Secret Army*, 301-02.

94. Interrogation of Bach-Zelewski, IMT/NA.

95. Ibid.

96. Records of German Field Command Armies, AOK 9, Kriegstagebuch Nr. 11, NA.

97. Iranek-Osmecki, *Unseen and Silent*, 242-43.

98. Bór, *Secret Army*, 286, 289.

99. Ibid., 316-17.

100. Message, Bach-Zelewski to Commander, Army Group Middle, 29 Aug. 1944, in AOK 9/NA.

101. Message, Bach-Zelewski to Commander, Army Group Middle, 29 Aug. 1944, in ibid.; interrogation of Bach-Zelewski, IMT/NA.

102. Margules, *Przyczółki Warszawskie*, 47 n.18; Heiber, *Hitler's Lagebesprechungen*, 626-27.

103. Iranek-Osmecki, *Unseen and Silent*, 222-36.

104. Interrogation of Bach-Zelewski, IMT/NA.

105. U.S. Counsel, *Nazi Conspiracy and Aggression*, Supplement A, 802-03.

106. AOK 9/NA; Pomian, *Warsaw Rising*, 20-22.

107. Korboński, *Fighting Warsaw*, 387.

108. Pomian, *Warsaw Rising*, 22-23.

109. See messages between Bór and Rohr and Bór and Reinhardt in AOK 9/NA.

110. Bruce, *Warsaw Uprising*, 192.

111. Krannhals, *Warschauer Aufstand*, 154-57.

112. Bór, *Secret Army*, 342-43; Kirchmayer, *Powstanie Warszawskie*, 504-05; Rokossovsky says the Soviet Air Force flew 4,821 sorties—2,535 of them with supplies—on behalf of the insurgents during the period 13 September-1 October. Rokossovsky, *A Soldier's Duty*, 261.

113. Pomian, *Warsaw Rising*, 23, 25.

114. AOK 9/NA; Krannhals, *Warschauer Aufstand*, 155-61; Bruce, *Warsaw*

Uprising, 191-92. The Russians blamed much of the failure of Berling's troops on the AK. Rokossovsky, *Soldier's Duty*, 262.

115. Krannhals, *Der Warschauer Aufstand*, 162.

116. Pełczyński, "O Powstaniu Warszawskim," 3-16; Bór, *Secret Army*, 345-47.

117. Letter, with report, Anderson to Spaatz, 9 Oct. 1944, in Spaatz Papers, Box 182, in Manuscript Division, Library of Congress; Daily Int/Tops Summary No. 243, Allied Expeditionary Force in USAF Historical Archives, Maxwell AFB, Ala,; Strzetelski, *Bitwa o Warszawe*, 122. Before Stalin gave his consent to the United States to use Soviet air bases, Harry Hopkins, Roosevelt's advisor, was against getting involved in helping the Poles for fear of jeopardizing United States-Soviet relations. Hopkins told on AAF officer that he would even withhold cables from Churchill to Roosevelt because the prime minister was urging him to send a supply mission to the Poles. See Lukas, *Strange Allies*, 80-81.

118. Krannhals, *Warschauer Aufstand*, 166-67.

119. Bór, *Secret Army*, 359. See messages on conditions in Warsaw in Pomian, *Warsaw Rising*, 17-34.

120. *New Statesman and Nation*, 2 Sept. 1944, 148.

121. Bruce, *Warsaw Uprising*, 197.

122. Ibid., 198-200; Kliszko, *Powstanie Warszawskie*, 77, 302-14; Sawicki, *Przed Polskim Prokuratorem*, 63-64.

123. Bór, *Secret Army*, 362-63; Pomian, *Warsaw Rising*, 35.

124. Interrogation of Bach-Zelewski, IMT/NA; AOK 9/NA.

125. Bór, *Secret Army*, 361-81; Sawicki, *Przed Polskim Prokuratorem*, 62-68; Pomian, *Warsaw Rising*, 80-81.

126. Interrogation of Bach-Zelewski, IMT/NA.

127. Komisja Historyczna, *PSZ* 3:819, 824. An additional 600 casualties in the Kampinos Forest raise the total to 22,200.

128. Interrogation of Bach-Zelewski, IMT/NA.

129. Krannhals, *Warschauer Aufstand*, 215; Kirchmayer, *Powstanie Warszawskie*, 424.

AFTERWORD

1. Gardner, review of *Sophie's Choice*, 16-17.

2. Nordon, review of *Poland*, 43.

3. Rosenfeld and Greenberg, *Confronting the Holocaust*, 8ff.

4. *Encyclopedia Judaica*, 8:890.

5. Dawidowicz, *Holocaust and Historians*, 141.

6. Friedman, *Roads to Extinction*, 559; Lichten, review of *Roads to Extinction*, 216-19.

BIBLIOGRAPHY

ARCHIVAL MATERIALS

United States

Franklin D. Roosevelt Library, Hyde Park, New York
　　The Biddle Report

Hoover Institution on War, Revolution, and Peace, Stanford, California
　　Jan Ciechanowski Papers
　　Stanisław Mikołajczyk Papers

Library of Congress, Washington, D.C.
　　Carl Spaatz Papers

National Archives, Washington, D.C.
　Records of:
　　German Field Command Armies
　　International Military Tribunal
　　Office of Strategic Services
　　Reich Leader of the SS and Chief of the German Police
　　United States Department of State
　　War Department General Staff

United States Air Force Historical Archives, Maxwell Air Force Base, Alabama
　　Miscellaneous Files

YIVO Institute for Jewish Research, New York, New York
　　Zylberberg Collection

Great Britain

Anglo-Jewish Association, London
　　Files relating to Jews and Poles

Board of Deputies of British Jews, London
　　Files relating to Jews and Poles

General Sikorski Historical Institute, London (now Polish Institute and General Sikorski Historical Museum)
Archiwa:
    Ambasady Polskiej (Londyn)
    Ministerstwa Spraw Wewnętrznych
    Naczelnego Wodza
    Prezesa Rady Ministrów
    Prezydenta R.P.
    Rady Narodowej
    Spraw Żydowskich

Polish Underground Study Trust, London
    Akta dotyczące Spraw Żydowskich
    Akta zawierające Depesze wymieniane pomiędzy
    Polskim Rządem w Londynie i Polskimi
    Władzami Podziemnymi.

Public Record Office, Kew, Richmond
Records of:
    Air Ministry
    Foreign Office
    Home Office
    Prime Minister's Office
    War Cabinet

Poland

Central Archives, Central Committee of the Polish United Workers Party, Warsaw
    Archiwum Żydowskie

INTERVIEWS

Helena Chorażyczewska, 17 Sept. 1984
Rachel and Karol Cymber, 18 July 1983
Joseph Friedenson, 13 June 1984
Staszek Jackowski, 30 July 1984
Rev. Jan Januszewski, 1 Aug. 1982
Stefan Korboński, 7 June 1982
Dr. Joseph Kutrzeba, 17 Sept. 1984
Pelagia Łukaszewska, 10 July 1983
Stanisław Makuch, 17 Sept. 1984
Michalina Tuśkiewicz, 18 Sept. 1984

CORRESPONDENCE

E. Barbarska, June 8, 1984.
Zofia Gruszczyńska, 12 Oct. 1982

Jan Karski, 12 Nov. 1982
George Lerski, 14 Dec. 1983
Count Edward Raczyński, 21 June 1984
Wenceslas Wagner, 20 Nov. 1982
Henryk Woliński, July 1984
Wacław Zajączkowski, 5 June 1984

UNPUBLISHED MANUSCRIPTS, PUBLISHED DOCUMENTS, OFFICIAL HISTORIES

American Jewish Commission on the Holocaust. "American Jewry during the Holocaust." 1984.
———. "Interim Report." 1984.
Apenszlak, Jacob ed. *The Black Book of Polish Jewry*. New York: Roy Publishers, 1943.
Bacon, Gershon Chaim. "Agudath Israel in Poland, 1916-1939: An Orthodox Jewish Response to the Challenge of Modernity." Ph.D. diss., Columbia University, 1979.
Central Commission for Investigation of German Crimes in Poland. *German Crimes in Poland*. 2 vols. New York: Howard Fertig, 1982.
Dallin, Alexander. "The Kamiński Brigade: A Case Study of German Military Exploitation of Soviet Disaffection." Unpublished manuscript. Study for Human Resources Research Institute, Air University, Maxwell Air Force Base, Alabama, 1952.
General Sikorski Historical Institute. *Documents on Polish-Soviet Relations, 1939-1945*. 2 vols. London: Heinemann, 1961-67.
Heiber, Helmut, ed. *Hitler's Lagebesprechugen: Die Protokollframente Seiner Militarischen Konferenzen, 1942-1945*. Stuttgart: Deutsche Verlags-Anstalt, 1962.
Komisja Historyczna Polskiego Sztabu Głownego w Londynie. *Polskie Siły Zbrojne w Drugiej Wojnie Światowej*. vol. 3, *Armia Krajowa*. London: Instytut Historyczny im. Gen Sikorskiego, 1950.
Polish Ministry of Information. *The Black Book of Poland*. New York: G.P. Putnam's Sons, 1942.
Polish Research Center. *German Failures in Poland*. London, 1942.
Pomian, Andrzej, ed. *The Warsaw Rising: A Selection of Documents*. London, 1945.
Republic of Poland. *German Occupation of Poland: Extract of Note Addressed to the Allied and Neutral Powers*. New York: Greystone Press, 1942. (Cited as *Polish White Book.*)
———. *Polish-Soviet Relations, 1918-1943: Official Documents*. Washington, D.C. [1943].
Sawicki, Jerzy. *Przed Polskim Prokuratorem: Dokumenty i Komentarze*. Warsaw: Iskry, 1958.

Studium Polski Podiemnej. *Armia Krajowa w Dokumentach, 1939-945.* 4 vols. London: Studium Polski Podziemnej, 1970-77.

Trial of the Major War Criminals before the International Military Tribunal. 42 vols. Nuremberg, 1947-49.

Trials of War Criminals before the Nuernberg Military Tribunals under Control Council Law No. 10, Nuernberg, October 1946-April 1949. 15 vols. Washington, D.C.: G.P.O., 1949-53.

U.S. Department of State. *The Department of State Bulletin,* 1942-1944.

————. *Foreign Relations of the United States: Diplomatic Papers, 1939.* Vol. 1, *General.* Vol. 2, *General, the British Commonwealth and Europe.* Washington, D.C.: G.P.O., 1956.

————. *Foreign Relations of the United States: Diplomatic Papers, 1941.* Vol. 1, *General: The Soviet Union.* Washington, D.C.: G.P.O., 1958.

————. *Foreign Relations of the United States: Diplomatic Papers, 1942.* Vol. 1, *The British Commonwealth, The Far East.* Vol. 3, *Europe.* Washington, D.C.: G.P.O., 1960, 1961.

————. *Foreign Relations of the United States: Diplomatic Papers, 1943.* Vol. 1, *General.* Vol. 3, *The British Commonwealth, Eastern Europe, the Far East.* Washington, D.C.: G.P.O., 1963.

U.S. Office of United States Chief of Counsel for Prosecution of Axis Criminality. *Nazi Conspiracy and Aggression.* 10 vols. Washington, D.C.: G.P.O., 1946.

MEMOIRS, AUTOBIOGRAPHIES, RECOLLECTIONS

Aleksandrowicz, Julian. *Kartk: z Dziennika doktora Twardego.* Cracow: Wydawnictwo Literackie, 1962.

Anders, W. *An Army in Exile: The Story of the Second Polish Corps.* London: Macmillan, 1949.

Bezwińska, Jadwiga, and Czech, Danuta, comps. *KL Auschwitz Seen by the SS: Hoss, Broad, Kremer.* Auschwitz: Publications of Państwowe Muzeum w Oświęcimu, 1972.

Bór-Komorowski, T. *The Secret Army.* New York: Macmillan co., 1951.

Cannistraro, Philip, et al., eds., *Poland and the Coming of the Second World War: The Diplomatic Papers of A.J. Drexel Biddle, Jr., United States Ambassador to Poland, 1937-1939.* Columbus: Ohio State Uni. Press, 1976.

Chciuk, Andrzej, ed. *Saving the Jews in War-Torn Poland, 1939-1945.* Victoria, Australia: Wilke and Co., 1969.

Churchill, Winston S. *Closing the Ring.* Boston: Houghton Mifflin and Co., 1951.

Ciechanowski, Jan. *Defeat in Victory.* Garden City, N.Y.: Doubleday and Co., 1947.

Gładysz, Antoni. *Piekło Na Ziemi: Wspomniennia z lat 1939-1945.* Doylestown, Pa.: Nakładem Wydawnictwo Promyk, 1972.

Guderian, Heinz. *Panzer Leader.* Trans. Constantine Fitzgibbon. New York: E.P. Dutton and Co., 1952.

Hilberg, Raul, et al. *The Warsaw Diary of Adam Czerniaków: Prelude to Doom.* New York: Stein and Day, 1979.

Hirszfeld, Ludwik. *Historia Jednego Życia.* Warsaw: Pax, 1957.

Hull, Cordell. *The Memoirs of Cordell Hull.* 2 vols. New York: Macmillan, 1948.

Iranek-Osmecki, George, trans. *The Unseen and Silent: Adventures from the Underground Movement Narrated by Paratroops of the Polish Home Army.* London: Sheed and Ward, 1954.

Jędrzejewicz, Wacław, ed. *Diplomat in Paris, 1936-1939: Papers and Memoirs of Juliusz Łukasiewicz, Ambassador of Poland.* New York: Columbia Univ. Press, 1970.

Karski, Jan. *Story of a Secret State.* Boston: Houghton Mifflin Co., 1944.

Korboński, Stefan. *Fighting Warsaw: The Story of the Polish Underground State, 1939-1945.* Trans. F.B. Czarnomski. n.p.: Minerva Press, 1968.

Korczak, Janusz. *The Warsaw Ghetto Memoirs of Janusz Korczak.* Trans. E.P. Kulawiec. Washington, D.C.: Univ. Press of America, 1979.

Kot, Stanisław. *Conversations with the Kremlin and Dispatches from Russia.* Trans. H.C. Stevens. London: Oxford University Press, 1963.

Kozłowski, Adam. *Ucisk i Strapienie: Pamiętnik Więźnia, 1939-1945.* Cracow: Wydawnictwo Apostolstwa Modlitwy, 1967.

Kukiel, Marian. *General Sikorski: Żolnierz i Mąż Stanu Polski Walczącej.* London: Instytut Polski, 1970.

Kulkielko, Renya. *Escape from the Pit.* New York: Sharon Books, 1947.

Lenz, John M. *Christ in Dachau or Christ Victorious.* Vienna: Missionsdruckerei St. Gabriel, 1960.

Lerski, Jerzy. *Emisariusz 'Jur.'* London: Polish Cultural Foundation, 1984.

Malak, O. Henryk Maria. *Klechy w Obozach Smierci.* 2 vols. London: Veritas, n.d.

Mikołajczyk, Stanisław. *The Rape of Poland: Pattern of Soviet Aggression.* New York: McGraw-Hill, 1948.

Miłosz, Czesław. *Nobel Lecture.* New York: Farrar, Straus, Giroux, 1980.

Mitkiewicz, Leon. *Z Gen. Sikorskim na Obczyźnie.* Paris: Instytut Literacki, 1968.

Nicolson, Harold. *The War Years, 1939-1945.* Vol. 2, *Diaries and Letters.* Ed. Nigel Nicolson. New York: Atheneum, 1967.

Nowak, Jan. *Courier from Warsaw.* Detroit, Mich.: Wayne State Univ. Press, 1982.

Orska, Irene. *Silent Is the Vistula: The Story of the Warsaw Uprising.* Trans. Marta Erdman. New York: Longmans, Green and Co., 1946.

Pat, Jacob. *Ashes and Fire.* New York: International Universities Press, 1947.

Pinkus, Oscar. *The House of Ashes.* Cleveland, Ohio: World Publishing Co., 1964.

Pomian, John, ed. *Jozef Retinger: Memoirs of an Eminence Grise.* Sussex, 1972.

Raczyński, Edward. *In Allied London.* London: Weidenfeld and Nicolson, 1962.

Ringelblum, Emmanuel. *Notes from the Warsaw Ghetto: The Journal of Emmanuel Ringelblum.* Ed. and trans. Jacob Sloan. New York: McGraw-Hill, 1958.

————. *Polish-Jewish Relations during the Second World War*. Ed. Joseph Kermish and Shmuel Krakowski. New York: Howard Fertig, 1976.

Rokossovsky, K. *A Soldier's Duty*. Moscow: Progress Publishers, 1970.

Rudnicki, K.S. *The Last of the War Horses*. London: Bachman and Turner, 1974.

Shatyn, Bruno. *A Private War: Surviving in Poland on False Papers, 1941-1945*. Trans. Oscar E. Swan. Detroit, Mich.: Wayne State Univ. Press, 1985.

Sosnkowski, Kazimierz. *Materiały Historyczne*. London: Gryf Publications, 1966.

Staden, Wendelgard von. *Darkness over the Valley: Growing Up in Nazi Germany*. New Haven, Conn.: Ticknor and Fields, 1981.

Stroop, Juergen. *The Stroop Report: The Jewish Quarter of Warsaw Is No More!* Trans. Sybil Morton. New York: Pantheon Books, 1979.

Sweet-Escott, Bickham. *Baker Street Irregular*. London: Methuen and Co., 1965.

Tec, Nechama. *Dry Tears: The Story of a Lost Childhood*. New York: Oxford Univ. Press, 1984.

Zadrożny, Stanisław. *Tu-Warszawa: Dzieje Radiostacji Powstanczej 'Błyskawica.'* London: Nakładem Księgarni Orbis, 1964.

Zagorski, W. *Seventy Days*. Trans. John Welsh. London: Frederick Muller, 1957.

Zaremba, Zygmunt. *Wojna i Konspiracja*. London: B. Świderski, 1957.

SECONDARY WORKS

Ainsztein, Reuben. *Jewish Resistance in Nazi-Occupied Eastern Europe*. New York: Barnes and Noble, 1974.

Arczyński, Marek, and Balcerak, Wiesław. *Kryptonim Żegota: Z Dziejów Pomocy Żydom w Polsce, 1939-1945*. Warsaw: Czytelnik, 1983.

Arendt, Hannah. *Eichmann in Jerusalem: A Report on the Banality of Evil*. New York: Viking Press, 1963.

Atholl, Duchess of. *The Tragedy of Warsaw and Its Documentation*. London: John Murray, 1945.

Bartelski, Lesław. *Mokotów, 1944*. Warsaw: Wydawnictwo Ministerstwa Obrony Narodowej, 1971.

Bartoszewski, Władysław. *The Blood Shed Unites Us: Pages from the History of Help to the Jews in Occupied Poland*. Warsaw: Interpress Publishers, 1970.

————. *Warsaw Death Ring, 1939-1945*. Warsaw: Interpress Publishers, 1968.

Bartoszewski, Władysław, and Lewin, Zofia. *The Samaritans: Heroes of the Holocaust*. New York: Twayne Publishers, 1970.

Bauer, Yehuda. *American Jewry and the Holocaust: The American Jewish Joint Distribution Committee, 1939-1945*. Detroit, Mich.: Wayne State Univ. Press, 1981.

————. *A History of the Holocaust*. New York: Franklin Watts, 1982.

————. *The Holocaust in Historical Perspective*. Seattle: Univ. of Washington Press, 1978.

Bethell, Nicholas. *The War That Hitler Won: The Fall of Poland, September, 1939.* New York: Holt, Rinehart and Winston, 1972.

Bettelheim, Bruno. *The Informed Heart: Autonomy in a Mass Age.* Glencoe, Ill.: Free Press, 1962.

Borkiewicz, Adam. *Powstanie Warszawskie.* Warsaw, 1957.

Borowski, Tadeusz. *This Way for the Gas, Ladies and Gentlemen.* Trans. Barbara Vedder. New York: Penguin, 1976.

Borowy, Wacław. *Okres Powstania 1944r. w Bibliotece Uniwersyteckiej w Warszawie.* Warsaw: Państwowy Instytut Wydawniczy, 1965.

Borwicz, Michael. "Factors Influencing the Relations between the General Polish Underground and the Jewish Underground," in *Jewish Resistance during the Holocaust: Proceedings of the Conference on Manifestations of Jewish Resistance, Jerusalem, April 7-11, 1968.* Jerusalem: Yad Vashem, 1971.

———. *100 Years of Jewish Life in Poland.* Paris: Centre D'Etudes Historiques, 1955.

Braham, Randolph. *The Politics of Genocide: The Holocaust in Hungary.* 2 vols. New York: Columbia Univ. Press, 1981.

Broszat, Martin. *Nationalsozialistische Polenpolitik, 1939-1945.* Stuttgart: Deutsche Verlags-Anstalt, 1961.

———. *Zweihundert Jahre deutsche Polenpolitik.* Munich: Ehrenwirth, 1963.

Bruce, George. *The Warsaw Uprising, 1 August—2 October 1944.* London: Rupert Hart-Davis, 1972.

Checiński, Michael. *Poland: Communism, Nationalism and Anti-Semitism.* New York: Karz-Cohl Publishing Co., 1982.

Ciechanowski, Jan M. *Powstanie Warszawskie: Zarys Podłoża Politycznego i Dyplomatycznego.* London: Odnowa, 1971

———. *The Warsaw Uprising of 1944.* Cambridge: Cambridge Univ. Press, 1974.

Ciołkosz, Adam. *Walka o Prawde: Wybór Artykułów, 1940-1978.* London: Polonia Book Fund, 1983.

Coleman, Marion M., ed. *The Polish Land: An Anthology in Prose and Verse.* Trenton, N.J.: White Eagle Publishing Co., 1943.

Datner, Szymon. "Destruction of Warsaw," in *1939-1945: War Losses in Poland.* Posen: Wydawnictwo Zachodnie, 1960.

Davies, Norman. *God's Playground: A History of Poland.* Vol. 2, *1795 to the Present.* New York: Columbia Univ. Pres, 1982.

Dawidowicz, Lucy S. *The Holocaust and the Historians.* Cambridge: Harvard Univ. Press, 1981.

———. *The War against the Jews.* New York: Holt, Rinehart and Winston, 1975.

Deschner, Gunther. *Warsaw Uprising.* New York: Ballantine Books, 1972.

Dobroszycki, Lucjan. *Centralny Katalog Polskiej Prasy Konspiracyjnej, 1939-1945.* Warsaw: Wydawnictwo Ministerstwa Obrony Narodowej, 1962.

Domagala, Jan. *Ci, Ktorzy Przeszli Przez Dachau: Duchowni w Dachau.* Warsaw: Pax, 1957.

Donat, Alexander. *The Holocaust Kingdom.* New York: Holt, Rinehart and Winston, 1965.

Duraczyński, Eugeniusz. *Wojna i Okupacja: Wrzesień 1939—Kwiecień 1943.* Warsaw: Wiedza Powszechna, 1974.

Dziewanowski, M.K. *The Communist Party of Poland: An Outline of History.* Cambridge: Harvard Univ. Press, 1959.

Elkins, Michael. *Forged in Fury.* New York: Ballantine Books, 1971.

Falconi, Carlo. *The Silence of Pius XII.* Boston: Little, Brown, 1970.

Farago, Ladislas. *The Game of the Foxes: The Untold Story of German Espionage in the United States and Great Britain during World War II.* Toronto: Bantam Books, 1973.

Fein, Helen. *Accounting for Genocide: National Responses and Jewish Victimization during the Holocaust.* New York: Free Press, 1979.

Foot, M.R.D. *Resistance: European Resistance to Nazism, 1940-1945.* New York: McGraw-Hill Book Co., 1977.

Friedenson, Joseph, and Kranzler, David. *Heroine of Rescue: The Incredible Story of Recha Sternbuch Who Saved Thousands from the Holocaust.* New York: Mesorah Publications, 1984.

Friedlander, Henry, and Milton, Sybil, eds. *The Holocaust: Ideology, Bureaucracy and Genocide.* Millwood, N.Y.: Kraus International Publications, 1980.

Friedlander, Saul. *Pius XII and the Third Reich: A Documentation.* New York: Alfred A. Knopf, 1966.

Friedman, Philip. *Roads to Extinction: Essays on the Holocaust.* New York: Holocaust Library, 1980.

———. *Their Brothers' Keepers.* New York: Holocaust Library, 1978.

Garliński, Józef. *Fighting Auschwitz.* London: Julian Friedmann, 1975.

———. *Hitler's Last Weapons: The Underground War Against the V-1 and V-2.* New York: Times Books, 1978.

———. *Oświęcim Walczący.* London: Odnowa, 1974.

———. *Poland, SOE, and the Allies.* London: George Allen and Unwin, 1969.

———. *Polska w Drugiej Wojnie Światowej.* London: Odnowa, 1982.

Gilbert, Martin. *Auschwitz and the Allies.* New York: Holt, Rinehart and Winston, 1981.

Gross, Jan Tomasz. *Polish Society under German Occupation: The General-Gouvernement, 1939-1944.* Princeton, N.J.: Princeton Univ. Press, 1979.

Gumkowski, Janusz, and Leszczyński, Kazimierz. *Poland under Nazi Occupation.* Warsaw: Polonia Publishing House, 1961.

Gutman, Yisrael. *The Jews of Warsaw, 1939-1943: Ghetto, Underground, Revolt.* Bloomington: Indiana Univ. Press, 1982.

Gutman, Yisrael, and Zuroff, Efraim, eds. *Rescue Attempts during the Holocaust: Proceedings of the Second Yad Vashem International Conference, Jerusalem, April 8-11, 1974.* Jerusalem: Yad Vashem, 1977.

Haestrup, Jorgen. *European Resistance Movements, 1939-1945: A Complete History.* Westport, Conn.: Meckler, 1981.

Hanson, Joanna K.M. *The Civilian Population and the Warsaw Uprising of 1944*. Cambridge: Cambridge Univ. Press, 1982.

Harris, Whitney R. *Tyranny on Trial: The Evidence at Nuremberg*. Dallas, Tex.: Southern Methodist Univ. Press, 1954.

Heller, Celia. *On the Edge of Destruction: Jews of Poland between the Two World Wars*. New York: Schocken Books, 1980.

Hilberg, Raul. *The Destruction of the European Jews*. Chicago, Ill.: Quadrangle Books, 1961.

Hrabar, Roman, et al. *The Fate of Polish Children during the Last War*. Warsaw: Interpress, 1981.

Iranek-Osmecki, Kazimierz. *He Who Saves One Life*. New York: Crown Publishers, 1971.

Irving, David. *Accident: The Death of General Sikorski*. London: William Kimber, 1967.

Jurewicz, Lesław. *Zbrodnia Czy Początek Wojny Domowej*. London: Poets and Painters Press, 1980.

Kamenetsky, Ihor. *Secret Nazi Plans for Eastern Europe: A Study of Lebensraum Policies*. New York: Bookman Associates, 1961.

Kirchmayer, Jerzy. *Powstanie Warszawskie*. Warsaw: Książka i Wiedza, 1970.

Kliszko, Zenon. *Powstanie Warszawskie: Artykuły, Przemowienia, Wspomnienia, Dokumenty*. Warsaw: Książka i Wiedza, 1967.

Koehl, Robert. *RKFDV: German Resettlement and Population Policy, 1939-1945*. Cambridge: Harvard Univ. Press, 1957.

Korboński, Stefan. *The Polish Underground State: A Guide to the Underground, 1939-1945*. Trans. Marta Erdman. Boulder, Colo.: East European Quarterly, 1978.

Krakowski, Shmuel. *The War of the Doomed: Jewish Armed Resistance in Poland, 1942-1944*. New York: Holmes and Meier, 1984.

Krannhals, Hanns von. *Der Warschauer Aufstand, 1944*. Frankfurt am Main: Bernard & Graefe Verlag fur Wehrwesen, 1962.

Kren, George M., and Rappoport, Leon. *The Holocaust and the Crisis of Human Behavior*. New York: Holmes and Meier, 1980.

Kurzman, Dan. *The Bravest Battle: The 28 Days of the Warsaw Ghetto Uprising*. Los Angeles, Calif.: Pinnacle Books, 1976.

Kwiatkowski, Jan K. *Komuniści w Polsce: Rodowód, Taktyka, Ludzie*. Brussels: Polski Instytut Wydawniczy, 1946.

Landau, Ludwik. *Kronika Lat Wojny i Okupacji*. 3 vols. Warsaw: Państwowe Wydawnictwo Naukowe, 1962-63.

Laqueur, Walter. *The Terrible Secret: Suppression of the Truth about Hitler's Final Solution*. Boston: Little, Brown and Co., 1980.

Leslie, R.F., ed. *The History of Poland since 1863*. Cambridge: Cambridge Univ. Press, 1980.

Levin, Nora. *The Holocaust: The Destruction of European Jewry, 1933-1945*. New York: Schocken Books, 1973.

Lewandowska, Stanisława. *Polska Konspiracyjna Prasa Informacyjno-Polityczna, 1939-1945*. Warsaw, Czytelnik, 1982.

Lewandowski, Józef. *Swedish Contribution to the Polish Resistance Movement during World War Two (1939-1942)*. Stockholm: Uppsala, 1979.

Lukas, Richard C. *Eagles East: The Army Air Forces and the Soviet Union, 1941-1945*. Tallahassee: Florida State Univ. Press, 1970.

————. *The Strange Allies: The United States and Poland, 1941-1945*. Knoxville: Univ. of Tennessee Press, 1978.

Madajczyk, Czesław. *Hitlerowski Terror na Wsi Polskiej, 1939-1945*. Warsaw: Państwowe Wydawnictwo Naukowe, 1965.

————. *Polityka III Rzeszy w Okupowanej Polsce*. 2 vols. Warsaw: Państwowe Wydawnictwo Naukowe, 1970.

Malinowski, Marian, *W Obronie Stolicy*. Warsaw: Wydawnictwo Ministerstwa Obrony Narodowej, 1960.

Marczak-Oborski, Stanisław. *Teatr Czasu Wojny: Polskie Życie Teatralne w Latach II Wojny Światowej, 1939-1945*. Warsaw: Państwowy Instytut Wydawniczy, 1967.

Margules, Józef. *Przyczółki Warszawskie*. Warsaw: Wydawnictwo Ministerstwa Obrony Narodowej, 1962.

Mark, Ber. *Powstanie w Getcie Warszawskim*. Warsaw: Wydawnictwo Idisz Buch, 1963.

————. *Uprising in the Warsaw Ghetto*. Trans. Gershon Freidlin. New York: Schocken Books, 1975.

Masson, Madeleine. *Christine: A Search for Christine Granville*. London: Hamish Hamilton, n.d.

Mendelsohn, Ezra. *The Jews of East Central Europe between the World Wars*. Bloomington: Indiana Univ. Press, 1983.

Michel, Henry. *The Shadow War: European Resistance 1939-1945*. New York: Harper and Row, 1972.

Mistecka, S. Maria Lucyna. *Zmartwychwstanki w Okupowanej Polsce, 1939-1945: Ośrodek Dokumentacji i Studiów Społecznych*. Warsaw: Wydawnictwo ODISS, 1983.

Morley, John. *Vatican Diplomacy and the Jews during the Holocaust, 1939-1943*. New York: Ktav Publishing House, 1980.

Morse, Arthur D. *While Six Million Died: A Chronicle of American Apathy*. New York: Random House, 1968.

Musiol, Teodor. *Dachau, 1933-1945*. Katowice: Wydawnictwo Śląsk, n.d.

Nurowski, Roman. *1939-1945: War Losses in Poland*. Poznań: Wydawnictwo Zachodnie, 1960.

Orlicki, Józef. *Szkice z Dziejów Stosunków Polsko-Żydowskich, 1918-1948*. Szczecin: Krajowa Agencja Wydawnicza, 1983.

Ostaszewski, Jan. *Powstanie Warszawskie*. Rome, 1945.

Pawełczyńska, Anna. *Values and Violence in Auschwitz: A Sociological Analysis*. Trans. Catherine S. Leach. Berkeley: Univ. of California Press, 1979.

Penkower, Monty N. *The Jews Were Expendable: Free World Diplomacy and the Holocaust*. Urbana: Univ. of Illinois Press, 1983.

Piekalkiewicz, Janusz. *Secret Agents, Spies and Saboteurs: Famous Undercover Missions of World War II*. New York: William Morrow Co., 1969.

Pobóg-Malinowski, Władysław. *Najnowsza Historia Polityczna Polski*. Vol. 3, *1864-1945*. London: n.p., 1960.

Podlewski, Stanisław. *Przemarsz Przez Pieklo*. Warsaw: Instytut Wydawniczy Pax, 1957.

Poliakov, Leon, *Harvet of Hate: The Nazi Program for the Destruction of the Jews of Europe*. New York: Holocaust Library, 1979.

Pospieszalski, Karol. *Polska pod Niemieckim Prawem*. Poznań: Wydawnictwo Instytutu Zachodniego, 1946.

Przygoński, Antoni. *Z Problematyki Powstania Warszawskiego*. Warsaw: Wydawnictwo Obrony Narodowej, 1964.

Rashke, Richard. *Escape from Sobibor*. Boston: Houghton Mifflin Co., 1982.

Ravel, Aviva. *Faithful Unto Death: The Story of Arthur Zygielbaum*. Montreal: Arthur Zygielbaum Branch of the Workman's Circle, 1980.

Reitlinger, Gerald. *The Final Solution: The Attempt to Exterminate the Jews of Europe, 1939-1945*. New York: Beechhurst Press, 1953.

——. *The SS: Alibi of a Nation, 1922-1945*. New York: Viking Press, 1957

Rosenfeld, Alvin H., and Greenburg, Irving. *Confronting the Holocaust: The Impact of Elie Wiesel*. Bloomington: Indiana Univ. Press, 1978.

Schwarzbart, Isaac I. *The Story of the Warsaw Ghetto Uprising: Its Meaning and Message*. New York: World Jewish Congress, 1953.

Stebelski, Adam. *The Fate of Polish Archives during World War II*. Warsaw: Central Directorate of State Archives, 1964.

Stein, George H. *The Waffen SS: Hitler's Elite Guard at War*. Ithaca, N.Y.: Cornell Univ. Press, 1966.

Steinberg, Lucien. *The Jews Against Hitler (Not as a Lamb)*. London: Gordon and Cremonesi, 1978.

Steven, Stewart. *The Poles*. New York: Macmillan Co., 1982.

Strzetelski, Stanisław. *Bitwa o Warszawe (1 Sierpnia—2 Października 1944 r): Fakty i Dokumenty*. New York: Komitetu Narodowego Amerykanów Pochodzenia Polskiego, 1945.

Terry, Sarah Meiklejohn. *Poland's Place in Europe: General Sikorski and the Origin of the Oder-Neisse Line, 1939-1943*. Princeton, N.J.: Princeton Univ. Press, 1983.

Tetens, T.H. *The New Germany and the Old Nazis*. New York: Random House, 1961.

Wagner, Wolfgang. *The Genesis of the Oder-Neisse Line: A Study in the Diplomatic Negotiations during World War II*. Stuttgart: Brentano Verlag, 1957.

Wandycz, Piotr. *The United States and Poland*. Cambridge: Harvard Univ. Press, 1980.

Wasserstein, Bernard. *Britain and the Jews of Europe, 1939-1945*. Oxford: Clarendon Press, 1979.

Weinberg, Gerhardt. *The Foreign Policy of Hitler's Germany: Starting World War II, 1937-1939*. Chicago, Ill.: Univ. of Chicago Press, 1980.

Weinryb, Bernard. *The Jews of Poland: A Social and Economic History of the Jewish Community in Poland from 1100 to 1800*. Philadelphia, Pa.: Jewish Publication Society of America, 1972.

Weydenthal, Jan B. de. *The Communists of Poland: An Historical Outline*. Stanford, Calif.: Hoover Institution Press, 1978.

Woytak, Richard A. *On the Border of War and Peace: Polish Intelligence and Diplomacy in 1937-1939*. Boulder, Colo.: East European Quarterly, 1979.

Wroniszewski, Józef K. *Ochota: 1944*. Warsaw: Wydawnictwo Ministerstwa Obrony Narodowej, 1970.

Wroński, Stanisław, and Zwolakowa, Maria. *Polacy i Żydzi, 1939-1945*. Warsaw: Książka i Wiedza, 1971.

Wytwycky, Bohdan. *The Other Holocaust: Many Circles of Hell*. Washington, D.C.: Novak Report, 1980.

Zarski-Zajdler, Władysław. *Martyrologia Ludności Żydowskiej i Pomoc Społeczeństwa Polskiego*. Warsaw: 1968.

Zawodny, J. K. *Nothing But Honour: The Story of the Warsaw Uprising, 1944*. Stanford Calif.: Hoover Institution Press, 1978.

Żenczykowski, Tadeusz. *General Grot: U Kresu Walki*. London: Polonia Book Fund, 1983.

ARTICLES AND PERIODICALS

Armstrong, John A. "Collaborationism in World War II: The Internal Nationalist Variant in Eastern Europe." *Journal of Modern History* 40 (Sept. 1968): 396-410.

Bauer, Yehuda. "When Did They Know?" *Midstream* (Apr. 1968): 51-58.

Bednarczyk, Tadeusz. "35 Rocznica Powstania w Getcie Warszawskim." *Życie Literackie* (16 Apr. 1978): 8-9.

Bór-Komorowski, T. "The Unconquerables." *Reader's Digest* (Feb. 1946): 127-68.

Breitman, Richard, and Kraut, Alan M. "Who Was the Mysterious Messenger?" *Commentary* 76 (Oct. 1983): 44-47.

Ciołkosz, Adam. "Broń dla Getta Warszawy." *Zeszyty Historyczne* (1969): 15-44.

Fox, John P. "The Jewish Factor in British War Crimes Policy in 1942." *English Historical Review* 92 (Jan. 1977): 82-106.

Gardner, John. Review of *Sophie's Choice*, by William Styron. *New York Times Book Review*, 27 May 1979, 16ff.

Garliński, J. "The Polish Underground State." *Journal of Contemporary History* 10 (Apr. 1975): 219-59.

Gongola, Leon. "A Jewish View of Poles and Germans." *Perspectives* (July-Aug. 1979): 503.

Gruber, Ruth. "The Heroism of Staszek Jackowski." *Saturday Review* (15 Apr. 1967): 19-21, 44.

"Holocaust." *Encyclopedia Judaica* 8 (1972): 890-91.

Iranek-Osmecki, Kazimierz. "Przyczynki do Powstania Warszawskiego." *Kultura* 11/73 (1953): 99-105.

———. "Ptaszki-Zrutki." *Kultura* 1/27 (1950): 133-39.

Iranek-Osmecki, Kazimierz, et al. "The Polish Government-in-Exile and the Jewish Tragedy during World War II." *Wiener Library Bulletin* 29 (1976): 62-67.

Krakowski, S. "The Slaughter of Polish Jewry—A Polish 'Reassessment.'" *Wiener Library Bulletin* 26 (1972): 13-20.

Kulski, W.W. Review of *Great Britain, the Soviet Union and the Polish Government-in-Exile, 1939-1945*, by George V. Kacewicz. *Polish Review* 26 (1981): 123-27.

Kusielewicz, E. "Some Thoughts on the Teaching of the Holocaust." *Perspectives* 14 (Mar.-Apr. 1984): Insert D.

Lewin, Issac. "Attempts at Rescuing European Jews with the Help of Polish Diplomatic Missions during World War II." *Polish Review* 22, no. 4 (1977): 3-23.

———. "Attempts at Rescuing European Jews with the Help of Polish Diplomatic Missions during World War II: Part II." *Polish Review* 24, no. 1 (1979): 46-61.

———. "Attempts at Rescuing European Jews with the Help of Polish Diplomatic Missions during World War II: Part III." *Polish Review* 27, nos. 1-2 (1982): 99-111.

Lichten, Joseph L. Review of *Roads to Extinction*, by Philip Friedman. *Polish Review* 27, nos. 3-4 (1982): 216-19.

Luczak, Czesław. "Aktion Warschau: Plunder of Polish Property by Heinz Reinefahrt's Detachments in Warsaw during the Uprising." *Polish Western Affairs* 9 (1968): 163-68.

Lukas, Richard C. "The RAF and the Warsaw Uprising." *Aerospace Historian* 22 (Dec. 1975): 188-94.

Madajczyk, C. "Generalplan Ost." *Polish Western Affairs* 3, no. 2 (1962): 391-442.

Mitkiewicz, Leon. "Powstanie Warszawskie—z Mojego Notatnika w Waszyngtonie." *Zeszyty Historyczny* 1 (1962): 113.

"Nazi Army on Polish Soil, The." *Living Age* 358 (May 1940): 213-16.

New Stateman and Nation. 2 Sept. 1944.

Nordon, Haskell. Review of *Poland*, by James Michener. *New York Times Book Review* 88 (20 Nov. 1983): 43.

Oliner, Samuel P. "The Unsung Heroes in Nazi-Occupied Europe: The Antidote for Evil." *Nationalities Papers* 12, no. 1 (Spring 1984): 129-36.

Pelzyński, T. "O Powstaniu Warszawskim: w Związku z Artykułem St. Okeckiego." *Bellona* 3 (1955): 3-16.

Peszke, Michael Alfred. "The Polish Armed Forces in Exile, Part I: September 1939-July 1941." *Polish Review* 26, no. 1 (1981): 67-113.

Polish Fortnightly Review. 1942-44.

Rudowski, Witold, and Zablotniak, Ryszard. "Clandestine Medical Studies in Poland, 1939-1945." *Journal of the Royal College of Surgeons of Edinburgh* 23 (July 1978): 239-52.

Taub, Walter. "Warsaw Tragedy." *Collier's* (17 Mar. 1945): 17, 79-80.

Woytak, Richard, and Kasparek, Christopher. "The Top Secret of World War II.' *Polish Review* 28 (1983): 98-103.

Wynot, Edward D. "'A Necessary Cruelty': The Emergence of Official Anti-Semitism in Poland, 1936-1939." *American Historical Review* 76, no. 4 (Oct. 1971): 1035-58.

NEWSPAPERS

Biuletyn Informacyjny
Frankfurter Zeitung
Gwardia Ludowa
Gwardzista
Informator (WRN)
New York Times
Nowe Drogi
Rzeczpospolita Polska
San Francisco Chronicle
Times, The (London)
Żywią i Bronią

APPENDIX A

Zegota: A Conspiracy of Good

In September 1995, a group of Poles, Jews and Polish Americans assembled in Warsaw to recognize publicly for the first time on Polish soil the extraordinary achievement of Zegota, the code name for the *Rada Pomocy Zydom* (Council for Aid to Jews). They did this by unveiling a black granite stone, inscribed in Polish, Hebrew and English, which recognized the uniqueness of Zegota, the only organization of its kind in German-occupied Europe that exclusively aided Jews with funds provided by its government.[1] After the war, Joseph Lichten, a distinguished Jewish leader, said that Zegota was "one of the most beautiful chapters in the story of help to the Jews not only in Poland but in all of Nazi-occupied Europe."[2]

Ever since the German invasion and occupation of Poland in 1939, Poles who knew Jews as friends, neighbors and colleagues helped them in various ways. Soon this assistance became more organized as various cells, often composed of Polish political parties, appeared. This was especially true of such groups as the Polish Socialists, who had strong links with members of the Jewish Bund. Other groups especially active in relief work shortly after the Germans imposed their ruthless domination over the country included the Democratic Party, the Union of Polish Syndicalists, the Front for Reborn Poland, and the Communists. But as the intentions of the Germans to annihilate the Jews became increasingly evident to the Polish people, it became equally obvious that assistance to the Jews had to be coordinated, organized, and funded on a broader national basis. The representative of the Polish government in Poland, the Government Delegate, responded to the growing public demand and established the Provisional Committee for Assistance to Jews, sometimes

Zofia Kossak-Szczucka   **Tadeusz Rek**   **Julian Grobelny**

referred to as the Konrad Zegota Committee, on September 27, 1942. It
was jointly headed by Zofia Kossak-Szczucka, the chairperson of the
Front for Reborn Poland, and Wanda Krahelska-Filipowicz, who had been
active in the socialist movement even before World War I and also had
ties with the Democratic Party.[3]

Like other social activists, Kossak-Szczucka had been personally
active in aiding Jews before the establishment of the Provisional
Committee. Despite the fact that this well-known Catholic novelist had
ambivalent feelings about Jews, she, like the vast majority of Poles,
condemned the German slaughter of the Jewish people. She expressed her
strong feelings in a leaflet, entitled "Protest," which summoned all Poles
to condemn unequivocally German crimes against the Jews. "We do not
want to be Pilates," she declared. "We are filled with sympathy,
indignation, and horror. Our Christian conscience bids us to protest.
Whoever does not join in this protest—is not a Catholic."[4]

In the two-month existence of the fledgling organization, the
Provisional Committee assisted about 200 Jews, 70 percent of whom were
children.[5]

On December 4, 1942, the Provisional Committee disbanded itself,
clearing the way for the establishment by the Government Delegate on
the same day of the Council for Aid to Jews, or Zegota, as it was known
in underground circles. In contrast to its predecessor, the new organization
had a broader political and social base. The presidium of Zegota
represented the moderate-left of the Polish political spectrum. Julian
Grobelny, a Socialist, was president; Tadeusz Rek of the Peasant Party,

Leon Feiner   Adolf Berman   Ferdynand Arczynski

was one of the two vice-presidents; Dr. Leon Feiner, a representative of the Bund, was the second vice-president; Dr. Adolf Berman of the Jewish National Committee (*Zydowski Komitet Narodowy*) was secretary; Marek Arczynski of the Democratic Party served as treasurer. Other important members of the presidium included Emilia Hizowa of the Democratic Party, and Ignacy Barski and later Wladyslaw Bartoszewski of the Front for Reborn Poland. Witold Bienkowski, who headed the Jewish Affairs Division in the office of the Government Delegate, served as the government's representative on Zegota.[6]

The leaders of Zegota were a remarkable group of social activists who dedicated their lives to saving as many Jews as possible. Julian Grobelny, who personally went through the streets of Warsaw searching for Jewish waifs, had fought for Polish independence prior to 1919. When World War II broke out, he joined the resistance and used the same pseudonym, "Trojan," by which he was known during the Silesian uprisings before World War I.[7]

Tadeusz Rek, who came from a peasant background, earned a law degree from the University of Warsaw. The Germans arrested and imprisoned him in Auschwitz and Neuengamme early in the war. After his release from confinement, Rek worked for the Polish underground press and soon joined Zegota.[8]

Ferdynand Arczynski was a former editor of a Cracow daily and, like Grobelny, had been involved in the Silesian uprisings. A tireless worker, Arczynski also headed the important legalization bureau of Zegota and supervised liaison with branches in Cracow and Lwow.[9] Dr. Leon Feiner was an attorney and a Bundist activist. He looked like a member of the Polish aristocracy, which made it easier for him to move freely through the streets of Warsaw on forged identity papers.[10]

Dr. Adolf Berman, a member of the Po'alei Zion Left, directed CENTOS (*Centralna Zwiazku Towarzystw nad Sierotami*), the leading Jewish organization involved in a variety of welfare activities for children. In Warsaw, CENTOS ran approximately 100 establishments offering relief to 40,000-45,000 children. He left the Warsaw Ghetto to represent the Jewish National Committee, a federation of several Zionist groups on the presidium of Zegota.[11] His brother, Jakub Berman, was a Communist who, as a leading official in the postwar Communist-dominated government in Poland, was responsible for the arrest, imprisonment and execution of Poles who had been loyal during the war to the democratic government of Poland in exile in London. Many of Berman's victims had been members of Zegota.[12]

These leaders, along with hundreds of others affiliated with Zegota, were idealists and activists. As two historians of the organization wrote, "Activists are by nature people who know people." All of the individuals involved in Zegota had a wide circle of friends and associates who had been active in various organizations.[13] Building upon these existing underground political, social, professional and military networks, Zegota broadened its reach in the vicinity of Warsaw, established regional councils in Cracow and Lwow, and cooperated with groups in Lublin and Zamosc.[14] As one Zegota member remarked, "There were many silent sacrificial anonymous Poles who provided great service to the *Rada [Pomocy Zydom]*."[15]

Zegota carried out an impressive program of aid on a national basis. It provided Jews with forged documents, money, housing, and medical assistance. It contacted Jews in ghettos and work camps, bringing them food, clothing and money. In many instances, Zegota operatives arranged escapes from ghettos and camps to Polish safe havens. And, as has been seen, Zegota took part in helping the Polish military and political underground combat the activities of blackmailers.

No Jew who tried to pass for a Christian could do so without holding proper legal documents. A Jew needed a *Kennkarte* or identity card, issued by German authorities, which certified his Polish nationality. He also required an *Arbeitskarte* or work certificate, a residence certificate, a record of his baptism and, if married, a marriage certificate. These documents converted Jews into Poles and allowed them to live and work outside of the ghetto.

As thousands of Jews fled into hiding, the only way to "legalize" them was to resort to forgeries. "How much effort and nerves went into making one document!" Wladyslawa Choms, a Zegota leader in Lwow, commented. "With time we became more experienced."[16]

The Warsaw Council of Zegota initially obtained its documents from shops producing documents for the AK. Later, the Council derived most of its forgeries from two privately owned shops. Henryk Weiss ran one of them. His shop had an impressive collection of printing machines, chemicals, stamps, and photographic equipment. Working with a small staff, Weiss' operation produced several sets of forged documents every day for Zegota. Weiss excelled at forging the signatures of all German officials except Ludwik Fischer, the Governor of Warsaw. When Weiss required Fischer's signature on a document, he called Zbigniew Rachwald, an AK specialist, to do the job. Weiss' forgeries were so convincing that none of his documents was ever questioned by German authorities.[17] "The fury of the Gestapo at our graphic skills was correspondingly great for they realized what was going on," Choms said.[18]

The starting point for a Jew's new identity was a birth certificate which was usually provided by a priest. Initially, the certificates were authentic, belonging to Poles who had died. The birth certificate had to match the Jewish recipient by age and sex. The demand for these documents was so enormous that priests had to issue fictitious ones. The risk for the clergy was equally great: thirty-three priests lost their lives for engaging in this activity.[19]

As historians of Zegota have observed, "The choice of the church from which a birth certificate was issued was also the beginning point for a whole new biography. It was not enough to have papers. Their owners also had to have a story to go with them." Jews had to master the facts of their new identity in order to respond convincingly to German interrogators who prowled the streets in search of victims.[20]

Since identification papers required a photograph of the bearer, this sometimes posed problems because old photos had little resemblance to individuals who had been victims of hunger and deprivation. New photographs often had to be retouched to eliminate telltale Semitic features.[21]

Forgers made every effort to invent Polish names for Jews that came close to their original ones to enable them to absorb their new identities more easily. For example, Berlinski became Jelenski; Rozenfeld, Rozynski. One woman's Polish was so poor that in order not to cast suspicion on herself, the forger gave her a name that enabled her to pose as a White Russian.[22]

Prior to the Warsaw Uprising of 1944, the number of forged documents supplied by shops in Warsaw to Zegota totalled at least 50,000, of which 80 percent got to Jewish hands at no cost to them. The remaining documents were lost or did not reach the Jews for whom they were intended.[23]

The Cracow Council of Zegota had fewer problems meeting the demand for forged documents because the need for them was not as great as in the Polish capital, to which Jews from other areas of the country flocked. Moreover, the shops which produced the forgeries in Cracow had worked closely with Polish political parties there since the early days of the occupation. Thanks to Polish railroad workers, documents produced in Cracow found their way to Jews in Lwow.[24]

Among the beneficiaries of forged documents were members of the Jewish military underground. One of its prominent leaders, Yitzhak Zuckerman, remarked, "Those documents we got from the Polish underground, Zegota, AK or AL, were made in special cells for forgery, in a mass production process. For example, a document like mine would have been good enough for a member of the Polish underground."[25]

Of the thousands of Jews whose lives were saved by the forged documents they received from Zegota, none had a more astonishing story than the Jewish women whose forgeries allowed them to join transports of Polish workers destined for forced labor in Germany. As one Zegota member commented, "A large number of Jewish women with Polish names went to the Reich. They found refuge in the lair of the enemy."[26]

Unfortunately, not everyone benefited from the forged documents they possessed. In Zamosc, Zegota provided documents and money to a group of ten Jews, who worked in an iron works, to enable them to flee. But the leader of the group informed Zegota that they chose not to escape because the Germans had assured them their lives would be spared. Shortly afterward, the Germans killed the entire group during the liquidation of the Zamosc Ghetto.[27] This naivete of Jews astonished Poles who, after the liquidations during the summer of 1942, visited the Warsaw Ghetto and heard Jews express similar sentiments.[28]

Legalization was one of the most important services Zegota provided to the Jewish people. The process required a large number of people, especially skilled technicians and experts to produce the documents and courageous couriers, who most often were women, to deliver them to their recipients. Stanislaw Gajewski, a Polish Jew who obtained false documents to save his family and friends, remarked: "About Zegota, the cells, the documentation, it took large numbers of people—not only those who rescued but all in the organization—priests, forgers, couriers, and so on. We'll never know the number. Now it is too difficult."[29]

Long before the creation of Zegota, Polish families and organizations helped Jewish children. Some of the major organizations included convents, orphanages, social welfare departments, and the Central Welfare Council. Two extraordinary women, Irena Sendler and Irena Schultz, tirelessly worked for the Central Welfare Council before being recruited by Zegota. Both women brought food, money and medicine to approximately 3,000 Jews in the Warsaw Ghetto. To be sure, many of the beneficiaries were children. Schultz not only saved many Jews under the auspices of Zegota but also personally hid several Jewish professors and physicians from the University of Warsaw. Her home near the walls of the Warsaw Ghetto was a critical assembly point to hide Jewish children. Even during the uprising in 1943 she personally rescued Jewish children from the burning ghetto.[30]

The leaders of Zegota wisely selected Irena Sendler to head the children's bureau of the organization. Her vast experience in rescuing children from the Warsaw Ghetto and her extensive contacts proved decisive in the success of Zegota's relief work. But in the fall of 1943, the Gestapo arrested and sentenced Sendler to death. Since she had hidden a portion of the archives of Zegota in her apartment and was the only individual who had memorized the whereabouts of the Jewish children under the organization's care, Julian Grobelny, Zegota's president, did everything he could to save her life. His bribe to German officials succeeded. The day of her scheduled execution, the Germans blasted her name over megaphones in Warsaw's streets. That day dramatically changed Sendler's life because thereafter she no longer could work and live freely. She had to go underground, changing her identity and address, and to live like the Jewish children she loved so much.[31] Sendler's children's bureau acted as a coordinating agency which identified the children who needed assistance and found a variety of places where they could be hidden—convents, special care centers like the Home of Father Gabriel Boduen, agencies run by the Central Welfare Council and, of course, private homes. In Warsaw, Zegota cared for approximately 2500 children, not counting an additional 100 youngsters whom it placed with partisans outside of the city. Approximately 50 percent of the children found homes with Polish families while the other half found shelter in religious and secular institutions.[32]

Child rescue was also a major priority of Cracow's Zegota but apparently no special register, analogous to Sendler's in Warsaw, was ever kept. A similar situation existed in Lwow where Wladyslawa Choms and her co-workers actively engaged in helping adults and children on both sides of the ghetto walls. Choms smuggled Jewish children from the Lwow Ghetto through sewers and in garbage wagons. Jewish mothers, seeing that they were doomed, gave the children to Choms, whom they called "The Angel of Lwow." Sometimes, sackfuls of bread were smuggled into the ghetto and the empty sacks were used later to carry Jewish children to the Polish side of the city where they found homes with Polish families or nuns. In addition to finding homes for Jewish youngsters, Choms personally cared for 60 boys and girls.[33]

The Polish clergy—priests, monks and nuns—worked closely with Zegota in caring for Jewish children. Among the clergy, nuns were in the best position to care for them on a prolonged basis. Often their convents were scattered in some of the more remote areas of the country, which lessened the risk of constant Gestapo scrutiny. One of many orders of nuns devoted to helping children was the Little Servant Sisters of the Immaculate Conception. One of the nuns of the order, upon receiving a prearranged code word from Zegota, regularly went to Warsaw to escort children back to the convent.[34]

Probably as many as two-thirds of the religious communities in Poland hid Jewish children and adults during the German occupation. Szymon Datner, a distinguished Jewish historian, writing about Polish nuns, said: "No other sector was so ready to help those persecuted by the Germans... this attitude, unanimous and general, deserves recognition and respect."[35]

Zegota considered finding housing for Jews a basic, if not the most important, form of aid to Jews because the life of a Jew depended upon a place to live. Describing this aspect of Zegota's work, one historian has said, "None of the accounts given by people in one way or the other to Zegota fail to make a reference to a persistent hunt for a room, for a corner of a room, for some place to hide in."[36]

Since Germans executed Poles for contacts with Jews and extended the death penalty for helping them to the offender's entire family, including children, the major difficulty facing Zegota operatives was to deal with the fear Poles naturally had about sheltering Jews. As one Polish research group correctly observed, "It is clear that conditions for assisting Jewish people were the most difficult in Poland and that dangers faced by potential rescuers the gravest."[37]

Zegota made it clear to owners of premises that the people who were to reside with them were Jews, not Christians, because as Teresa Prekerowa has said, "It would be a disloyal exposure of people's lives to risks." Only in special circumstances did some Zegota members break this rule.[38]

Some Poles accepted Jews without financial payment. Others, whose material situation was inadequate, needed money to feed and care for their charges. Some Poles required higher rents from Jews than other lodgers because of the huge risks they took in hiding them. If Jews resided with a Polish family, the Poles could not receive their customers at home in connection with an illegal activity which many people depended upon to survive the war. Zegota understood these considerations and financially underwrote the housing of many Jews in private homes. But it categorically opposed people who tried to make a lucrative business out of leasing premises to Jews. The number of people involved in this activity was small because few Jews could afford to pay exorbitantly high rents.[39]

Irena Staskowa, who worked for Zegota, was a typical example of a Pole who housed Jews. She hid many Jewish people for varying lengths of time. One Jewish woman, who resided with her for one or two months, could not stand the isolation from her own people and returned to the ghetto. Staskowa followed the maxim, so common among Polish humanitarians, "For one Jew, you lose your head; for several Jews, it's the same head." On one occasion, Staskowa escorted a Jewish girl from a place outside the ghetto when some informers spotted her. "Madam, you forgot to put on your armband," one of them said. Staskowa rebuffed them with coarse epithets and created such a commotion that the informers fled the area. The incident allowed the Jewish girl to meld into the crowd. She later found a home and lived and worked as a Pole for the remainder of the occupation.[40]

Dr. Jan Zabinski, who headed the Warsaw Zoological Gardens, and his wife, Antonina, hid about twenty people, many of them friends and colleagues. Only when their financial burden became enormous did the Zabinskis accept material help from Zegota.[41]

Despite the fact that Cracow was the capital of the General Government and crawled with German police, Polish Socialists alone had managed to assemble 150 shelters for Jews.[42]

Sometimes Jews with a Semitic appearance had to be accommodated in special hideouts, places built in apartments and homes. Some of these were used only in times of imminent danger; others were occupied on a permanent basis. Emilia Hizowa, an architectural engineer, excelled in designing these hideouts, which had to go unnoticed during a Gestapo search. Two market gardeners, Mieczyslaw Wolski and Wladyslaw Marczak, built one of the largest of these hideouts that enabled thirty Jews to hide from the enemy. Historian Emmanuel Ringelblum was one of its occupants. Unfortunately, the Germans discovered the hideout and killed everyone, including their Polish protectors.[43]

The Dippel family, on the other hand, was more successful. They hid 52 Jews in a cellar. The difficulty in accommodating so many people—providing food, medicine and clothing—was overwhelming. Zegota underwrote much of the cost of their upkeep.[44]

Hideouts for Jews dotted the Polish countryside. Peasants often gave careful thought to their location. In one village, the hideout was a barn. In case of danger, Jews could escape through a screen of thick bushes and shrubs to a stable and from there, to an underground trench. In another place, the entry to the hideout was under the bed of the proprietor. By lifting up a floorboard, a person found his way to a stable and from there to a pigsty, covered with straw. Often in forests Jews hid in bunkers which, like fox dens, had two entrances. If there were children in a hiding place when the Germans approached it, parents sometimes gave them luminal in order to put them to sleep. Otherwise, adults ran a grave risk that the cries of the children would alert the Germans to the hiding place.[45]

Rarely did Jews stay only in one shelter during the German occupation. They usually had to move at least a few times. Some Jews moved a dozen or more times. The N. Gross family lived in 43 households during the war.[46]

There was a severe shortage of physicians in Poland because almost 40 percent of them had died during the war. Nevertheless, through its medical bureau, which functioned until the Warsaw Uprising of 1944, Zegota provided medical assistance to Jews in need. Dr. Ludwik Rostkowski, a member of the underground Coordinating Committee of Democratic and Socialist Physicians, organized dozens of medical doctors who regularly made calls to ailing Jews. In Warsaw, Zegota set up secret post-boxes where Zegota members deposited cards containing the names, addresses, and descriptions of the illnesses of Jews. A few times every week a Zegota courier retrieved the cards and gave them to Dr. Rostkowski, who evaluated them and dispatched a physician in the appropriate specialty to the patient.[47]

Itzhak Zuckerman said, "You couldn't prevent diseases and, in such cases, we had gentile doctors on the Aryan side.... But you could generally ask for a doctor from Zegota. I'm sure that if I had called for someone, he would have come. For Jews, who were seriously ill, there was a cell of loyal doctors who would be informed and they would appear."[48]

Zegota physicians were also available to remove the signs of circumcision and tattoos from Jews who had escaped from concentration camps.[49] One Polish physician, a former anti-Semite, provided medical care to members of the Jewish Fighting Organization after the uprising in Bialystok in August 1943. The Jewish commander, Mordecai Tenenbaum, trusted the Pole with the archives of the Jewish underground.[50]

Poles organized a number of clandestine pharmacies, some with Zegota ties, that dispensed medicine to ailing Jews. In Cracow, the Germans allowed Tadeusz Pankiewicz, a Polish pharmacist, to remain in the ghetto and operate his pharmacy. Pankiewicz's Eagle Pharmacy became a legend in its time because it served as an observation post to document German crimes inside the ghetto and provided an important link between Jews and Poles. The pharmacy became a social and intellectual center for Jews anxious for a respite from the grim life around them. Rabbis even trusted Pankiewicz to hide sacred texts from the Germans.[51]

As suggested earlier, Zegota regularly dispatched couriers to contact Jews in ghettos and camps throughout the country. Stefan Sendlak, assisted by Tadeusz and Ewa Sarnecki, played a major role in Zegota's courier operations. Zegota's couriers usually brought money, food, and mail to ghettos and camps and returned with letters from the prisoners for friends and family. This correspondence was important in revealing to the world the horrible conditions which the Jews had to endure.[52]

Couriers also rescued a number of Jews from ghettos and camps, including Auschwitz, an activity that Jewish leaders in Poland regarded as critically significant. Adolf Berman, head of the Jewish National Committee, said: "The most important thing, so all this won't be so hopeless, would be to extract a small group from these hellish camps and to save them for the future."[53]

Jozefa Rysinska and Ada Prochnicka were well known couriers who personally escorted several Jews to safety. One young Jewish girl, Janina Hescheles, confined in the Janowska camp, despaired that she would ever be free again. Rysinska rescued her and found a Polish home for her. But couriers paid a high price for their dangerous work. The Gestapo killed Prochnicka and sent Rysinska to Plaszow prison.[54]

Stefan Malecki, who had received permission from the Polish underground to work as a member of the Blue Police, helped Zegota facilitate several flights of Jews from ghettos. A bold man, Malecki abducted a Zegota courier who had been confined in Gestapo headquarters and led him to safety. He had heard of the arrest and confinement of the distinguished Jewish educator, Henryk Rowid, in the Cracow Ghetto. Malecki arranged a way for Rowid to flee from the ghetto but the Jew, believing nothing would happen to him, rejected the offer. Rowid spurned a subsequent effort to free him by another Zegota member. The Germans ended up murdering him.[55]

Zofia Mycko was another courageous Pole who saved Jews referred to her by Zegota and by individuals. Employed by the German firm, Sudbau, Mycko was in a unique position which allowed her to help Jews and Poles to flee to other countries in the company's transports. She allegedly assisted an estimated 3,000 people, of whom several hundred were Jewish. Jews who were unable either to escape from Poland or to find suitable housing lived with Mycko.[56]

Franciszek Krzyzak helped about 50 Jews, including the nuclear physicist Ludwik Wertenstein, who had been earlier sheltered by a Zegota member, flee to Hungary. After a risky trip for Krzyzak and Wertenstein, the scholar found a home in Hungary, only to die a few hours before the Soviets occupied the country.[57]

Keenly sensitive to the need of securing broad support from Polish society in the effort to assist Jews, Zegota was one of the key Polish elites, along with other groups within the political and military underground, that urged the Polish Government-in-Exile and the underground to help the Jewish people as much as possible. To counteract the opinion expressed in some of the underground nationalist publications urging Poles not to concern themselves with the plight of the Jews, Zegota published in 1943 three issues of the *Kommunikaty Prasowe* (Press Service News) which informed Poles about the liquidation of Jewish camps in Lublin, the Jewish Uprising in Bialystok and other events.[58]

In three leaflets published in May, August, and September 1943, Zegota quoted pronouncements by General Wladyslaw Sikorski, the Polish premier, and Stanislaw Jankowski, the Government Delegate for the Homeland, which urged Poles to help Jews. They also condemned the activities of informers. A fourth Zegota leaflet, published under the bogus authorship of a German resistance movement, warned Germans who perpetrated crimes against Jews. Zegota distributed the leaflets to homes and offices and posted them on walls in Warsaw.[59]

Zegota also printed and circulated pamphlets dealing with the plight of the Jewish people. Published with the assistance of the AK, one pamphlet, written by Maria Kann, was especially powerful. Entitled *Na Oczach Swiata* (In the Eyes of the World), it addressed not only Poles but also the people of the world:

> It is imperative to stop the criminals immediately by force because no revenge will ever bring the exterminated nations back to life. Nor will it make up for moral wrongs. Each day brings annihilation and wreaks terrible havoc, putting Europe back by many centuries. The whole world is responsible for this, for its weakness, its spiritual sloth, its egoism.
>
> When the day of victory dawns, the only expiation for this failure to resist evil will be to rebuild the world that the ideals, proclaimed by the democracies, will at least become realized and a similar tragedy shall never recur anywhere.[60]

According to Kazimierz Iranek-Osmecki, one of the leaders of the AK, "This was the first strong public expression of Polish opinion accusing the West of inactivity and of passively standing by while a crime, unheard of in the annals of humanity, was being perpetrated."[61]

The publication efforts of Zegota and other Polish underground groups was also intended to counteract German anti-Semitic propaganda which deluged the Poles in the press and on placards and megaphones in town squares. It was commonplace to see posters vilely equating Jews with lice and typhus. But some astute German officials observed that their anti-Semitic propaganda was counter-productive because it brought loathing from most Poles and encouraged sympathy and compassion for Jews.[62]

At the same time the Germans also conducted a campaign of anti-Polonism for Jewish audiences. Even in work camps, the Germans herded Jews into rooms to view German films that depicted Poles, not Germans, as their oppressors. One former Zegota activist poignantly commented on the enduring success of this anti-Polish campaign in the works of some western writers published after the war: "More or less to this day Goebbels' propaganda continues to slander Poles."[63]

The Polish government provided approximately 90 percent of the funds for Zegota's operations. Jewish organizations in Poland and abroad contributed the remainder. The Government Delegate's initial grant to Zegota amounted to 150,000 zlotys in January 1943, and increased to 900,000 zlotys in April 1943, during the Warsaw Ghetto Uprising. Monthly allocations leveled off to 550,000 zlotys from June to October 1943, but increased to 1,000,000 zlotys by January 1944. Allocations swelled to 2,000,000 zlotys in July 1944. During the Warsaw Uprising of

1944, Zegota did not receive any funds. To make up for the necessary lapse, the Government Delegate allocated 8,000,000 zlotys in November and 6,000,000 in December 1944. Zegota also provided funds to the Bund and Jewish National Committee to help Jews under their care until Jewish organizations abroad began to send them funds during the last half of 1943.[64]

By 1944, about 4,000 Jews received financial aid from Zegota but the number of Jews who received other forms of assistance was substantially greater.[65] As has been seen, Zegota distributed 50,000 forged documents and 80 percent reached Jewish hands. At least 40,000-50,000 Jews, about half of the Jews who survived the Holocaust in German-occupied Poland, benefitted from some form of aid from Zegota.[66]

Like the western democracies, Jewish organizations abroad awakened belatedly to the cataclysm that engulfed their kinsmen. Funds for the Bund and Jewish National Committee in Poland began to arrive from Jewish groups in the West at a time when the bulk of Polish Jewry had already been annihilated by the Germans. Adolf Berman told Ignacy Schwarzbart early in November 1943 that there were no more than 250,000-300,000 Jews left in Poland. And, he added, "In a few weeks there will not be any more than 50,000 of us."[67] At the same time, he told Jewish leaders in Palestine, "There aren't many of us left. The majority are gone. The Germans destroy the remainder of the Jews in camps which they have hermetically sealed."[68]

Zegota never possessed adequate funds to meet the huge demands placed upon it. In October 1943, officials noted that allocations from the Government Delegate allowed it to give 250-500 zlotys monthly to a Jew in hiding. These funds, they complained, were inadequate to maintain existing services, not to mention assuming the additional burden of providing for "new" people who needed help. "The matter is urgent," Zegota declared.[69]

In March 1944, the Jewish National Committee ran out of funds to provide for Jews under its care and consequently stopped its monthly donation to Zegota. The same month, Zegota bluntly told the Government Delegate that the situation was "catastrophic." Zegota specifically called attention to the plight of 8,000 Jews in a work camp near Cracow. It also wanted to rescue 200 Jewish children from Plaszow, which required 1,000,000 zlotys to bribe German guards.[70]

The costs of aiding Jews were so enormous they went beyond the capabilities of the Polish government, Zegota and the Polish people to deal with the problem. One Polish leader involved in Zegota estimated that it cost 5,000,000 zlotys every month to maintain 10,000 Jewish orphans. To free one Jew cost 6,000-15,000 zlotys.[71]

On its part the Jewish National Committee in Warsaw was critical of Jewish organizations abroad for not providing sufficient funds to save more Jews. In one message, it asked, "Does the American Joint no longer function? Why doesn't it send money?" In a letter to a friend, one Polish Jew echoed the sentiments of many Jews when he criticized Jews in Great Britain and the United States for allowing the mass murder of their kinsmen in Poland.[72]

Itzhak Zuckerman agreed: "What we got from abroad was a tiny sum in relation to our needs, a few tens of thousands of dollars. It's hard to comprehend how Jews in Eretz Israel and in the Western [sic] world didn't comprehend what ransom meant. We didn't have any other sources."[73]

In late October 1943, a Zegota protocol, which registered no objections from its Jewish representatives, criticized not only the inadequate response of international Jewry to the plight of Jews in Poland but also the improvidence of Polish Jews themselves for failing to provide for the dark days when funds would be needed to save their lives.[74]

But budgetary limitations were obviously not the only or even the most significant problem facing Zegota and the Polish underground in saving Jews. German determination to kill the Jews with the apparatus of terror at their disposal was the dominant factor that Jews themselves recognized in limiting Jewish survival. As top leaders of the underground told Jan Karski, a Polish emissary who in 1942 gave an eyewitness account to western statesmen concerning the plight of the Jews: "We want you to tell the Polish government, the Allied governments and great leaders of the Allies that we are helpless in the face of the German criminals. We cannot defend ourselves, and no one in Poland can defend us. The Polish underground authorities can save some of us, but they cannot save the masses. We are being systematically murdered. Our entire people will be destroyed. This cannot be prevented by any force in Poland, neither the Polish state nor the Jewish Underground. Place this responsibility on the shoulders of the Allies." Dr. Emmanuel Scherer, who represented the Bund on the Polish National Council, echoed the same sentiments: "I fully realize that the main part of the work is beyond the limited possibilities of the Polish state."[75] Itzhak Zuckerman, who had first-hand experience with the situation in Poland, agreed: "After all, there were thousands of Jews. There was no solution for the masses."[76]

Despite the accurate observations of Jewish leaders in Poland, western Jews had curious, if not bizarre, ideas about Polish capabilities to rescue large numbers of their kinsmen. These naive notions revealed a lack of understanding of the ruthlessness of German policies aimed at the Polish people. Ignacy Schwarzbart, a Zionist who served on the Polish National Council in London, displayed this lack of realism when he airily asserted, "Since allied [sic] governments are reluctant to do anything, help can practically come only from the Gentile population in Poland by taking out the Jews from ghettos and hiding them."[77]

Since no organization existed in Poland that was capable of saving large numbers of surviving Jews, Zegota as early as July 1943 urged a major international effort by the great powers to initiate an exchange of Jews for German citizens residing on territory of the Allied powers.[78] Only a massive sustained political and military effort by the great powers might have saved more Jews. But that was never attempted.

The delays often incurred in transferring funds, deposited by Jewish organizations with the Polish government in London for the Bund, the Jewish National Committee and others, seriously strained Polish-Jewish relations. In March 1944, the Government Delegate warned that failure of Polish authorities in London to transmit funds from Jewish groups abroad risked serious political repercussions. It seems that the rigidity of the Polish bureaucracy made a difficult problem even more severe.[79]

But most of the irregularities can be explained by the incredible difficulty of transferring money from England to Poland. Unlike Belgium, where the Committee for the Protection of Jews in Belgium could simply draw on funds from Belgian banks,[80] Poland was a different matter altogether. Money had to be sent by aircraft flying over hundreds of miles of German-dominated territory to a country that was under a brutal tyranny unknown in most of Europe.

The Polish government transferred all funds to Poland through the Sixth Bureau of the Polish Army, which dropped parachutists wearing special belts. Each belt had an identification sign which indicated the amount of money and a coded address of the recipient. A former AK officer explained the operation:

> Notification from London about the arrival of civilian money consignments was sent to Poland by two channels. The Sixth Bureau of the Polish G.H.Q. in a coded message informed the Home Army command of the arrival of aircraft, giving the dropping zone, the identification sign, and the amount and destination of aid. At the same time, the Polish ministry of the interior informed the government delegate, also by coded message, of what sums had

been dispatched for the civilian authorities.[81]

After a parachute drop, the AK collected the belts and carried them to a special Home Army unit in Warsaw in charge of liaison with London. From there the AK packed the money in secret containers and delivered them to the Government Delegate's office, the clearance point for distribution of funds to designated recipients.[82]

Transferring money to Poland was obviously complicated and dangerous. Little wonder that all funds did not reach their intended beneficiaries. Out of 858 aircraft missions to Poland, only 56 percent made successful parachute drops. When a successful landing took place, parachutists had to contend with the Germans who prowled the drop zones. "Thus, large sums were discovered in hideouts or confiscated while in transport from one location to another," Iranek-Osmecki said. "Nazi controls and searches were a nightmare, seriously hampering the work of the underground." When the Germans found money during a search, it also meant the loss of Home Army personnel and employees of the Government Delegate's office. No precise figures are available on funds destined for Jewish organizations in Poland that were lost in transit.[83]

Since its inception, Zegota had urged the Polish government to organize a general committee in the West for aid to Jews to alert public opinion to the plight of the Jews and to raise funds for their relief. "The needs are great; greater resources are essential," Zegota declared.[84] Finally, if belatedly, in the midst of serious strain with Jews over Jewish desertions from the Polish Army, the Polish government in the spring of 1944 organized the Council for the Rescue of the Jewish Population in Poland.[85] Zegota hoped that now greater funds would be available to help Jewish survivors. But, by the time the Rescue Council began serious deliberations in London, the Poles rose up against the Germans in Warsaw in August 1944 in the bloodiest sustained urban struggle against an enemy during World War II. The two-month insurrection destroyed the Polish capital, and, with it, the center of Polish relief activity in Poland for Jews. Although Zegota continued its relief work outside of Warsaw on a reduced basis, it was apparent that Jews who survived the German terror in Poland would be helped more by the military defeat of the Germans by the Soviets than by the newly formed Rescue Council in London. By January 1945, the Soviets had occupied most of Poland and Jews began to emerge from hiding and from the camps.

Despite their own belated response to the plight of their kinsmen, Jews in the West and in Palestine were unreasonably critical and demanding of the Polish government and the Polish people in their efforts to aid Jews.[86] At the same time, they saw nothing incongruous in their lack of support for Poland in its struggle with the Soviet Union for political independence and territorial integrity. Even the execution of prominent Polish Jews by the Soviets did not dampen the support of many Jews for the Soviet Union.

Wladyslaw Banaczyk, speaking at a meeting of the newly formed Rescue Council shortly after the issue of Jewish deserters from the Polish Army had so badly strained Polish-Jewish relations, reminded its members, several of whom were Jewish:

> Without underestimating the efforts and achievements of Jewish organizations it may be stated that it was the Polish Government who first organized active help and relief for the Jews of Poland. In this task they were fully supported by the Polish people in occupied Poland, ...they do it as a duty towards humanity and towards Poland and do not care particularly for appreciation. ...All attempts at arousing the opinion of the world and of Jewry against us will not and cannot distract us from the path... to help and rescue as many Jews in Poland as it is possible.[87]

Most Jews who survived the German occupation of Poland were saved by Poles unconnected with Zegota. Recent estimates of the number of Jewish survivors in Poland range from 40,000-50,000 to 100,000-120,000, though one estimate of the Polish underground placed the figure at 200,000. Tadeusz Bednarczyk, who was active in the Polish underground and had close contact with the Warsaw Ghetto, estimated that 300,000 Jews survived the Nazis in Poland. Wladyslaw Zarski-Zajdler stated that at one point during the German occupation there were as many as 450,000 Jews sheltered by Poles, but not all of them survived the war.[88] His estimate is close to that offered after the war by the former foreign minister of the Polish government, Count Edward Raczynski.[89]

As has been seen, it was the degree of German control over Poland, not anti-Semitism, which was the decisive factor in influencing the number of Jews who survived the war. The Netherlands, which had few Jews and less anti-Semitism than Poland, experienced about the same percentage of Jewish losses as Poland. On the other hand, Romania, which had an anti-Semitic history, had a relatively low rate of Jewish losses.[90]

It is difficult to draw precise conclusions concerning the number of Poles actively involved in aiding Jews. Ringelblum estimated that in Warsaw alone 40,000-60,000 Poles were involved in hiding Jews. As Polish scholar Wladyslaw Bartoszewski has pointed out, however, there were thousands of Poles who had been engaged in aiding Jews but, despite their best efforts, had been unable to save them. These people are not included in Ringelblum's guess. Bartoszewski states that "at least several hundred thousand Poles of either sex and of various ages participated in various ways and forms in the rescue action."[91] Historian Teresa Prekerowa caps the figure at 360,000 Polish citizens who aided Jews.[92]

These estimates are probably too conservative. Even if one accepts the lowest range of Jewish survivors in Poland (40,000-50,000), the evidence suggests that they constituted only about 50 percent of those who had been sheltered and survived the war. This means that a minimum of 80,000-100,000 Jews had been in hiding. There is also evidence to suggest that an average of 10-12 people, including children, were directly or indirectly involved in helping one Jew. This suggests that at least 800,000-1,200,000 Poles aided Jews. However, if the higher estimate of Jewish survivors in Poland is accepted, obviously the calculations substantially increase the number of Polish rescuers to the 2-3 million range. None of these estimates should be engraved in stone. All World War II statistics, including the oft-repeated figure of 6 million Jewish losses, should be subjected to revision, downward or upward, as the findings of additional research become available.

A significant minority of Poles helped Jews during the German occupation. Poles were no different from western Europeans, where only small minorities in much less threatening circumstances aided Jewish refugees. The Polish record of aid to Jews was better than other eastern Europeans subjected to German occupation and oppression. And, as Jewish historian Walter Laqueur has stated, "A comparison with France would be by no means unfavorable to Poland."[93]

A Pole once said that Hamlet's "To be or not to be" never had greater meaning than it did during the time of the German occupation of Poland. The men and women of Zegota were among those Poles who responded to the defining challenges of that day by risking their lives and the lives of their families for other human beings. They are among the true moral giants of our time. The just reward for these heroes and heroines is to remember who they are and what they did. By doing that, the real significance of Zegota will not be lost.

Notes to Appendix A

1. *Gazeta Wyborcza*, September 28, 1995; *Rzeczpospolita-Warszawa*, September 28, 1995; Zegota Monument program, September 27, 1995. A Polish American Committee, chaired by Bozenna Urbanowicz Gilbride, spearheaded and raised funds for the monument. Other members of the committee included John Gmerek and Frank Milewski.

2. Kazimierz Iranek-Osmecki, *He Who Saves One Life* (New York: Crown Publishers, 1971), p. xii.

3. Teresa Prekerowa, *Konspiracyjna Rada Pomocy Zydom w Warszawie 1942-1945* (Warsaw: Panstwowy Instytut Wydawniczy, 1982), pp. 51-57; Teresa Prekerowa, "The Relief Council for Jews in Poland, 1942-1945, p. 2. Speech delivered at the Conference on Polish-Jewish Relations in Modern History, Oxford, 1984. Prekerowa's speech is a useful synthesis of her book on Zegota.

4. Report of the Polish Ministry of Interior, July 1-December 1, 1942, in Office of Strategic Services, RG 226, National Archives.

5. Report of the Provisional Committee for Aid to Jews for the period 27 September 1942 to 4 December 1942 in Library, Polish Underground Study Trust, London, England. Hereinafter cited as PUST.

6. Prekerowa, *Konspiracyjna Rada Pomocy Zydom*, pp. 59-60; 67-68.

7. *Ibid.*, pp. 72-73; *Biuletyn ZIH*, 1963, No. 45-46, pp. 234ff.

8. Prekerowa, *Konspiracyjna Rada Pomocy Zydom*, p. 73.

9. *Ibid.*, p. 74. Also see Marek Arczynski and Wieslaw Balcerak, *Kryptonim Zegota: z Dziejow Pomocy Zydom w Polsce, 1939-1945* (Warsaw: Czytelnik, 1983).

10. Irene Tomaszewski and Tecia Werbowski, *Zegota: The Rescue of Jews in Wartime Poland* (Montreal: Price-Patterson Ltd., 1994), p. 45.

11. Richard C. Lukas, *Did the Children Cry? Hitler's War Against Jewish and Polish Children, 1939-1945* (New York: Hippocrene, 1994), p. 51; Prekerowa, *Konspiracyjna Rada Pomocy Zydom*, p. 74.

12. Tadeusz Piotrowski, "Kielce and the Postwar Years," in *Kielce-July 4, 1946: Background, Context and Events* (Toronto: Educational Foundation in North America, 1996), pp. 32-33.

13. Tomaszewski and Werbowski, *Zegota*, pp. 46-47.

14. Richard C. Lukas, *The Forgotten Holocaust: The Poles Under German Occupation, 1939-1944* (New York: Hippocrene, 1990), p. 147.

15. Zeznanie, Stefan Sendlak, in Syg. 3973, Zydowski Instytut Historyczny, Warsaw, Poland. Hereinafter cited as ZIH.

16. Iranek-Osmecki, *He Who Saves One Life,* p. 50.

17. Prekerowa, *Konspiracyjna Rada Pomocy Zydom*, pp. 152ff.

18. Iranek-Osmecki, *He Who Saves One Life.*, p. 50.

19. Tomaszewski and Werbowski, *Zegota*, pp. 58-59.

20. *Ibid.*, p. 59.

21. Prekerowa, *Konspiracyjna Rada Pomocy Zydom*, p. 159

22. *Ibid.*, p. 160.

23. *Ibid.*, p. 161.

24. Tadeusz Seweryn, "Wielostronna Pomoc Zydom w Czasie Okupacji Hitlerowskiej," *Przeglad Lekarski* (1967), No. 1, pp. 164, 178.

25. Yitzhak Zuckerman, *A Surplus of Memory: Chronicle of the Warsaw Ghetto Uprising*, trans. Barbara Harshev (Berkeley: University of California Press, 1993), p. 486.

26. Zeznanie, Stefan Kalinowski, in Syg. 5376, ZIH.

27. Zeznanie, Stefan Sendlak, in Syg. 3973, ZIH.

28. "Zydzi," December, 1942, in Delegatura Rzadu RP 202/XV-2, p. 87, Archiwum Akt Nowych, Warsaw, Poland. Hereinafter cited as AAN.

29. Quoted in Tomaszewski and Werbowski, *Zegota*, pp. 153, 156. Wanda Draczynska, a member of the AK, observed: "In Warsaw, most people had some affiliation with an underground organization, even if they did not formally take an oath." Richard C. Lukas, ed., *Out of the Inferno: Poles Remember the Holocaust* (Lexington: University Press of Kentucky, 1989), pp. 59-60.

30. Lukas, *Did the Children Cry?* p. 174; Obituary, written by the Zydowski Instytut Historyczny w Polsce, in author's files.

31. Oswiadczenie, Helena Grobelna, in Syg. 6313, ZIH; Lukas, *Did the Children Cry?* p. 179. Wanda Sokolowska was another remarkable woman who helped hundreds of Jewish children out of the Warsaw Ghetto. In 1994, she was the subject of an Israeli documentary, entitled "Wanda's List." Zygmunt Zielinski, "Rescue Efforts on Behalf of Jews by the Roman Catholic Church in German-Occupied Poland," typescript, October, 1994, in author's files.

32. Lukas, *Did the Children Cry?* pp. 178-79.

33. Prekerowa, "The Relief Council for Jews in Poland," p. 14; Lukas, *Did the Children Cry?* pp. 179-80.

34. Lukas, *Did the Children Cry?* pp. 183-88.

35. *Ibid.*, pp. 184, 189.

36. Sprawozdanie z Dzialalnosci Rady Pomocy Zydom przy Pelnomocniku Rzadu w Kraju za Czas od Grudnia 1942 do Pazdziernika 1943, in Delegatura Rzadu RP 202/XV-2, pp. 365-71, AAN; Prekerowa, "The Relief Council for Jews in Poland," p. 9.

37. The Main Commission for the Investigation of Crimes Against the Polish

Nation, et. al., *Those Who Helped: Polish Rescuers of Jews during the Holocaust*, Part I (Warsaw: 1993), pp. 16-17.

38. Prekerowa, "The Relief Council for Jews in Poland," p. 9.

39. *Ibid.*, p. 10.

40. *Biuletyn ZIH*, 1968, No. 65-66, pp. 200ff.

41. *Ibid.*, pp. 198ff; Zeznanie, Dr. Jan and Antonina Zabinski, in Syg. 5704, ZIH.

42. Seweryn, "Wielostronna Pomoc Zydom," p. 167.

43. Prekerowa, "The Relief Council for Jews in Poland," pp. 9-10.

44. Tomaszewski and Werbowski, *Zegota*, pp. 144-51.

45. Seweryn, "Wielostronna Pomoc Zydom," pp. 166, 174.

46. Lukas, *Did the Children Cry?* p. 156.

47. Prekerowa, *Konspiracyjna Rada Pomocy Zydom*, pp. 218-26.

48. Zuckerman, *Surplus of Memory*, p. 495.

49. Seweryn, "Wielostronna Pomoc Zydom," p. 174.

50. Philip Friedman, *Their Brothers' Keepers* (New York: Holocaust Library, 1978), p. 206.

51. Seweryn, "Wielostronna Pomoc Zydom," p. 173; Aleksander Bieberstein, *Zaglada Zydow w Krakowie* (Cracow: Wydawnictwo Literackie, 1985), pp. 94-99.

52. Zeznanie, Stefan Sendlak, in Syg. 3973, ZIH.

53. Sprawozdanie, Berman do Bundu w Londynie, November 15, 1943, in Delegatura Rzadu RP, 202/XV-2, pp. 99ff, AAN. One of the Jews who escaped from Auschwitz with Zegota's help was Szymon Zajdow. Seweryn, "Wielostronna Pomoc Zydom," p. 169.

54. Seweryn, "Wielostronna Pomoc Zydom," pp. 168-72.

55. *Ibid.*, pp. 169-70.

56. *Biuletyn ZIH*, 1968, No. 65-66, pp. 202-205.

57. Seweryn, "Wielostronna Pomoc Zydom," pp. 172-73.

58. Prekerowa, "The Relief Council for Jews in Poland," p. 17.

59. *Ibid.*; Sprawozdanie z Dzialalnosci Rady Pomocy Zydom.

60. Quoted in Iranek-Osmecki, *He Who Saves One Life*, pp. 144-45.

61. *Ibid.*, p. 145.

62. Seweryn, "Wielostronna Pomoc Zydom," pp. 179-80.

63. *Ibid.*, p. 180

64. Prekerowa, *Konspiracyjna Rada Pomocy Zydom*, pp. 112-32.

65. *Ibid.*, p. 111.

66. Lukas, *Forgotten Holocaust*, p. 150.

67. Depesza, ZKN do Schwarzbarta, November 15, 1943, in Delegatura Rzadu RP 202/XV-2, p. 378, AAN.

68. Depesza, Adolf do (Tel Aviv), November 15, 1943, in *ibid.*, p.115.

69. Depesza, Trojan and Borowski (no recipient indicated), October 8, 1943, in *ibid.*, pp. 356-58.

70. Depesza, Lasocki do Kalskiego, March 8, 1944; Depesza, Kalski do Muszynskiego, March 9, 1944; Depesza, RPZ do Pana Pelnomocnika Rzadu R.P.,

March 12, 1944, in *ibid.*, pp. 143, 204.

71. Lukas, *Forgotten Holocaust*, p. 149.

72. *Ibid.*

73. Zuckerman, *Surplus of Memory*, p. 448.

74. Protokol z Przyjecia Przedstawicieli Rady P.Z., (signed Wencki), October 28, 1943, in Delegatura Rzadu RP 202/XV-2, p. 117, AAN.

75. Lukas, *Forgotten Holocaust*, p. 149.

76. Zuckerman, *Surplus of Memory*, p. 478.

77. David Engel, *Facing a Holocaust: The Polish Government-in-Exile and the Jews, 1943-1945.* (Chapel Hill: University of North Carolina Press, 1993), p. 198, n. 17.

78. Depesza, Rada Pomocy Zydom do Rzadu Polskeigo, July 22, 1943, in Teka 78, poz. 176, PUST.

79. Depesza, Kalski do Muszynskiego, March 10, 1944; Depesza DR do Pana Prezesa Rady Ministrow, March 10, 1944; Depesza Hubert do Malickiego, March 18, 1944, in Delegatura Rzadu RP 202/XV-2, pp. 142, 148, AAN.

80. Prekerowa, *Konspiracyjna Rada Pomocy Zydom*, p. 125.

81. Iranek-Osmecki, *He Who Saves One Life*, p. 236.

82. *Ibid.*, p. 237.

83. *Ibid.*, pp. 237-38.

84. Depesza, Borowski, Marek, do Pelnomocnika Rzadu w Kraju, December 29, 1942, in Delegatura Rzadu RP 202/XV-2, pp. 84-86, AAN; Depesza, Wernic do Stema, January 8, 1943, in Teka 78, poz. 17, PUST.

85. Engel gives extensive coverage to the Relief Council but, curiously, says little about Zegota, which was a more significant organization. See the appropriate sections in *Facing a Holocaust*.

86. For example, see the memorandum sent by western Jewish leaders to the Polish government in March, 1943 in *ibid.*, pp. 226-27, n. 90. There are other examples cited in Engel's book.

87. Quoted in *ibid.*, p. 151.

88. Lukas, *Forgotten Holocaust*, p. 149.

89. Raczynski estimated that Poles had sheltered about 400,000 Jews during the war. Interview with Count Edward Raczynski, July 21, 1986, London, England.

90. Lukas, *Forgotten Holocaust*, p. 150.

91. *Ibid.*

92. *Tygodnik Powszechny*, March 29, 1987.

93. Lukas, *Forgotten Holocaust*, p. 150.

APPENDIX B

THEY WERE KILLED FOR THE HELP THEY GAVE*

These are excerpts from a report prepared by the Main Commission for the Investigation of Crimes Against the Polish Nation that document the deaths of 704 Polish people for helping Jews during World War II. The list does not include the so-called pacification of Polish villages by the Germans for rendering help to Jews.

In no sense is this list complete. It simply represents the effort of one official body to document Poles who died helping Jews. Estimates of the total number of Poles who died for the help they gave to Jews range from 2,000 to 50,000.

There is a huge discrepancy between the list prepared by the Main Commission for the Investigation of Crimes Against the Polish Nation and the number of people in the list who have been awarded posthumous medals by Yad Vashem, the Israeli organization which recognizes gentiles for helping Jews during the Holocaust. Out of 704 deceased Poles, only a fraction of them are recognized by Yad Vashem.

The discrepancy is partially explained by the criteria of Yad Vashem which requires testimonies from Jews who received assistance from

*The Main Commission for the Investigation of Crimes Against the Polish Nation, The Institute of National Memory and The Polish Society for the Righteous Among the Nations, THOSE WHO HELPED: POLISH RESCUERS OF JEWS DURING THE HOLOCAUST, Part II (Warsaw: 1996), pp. 48-132.

gentiles. When the Germans killed Polish rescuers along with their Jewish charges, there obviously was no one alive to make the required statements to Yad Vashem. This is why the number of Poles who helped Jews and those who died for it is greater than historians are able to document with any degree of accuracy.

9. ARASZKIEWICZ, Aleksandra, living in Cisie near Ceglow, Siedlce prov.

A sizable group of Jews from Ceglow took refuge in the village of Cisie (incl. from the Goldsztajn family Esther, Yoyne and Mendel and the baby girl, Jablonka), as well as fugitives who had escaped from the "death trains" traveling to Treblinka via Ceglow. On 28 June 1943 raids were carried out on the village by the military police from Minsk Mazowiecki, during which 25 Poles (incl. several railway workers) were taken from their homes together with the numerous sheltered Jews and murdered. The following were killed in Ceglow or Cisie village: Aleksandra Araszkiewicz, Marcin Dabrowski, Franciszek Fiutkowski, Aleksander Gasior, Henryk Gergera, Rozalia Jaworska with her 2 years old daughter, Tadeusz Lipinski, Zygmunt Malus, Stanislaw Pezyk, Tomasz Platek and Sylweriusz Platek, Edward Rzysko, Wladyslaw Saski, Eugeniusz Skwiecinski, Marian Smater, Piotr Smater, Jan Szczesny, Jozefa Szyperska, Aleksandra Wasowska, Jan Wasowski, Mieczyslaw Wasowski, Wladyslaw Wojcicki, Jan Zaganczyk and Ludwik Zajac. Wieslaw Walczewski was arrested on this day and shot in January 1944. The village was burnt down (cf. 92, 124, 141-142, 186-187, 332, 361, 456, 470-471, 536, 539, 560, 564-565, 597, 604, 630, 635-637, 677, 693, 696).

10. ARCHUTOWSKI, Roman, rector of the Archdiocesan Seminary in Warsaw, sent to Majdanek for aiding Jewish people; died after torture in October 1943.

11. ARCISZEWSKI, Albin, 45, living in Orlicz near Garbow, Lublin prov., executed in September 1943 for helping Jews from the camp at Antopol; he tried to save the lives of dr. Czerniak, his wife and 2 daughters, Isaac Elfenstein, Lena Mazurska and Itka Wolyniec.

12. AUGUSTYN, Jozef, living in Szerzyny, Tarnow prov.

13. AUGUSTYN, Jozefa, Jozef's wife. They sheltered 3 Jews from Szerzyny—the family of Elias and Hersh Haskel—for which they were shot together with the Jewish family on 4 February 1944 by the German military police.

14. AUGUSTYNIAK, Franciszek, 30, worker, living in Paulinow near Sokolow Podlaski, Siedlce prov., shot by an SS unit on 24 February 1943

together with a group of 14 people who were victims of a provocation: several weeks earlier they rendered help to a Nazi agent, who pretended to be a Jewish fugitive; together with Augustyniak in Paulinow died also: Zygmunt Dryga, Franciszek Kirylski, Jozef, Ewa and Stanislaw Kotowski, Stanislaw Piwko, Jan Sliwinski, Aleksandra Wiktorzak (cf. 111, 216, 259-261, 469, 609, 648); Stanislaw Kusiak and Stanislaw Mazurek died in the Treblinka camp (cf. 314, 374); and Czeslaw Borowy, Jan Brzozowski and Stanislaw Henduszko died while digging trenches (cf. 43, 57, 166).

15. BACZEWSKA, Honorata, 30, teacher, living in Lublin, underground liaison officer and Home Army (AK) press carrier; murdered for sheltering Jews early in 1945 by Ukrainian nationalists.

16. BANASZEK, Marianna, c. 50, living in Pustelnik near Marki, Warsaw prov.

17. BANASZEK, Stanislawa, daughter

18. BANASZEK, Wladyslaw, son, murdered in October 1943 for concealing a Jewish family of 3 of unknown identity. The Jewish family, informed of the threat of a raid on the house, escaped.

19. BARAN, Adam, 29, living in Hucisko near Glogow Malopolski, Rzeszow prov.

20. BARAN, Szczepan, 36

On 10 June 1943 a division of the German military police from Rzeszow surrounded the village of Hucisko and murdered 21 inhabitants of this village and the neighbouring village of Przewrotne in retaliation for sheltering Jews. The following died: Adam Baran, Szczepan Baran, Franciszek Beskur, Jadwiga Chezalik, Franciszek Drag, Anna Dworak and 7 members of her family: Anna (younger), Jan, Katarzyna, Maria, Michal, Stefania and Zofia; Adam, Jozef and Marcin Gut, Marcin Kolano, Jakub Rumak, Jozef Rumak, Jozef Sluja and Adam Susich. As part of their repressive measures, the Germans burnt down 17 houses and numerous service buildings (cf. 31, 61, 110, 113-120, 161-163, 222, 521-522, 563, 589). Similar measures were carried out two times in the village of Przewrotne (cf. 49-51, 70-71).

21. BARAN, Rozalia, living in Modryn near Hrubieszow, Zamosc prov., in December 1942 beaten up and then murdered for rendering her "Kennkarte" accessible to a Jewess, who using it went to work in Germany and was recognized there and captured.

22. BARANEK, Wincenty, 46, farmer, living in Siedliska near Miechow, Kielce prov.

23. BARANEK, Lucja, 35, Wincenty's wife

24. BARANEK, Henryk, 12, son

25. BARANEK, Tadeusz, 10, son

26. BARANEK, Katarzyna, mother of Wincenty, murdered by the military police on 15 March 1943 together with Katarzyna Kopec, mother of Lucja and the Jews they were sheltering: Pinczowski, Skowron, Sybirski and Weitzman (cf. 228).

27. BARGLIK, Maria, 51, farmer, living in Tokarnia, Cracow prov., killed on 6 March 1944 following sentence passed by a special court (Sondergericht) at Szaflary for sheltering the 6-member family of Samuel Steinberg.

28. BARGLIK, Stefan, living in Tokarnia, Cracow prov., shot on the strength of the special court verdict of the SS and Police Commander (Standgericht) in Cracow for "fostering Jews and rendering shelter to them"; execution of the verdict was pronounced on 21 February 1944.

44. BORYCKI, Stanislaw, 44, farmer, living in Boisko near Lipsko, Radom prov.

45. BORYCKA, Zofia, 38, Stanislaw's wife

46. BORYCKI, Zbigniew, son, shot on 2 January 1943 in their own farm for rendering help to Jews; their farm was burned down. At the same time Krawczyk family was also killed (cf. 279-281).

47. BRAJA, Wladyslaw, living in Rowne near Dukla, Krosno prov., executed in August or September 1943 for concealing 3 Jewish people.

48. BRONISLAWSKI, Edward, living in Warsaw, shot on 21 April 1943—during the third day of the Ghetto Uprising—when as a liaison officer of the Gwardia Ludowa (People's Guard) he tried to supply guns to the Jewish fighters. His wife Wiktoria and his son Zbigniew were arrested. Their subsequent fate is unknown.

49. BRUDZ, Antoni, 24, living in Przewrotne near Glogow Malopolski, Rzeszow prov.

50. BRUDZ, Wojciech, 34

51. BRUDZ, Walenty, 57. On 13 March 1943 a division of the German police, under the supervision of Gestapo functionnaries, killed c. 30 people in the village of Przewrotne for sheltering Jewish people. Along with the members of the Brudz family were killed: Andrzej Drag, Franciszek Drag, Wojciech Drag, Michal Gawel, Adam Organisciak and 6 members of his family: Andrzej, Aniela, Franciszek, Jozef (born in 1906), Jozef (born in 1912) and Wojciech; Lukasz Pomykala, Wojciech Pomykala, Antoni Rusin, Jan Walc, Franciszek Wanoska, Franciszek Wilk, Jozef Wilk (cf. 108-109, 110, 136, 427-433, 476-477, 525, 629, 633, 650-652). It has proved impossible to establish the names of other victims.

A second execution in Przewrotne took place on 9 May 1943 (cf. 70-71), as well as in the nearby village of Hucisko on 10 June 1943 (cf. 19-20).

52. BRUHL, Hanna, living in Milanowek, Warsaw prov., shot on 17 May 1943 by military policemen from Grodzisk Mazowiecki in the "Anielin" villa of Milanowek together with the 4 Jewish people she had been sheltering (2 men, 2 women).

53. BRUST, Jan, living in Rakow near Czestochowa, shot in the first half of 1944 at the Hasag-Eisenhutte A.G. camp for distributing money and food and passing of correspondences to Jewish inmates, as part of the campaign carried out by the Relief Council for Jews and the Jewish underground.

54. BRYNKUS, Cyryl, 44, living in Spytkowice near Oswiecim, Cracow prov., arrested on the 15 November 1943 for help rendered to Jewish population; put in jail in Zakopane, later transferred to Plaszow camp and then to Montelupich prison in Cracow. Shot in Cracow on 28 May 1944.

55. BRYS, Johan, railwayman, living in Sosnowiec, Katowice prov., he helped fugitives from the Sosnowiec ghetto; some of them he transported to Hungary. For this activity he was arrested in 1944 by Gestapo officers and sent to the concentration camp Auschwitz, where from he never came back. Posthumously awarded the medal "Righteous Among the Nations."

56. BRZOZOWSKA, Zofia, living in Kobylka, Warsaw prov., shot on 1 September 1943 by members of the Gestapo together with 2 Jewish men sheltered on her property (one of them was Goldberg, owner of the tannery in Wolomin).

57. BRZOZOWSKI, Jan, 16, living in Paulinow near Sokolow Podlaski, Siedlce prov., shot on the 24 February 1943 while digging trenches near Sokolow Podlaski as one of the 14 persons who happened to be victims of a provocation: several weeks earlier they rendered help to a Nazi agent, who pretended to be a Jewish fugitive (cf. 14).

58. BUSZKO, Henryk, 30, farmer, living in Liza Stara near Bialystok, murdered on 21 September 1943 by gendarmes from the post in Pietkowo for help rendered to Jews hiding after escape from a transport to Treblinka camp.

59. BUZOWICZ, Wincenty, living in Radom.

60. BUZOWICZ, Anna, Wincenty's wife, on 3 April 1943 sentenced to death by a special court (Sondergericht) in Radom for helping the Jewish women Sala Rubinowicz and Else Schwarzman. Wiktoria Paduch, Jan Pinkus, Zenon Polonski and Maria Rozanska were also sentenced to

death in the same case (cf. 442, 466, 475, 517).

61. CHEZALIK, Jadwiga, 41, farmer, living in Hucisko near Glogow Malopolski, Rzeszow prov., killed on 10 June 1943 in a mass execution for sheltering Jewish people in which 21 villagers died (cf. 19-20).

62. CHEC, Franciszek, 17, living in Tomaszowice near Jastkow, Lublin prov., foster-child of Leonard Pietrak, killed together with him and his family on 28 February 1944 for sheltering 2 Jewish men (cf. 461-463).

63. CHOLEWINSKI, Marcin, 30, living in Grzymalkow near Kielce, shot on 19 October 1942 for supplying food to the Radoszyce ghetto.

64. CHOREW, Wlodzimierz, from Bereza Kartuska (city incorporated after the war into the Soviet Ukraine)

65. CHOREW, (Christian name unknown), mother

66. CHOREW, (Christian name unknown), father, executed in autumn 1943 together with the Jewish woman they were sheltering, Leycha Kaplan.

67. CHOWANIAK, Karol, farmer, living in Zawoja near Makow Podhalanski, Bielsko prov.

68. CHOWANIAK, Tekla, Karol's wife. Karol Chowaniak was arrested in May 1943 together with 4 sheltered Jews (Kuczko family among others) who were shot on the spot. Karol had gone through several week long investigation in the Gestapo prison "Palace" in Zakopane, and then was sent to Auschwitz camp; Tekla Chowaniak arrested shortly afterwards together with her foster-child, Karolina Marek; both were sent directly to Auschwitz. All three of them died there (cf. 368).

69. CHRACA, Karol, 46, living in Wroblowka, Nowy Sacz prov., executed by the Gestapo on 20 May 1942 in Czarny Dunajec together with Jozef Lehrer and his daughter, for supplying food to the Lehrers and other Jewish people in hiding.

70. CHUBRO, Marcin, 37, living in Przewrotne near Glogow Malopolski, Rzeszow prov.

71. CHUBRO, Michal, 53. On 9 May 1943, following orders issued by the Gestapo, a division of the military police from Rzeszow surrounded the village of Przewrotne and murdered 16 Poles for sheltering Jewish people. Apart from Marcin and Michal Chubro, the following died: Andrzej Gola, Antoni Granat, Ludwik Gut, Jozef Kus, Pawel Laska, Jan Marszal, Jozef Tryburski (cf. 148, 152, 164, 317, 323, 371. 618). The names of the other 7 victims have not been established. Similar executions took place in Przewrotne on 13 March 1943 (cf. 49-51), as well as in the nearby village of Hucisko on 10 June 1943 (cf. 19-20).

72. CHYBOWSKI, Franciszek, 60, living in Rzedowice near Ksiaz

Wielki, Kielce prov.

73. CHYBOWSKA, Julia, 54, Franciszek's wife, shot on 5 March 1943 for sheltering Jewish people.

74. CIESIELSKI, Jozef, 19, farmer, living in Boisko near Lipsko, Radom prov., shot on 7 November 1943 in a group of 3 persons for help rendered to Jewish population (cf. 283, 582).

75. CIESLAK, Wojciech, living in Leka Szczucinska, Tarnow prov., shot on 21 March 1943 for sheltering in his house a Jewish woman from Pacanow.

76. CIOLKOSZ, Feliks, 58, living in Markuszowa near Wisniowa, Rzeszow prov.

77. CIOLKOSZ, (Christian name unknown), 50, Feliks's wife

78. CIOLKOSZ, Jan, 26, son, shot in June 1943 by military policemen from Wisniowa for helping Jewish people who had taken refuge in the nearby woods (cf. 426).

79. CYPARSKA, Stefania Janina, 25, living in Wydrna, Krosno prov.

80. CYPARSKI, Alfred Fryderyk, 6, son

81. CYPARSKA, Stanislawa, 3, daughter

82. CYPARSKI, Tadeusz, 6 months, son, murdered in March 1944 for rendering help to Jews by Stefania.

83. CYPARSKI, Wojciech, 30, living in Krzemienna, Krosno prov., shot in early March 1944 by Gestapo officers for rendering help to Jews and Soviet POWs.

84. CZAPLA, Stanislaw, 30, farmer, living in Swiesielice, Radom prov., murdered on 7 December 1942 by gendarmes from unit stationed in Ciepielow for help rendered to Jews. Together with him died: Bronislaw Dobron, Stanislaw Nowotnik, Marianna Skwira, Wojciech Skrzak and members of Wdowiak and Wojewodka families (cf. 102, 403, 557, 561, 638-640, 660-665).

85. CZERSKA, Janina Wanda, 56, living in Warsaw, sheltered 7 Jews in her house in Milanowek: Jadwiga Minska (whose husband Ignacy was killed in Katyn) and 6 other persons who are known only by their assumed names: Cholewinski (married couple and their 2 sons) and Kordonski (married couple). In the autumn of 1943 five of them and J.W.Czerska were arrested. There is no trace of the Jews, and Czerska was transferred on 5 October from Pawiak prison to the Auschwitz camp where she died on 20 February 1944.

86. CZERWONKA, Franciszek, 56, farmer, living in Pawlosiow near Jaroslaw, Rzeszow prov.

87. CZERWONKA, Julia, 55, Franciszek's wife

88. CZERWONKA, Stanislaw, 18, son, shot on 7 July 1943 by Gestapo for sheltering Jews.

89. DABOWSKI, Krzysztof, 44, farmer, living in Dlugoleka near Knyszyn, Bialystok prov., murdered on 5 May 1945, already after the liberation, in connection with the unselfish sheltering of 7 Jews from Knyszyn since September 1942. (They were: Ber Slodki with his wife Fruma; their daughter Szosza and son-in-law Abram Krawiec, rabbi; Gerson Krawiec, his wife Lenta and their son, Szmuel). All of them left Poland after the war. Dabowski however was killed by bandits who demanded large sums of money from him, which—in their opinion—he must have earned for sheltering the Jews. Posthumously awarded the medal "Righteous Among the Nations."

104. DOMANSKI, Piotr, 76, farmer, living in Rzazew near Zbuczyn, Siedlce prov.

105. DOMANSKI, Franciszek, 37, farmer, Piotr's son

106. DOMANSKI, Antoni, 32, farmer, Piotr's son, shot by the military police on 8 April 1943 for sheltering Jews and partisans.

107. DOMERADZKI, Jan, living in Trebaczew near Sadkowice, Skierniewice prov., shot on 11 December 1943 with his neighbours—the Szczepaniak family—for helping a Jewish family. The father of this family was also shot, the fates of remaining family members being unknown (cf. 594-596).

108. DRAG, Andrzej, 48, living in Przewrotne near Glogow Malopolski, Rzeszow prov.

109. DRAG, Wojciech, 42, on 13 March 1943 shot in the village of Przewrotne in a group execution for sheltering Jews (cf. 49-51).

110. DRAG, Franciszek, 31, living in Przewrotne near Glogow Malopolski, shot on 10 June 1943 in the village of Hucisko (cf. 19-20).

111. DRYGA, Zygmunt, 54, living in Paulinow near Sokolow Podlaski, Siedlce prov., shot in Paulinow by an SS unit on 24 February 1943 together with a group of 14 people who were victims of a provocation: several weeks earlier they rendered help to a Nazi agent, who pretended to be a Jewish fugitive (cf. 14).

112. DUDKIEWICZ, Aleksander, living in Gniazdowo near Lochow, Siedlce prov., killed in autumn 1942 in Gniazdowo together with a Jewish sheltered fugitive with the surname Frydman.

113. DWORAK, Katarzyna, 60, living in Hucisko near Glogow Malopolski, Rzeszow prov.

114. DWORAK, Maria, 56

115. DWORAK, Michal, 57

116. DWORAK, Anna, 30

117. DWORAK, Jan, 29

118. DWORAK, Anna, 21

119. DWORAK, Stefania, 16

120. DWORAK, Zofia, 52, living in Przewrotne near Glogow Malopolski, killed on 10 June 1943 in a group execution for sheltering Jewish people (cf. 19-20).

121. DZIAK, Antoni, living in Bedzienica near Iwierzyce, Rzeszow prov., arrested and later executed on 27 October 1943 for sheltering 5 Jewish males: 3 young boys (Bendys brothers), Faust (30 years) and Meler (40), while Dziak's wife, Zofia, managed to escape.

122. FEDOROWICZ, Jakub, living in Kaweczyn, Skierniewice prov., shot in the spring of 1944 for sheltering Abraham Rosenberg and his son as well as other Jewish people. Also shot was Stanislaw Trojanowski, his associate, and the Jews, of which only one succeeded in getting away (cf. 616).

123. FILIPEK, Katarzyna, 47, farmer, living in Tokarnia near Nowy Targ, Cracow prov., murdered in January 1944 by Germans in result of denunciation; since July 1943 she sheltered 6 Jews (they were: Samuel Szternlicht, his 2 daughters, son-in-law and 2 grandchildren); all of them died. Filipek was posthumously awarded the medal "Righteous Among the Nations."

137. GAWRON, Czeslaw, 20, living in Wola Przybyslawska near Garbow, Lublin prov.

138. GAWRON, Leonard, 21, Czeslaw's brother, murdered on 10 December 1942 together with the Aftyka family for helping Jews (cf. 3-6).

139. GAWRYCH, Jan, 50, forester from Czarna near Minsk Mazowiecki, Siedlce prov., shot on 30 March 1943 together with a group of Jews whom he rendered help—partisans and 2 fugitive Soviet POWs; together with them also died Stanislaw Skuza and Dawid Rutkowski cooperating with Gawrych (cf. 526, 558).

140. GAWRYS, Piotr, 20, living in Polomia near Tarnow, Rzeszow prov., murdered on 9 September 1943 together with a group of 8 Poles sheltering Jews (cf. 508-512).

141. GASIOR, Aleksander, farmer, living in Cisie near Ceglow, Siedlce prov.

142. GERGERA, Henryk, farmer, both people were shot on 28 June in a group of 25 people for help organized by the village in sheltering Jews (cf. 9).

143. GERULA, Michal, farmer, living in Lozinka Dolna, Cracow

prov., shot on 23 February 1944 on the strength of the special court (Standgericht) verdict of the SS and Police Commander in Cracow for sheltering Jews.

144. GIELAROWSKI, Bartlomiej, living in Trzebuska near Sokolow Malopolski, Rzeszow prov., in summer of 1943 shot together with Karolina Marciniec who was living at the same address and the 5 people of Jewish nationality from Sokolow Malopolski sheltering with them (cf. 133).

145. GLONIAK, Walenty, 50, living in Biala near Tyczyn, Rzeszow prov.

146. GLONIAK, Jozef, 21, son, shot on 15 October 1943 together with 3 sheltered Jews from Tyczyn.

147. GNIDULA, Jozef, 70, farmer, living in Majdan Nowy near Ksiezpol, Zamogc prov., shot on 29 December 1942 with his cousin, Anna Margol, for sheltering the Jewish woman Boruch (no first name). Boruch, having been captured and beaten by the military police, and being promised her life would be spared, gave away the names of her shelterers and others who had helped her. The following perished as a result: Katarzyna and Jozef Kowal, Anastazja and Maria Lubiarz as well as Kazimierz Szabata. Boruch was also killed (cf. 262-263, 344-345, 370, 592).

148. GOLA, Andrzej, 41, living in Przewrotne near Glogow Malopolski, Rzeszow prov., shot on 9 May 1943 with 15 other inhabitants of the village for sheltering Jews (cf. 70-71).

149. GOLEN, Eleonora, living in Jaslo, Krosno prov., shot together with another Pole in 1943 by officers of the German police and SS for sheltering a 12 year old Jewish boy; the boy died together with them.

150. GRABOWSKA, Irena, living in Piastow, Warsaw prov. From April 1942 she was sheltering a small group of Jews while helping many others: together with her mother she gave refuge to the family Mortkowicz, noted publishers and booksellers from Warsaw. On 7 February 1944 she was arrested and following brutal questioning was shot on 26 April of that year.

168. HOLTZER, Marianna, 61, Jozef's wife, killed by military policemen from the police-station at Rachanie on 2 November 1942 for attempting to protect the lives of c. 12 Jewish people who had been legally employed on their lands. After killing the Holtzers the Germans also shot the Jews.

169. INGLOT, Zofia, living in Wola Komborska near Krosno, shot in October 1943 by SS officers for sheltering 2 Jews; together with her

died: Janina Kwolek as well as Jozef and Katarzyna Prejzner and both sheltered Jews (cf. 319, 481-82).

170. IRZEK, Julia, living in Lwow (city incorporated after the war into the Soviet Ukraine), sentenced by a special court (Sondergericht) to death for helping Jews; information of the death sentence was given in the public notice issued by the Commander of the SS and the Galicia District Police on 14 December 1943.

171. IWANSKI, Roman, living in Warsaw, as soldier of the Home Army (AK) associated organization, he fought together with members of the Jewish Military Union (ZZW) during the Warsaw Ghetto Uprising, and was shot on 27 April 1943 on Muranowski Sq.

172. IWANSKI, Zbigniew, living in Warsaw, as member of the Home Army associated organization, he fought against the German troops on Karmelicka Str. in Warsaw. Perished on 3 May 1943 while conducting 15 people from the burning ghetto.

173. IZDEBSKI, Mieczyslaw, 28, farmer, living in Zienki near Wlodawa, Lublin prov., murdered in the spring of 1943 together with Kupersztok family of 5 (Nata, her husband and 3 children aged 10-18 years old). Neighbours saved three year old daughter of Izdebski.

174. JABLKOWSKA, Helena, PPS (Polish Socialist Party) member, living in Warsaw. She sheltered many Jews, incl. Bardach family, for which she was arrested on 6 January 1944 and shortly shot.

175. JAJESNICA, Jozef, living in Kalusz, former Stanislawow prov. (place incorporated after the war into the Soviet Ukraine)

176. JAJESNICA, Maria, Jozef's wife

177. JAJESNICA, Jan, 10, son. Maria, owner of a brickworks, allowed a group of 4 refugees, who had escaped from a Jewish transport, to take shelter in a building on her property. Pursuing German soldiers forced the Jajesnica family into this building and burnt all 7 people alive.

178. JAKUBOWSKA, Walentyna, farmer, living in Poplawy near Bransk, Bialystok prov., murdered on 12 April 1943 by gendarmes from Bransk; together with her died 2 sheltered by her Jewish children: Lejb (11) and Fajwel (13) Dolinski.

179. JANICZEK, Jan, 46, living in Warsaw, employee of the Polish Savings Bank (PKO); he gave shelter in his own home to the Jew Grossman. Both people were arrested and perished in Gross-Rosen (Janiczek on 4 December 1944).

180. JANTON, Jan, 31, living in Wola Brzostecka near Brzostek, Tarnow prov., supplied food to the Fish family 6 of whom were hiding in the woods (mother, Henia, c. 60, daughters Baily, 23, Rosa, 26, and Ester,

28, son Moses, 30, as well as the Baily's baby-girl). As the result of denunciation all, including Janton were killed on 8 December 1942 and buried in a common grave in the woods. Janton was awarded posthumously with the medal "Righteous Among the Nations."

181. JANUS, Helena, 40, wife of Bronislaw, living in Dzwonowice near Pilica, Katowice prov.

182. JANUS, Maria, 22, daughter of Bronislaw

183. JANUS, Krzysztof, 3, son of Bronislaw. Helena and her husband Bronislaw sheltered the Jewish families, Berlinski and Rusinek (6 people). On 12 January 1945 a group of military police and Gestapo discovered the Jewish refugees and killed everyone present at the time, incl. Bronislaw's sister, Zofia Madej, her husband and her daughter. Only Bronislaw Janus, absent at that time, escaped with his life (cf. 351-353).

184. JAROSZYNSKI, Bronislaw, living in Stryj (place incorporated after the war into the Soviet Ukraine), sentenced to death "for conspiring with Jews" by a special court of the Commander of the SS and the Galician District Police-Standgericht (public announcement from 28 January 1944).

185. JASINSKI, Antoni, living in Warsaw, shot together with the Jewish couple (he an engineer, she a dentist) he had given refuge in his flat; the tragedy resulted from the dentist's insufficient caution in selecting patients she treated.

186. JAWORSKA, Rozalia, living in Cisie near Ceglow, Siedlce prov.

187. JAWORSKA, (Christian name unknown), 2, daughter, shot on 28 June 1943 in Ceglow in a group of 25 inhabitants of Cisie village for sheltering Jews (cf. 9).

188. JELONEK, Jozef, living in Zajaczkow near Ciepielow, Radom prov., shot in January 1943 with the family of Gabriel Wolowiec for helping Jews (cf. 668-673).

189. JEWTUSIK, Opanas, living in Lwow (city incorporated after the war into the Soviet Ukraine), sentenced to death by a special court of the Commander of the SS and the Galician District Police (Standgericht) for helping Jews (official announcement from 28 January 1944).

190. JEDRZEJCZYK, Jozef, 27, farmer, living in Matysowka near Rzeszow, for help rendered to Jews shot on 15 October 1943 by Gestapo officers near police station in Tyczyn.

191. JEDRZEJEWSKI, Jozef, 27, living in Matysowka near Tyczyn, Rzeszow prov., shot on 15 October 1943 in Tyczyn in a group of 5 Poles, some of whom had been brought from surrounding localities, and given the death sentence for helping Jewish people (cf. 211, 443).

192. JOC, Jan, 61, farmer, living in Metow near Lublin.

193. JOC, Jadwiga, 57, Jan's wife, murdered in November 1943 for supplying food to Jews hiding in nearby forest.

194. JOZEFEK, Bronislaw, living in Lwow (city incorporated after the war into the Soviet Ukraine)

195. JOZEFEK,Kazimierz

196. JOZEFEK, Maria, sentenced to death by a special court of the Commander of the SS and the Galician District Police (Standgericht) for sheltering Jews; their names were placed on official announcements issued on 14 December 1943 and 28 January 1944.

197. JUSZCZYK, Franciszek, 55, living in Bialobrzegi, Radom prov.

198. JUSZCZYK, Wiktoria, 45, Franciszek's wife

199. JUSZCZYK, Stefan, 23, son

200. JUSZCZYK, Weronika, 20, daughter

201. JUSZCZYK, Boleslaw, 17, son

202. JUSZCZYK, Helena, 15, daughter. They rendered help to a Nazi agent, who pretended to be a Jewish fugitive (cf. 14).

217. KLIS, Michal, Polish police officer, living in Cracow, arrested on 11 September 1943 and shot for participation in preparation of false docments for Jews in hiding.

218. KLUBA, Stanislaw, living in Kamyk near Lapanow, Tarnow prov., sheltered 3 Jews (incl. Moses Landner and Irena Rajs); on 4 December 1943 the military police discovered the hide-out; the Jewish fugitives were shot immediately, Kluba on 20 January 1944. Posthumously awarded the medal "Righteous Among the Nations."

219. KMIEC, Anna Zofia, 51, living in Radgoszcz-Poreba, Tarnow prov.

220. KMIEC, Bronislaw, 19, Anna Zofia's son, shot on 28 November 1942 for sheltering Jews, incl. a son of a baker from Radgoszcz. Anna Zofia's baby grandchildren, Bronislawa and Janina Soltys also died, as well as Tomasz and Bronislawa Juzba (cf. 203-204, 574-575).

221. KOGUT, Anna, living in Dabrowa Tarnowska, Tarnow prov., shot by German gendarmes in September 1944 together with sheltered by her Jewish Metzger family of 3.

222. KOLANO, Marcin, 36, living in Hucisko near Glogow Malopolski, Rzeszow prov., on 10 June 1943 killed in a mass execution for sheltering Jews (cf. 19-20).

223. KOLBUSZEWSKI, Kazimierz, 58, prof. at the University of Lwow (city incorporated after the war into the Soviet Ukraine), arrested in 1942 and murdered on 20 February 1943 in Majdanek for giving

medical help to a Jewish woman, his former house servant.

224. KOMARNICKA, Leokadia, professor's wife, living in Warsaw, helped Jewish people, leading them out of the ghetto and sheltering in her own home or finding for them flats where they might take refuge, as well as sharing with them all she had. She travelled to Lowicz to collect a debt owed to one of them where she was betrayed as a "Jewish guardian" by the debtor; she was shot by the Gestapo.

225. KONIECZNA, Natalia, living in Giebultow near Ksiaz Wielki, Kielce prov.

226. KONIECZNA, (Christian name unknown), Natalia's daughter, shot in May 1944 together with 7 unidentified sheltered people of Jewish background; the husband of Natalia managed to escape.

227. KOPACZ, Stanislaw, farmer; living in Szynwald, Tarnow prov., in 1942-1944 he sheltered several Jews; he was shot together with them as a result of them being discovered during pacification of Szynwald in August 1944.

228. KOPEC, Katarzyna, 58, living in Siedliska near Miechow, Kielce prov., mother of Lucja Baranek, murdered together with her whole family on 15 March 1943 for sheltering 4 Jews, who were also killed (cf. 22-26).

229. KORDULA, Henryka, 13, living in Rekowka near Ciepielow, Radom prov. On 6 December 1942 the military police executed 33 inhabitants from Rekowka and Ciepielow for sheltering Jews; among others, the entire Kosior family and Henryka Kordula, who happened to be visiting at the Kosior's, were killed (cf. 243-256).

230. KOSIARCZYK, Wiktoria, farmer, living in Skrzynice near Jablonna, Lublin prov.

231. KOSIARCZYK, Andrzej, 28, farmer, Wiktoria's son

232. KOSIARCZYK, Katarzyna, 27, cousin, shot on 9 October 1943 in Bystrzejowice in the house of Wiktoria's daughter, Zofia and her husband, Roman Kucharski, who had been sheltering 5 Jewish people; all 10 people were killed (cf. 299-300).

233. KOSIBA, Wojciech, 71, living in Hankowka near Jaslo, Krosno prov., shot by gendarmes in June 1944 for help rendered to Ryfka and Salka Saul, who also died.

234. KOSIELSKI, Franciszek, farmer, living in Rzyczyn near Garwolin, Siedlce prov.

235. KOSIELSKA, Katarzyna, Franciszek's wife

236. KOSIELSKA, Bronislawa, daughter

237. KOSIELSKA, Genowefa, daughter

238. KOSIELSKA, Leokadia, daughter

239. KOSIELSKA, Zofia, daughter

240. KOSIELSKI, Czeslaw, son

241. KOSIELSKI, Lucjan, son

242. KOSIELSKI, Stanislaw, son, the Kosielski family sheltered Jews in their farm; the sons were members of Gwardia Ludowa (People's Guard). On 7 March 1944 gendarmes discovered the Jews during the search they carried out and murdered them together with the whole Kosielski family.

243. KOSIOR, Wladyslaw, 42, living in Ciepielow, Radom prov.

244. KOSIOR, Karolina, 40, Wladyslaw's wife

245. KOSIOR, Aleksander, 18, son of Wladyslaw

246. KOSIOR, Tadeusz, 16, son of Wladyslaw

247. KOSIOR, Wladyslawa, 14, daughter of Wladyslaw

248. KOSIOR, Mieczyslaw, 12, son of Wladyslaw

249. KOSIOR, Irena, 10, daughter of Wladyslaw

250. KOSIOR, Adam, 6, son of Wladyslaw

251. KOSIOR, Stanislaw, 40, living in Rekowka near Ciepielow

252. KOSIOR, Maria, 27, Stanislaw's wife

253. KOSIOR, Jan, 8, son of Stanislaw

254. KOSIOR, Mieczyslaw, 5, son of Stanislaw

255. KOSIOR, Marian, 4, son of Stanislaw

256. KOSIOR, Teresa, 3, daughter of Stanislaw. On 6 December 1942 the military police burnt alive 33 people from the neighbouring villages of Ciepielow and Rekowka. The group killing was the result of members of the Volksdeutsch community denouncing their Polish neighbours for sheltering and feeding 6 Jews. The entire Kosior family was killed. Tadeusz Kosior attempted to escape from the burning barn, but was pursued and thrown back into the flames. Obuchiewicz, Kowalski and Skoczylas families, other Poles, as well as sheltered Jews were also killed in the massacre (cf. 229, 257, 267-273, 405-410, 553-554)

257. KOSCINSKA, Marianna, 68, living in Rekowka near Ciepielow, Radom prov., mother-in-law of Piotr Skoczylas, killed on 6 December 1942 with the Skoczylas and Kosior families (cf. 243-256, 553-554).

258. KOTFIS, Wojciech, 70, living in Uszew near Gnojnik, Tarnow prov., shot by the military police in May 1944 with the Jewish people he was sheltering, Federgrun and Goldberg with 3 children.

259. KOTOWSKI, Jozef, 56, farmer, living in Paulinow near Sokolow Podlaski, Siedlce prov.

260. KOTOWSKA, Ewa, 54, Jozef's wife

261. KOTOWSKI, Stanislaw, 25, farmer, son, shot by an SS unit on

24 February 1943 together with a group of 14 people who were victims of a provocation: several weeks earlier they rendered help to a Nazi agent, who pretended to be a Jewish fugitive (cf. 14).

285. KRYSIEWICZ, Stanislaw, farmer, living in Waniewo near Narew, Bialystok prov.

286. KRYSIEWICZ, Wiadyslawa, 37, Stanislaw's wife, shot by the military police from Tykocin in September 1943 for sheltering the following Jewish fugitives: Leyser Rozanowicz and his wife, Benjamine Rozanowicz and his wife, Shloma Jaskolka and his wife, Olsha, from Sokoly and a young Warsaw woman, all of whom also perished. 5 young children belonging to the Krysiewicz family were taken into the homes of neigbours.

287. KRZYSZTANIAK, Wladyslaw, living in Faliszowka, Krosno prov., killed on 21 November 1943 with the Jewish people sheltered in his house (incl. 2 adult women and a 5 year old child).

288. KSIAZEK, Boleslaw, farmer, living in Olesin near Debe Wielkie, Siedlce prov., shot on 12 May 1943 by the military police together with the Jewish fugitive named Idel sheltered in the house.

289. KSIAZEK, Franciszek, 50, living in Wierzbica near Kozlow, Kielce prov.

290. KSIAZEK, Julia, 40, Franciszek's wife

291. KSIAZEK, Jan, 21, son

292. KSIAZEK, Zygmunt, 18, son, shot on 29 January 1943 with 2 other families from Wierzbica for sheltering 3 Jews (surname Wandelsman), who were also killed. The fugitives' son-in-law, Naftul, having been captured and forced through beating to give information gave away the hide-out (cf. 294-298, 401-402, 439).

293. KUBICKA, Zofia, living in Pantalowice near Kanczuga, Przemysl prov., shot on 4 December 1942 with her parents and other villagers for helping a group of c. 12 local Jewish people who had taken refuge in the nearby woods (cf. 93-96).

294. KUCHARSKA, Anna, living in Wierzbica near Kozlow, Kielce prov.

295. KUCHARSKI, Mieczyslaw, 15, son

296. KUCHARSKI, Boleslaw, 9, son

297. KUCHARSKI, Jozef (twin), 7, son

298. KUCHARSKI, Stefan (twin), 7, son, shot on 29 January 1943 by the German military police with the Ksiazek and Nowak families and 2 Jewish fugitives from the Wandelsman family. The following survived the massacre: the Kucharski father, Izydor and 13 years old Bronislaw,

who following the Germans' departure, recovered consciousness, although Izydor lost an eye and Bronislaw completely lost his sight. Anna's mother, Julianna Ostrowska, was shot with the Kucharskis. The Wandelsman son-in-law, Naftul, had been forced by torture to give away the hide-out's location (cf. 289-292, 439).

299.KUCHARSKI, Roman, 31, farmer, living in Bystrzejowice near Piaski, Lublin prov.

300. KUCHARSKA. Zofia, 23, Roman's wife, killed by the military police on 9 October 1943 in their own home for sheltering Jews who were also killed while trying to escape; Andrzej, Katarzyna and Wiktoria Kosiarczyk were also executed; the 5 year old Kucharski son, Jozef, was injured, as a result of which he remained an invalid for the rest of his life. The farmhouse and buildings belonging to the Kucharskis, together with their livestock were burned (cf. 230-232).

301. KUCHARSKI, Stanislaw, 53, living in Debska Wola near Starachowice, Kielce prov., sentenced to death by a special court (Sondergericht) in Radom on 7 May 1943 on the grounds that "a certain Jewish woman, who had escaped from the ghetto, was sheltered in his house." The sentence was carried out on 25 September 1943.

338. LODEJ, Wladyslaw, 38, farmer, son of Wojciech and Marianna, coorganized a camp in the Kutera forest-range for c. 40 Jews from Ilza, which camp he, together with his family, helped supply with food; he was killed on 31 December 1942

339. LODEJ, Wiktoria, Wladyslaw's wife

340. LODEJ, Edward, 14, son

341. LODEJ, Janina, 12 daughter

342. LODEJ, Wladyslaw, 8, son

343. LODEJ, Stanislaw, 6, son. The entire family was arrested in Lubien on 21 December 1942 and was killed in the forest near Ilza.

344. LUBIARZ, Anastazja, 43, farmer, living in Majdan Nowy near Ksiezpol, Zamosc prov.

345. LUBIARZ, Maria, 76, Anastazja's mother-in-law, killed on 29 December 1942 by military policemen from Bilgoraj for sheltering and feeding Jews; they were betrayed by a young woman under their care who was captured and tortured by the Germans and gave information when promised her own life would be spared. The husband and son of Anastazja succeeded in concealing themselves. The Germans burnt down the farmhouse and buildings (cf. 147).

346. LUCZYK, Gabriel, farmer, living in Lopuszka Wielka near Przeworsk, Przemysl prov., shot in the autumn of 1943 together with 7

Jews (hiding in nearby forest since 1942) whom he rendered help.

347. LUKACZ, Eugeniusz, chemist, living in Lutowiska, Krosno prov.

348. LUKACZ, Janina, Eugeniusz's wife, arrested in the middle of 1943 for helping the Jewish families: Luterman, Rand and Fish. Eugeniusz died in Dachau, Janina in Tarnow prison.

349. MACHUL, Jan, farmer, living in Cezaryn near Pulawy, Lublin prov., shot on 3 July 1943 together with 2 Jews he was sheltering.

350. MACHULSKI, Jan, living in Schabojewo near Zawidz, Plock prov., killed by the military police on 8 May 1942 in Schabojewo for sheltering 3 Jewish women: Choma Dygala, Alka Alterowicz and Ida Alterowicz.

351. MADEJ, Mieczyslaw, living in Dzwonowice near Pilica, Katowice prov.

352. MADEJ, Zofia, Mieczyslaw's wife

353. MADEJ, Krystyna, 2, daughter, killed by the Germans on 12 January 1943 in the house of Zofia's brother, Bronislaw Janus, together with his family and 6 sheltered Jews (cf. 181-183).

354. MADUZIA, Jozef, living in Jaworze Dolne near Pilzno, Tarnow prov., shot by the Gestapo and soldiers of the Wehrmacht in a group of 4 farmers and 6 sheltered Jews (cf. 208).

355. MAJKUT, Antoni, farmer, living in Grodzisko Gorne, Cracow prov., sentenced to death for sheltering Jews; verdict passed by the special court (Standgericht) of the SS and Police Commander in Cracow and pronounced on 23 February 1944.

356. MALARECKI, Michal, living in Daleszyce, Kielce prov., arrested in summer 1943 for transporting—together with Stanislaw Furmanek—Jews from Daleszyce to Chmielnik; he died following torture in a prison (cf. 127).

357. MALEWSKA, Wiktoria, living in Lwow (city incorporated after the war into the Soviet Ukraine), shot in Ludzmierz on 6 March 1944 together with 2 other women and 3 men of unknown names for help rendered to Jewish people.

385. MINIEWSKI, Stefan, farmer, living in Szczurowice, Tarnopol prov., together with several members of his family he rendered help to Jews hiding in the forest by supplying them with food; in his own farm premises he sheltered 2 Jews (they were: Izak Parnas and Izak Szterling), who managed to live there to see the end of the war. However, when in 1944 news about how they survived was spread around, Stefan Miniewski was murdered by the Ukrainian nationalists. Posthumously awarded the

medal "Righteous Among the Nations."

386. MLYNARSKI, Jozef, 34, farmer, living in Bystrzejowice near Piaski, Lublin prov. From September 1942 he sheltered 5 Jews in a dugout below his house, incl. the Honig family from Piaski; arrested in January 1943 after being betrayed by an informant; even though the Germans failed to find the shelter and its Jewish occupants, he was sent to Majdanek where he perished.

387. MORAWSKI, Eugeniusz, living in Warsaw, killed on 19 April 1943—in the first day of the Warsaw Ghetto Uprising—when fighting with his Home Army (AK) unit at the ghetto walls in Bonifraterska Str.; the attempt to make an opening in the wall was unsuccessful.

388. MROZKOWSKI, Antoni, living in Ciepielow, Radom prov., shot in winter of 1942/1943 near the so-called Gorki (headquarters of the military police in Ciepielow) for "conspiring with Jews."

389. MURZEWSKI, Stanislaw, farmer, living in Laskarzew near Garwolin, Siedlce prov., shot by gendarmes on 21 December 1943 under a charge of rendering help to Jews.

390. NALEWAJKA, Jan, living in Wola Przybyslawska near Garbow, Lublin prov.

391. NALEWAJKA, Julia, Jan's wife, burned alive on 10 December 1942 in their own home together with their 3 children and sheltered Jews (cf. 3-6).

392. NEY, Julian, doctor in Jaslo, Krosno prov., killed by members of the Gestapo for saving from certain death a Jewish woman from Jaslo—Sara Diller. Posthumously awarded the medal "Righteous Among the Nations."

393. NIECPON, Jan, 56, living in Zolynia near Lezajsk, Rzeszow prov., shot by local gendarmes in May 1944 together with a Jewess whom he sheltered and who was a fugitive from Bialobrzegi.

394. NIELACNY, Wiadyslaw, 42, worker, living in Chorzenice near Radomsko, Czestochowa prov., arrested in March 1943 and then shot for help rendered to Jews.

395. NIEPSUJ, Anna, 45, living in Klikowa, Tarnow prov., murdered by members of the Gestapo from Tarnow on 8 April 1943 together with 2 sheltered Jews.

396. NIZIOL, Aniela, 50, living in Lancut, Rzeszow prov., arrested for sheltering Wolkenfeld family; shot in the building of the tribunal on 24 August 1942.

397. NOWAK, Maria, 18, farmer, living in Podszkodzie near Ostrowiec Swietokrzyski, Kielce prov. On 6 April 1943 a search, resulting

from a denunciation, was carried out in the Nowak house by military police from Ostrowiec. Even though no sheltered Jews were discovered, they having taken refuge elsewhere, Maria, together with Leokadia Swarlinska, mother of a 3 year old child, were taken away and sent to the concentration camps. Leokadia survived, but Maria perished.

398. NOWAK, Tadeusz, 39, living in Skarzysko-Kamienna, Kielce prov., hanged in public at the Hasag-Werke factory in Skarzysko for smuggling food for the Jews forced to work there.

399. NOWAK, Teofil, living in Posadza near Koniusza, Cracow prov.

400. NOWAK, (Christian name unknown), 2, Teofil's daughter, killed on 22 June 1943 for Teofil's involvement in aiding Jewish people; Maria and Stanislaw Wierzbanowski, Zebala (no first name) and Katarzyna Zmuda with her children were shot at the same time (cf. 644-645, 698, 702-704).

401. NOWAK, (Christian name unknown), living in Wierzbica near Kozlow, Kielce prov.

402. NOWAK, (Christian name unknown), daughter, shot on 29 January 1943 for sheltering members of the Jewish Wandelsman family, who were also killed (cf. 289-292).

403. NOWOTNIK, Stanislaw, 45, farmer, living in Swiesielice, Radom prov., murdered on 7 December 1942 in a group of 14 people by gendarmes from unit stationed in Ciepielow for help rendered to Jews (cf. 84).

404. NOYSZEWSKA, Ewa, Mother Superior from the nunnery of the Immaculate Conception, Slonim (place incorporated after the war into the Soviet Ukraine), shot in 1941 with sister Marta Wolowska for sheltering Jews in the nunnery (cf. 674).

405. OBUCHIEWICZ, Piotr, 58, living in Ciepielow, Radom prov.,

406. OBUCHIEWICZ, Helena, 35, Piotr's wife

407. OBUCHIEWICZ, Wladyslaw, 6, son

408. OBUCHIEWICZ, Zofia, 3, daughter

409. OBUCHIEWICZ, Janina, 2, daughter

410. OBUCHIEWICZ, (Christian name unknown), 7-month old baby, On 6 December 1942 a division of the military police burned alive 33 villagers from Ciepielow and Rekowka, incl. the Obuchiewicz family, for sheltering Jewish people (cf. 267-273).

411. OCHMINSKI, (Christian name unknown), living in Wola Przybyslawska near Garbow, Lublin prov., burned alive on 10 December 1942 with 4 members of his family in a mass execution carried out in the village where Jews had been sheltered (cf. 3-6).

412. OLESIUK, Wojciech, 53, farmer, living in Chominna near Lomazy, Biala Podlaska prov.

413. OLESIUK, Stefania, 40, Wojciech's wife

414. OLESIUK, Piotr, 14, son

415. OLESIUK, Stefan, 9, son

416. OLESIUK, Szymon, 3, son, shot on 7 November 1943 in Chominna village by military policemen from Wisznice for sheltering a Jew who also perished.

417. OLSZEWSKA, Maria, 42, living in Skornice near Konskie, Kielce prov.

418. OLSZEWSKA, Janina, 30, wife of Henryk

419. OLSZEWSKA, Krystyna, 9, Janina's daughter

420. OLSZEWSKA, Zofia, 1, Janina's daughter

421. OLSZEWSKI, Bogdan, 2, Janina's son

422. OLSZEWSKI, Jan, 5, Janina's son

423. OLSZEWSKI, Marian, 10, Maria's son

424. OLSZEWSKI, Leon, 19, Maria's son

425. OLSZEWSKI, Henryk, 33, Maria's step-son. On 16 April 1943 the Germans discovered 11 members of the Weintraub family sheltered by the Olszewskis in a specially built dug-out. Henryk and Leon were taken away by police and their fate is unknown; the seven other members of the family were killed in their own house.

464. PIETRZYKOWSKI, Jozef, doctor in Bobowa, Nowy Sacz prov., arrested and shot at the turn of 1942 for providing medical aid to a Jewish child.

465. PILAWSKI, Wladyslaw, living in Domaradz near Krosno, shot by German gendarmes on 26 June 1942 for help rendered to Jews.

466. PINKUS, Jan, living in Radom, sentenced with several other people to death on 3 April 1943 by a special court (Sondergericht) in Radom for helping the Jewish women Sala Rubinowicz and Elka Szwarcman (cf. 59-60).

467. PIRGA, Aleksandra, farmer, living in Kozlowek near Strzyzow, Rzeszow prov., shot by gendarmes together with a group of other people in June 1943 in Markuszowa village for rendering help to Jews hiding in the forest (cf. 426).

468. PISKOREK, Kazimierz, railway driver, living in Kowel (city incorporated after the war into the Soviet Ukraine), killed by the military police for helping Jewish refugee Szpulman: at the turn of 1942 he took him by train from Kovel to Chelmno. A Jewish family being sheltered by Piskorek escaped.

469. PIWKO, Stanislaw, 31, farmer, living in Paulinow near Sokolow Podlaski, Siedlce prov., shot by an SS unit on 24 February 1943 in Paulinow together with a group of 14 people who were victims of a provocation: several weeks earlier they rendered help to a Nazi agent, who pretended to be a Jewish fugitive (cf. 14).

470. PLATEK, Sylweriusz, living in Cisie near Ceglow, Siedlce prov.

471. PLATEK, Tomasz, Sylweriusz's brother, shot on 28 June 1943 in a group of 25 villagers for sheltering Jews (cf. 9).

472. PLAWCZYNSKA, Janina, over 70, living in Warsaw, died with Rena Laterner for helping Jewish insurgents to contact underground members on the "Arian" side and in sheltering them (cf. 324).

473. PODGORSKI, Piotr, 39, village watchman, living in Wierbka near Pilica, Katowice prov., shot by Gestapo officers in early January 1943 for withholding information from the authorities about Jews being sheltered by Maria Rogozinska (cf. 514-515).

474. POKROPEK, Stefan, living in Warsaw, supplied arms to the Warsaw ghetto. On 7 July 1943 he committed suicide when the military police forced the way into his flat where he had been sheltering the insurgent Tuvie Szejngut and hoarding arms for the Jewish Fighting Organization (ZOB).

475. POLONSKI, Zenon, 20, living in Kozienice, Kielce prov., sentenced on 3 April 1943—together with a number of other people—to death, by a special court (Sondergericht) in Radom, for helping the Jewish women Sala Rubinowicz and Elka Szwarcman, who had escaped from the Radom ghetto (cf. 59-60).

476. POMYKALA, Lukasz, 47, living in Przewrotne near Glogow Malopolski, Rzeszow prov.

477. POMYKALA, Wojciech, 26, killed in a mass execution on 13 March 1943 carried out in revenge for sheltering and feeding Jews (cf. 49-51).

511. REBIS, Wiktoria, 24, daughter

512. REBIS, Karol, 19, son, murdered together with 9 Jews sheltered by them caught during search of the house on 9 September 1943 by German police from Debica; together with the Rebis family died Piotr Gawrys, maid Zofia Miela and 2 other Poles unknown by name (cf. 140, 382).

513. ROGINSKA, Janina, living in Wegrow, Siedlce prov., shot on 15 June 1943 by military policemen from Wegrow when, during a search, Jewish fugitives were discovered in her barn (incl. Moshe Ptak), all of whom were also shot. Posthumously awarded the medal "Righteous

Among the Nations."

514. ROGOZINSKA, Maria, 40, worker, living in Wierbka near Pilica, Katowice prov.

515. ROGOZINSKI, Jan, 5, son. There was a group of Jews sheltered in the cellars of their house; early in January 1943 when the Rogozinski family was away, Gestapo officers were brought there by volksdeutsch neighbours and discovered the hiding place of the Jews; murdered all of them together with Piotr Sendra, who was there at the time and a night watchman, Piotr Podgorski. The Gestapo officers threatened that the whole village would be punished if Rogozinskis didn't show up. The intimidated inhabitants of the village gave them away to the Germans. Both of them were killed on 15 January 1943 (cf. 473, 543)

516. ROKICKI, Stanislaw, living in forester's lodge Czarna near Minsk Mazowiecki, Siedlce prov., shot on 13 March 1943 together with 5 sheltered Jews: Teresa Powazek and her husband, Helena Szpindler and her mother and Abram Slomka as well as with 2 fugitive Soviet POWs.

517. ROZANSKA, Maria, living in Radom, on 3 April 1943 sentenced—together with several other people—to death by a special court (Sondergericht) in Radom, for helping the Jewish women Ela Szwarcman and Sala Rubinowicz (cf. 59-60).

518. RUCHALA, Jozef, living in Librantowa near Nowy Sacz

519. RUCHALA, Weronika, Jozef's wife, shot for supplying food to Jews hiding in a forest.

520. RUDECKA, Maria, 48, owner of an estate in Wodzislaw near Sedziszow, Kielce prov., shot on 27 April 1943 for repeated help rendered to Jewish people.

521. RUMAK, Jakub, 34, living in Przewrotne near Glogow Malopolski, Rzeszow prov.

522. RUMAK, Jozef, 31, shot on 10 June 1943 in a mass execution for sheltering Jews in the village of Hucisko (cf. 19-20).

523. RUMIN, Maria, farmer, living in Popradow near Nowy Sacz

524. RUMIN, Jan, son, shot for sheltering 5-persons of the Jewish Kaufer family from Zawada; the Jews were also killed.

525. RUSIN, Antoni, 41, living in Przewrotne near Glogow Malopolski, Rzeszow prov., murdered on 13 March 1943 in a group of 30 Poles for helping Jewish people (cf. 49-51).

526. RUTKOWSKI, Dawid, living in Ignacow, Siedlce prov., shot on 30 March 1943 together with Jan Gawrych and Stanislaw Skuza and a group of Jewish partisans, whom they helped (cf. 139).

527. RUTKOWSKI, Wladyslaw, living in Chodnow near Biala

Rawska, Skierniewice prov., murdered by Gestapo officers early in January 1943 for cooperation in helping a group of Jews in the home of Maria Rogozinska (cf. 514-515).

544. SEDLAKOWSKA, Janina, living in Zwierzyniec, Zamosc prov., murdered on 24 October 1942 for help rendered to Jews.

545. SEKOWSKA, Magdalena, living in Przemysl. On a number of occasions, Sekowska hid in her flat, on the corner of Janowska and Grodzka Str., young Jewish fugitives from Lwow. Jews escaped from the Lwow ghetto to the Lyczakow Cemetery, from which Sekowska's son-in-law, a mechanic on the railways, brought them to Przemysl. Sekowska was arrested by the Gestapo in 1942, beaten and tortured, she was taken to Auschwitz where soon after she perished.

546. SIEWIERSKI, Stefan, 19, living in Warsaw, socialist activist in a youth organization, captured in May 1943 while conducting Jews out of the ghetto to the woods. He died in the Gestapo prison on Szuch Ave. in Warsaw, after being tortured. Posthumously awarded the medal "Righteous Among the Nations."

547. SINIARSKI, Stanislaw, 45, farmer, living in Lutkowka near Mszczonow, Skierniewice prov.

548. SINIARSKA, Marianna, 43, Stanislaw's wife

549. SINIARSKI, Marian Jozef, 16, son

550. SINIARSKA, Irena, 9, daughter

551. SINIARSKI, Edward, 8, son. The Siniarski family was shot on 10 March 1944 by military policemen from Mszczonow for sheltering 3 Jews (Lipszyc, his wife and child), who were also executed.

552. SKALSKI, Stanislaw, 50, teacher, living in Leczyca, Plock prov., arrested in 1942 by Gestapo officers for organizing escape possibilities for Jews. He died as a result of beatings and tortures being applied to him.

553. SKOCZYLAS, Piotr, living in Rekowka near Ciepielow, Radom prov.

554. SKOCZYLAS, Leokadia, 8, Piotr's daughter, burned alive on 6 December 1942 by military policemen in a group of villagers for sheltering and feeding Jews; their farm buildings were burnt down. The group execution was carried out on the same day in Rekowka and in nearby Ciepielow (cf. 243-256, 257).

555. SKOLIMOWSKI, Alfons, 31, farmer, living in Roguziec near Mordy, Siedlce prov., shot on 2 March 1943 in Roguziec by the military police for sheltering Jews.

556. SKLADOWSKA, Halina, living in Lwow (city incorporated

after the war into the Soviet Ukraine), sentenced to death for helping Jews (public announcement issued by the Commander of the SS and the Galician District Police on 14 December 1943).

557. SKRZAK, Wojciech, 50, farmer, living in Swiesielice, Radom prov., murdered on 7 December 1942 in a group of 14 people by gendarmes from unit stationed in Ciepielow for help rendered to Jews (cf. 84).

558. SKUZA, Stanisiaw, living in Ignacow, Siedlce prov., shot on 30 March 1943 together with Jan Gawrych and Dawid Rutkowski as well as with group of Jewish partisans whom they rendered help (cf. 139).

559. SKWARA, Irena, living in Warsaw, shot as she was leaving Warsaw in September 1944 before the collapse of the uprisiing, accompanied by Waclaw Turski-Teitelbaum whom she had sheltered and who was identified by a German checkpoint guard as a Jew. Turski was also executed.

607. SLEDZ, Jadwiga, living in Warsaw, arrested on 2 December 1943 together with her sisters, Anna Rycerz and Janina Zelichowska, as well as with her relation Helena Sledz for rendering help to Jewish families. Placed in Pawiak jail with the others, she was shot on 10 December 1943 in the ruins of the Warsaw ghetto (cf. 532, 606, 701).

608. SLIWA, Wladyslaw (or Wojciech), 26, former N.C.O., living in Kozlowek near Strzyzow, Rzeszow prov., shot by gendarmes together with a group of other people in June 1943 in Markuszowa village for rendering help to Jews hiding in the forest (cf. 426).

609. SLIWINSKI, Jan, 48, worker, living in Paulinow near Sokolow Podlaski, Siedlce prov., shot by an SS unit on 24 February 1943 in Paulinow together with a group of 14 people who were victims of a provocation: several weeks earlier they rendered help to a Nazi agent, who pretended to be a Jewish fugitive (cf. 14).

610. TATOMIR, Jan, 49, mason, living in Jaroslawice, Tarnopol prov. (place incorporated after the war into the Soviet Ukraine), he gave refuge, with his wife and daughter, to 6 Jewish people in a shelter dug under his house. He was killed on 1943 by the Germans. Posthumously awarded the medal "Righteous Among the Nations."

611. TOKARCZYK, Regina, 76, living in Pielgrzymka near Krosno.

612. TOKARCZYK, Karolina, 41, daughter, shot on 15 July 1943 in the field near their own home by officers of German police for sheltering Jews.

659. WODA, Kasper, people's movement activist, living in Gruszawa near Miechow, Cracow prov., arrested in November 1943 and sent to

Auschwitz where he died for sheltering Jews.

660. WOJEWODKA, Ignacy, 50, farmer, living in Swiesielice, Radom prov.

661. WOJEWODKA, Marianna, 45 farmer, Ignacy's wife

662. WOJEWODKA, Waclaw, 21, farmer, son

663. WOJEWODKA, Jan, 18, farmer, son

664. WOJEWODKA, Stanislaw, 12, son

665. WOJEWODKA, Jozef, 7, son, murdered on 7 December 1942 in a group of 14 people by gendarmes from the unit stationed in Ciepielow for help rendered to Jews (cf. 84).

666. WOLSKI, Jan, living in Gniewoszow, Radom prov., shot in August 1943 together with Jozef Suchecki for sheltering several Jews—fugitives from camp in Gniewoszow. The Jews were warned and managed to survive (cf. 587).

667. WOLSKI, Mieczyslaw, living in Warsaw. With his family he built an underground shelter in his backgarden on Grojecka Str., where from 1942 he gave refuge to 34 Jews, incl. the well-known historian Emanuel Ringelblum with wife and son. Most likely through betrayal, the shelter was discovered on 7 March 1944. Wolski, his nephew, Janusz Wysocki, and all the fugitives in the shelter were taken to Pawiak prison. The Jews were soon after shot in the ghetto ruins, while no traces of Wolski and Wysocki were ever found. Posthumously awarded the medal "Righteous Among the Nations" (cf. 690).

668. WOLOWIEC, Gabriel, farmer, living in Zajaczkow near Ciepielow, Radom prov.

669. WOLOWIEC, Stanislawa, Gabriel's wife

670. WOLOWIEC, Bronislawa, daughter

671. WOLOWIEC, Janina, daughter

672. WOLOWIEC, Leokadia, daughter

673. WOLOWIEC, Kazimiera, daughter. In January 1943, the military policemen from Ciepielow killed the entire family of Gabriel Wolowiec. He was arrested and executed earlier. The Wolowiec daughters were aged 3-12 years. Jozef Jelonek was arrested with them and also shot, together with the mentally underdeveloped servant Franciszek Zaborowski. The crime was carried out in response to the family's helping Jews in hiding (cf. 188, 692).

674. WOLOWSKA, Marta, nun, Slonim (place incorporated after the war into the Soviet Ukraine), killed in 1941 in the nunnery of the Immaculate Conception in Slonim—together with Mother Superior Ewa Noyszewska—for sheltering Jews (cf. 404).

675. WOZNIAK, Franciszek, living in Pawlow near Dabrowa Tarnowska, Cracow prov., murdered together with Michal Wojcik by gendarmes in the spring of 1943 for sheltering Jews and helping them to escape (by organizing, among other things, river crossings) (cf. 679).

676. WOZNIAK, Marian, living in Minsk Mazowiecki, Siedlce prov. killed in May 1944 for sheltering and helping Jews.

677. WOJCICKI, Wladyslaw, living in Cisie near Ceglow, Siedlce prov., killed in Ceglow on 28 June 1943 in a group execution of Cisie villagers—for sheltering Jews (cf. 9).

688. WYDMANSKI, Jozef, farmer, living in Krepa near Miechow, Cracow prov., shot by Gestapo on 23 September 1944 together with a Jew he was hiding. His farm was burned down.

689. WYSMULSKA, Zofia, farmer, living in Moszenki near Jastkow, Lublin prov., gave refuge to 4 Jews in an underground shelter and also provided additional 16, hiding in the nearby woods, with food and medicines. She was shot by the military police on 25 September 1943. Her husband Marian managed to escape; the sheltered Jews and Marianna Barszcz, Wysmulski's employee, were also killed (cf. 29).

690. WYSOCKI, Janusz, living in Warsaw, arrested on 7 March 1944 for helping Mieczyslaw Wolski to construct an underground shelter and for his part in giving refuge to 34 Jews living in that shelter; he died in unknown circumstances and was posthumously awarded the medal "Righteous Among the Nations" (cf. 667).

691. WYSOCZANSKA, (Christian name unknown), pharmacist, living in Sokal (place incorporated after the war into the Soviet Ukraine), murdered in February 1942 together with 3 Jewish girls sheltered by her.

692. ZABOROWSKI, Franciszek, 40, living in Zajaczkow near Ciepielow, Radom prov., killed in January 1943 by military policemen from Ciepielow with the Wolowiec family for sheltering Jews (cf. 668-673).

693. ZAGANCZYK, Jan, living in Cisie near Ceglow, Siedlce prov., killed on 28 June 1943 with numerous other Cisie villagers for help given to Jews (cf. 9).

694. ZAGORSKI, Piotr, farmer, living in Kozlowek near Strzyzow, Rzeszow prov., shot by gendarmes together with a group of other people in June 1943 in Markuszowa village for rendering help to Jews hiding in the forest (cf. 426).

695. ZAJAC, Franciszek, living in Wola Skrzydlanska near Limanowa, Nowy Sacz prov., sent to Dachau camp, where he died after a Jewess he was sheltering was discovered and murdered.

696. ZAJAC, Ludwik, living in Cisie near Ceglow, Siedlce prov., killed on 28 June 1943 with numerous other Cisie villagers for help given to Jews (cf. 9).

697. ZAJDEL, Karolina, living in Nadolno near Krosno, she was arrested at the end of 1944 by gendarmes who discovered in her house a sheltered Jew (shot while trying to escape); she was taken to the prison in Dukla and murdered there.

698. ZEBALA, (Christian name unknown), living in Posadza near Koniusza, Cracow prov., shot in a group of 8 Poles on 22 June 1943 in Posadza for sheltering Jews (cf. 399-400).

699. ZIELINSKA, (Christian name unknown), wife of an industrialist, living in Lwow (city incorporated after the war into the Soviet Ukraine), arrested in the autumn of 1942 for sheltering a 40 year old Jew, an industrialist of unknown name; sent to Majdanek camp, where from she never came back.

700. ZIELINSKA, Rozalia, 35, farmer, living in Gumniska near Debica, Tarnow prov., shot by gendarmes on 17 July 1943 for sheltering Samuel Wind, a taylor from Debica.

701. ZELICHOWSKA, Janina, living in Warsaw, arrested on 2 December 1943 together with her sisters Anna Rycerz and Jadwiga Sledz as well as with Helena Sledz for help rendered to Jewish families; all four were placed in Pawiak prison and on 10 December 1943 they were shot in the ruins of the Warsaw ghetto (cf. 607).

702. ZMUDA, Katarzyna, 40, living in Posadza near Koniusza. Cracow prov.

703. ZMUDA, Teresa, 18, daughter

704. ZMUDA, Zdzislaw, 10, son, shot on 22 June 1943 in Posadza in a group of 8 Poles for sheltering Jews (cf. 399-400).

APPENDIX C

RIGHTEOUS AMONG THE NATIONS—
Per Country And Ethnic Origin*
(as of 1 January 1995)

Poland	4,478
Netherlands	3,774
France	1,249
Belgium	685
Ukraine	431
Czech Rep. + Slovakia	301
Germany	294
Hungary	283
Lithuania	266
Greece	178
Italy	177
Russia	139
Yugoslavia (all regions)	135
Austria	78
Albania	48
Romania	46

* The Main Commission for the Investigation of Crimes Against the Polish Nation, The Institute of National Memory and The Polish Society for the Righteous Among the Nations, THOSE WHO HELPED: POLISH RESCUERS OF JEWS DURING THE HOLOCAUST, Part II (Warsaw: 1996), p. 209.

Latvia	35
Switzerland	19
Bulgaria	13
Denmark	12
England	9
Sweden	7
Moldavia	5
Norway	6
Spain	3
Armenia	3
Luxembourg	1
U.S.A.	1
Estonia	1
Brazil	1
Portugal	1
Japan	1
Turkey	1

TOTAL PERSONS   12,681

APPENDIX D

The posters and announcements which follow were originally published
in *Polacy-Zydzi, 1939-45.* S. Wronski and M. Zwolakowa. Warsaw: 1971.

BEKANNTMACHUNG

Betrifft:
Beherbergung von geflüchteten Juden.

Es besteht Anlass zu folgendem Hinweis:
Gemäss der 3. Verordnung über Aufenthalts-
beschränkungen im Generalgouvernement
vom 15. 10. 1941 (VO. Bl. GG. S. 595) unterliegen
Juden, die den jüdischen Wohnbezirk unbe-
fugt verlassen, der Todesstrafe.

Gemäss der gleichen Vorschrift unterliegen Perso-
nen, die solchen Juden wissentlich Unterschlupf gewähren, Beköstigung verabfolgen oder Nahrungsmittel verkaufen, ebenfalls der Todesstrafe.

Die nichtjüdische Bevölkerung wird da-
her dringend gewarnt:

1.) Juden Unterschlupf zu gewähren,
2.) Juden Beköstigung zu verabfolgen,
3.) Juden Nahrungsmittel zu verkaufen.

Tschenstochau, den 24. 9. 42.

OGŁOSZENIE

Dotyczy:

przetrzymywania ukrywających się żydów.

Zachodzi potrzeba przypomnienia, że stosownie do § 3 Rozporządzenia o ograniczeniach pobytu w Gen. Gub. z dnia 15. X. 1941 roku (Dz. Rozp. dla GG. str. 595) żydzi, opuszczający dzielnicę żydowską bez zezwolenia, podlegają karze śmierci.

Według tego rozporządzenia, osobom, które takim żydom świadomie udzielają przytułku, dostarczają im jedzenia lub sprzedają artykuły żywnościowe, grozi również kara śmierci.

Niniejszym ostrzega się stanowczo ludność nieżydowską przed:

1.) udzielaniem żydom przytułku,

2.) dostarczaniem im jedzenia,

3.) sprzedawaniem im artykułów żywnościowych.

Częstochowa, dnia 24. 9. 42.

Der Stadthauptmann
Dr. Franke

Der Kreishauptmann in Tarnow

BEKANNTMACHUNG!

Zur Durchführung der vom SS- und Polizeiführer in Krakau angeordneten Judenaussiedlungen wird folgendes bekannt gemacht:

§ 1

Am 16. IX. 1942 erfolgen Judenaussiedlungen.

§ 2

Jeder Pole, der in irgendeiner Form durch seine Handlung die Aussiedlung gefährdet oder erschwert, oder bei einer solchen Handlung Mithilfe ausübt, wird strengstens bestraft.

§ 3

Jeder Pole, der während und nach der Aussiedlung einen Juden aufnimmt oder versteckt, wird erschossen.

§ 4

Alle zum Betreten des Judenwohnbezirkes ausgestellten Passierscheine verlieren vom Tage dieser Bekanntmachung ihre Gültigkeit. Wer trotzdem das Ghetto betritt, wird strengstens bestraft und läuft Gefahr erschossen zu werden.

§ 5

Wer Sachen von Juden unmittelbar oder mittelbar kauft, geschenkt erhält oder sonst erwirbt wird strengstens bestraft.

Jeder Pole, der in Besitz von Juden gehörigen Sachen ist, ist verpflichtet, den Besitz sofort bei der Sicherheitspolizei in Tarnow anzumelden, widrigenfalls er mit strengster Bestrafung wie ein Plünderer zu rechnen hat.

§ 6

Während des Transportes der Juden vom Sammelplatz zum. Bahnhof ist das Betreten der Strassen verboten, durch welche der Transport geleitet wird.

Die Bewohner der Häuser der in Betracht kommenden Strassen und Plätze haben bei Annäherung des Zuges die Haustüren und Fenster zu verschliessen und jede Art der Beobachtung des Zuges zu unterlassen. Verstösse gegen diese Anordnung werden bestraft.

OBWIESZCZENIE!

W związku z zarządzonym przez Dowódcę SS i Policji w Krakau wysiedleniem żydów, ogłaszam co następuje:

§ 1.

W dniu 16. września 1942 r. odbędzie się wysiedlenie żydów.

§ 2.

Każdy Polak, który w jakikolwiek sposób utrudni akcję wysiedlenia, podlega najsurowszym karom.

§ 3.

Każdy Polak, który podczas lub po akcji wysiedlenia przyjmie żyda lub udzieli mu schronienia, zostanie rozstrzelany.

§ 4.

Przepustki, upoważniające do wstępu do dzielnicy żydowskiej tracą ważność z chwilą ukazania się niniejszego obwieszczenia. Osoby, które pomimo tego do dzielnicy żydowskiej wchodzą, podlegają surowym karom i narażają się na zastrzelenie.

§ 5.

Kto jakiekolwiek rzeczy bezpośrednio czy pośrednio od żydów kupuje, w podarunku odbiera albo w inny sposób wchodzi w posiadanie tychże, podlega surowym karom.

Każdy Polak, mający w posiadaniu rzeczy, stanowiące własność żyda, obowiązany jest fakt posiadania zgłosić natychmiast w Policji Bezpieczeństwa w Tarnowie, gdyż w przeciwnym razie będzie traktowany jako łupieżca i podlega najsurowszym karom.

§ 6.

Podczas transportu żydów z placu zbiórki na dworzec kolejowy zostaje dostęp dla ludności wzbroniony na ulice i place, przez które transport przechodzić będzie.

Przy zbliżaniu się transportu do danych ulic, mieszkańcy powinni zamknąć bramy wejściowe domów oraz okna i zaniechać obserwacji transportu.

Nieprzestrzegający powyższych przepisów podlegają surowym karom.

Tarnow, dnia 15. September 1942.

Der Kreishauptmann
i. v.
Dr. PERNUTZ.

GENERALGOUVERNEMENT
DISTRIKT RADOM
Der Stadt-Kommissar der Stadt Ostrowiec
(Kreishauptmannschaft Opatow)

BEKANNTMACHUNG

Es ist wiederholt festgestellt, dass geflüchtete Juden von Polen aufgenommen sind. Ich mache auf die 3. Verordnung über Aufenthaltsbeschränkung im Generalgouvernement vom 15. 10. 1941. VO. Bl. GG. S. 595 aufmerksam. Danach werden diejenigen Polen, die den geflüchteten Juden Unterschlupf oder Beköstigung gewähren oder ihnen Nahrungsmittel verkaufen, mit dem Tode bestraft. Ich weise hierauf letztmalig hin.

Ostrowiec, den 28. September 1942.

Der Stadtkommissar
(gez.) Motschall

GENERALNE GUBERNATORSTWO
DYSTRYKT RADOM
Komisarz Miasta w Ostrowcu
Starostwo Powiatowe w Opatowie

OGŁOSZENIE

Stwierdzono powtarzające się wypadki ukrywania się żydów uchodźców u polaków. Zwracam uwagę na 3 rozporządzenie z dnia 15. 10. 1941 (VO. Bl. GG. str. 595) w sprawie ograniczenia pobytu na terenie Generalnego Gubernatorstwa pouczam, że kto udziela żydom uchodźcom pomieszczenia i żywności lub sprzedaje żydom środki żywnościowe, będzie karany śmiercią. Pouczam jest ostateczne.

Ostrowiec, dnia 28 września 1942 r.

Komisarz Miasta
(—) Motschall

INDEX for text pages 1 to 272